KING of the HIGH
MISSOURI

by Jack Holterman

Library of Congress Catalog Card Number: 86-91137

ISBN: 0-934318-87-5

Design by DD Dowden

Publishing Consultant:
Falcon Press Publishing Co., Inc.,
Helena and Billings, Montana

FALCON
PRESS
PUBLISHING CO. INC.

Acknowledgements

This is a book about marginal people, and, more specifically, marginal families. In the current jargon of sociologists *marginal* is a term that refers to people who live their lives on the edges of two cultures, two ethnic groups, two religions, two social strata, and usually the margins turn out to be the cutting edges. They are people who have one foot in one world and one in another. Sometimes they lose all footing and slip into drink, drugs or fundamentalism. Sometimes they emerge as go-betweens, polyglots instead of monoglots, co-creators of the harmony of cosmos and chaos that makes the world go 'round. But the term *marginal* is pejorative to say the least, so in my own jargon for *margin* I am substituting the bolder word *frontier*. It fits the times and places I talk about in this book. And though the book is as true a story as I can make it, it is not one for purists of any stripe. For what can purists know about the edges of things?

It has not been any easy book to write. In fact, it is a very complex story. But I have had the help of many people who have given me of their time, advice, information—and forebearance—all in our effort to understand better the margins or frontiers and the people who live on them. They have helped me also in sorting out the spoilers and the healers, for on the edges of things there will be many of both.

To the staff members of many libraries, archives and historical societies I owe a great deal of thanks for their patient attention to my persistent queries and even for information volunteered: The local libraries of Flathead County, Montana, at both Kalispell and Columbia Falls; the Montana Historical Society in Helena; the Eastern Washington State Historical Society in Spokane; the Smithsonian Institute of Washington, D.C.; the National Museum of American History; the Harvard-Smithsonian Observatory; Harvard University Library; Stanford University Library; the State Historical Society of North Dakota; the Historical Society of South Dakota; the State Historical society of Nebraska; the Missouri Historical Society; the Bradley University Library in Peoria (Special Collections); Peoria Public Library; Illinois State Historical Society; California Historical Society; the Historical Society of Pennsylvania, the War Library and Museum in Philadelphia; Coyle Free Library in Chambersburg, Pennsylvania; Idaho State Historical Society; the Boise Public Library; the Presbyterian Historical Society in Philadelphia; the Historical Foundation of the Presbyterian and Reformed churches in Montreat, North Carolina; the Graduate Theological Union Library of the San Francisco Theological Seminary Branch at San Anselmo, California; the Genealogical society of Utah; the Genealogical Society of the Kalispell Latter Day Saints; the Kansas State Historical Society; the William Andrews Clark Memorial Library of the University of California at Los Angeles (Montana Collection); the Archives of the Moravian College in Bethlehem, Pennsylvania; the Archives of the U.S. Military Academy at West Point, New York; the University of Cologne (Küln) in Germany; the Main State

Archives of Hesse in Wiesbaden (Hessisches Hauptstaatsarchiv); el Museo de Ciencias Naturales in Madrid, Spain; the Archives of the Grand Duke of Luxembourg; l'Administration des biens de S.A.R. le Grand-Duc de Luxembourg; and the staff of Falcon Press in Helena and Billings, Montana.

Among the many persons to whom I owe individual thanks for many favors, these should be inscribed in golden letters: Molly Culbertson Sedgewick of Kalispell for her reminiscences; Hugh A. Dempsey of Calgary for much correspondence and advice in particular about the Blood people; Barbara Knutson of Kalispell for repeatedly ferreting out arcane sources of information; O'Neil Jones of Bigfork, Montana, for information regarding Natawista and son Jack; Dave Walter of the Montana Historical Society for an endless stream of correspondence and suggestions; James H. Trott of Philadelphia (formerly of Fort Benton) for much research in the Presbyterian archives generously provided for my use; Beth Ladeau of Whitefish, Montana, for designing the Culberston genealogy chart and many suggestions; Terry Parsons for typing my manuscript in the presentable form I fail to achieve myself; Coralee Paull for research in St. Louis archives; Dr. Robert Schweitzer of the Württembergische Landesbibliothek in Stuttgart, Germany; Hans-Müller for research at the University of Cologne; Padre Ricardo Martínez de Velasco for investigations at the Museo de Ciencias Naturales in Madrid; professor Gertrude Lackschwitz and Anne Broeder-Cevrero for translations; Dave Flaccus and Caroline Patterson for editorial suggestions; Evelyn Sheets of Trenton, Missouri; Mike Olinger of West Glacier; Father A. Duhaime, O.M.I. of Cardston, Alberta; Professor Jean Schoos for help in the Luxembourg archives; Jeannette Erickson for suggestions regarding the Culbertson genealogy; Dick Strong of the U.S. Forest Service; Owen Gingerich of the Harvard-Smithsonian Observatory; Kenneth W. Rapp of the Archives of the U.S. Military Academy at West Point; Joel Overholser of Fort Benter for comments on the original manuscript of this book; Gloria Culbertson of Oregon; Kathy Lucke for photos from the estate of Mollie Culbertson Sedgwick; Mr. and Mrs. Carson Boyd of Browning, Montana; and many descendents of Blackfeet and Sioux families mentioned in my narrative, some now departed far beyond the reach of my expressions of gratitude.

One of my own regrets about this book is that it has to deal so much with spoilers and spoiliation and so little with healers. But I cannot invent history. And perhaps just in posing the question there is a measure of healing.

Jack Holterman

CONTENTS

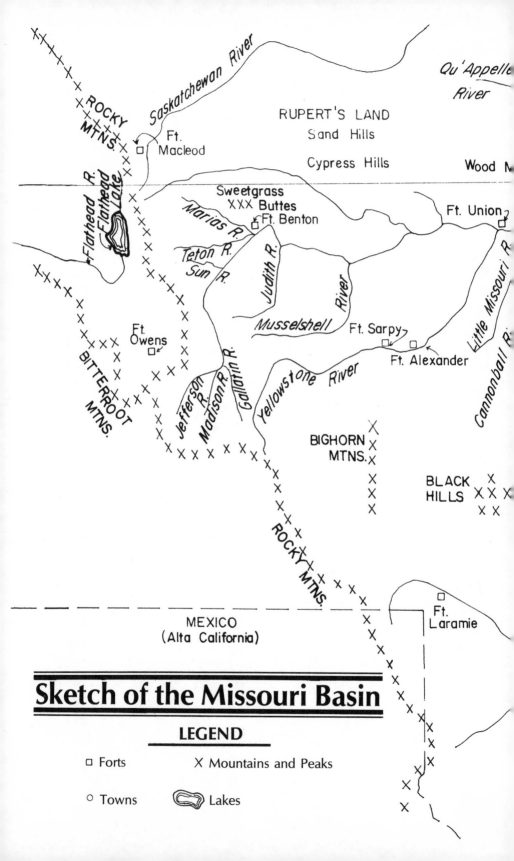

Sketch of the Missouri Basin

LEGEND

□ Forts   X Mountains and Peaks

○ Towns   Lakes

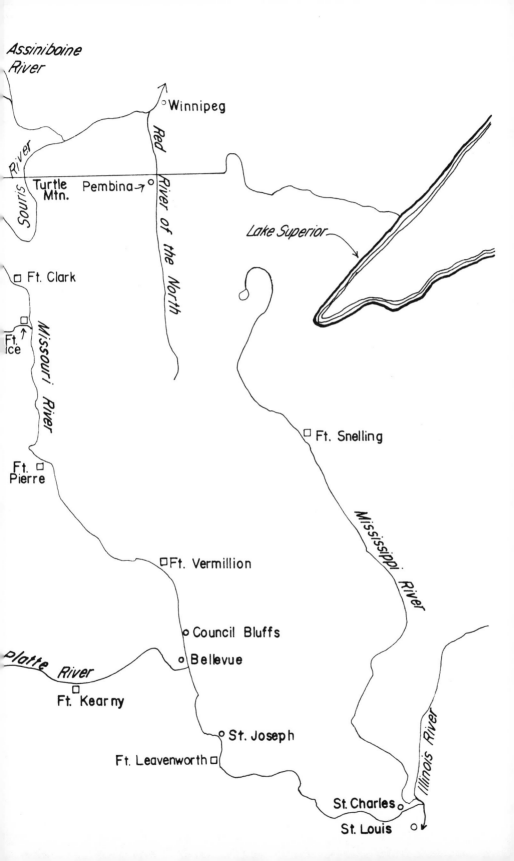

Prologue

At midnight of the 11th of November, 1799, on the very brink of the New World and the new century, the heavens put on a dramatic display that sent repercussions around the earth from that day to this. It began over the Americas, fading out eastward into the dawn of the 12th. In the Shining Mountains, at the Three Forks of the Missouri, the cosmic dance could have been visible only to secluded vision-questers or passing warparties—perhaps even that fateful warparty that spirited away the little Shoshoni princess and sold her as a slave. An hour later the spectacle would be breaking loose over Vera Cruz and two hours later over the rim of Venezuela, where the Baron von Humboldt stood aghast to behold the thousands of stars pouring out of the constellation Leo. In just the last fortnight the Baron had endured earthquakes, an eclipse of the sun and a sequence of "electric explosions" in the atmosphere, all to be climaxed by this ballet of the stars. And 1800 nautical miles eastward, the "shooting stars" appeared over Cologne and Paris shortly before the dawn-light outshone them, betraying the night-owls who tried to sneak home undetected.

No one knew then what meteors were, though Humboldt, the most learned man of his age, was making sharp guesses. From the good folk of Nueva Andalucía he discovered that similar occurrences had astounded them before— yes, just 33 years before—. . . Scientists like Humboldt asked the hard questions. The simple folk like the rest of us offered non-questions: Should the shooting stars and the new century be greeted with chants of *Dies irae* or cries of *Hallelujah*?

Your deeds are your children. They will return.
—Sioux proverb

...And when his wife died and left him in grief,
Shining Shirt scaled the highest peak, crying for a
vision. And the Great Spirit spoke in the mountain
tops, "Go walk in beauty and leave the rest to Me."
—Salish legend

Harper's Ferry, the junction of the Shenandoah with the Potomac and of the states Virginia,
West Virginia and Maryland. Permit to publish confirmed by U.S.N.P.S. Courtesy of National
Park Service. Photographer Hugo Skrastins, 1967.

CHAPTER I

Culbertson's Row

Frontiers, like the Kingdom of God, are within you and often beyond. This is the saga of some wanderers who crossed frontiers of all sorts, even the greatest frontier of all—the ocean. Over the ocean escaped the Scotch-Irish and other Jacobites after the collapse of the House of Stuart. The dreadful sea and the wild frontiers beyond it were better than prison, much better than leaving your detached head impaled on the top of Temple Bar.

Scotch-Irish they were, those three or four brothers Culbertson who came to America from Northern Ireland, and *northern* Northern Ireland at that, probably from Culbertson's Row near Ballymena. Calvinists to the bone, the scions of this family were eager to make it clear that they were more Scot than Irish: "You can always tell a Culbertson," said they, "—big ears, big feet, big nose. That shows you how much a Scot he really is." (Evidently, nothing was said for the feminine half of the family.) Their name may derive from St. Cuthbert, no more a Calvinist than was John Scotus of Duns, and some extremists would go so far as to claim the family's descent from the shockingly non-Calvinist dynasty of Stuart.

In 1743 or earlier they settled near the Conococheague Creek in the strategic region where the Virginias, Maryland, and Pennsylvania all converge toward the Potomac and the Shenandoah, the intersection of frontiers which were then still a-borning: North-South, East-West, slave-free, Celt-Saxon, Low Church-High Church. There between the Blue Ridge and the Alleghenies, one of the Culbertson brothers from Ulster sired three sons, all of whom were colonels in the Army of the Revolution and none of whom were Tories. "The Old Colonel" lined his men up on both sides of the brook, made them clasp hands across the waters and then, sipping Highland whiskey, swear a mighty Scottish oath of fealty. No doubt about it. If you broke an oath like that, you'd rot in hell. Robert Culbertson, Jr., also a colonel, married Annie Duncan and prayed at the Provincial Meeting House of Middle Spring. His prayers, of course, were answered bountifully with a dozen children, and so the new Culbertson's Row of Chambersburg was at once both populated and doomed eventually to split apart. But who would scorn a dozen descendants of Duncan, presumably the very same Duncan who fell by the hand of Macbeth in the testy times of 1040?

The eldest of the twelve was Joseph, born on Culbertson's Row but spirited away, not by his brothers like another Joseph I've heard about, but by the lure of fortune. And just as the ancient Joseph became a guardian of Pharoah's coffers, so too the new Joseph became a guardian of coffers, a banker in Philadelphia. (Though, by some accounts, he was just a merchant and inn-keeper.) A man of property and the work ethic, Joseph married Captain Finley's daughter Mary and by her sired his half-dozen: Robert, James, Alexander, Cyrus,

William, and Mary. Robert moved away from the Row and went to Cincinnati. James Finley Culbertson became printer and editor of the *Anti-Masonic Gazette* of Chambersburg, but then probably in the 1840s took off to Cincinnati like his brother.

Alexander, born May 16, 1809 at Chambersburg, was the in-between brother. Of Cyrus Duncan Culbertson we know less, William too moved away from the Row and became a physician in Indiana. Mary died young, and so in fact did Mary her mother.

Having tucked mother Mary away in her grave, Joseph cast about, banker-like, for a more profitable investment. Then by Frances Stuart from Harrisburg he begot his second quota: Michael(or Matthew) Simpson, Joseph, Thaddeus and Anna Mary. "M. Simpson," whose baptismal name is recorded differently in different accounts, was born in January 18, 1819, not quite nine months after the wedding. Joseph, Jr., fell from a horse and died young. Anna Mary, in her lady-like way, receded into obscurity. Of Thaddeus, born in 1823, we shall learn more as time goes by.

There are, of course, always two kinds of people in the world; the heroes and those who aren't. Joseph might have said: those who are good investments and those who are risks. Artistotle made a very dangerous distinction: those who are born to be masters and those who are born to be slaves (a polarization that would presently bring a great nation to cannibalize itself.) John Calvin drew his line between those predestined to glory and those predestined to hell. Cervantes, more empirical, labeled them the Haves and the Have-nots, thus leaving the puzzle still unresolved, for there are so many ways to have and so many to go without. American Indians prophets dichotomized the healers from the spoilers.

But by the 1830s many people were forming still another dichotomy: the folks who lived north of the Potomac and those who lived south of it. Such a division could play havoc with the lives of families close to the river on either side. Among these we may count the Culbertsons, for though Culbertson's Row was quite a ride from the Potomac, one of its access points was Shenandoah Falls (Harper's Ferry).

A rare jewel was Frances Stuart, commonly but uncritically pointed out as a direct descendent of none other than Mary, Queen of Scots. One of her admirers wrote: [1] "In her veins flowed the blood of the royal Stuarts, but none set a lighter value than she on that petty distinction. To those who knew her best, she was indeed, in a higher sense, the daughter of a king." And her hagiographers go on to call her "a mother among the fathers," an allusion to the founding fathers of the American Board of Foreign Missions and also to Frances' personal zeal on behalf of the heathen overseas. (The heathen, it seems, were always thought of as overseas or beyond the western frontier.) In those days, when the literary productions of genteel ladies had to be closely scrutinized by level-headed gentlemen to shield the public from feminine frivolities, Frances Stuart dared to compose under her own name an essay entitled "The Female Missionary Society of Dauphin County." In this distinguished society, the members pledged themselves to propagate the Gospel among "those poor savage tribes" that were otherwise doomed to perish. So, of course, when Frances' first-born turned out to be a male-child, like Isaac, nothing would do but that she dedicate him as a mere babe to God and the foreign missions. Michael she named him — Michael[2] of the flaming sword, the slayer of dragons.

---

[1] James Rose and Dr. Martin, listed in my bibliography. They both say the same thing.
[2] He was also called Matthew and Simpson but I'll settle for Michael.

In some ways, Michael Simpson seems the brother most like Alexander. I even imagine I see a likeness in their portraits. Perhaps Frances Stuart would not be wholly delighted with my comparison. Alec did not really belong to her, of course, and I suspect his father had never found him a good investment. For while his brothers were educated for the professions: the clergy, the military, medicine, journalism, poor Alec—or lucky Alec—received but a mediochre education sufficient for a clerk, or what was then called a "grammar schooling." Even so, he might well have enjoyed growing up in the midst of the Blue Ridge and the Alleghenies, where wolves and panthers still prowled the woods. Perhaps that was how he developed his skills as hunter and outdoorsman.

At this stage, there is no sign that anyone expected Alec to add luster to the family annals, whereas everyone, or at least Frances' "intimate friends" were aware of her special consecration of little Michael Simpson, none more so than the puzzled lad himself, for even his playmates dubbed him "missionary boy." As they frolicked on the village green or along the banks of the Susquehanna, they would mock him with glee (or ply him with cool pity) over the latest news about missionaries in Sumatra who had been devoured by cannibals. They probably fantasized about the poor victim being stewed in a big black pot. Alec, much older than Michael Simpson, certainly had no prospects to rival that.

But there was someone who did concern himself with Alec's prospects, and that was his uncle John Craighead Culbertson. Uncle John proved the key to Alec's future in the West. Having entered the Army from Pennsylvania for the war of 1812, John Craighead became a lieutenant already in the following year, eventually a captain, and was honorably discharged when the Army was reorganized in 1821. But the Army was still in his blood, and he made himself a sutler at Baton Rouge.

The sutler was a civilian accorded the rank of cadet and assigned singly to a military post (though each sutler might work in partnership with others). It was his job to sell the amenities to the troopers, the things that kept them contented far from home (food, clothes, whiskey, etc.). Though he sold for profit, he was under careful military regulations and was appointed by the Secretary of War. Sometimes there occurred some overlapping of sutlers' jurisdictions when troops on the move passed through posts assigned to other sutlers. Uncle John may have run into this problem in one of his early adventures along the Missouri River in the wake of the mislabeled "Yellowstone Expedition."

But on his first tour of duty with Alec, Uncle John took his nephew off to Florida when the boy was seventeen. Though it tells you in the history books that they went to the Indian Wars, there really was no Indian war in Florida in 1826. This was the interval between the first and second Seminole wars. Even before this time, the Indian cause had reached an impasse east of the Mississippi. It had already been lost, it would seem, when the great Tecumseh made his last desperate gamble. According to his devotees, he had stamped his foot and shaken the earth so that the valleys of the Ohio and Mississippi cracked open, belched forth sulphur fumes and sent the rivers rolling backwards. It was the Indian Apocalypse, and Tecumseh himself perished with his cause.

For the time being then, Alec lived in a season of relative tranquility. It is quite likely that he did get something of an introduction to Indian life in northern Florida, for he had but to look about him to observe a land made safe for slavery by an agressive Scotch-Irishman named Andrew Jackson, a land where blacks were in thraldom and Indians in hungry confinement. But Osceola was then still serving as an Army scout, and whites came south for a health resort. Even

Emerson was recovering his health in the Florida sun and paying his respects to the noted newly-weds, Napoleon's nephew and George Washington's niece. [3]

So we cannot conjure up visions of wild adventure for young Alec Culbertson. His uncle was a simple sutler to the First Regiment and Alec his simple clerk and apprentice. Their duties kept them shifting along the Gulf Coast between Pensacola and New Orleans.

The midlands, however, must have been something of an eye-opener for a country bumpkin like Alec. They were a far cry from the Anglo-Saxon world of the Puritan ethic plus (or versus) the Celtic Scotch-Irish world with its ethic of aggressiveness. In New Orleans, eastern sugar planters knocked elbows with scions of the original French families and the more recent Baratarians, Acadians and Spaniards.

Alec did have one wild adventure. While he was aboard a small schooner cruising out of New Orleans into Mobile Bay during December of 1826, his little ship was wrecked and he himself cast adrift on the deep for three to four hours. At last he was rescued by a cargo ship. Maybe that experience had something to do with his decision to turn to the shore, not to sea. In the spring of 1827 he headed up the Mississippi with a detachment of the First Infantry for Jefferson Barracks, near St. Louis.

It seems that his Uncle John struck St. Louis first, both some years ago and again shortly before or after Alec became a sutler on his own account. Neither of them would be welcomed with the fanfare with which St. Louis had greeted Lafayette and Prince Paul of Württemberg, but the Culbertsons, with their big Scottish ears and noses, were resourceful.

[3] Prince Achille Murat and Catharine Willis Gray. She was really the great-grandniece of Washington.

CHAPTER II

Lords of St. Louis

St. Louis was the focal point of various frontiers. It was a city of 7,000 inhabitants, the free and the bonded, a city of churches, warehouses, shanties, and mansions, of Creoles from Lower Louisiana or Vincennes, Canadians from Quebec, Hispanics from New Mexico, old Mexico and New Orleans, Germans as johnny-come-latelies from war-troubled Europe, Indians from many prairie tribes or even a few from the "mountains." The great trails led off from St. Louis to Sante Fe, to the Platte and the Great Lakes and to the Three Forks of the Missouri; to lands as mysterious as Xanadu. Yet there still were residents who could recall the days when St. Louis itself was almost as mysterious and as remote from civilization. And the founding family of St. Louis still reigned there in social glory—the family Chouteau.[4]

It all began when René Chouteau abandoned wife and son in New Orleans and sailed home to France. Madame Marie Thérèse Chouteau, quite undaunted, fled with her little René into the arms of a more gentlemanly émigré, Pierre. de Laclède Liguest. In 1763 Laclède and his unoffical stepson, young René Auguste Chouteau (who usually dropped his father's name René), ventured up the Mississippi, selected a site for a trading post on the wild west bank, the Right Bank, and named it in honor of the King, Louis XV, and his ancestor St. Louis IX. Then came the Spaniards who called the place San Luis de los Ilineses (St. Louis of the Illinois). The first Spanish governor of Upper Louisiana brought four bachelors to take French brides: Vásquez, Duralde, Álvarez, and Álvarez Ortiz. And so the city and its principal families began. Though it grew rapidly, one third of its population was soon comprised of slaves in spite of the Spanish law restricting slavery and forbidding the enslavement of Indians.

Never one to kowtow to church or state, the redoutable Madame Chouteau retained her slaves, both blacks and Indians, her legal husband's name and her extra-legal husband's rather elegant residence. Though she did condescend to a few inconveniences for the sake of appearances, no one was fooled. And when her husband René returned from France and summoned her back to New Orleans, Madame refused to go. One by one, Spanish officials deemed it discreet to avoid crossing Madame Chouteau, and so she and her family cultivated practical relations with the Spanish commandants Piernas, Leyba, Cruzat, Pérez, and Delassus. Madame herself lived well on into the American era, surviving by years not only Laclède, but no doubt many of her dour judges and traducers. In the end this beautiful and willful woman became the matriarch, the Chthonic Mother incarnate, the veritable founder of a huge and powerful family and even of St. Louis itself. As family biographers remind us, her progeny became intertwined by matrimony, finance and the fur trade with the families Ménard, Lab-

---

[4] Pronounced "shoe-toe." Mispronounced "show-toe."

Pierre Chouteau, Jr., "le Cadet". The Missouri Historical Society, Negative No. POR C-41.

badie, Gratiot, Cabanné, Cerré, De Muns, Papin, Pratte, Sarpy, with the Italian Vigo, the Tyrolese Berthold, the Parisian Saugrain. (And Saugrain for one had connections with Franklin, Guillotine and Gálvez.) No, it was not exactly what we can call a Creole mafia, but on Madame's demise there was quite an auction of slaves.

In accordance with old French law, the lordly Chouteaus retained their surname whether they were descended from old Chouteau himself or from his replacement, Laclède. The sons of Madame established the family fortune largely on trade with the Osage Indians. (René) Auguste built up an Osage monopoly, while his half-brother (Jean) Pierre claimed he too had been schooled in the *académie osage* and then quoted Horace to disprove his claim. Something of a benign tyrant, Pierre dominated the fur trade, vying with his Creole rivals like the Robidoux and La Barge. Pierre sired two sons, Auguste Pierre and Pierre le Cadet (the second-born), and despite the tradition of primogeniture (and perhaps because good-natured Auguste preferred Osage ladies) it was under the aegis of le Cadet, worthy grandson of Madame, that the family Chouteau became one of the wealthiest and most monopolistic in the early history of American capitalism.

Pierre le Cadet, tycoon, soul of the power structure, was at heart a true Southern gentleman and the ideal family man. Residing in a gracious Southern mansion with the proper quota of slaves and the traditional devoted Creole family, he was a good Catholic, of course—if somewhat in the style of oligarchs. His charismatic smile preserved just a hint of Machiavelli in one sly corner. In 1820 he was a delegate to the Missouri Constitutional Convention. Now he ran the fur trade which would eventually lead him into the railroad industry and the mines of Iron Mountain. Yes, Pierre le Cadet was one of the lords of St. Louis.

Another was General William Clark, Commissioner and Superintendent of Indian Affairs, erstwhile partner of Meriwether Lewis in the trek across the continent, and younger brother of George Rogers. The Clarks, of course, were an old Virginia family, and it was the elder brother, George Rogers, who got his foot in the Creole door during the Revolutionary War by his connections to Cerré and Gratiot. The story of George's frustrated romance with the sister of Commandant Piernas became something of a parlor legend in which the poor girl was sent off to a convent in Spain. But from George perhaps, William learned how to play the games and, like the old Spanish governors, stay on the good side of the Chouteaus. When noble dignitaries came calling in St. Louis—the Marquis de Lafayette, Karl Bernhard the Duke of Saxe-Weimar, Prince Paul of Württemberg it was General Clark or Pierre le Cadet or both who played host.

Uncle John Culbertson ran head-on into the Virginia Creole machine. In 1828 he addressed a letter to Vice-President Calhoun requesting clarification of his right to do business with the First Regiment wherever it might go, and so avoid overlapping of sutlers' jurisdictions. (John had been used to dealing with Calhoun as Secretary of State.) In the present instance he had crossed jurisdictions with James Kennerly of Virginia, partner to John O'Fallon and brother-in-law to General Clark. Uncle John had moved into terrain where the First Families of Virginia were marking off their turf on the Missouri frontier. But in such a touchy situation he must have handled himself with superb discretion because he came off with the confidence of his competitors and seems to have turned them into allies. Perhaps John had some previous connection with Pierre le Cadet that now served him well.

But what of those First Families from the Shenandoah and beyond—Kennerly, Fairfax, Hancock, Rogers, Radford, Byrd, O'Fallon, Clark? In Missouri these Virginians encountered another network of families similarly bound together by marriage and commerce, the French and Spanish Creoles. The impact was soon resolved, and it was not long before the First Families of Virginia began to intermarry with the First Families of Louisiana and Missouri. Business interests took precedence over the conflict of religions and cultures and did provide at least one variation on the old system of cousin-to-cousin marriages. Eventually we find Radford and Kennerly firmly wedded to Ménard and

Saugrain, even Clark to Chouteau. For the moment, at least, we'll give credit to John Craighead Culbertson for establishing a favorable accommodation with the Virginia-Missouri conglomerates as a basis on which his nephew could build his own accommodations. This alliance with Virginians on the Mississippi eventually lent a Southern tilt to Alec's world-view. Little wonder that the old chantey sings for those who are bound away, bound away from the rolling Shenandoah, far across the wide Missouri. . .

It is not possible to reconcile all the discrepancies in the accounts of Alec's youthful exploits, but according to one of these stories, he appears at the age of 20 for an interview in the reception hall of M. Pierre Chouteau le Cadet, manager of the American Fur Company in St. Louis. Le Cadet's offices are on the waterfront of the Mississippi, where he arrives in a coach with slaves. He sports a high collar, ruffled shirt and black swallow-tails. He is very handsome, charming, unscrupulous moving down the file of job-seekers with a query here, a caution there, and secretaries all a-bustle about him, jotting notes, admiring his every utterance and gesture: *Oui, monsieur, C'est ca, monsieur. . .* But Alec, poor Alec, is barefoot as he'd been in the Blue Ridge, with those big ugly Culbertson feet sticking out for all the world to behold. Yet that very day he gets a job as clerk for Pierre Chouteau le Cadet, scion of the founding family of St. Louis. If the story is true, one suspects Alec's influential uncle had something to do with it, especially since it is more certain from other evidence that Uncle John did give Alec a recommendation.

At any rate, Alec had set foot onto a battleground in the war between corporations. Four major fur companies had centered in St. Louis, each one eager to devour the others. There was Manuel Lisa's old Missouri Fur Company, followed by General Ashley's Rocky Mountain Fur Company. There was the French Company headed by the leading Creole families, Chouteau, Pratte and Cabanné. And there was the German Johann Jakob Astor's American Fur, the formidable AFC.[5] That had been three corporations too many and especially so after 1822 when William Clark, Agent and Commissioner of Indian Affairs, had thrown open to traders the rich lands of the Upper Missouri. (At that time, this was the country beyond the Big Sioux River. The concept of the Upper Missouri was elastic enough, however, to shift through the years.) Competition for these far regions changed quickly after 1822 from merely ferocious to indescribable as one by one AFC crushed out its rivals. Yet through it all M. Pierre Chouteau held his handsome head high. If French-German rivalry has proved historically disastrous, French-German amalgamation has often proved the opposite, and after Chouteau's merger with Astor, the single remaining barrier to the ascendency of American Fur was one man, Kenneth McKenzie. In 1828 AFC solved the problem of McKenzie by the only way possible, a second merger, this time with McKenzie's company, which now became the famous—or infamous—UMO, the Upper Missouri Outfit. The UMO was now the outmost branch of AFC, that monopolistic three-headed monster with the three heads named Chouteau, Astor and McKenzie.

So Alexander Culbertson began his service to the three-headed monster, even through he must still have been in part-time service to the Army as sutler. Northward he moved up the Mississippi again, as far as Fort Snelling along with four companies of Colonel Taylor. A mile from the fort, on the banks of the Mississippi, he built himself a house and continued as sutler to the Army and trader to the Indians for AFC, operating along the rivers St. Peter and Minnesota.

I am tempted to think that it must have been during the eight years around

---

[5] Astor planned to link his fur trade with the Columbia River, Hawaii and China.

Fort Snelling and modern Minneapolis that Alex encountered a couple of his future companions on the high Missouri. One was a young Frenchman from Bordeaux, Jean Baptiste Moncravie, now a sergeant at Fort Snelling, a man of many talents and *joie de vivre*. The other man was Malcolm Clarke, talented too, but joyless and the son of Lt. Nathan Clarke. Though it is possible the Clarkes had left the area before Alec reached it, there was clearly some contact between Clarkes and Culbertsons, with John Craighead Culbertson as the usual link in the chain. It was at Fort Snelling, as best we can tell, that he first encountered the third head of the monster that called itself AFC, Kenneth McKenzie, reigning monarch of the high Missouri. Whether this contact had anything to do with Alec's disillusionment, I cannot say, but when his contract ran out in 1832, Alec went with it. He did not renew.

There are other accounts of Alec's first tour of duty with AFC, 1829 to 1832. In one of these he serves as a clerk to Pierre le Cadet for a year and then is sent up the Missouri with James Kipp to winter near the Little Missouri (western North Dakota). There he proves himself to be a master of men. But neither this nor other versions of the story appear credible. I cannot but wonder whether such accounts confuse Alec with his Uncle John, who is more likely to have been a manager of men at that period and maybe any other. To early raconteurs, one Culbertson may have sounded as good as another.

Kenneth McKenzie, we should notice, was a kinsman of Canadian explorer Sir Alexander and had come from Scotland to serve as a clerk in the Northwest Fur Company.[6] Then he moved south into the States to form a partnership with James Kipp. He had, it appears, two daughters by an Indian mother, leaving them at a boarding school on the Red River. The outfit of McKenzie and Kipp was licensed in the States in 1822 for trade with the Sioux, Mandans, Crows, and Hidatsas. McKenzie himself set up headquarters at Fort Tecumseh. But lured to far horizons in 1828-29, he and Kipp established the most important of the Missouri River posts, Fort Union, at the mouth of the Yellowstone. Fort Union became McKenzie's new fiefdom, and there he ruled as a feudal lord in his castle. He had his own black slaves and his whipping post, and his word was law for uncountable miles around. He does not seem to have been very scrupulous about any law but his own. Somewhere along the line he had a son Owen by an Indian mother.

Such was the man upon whom Alex turned his back when he went home to Pennsylvania in 1832. Then he thought things over once more. Home was not really home any more. Culbertson's Row was something that belonged in the past, not the future. Besides, it had a problem that none of the biographers take into account. In 1832 that part of the country lay directly in the path of the on-sweeping pandemic of cholera. The disease seems to have sprung out of China or India by way of merchant ships to Marseilles or London. From England and Ireland it must have been carried, again by ship, into Quebec, and from Quebec, by land or canoe, to Detroit. Panic spread before it down into Ohio and over through New York and to Philadelphia itself. To young Alec Culbertson, even the tyrannical Kenneth McKenzie must have looked better than the cholera, which could strike you down with the thrust of the cobra.

So disillusioning as the frontier was, it still had a siren's call that lured Alec away from the Row once again, away from Chambersburg, from the Blue Ridge, from brother Michael Simpson, and back to St. Louis and Pierre Chouteau. This

[6] The North West Fur Company operated in British America, the rival to the Hudson's Bay Company. In 1804, NWC bought out its own maverick rival, XY Company, and in 1821 Hudson's Bay absorbed North West. So in the end it boiled down to HBC vs. AFC.

time he was accompanied by an old friend. Edwin Thompson Denig, a physician's son with enough Viking blood to give him a yen for novelty.

The fact was, Chouteau, Astor and McKenzie needed bright young men like these two at their remote outposts. In 1831, for instance, James Kipp had ventured far beyond even the Yellowstone and set up a make-shift post for the formidable Blackfeet Indians at the mouth of the Marias, and Pierre Chouteau himself, that same year, had taken the cruise of the steamer *Yellowstone* up the Missouri to Fort Tecumseh (later renamed Fort Pierre in his honor), but this was only the short run. In 1832 Pierre outdid himself by taking the full mountain run all the 2,000 miles to Fort Union, an inland voyage never before accomplished. George Catlin went along to record the trip in his paintings and writings. How wonderful to travel 100 miles a day!

But as one of the triumvrate, Pierre did not need to dabble in such adventure again. Now he knew well enough what lay beyond the gates he guarded at St. Louis. He could swivel back in his chair at his private waterfront offices and calmly contemplate the master-stroke, the double thrust for empire that he would deliver this very spring of 1833. He would put an end to the clumsy era of mackinaws and keel-boats by consolidating his grasp on the high Missouri with a system of steamboats. His own voyage last year proved it could be done. Now he would send two steamers up the river. And he chuckled to himself as he pondered his plan of paying off his employees up there with merchandise instead of cash. There were other lords of St. Louis, *mais oui*, and of American Fur as well, but there was only one Pierre Chouteau le Cadet.

CHAPTER III

Of Princes

The threads that intertwine to weave the story of the kings of the high Missouri are traced back to farther rivers and other kings. In a castle on the Rhine lived the sixth[7] child of the lord of Wied, a son who by the law of primogeniture had no promise of coming to power. Instead, he cast about for a different world to conquer and alighted happily on the kingdom of the natural sciences. The young Prince Alexander Philipp Maximilian zu Wied-Neuwied showed enthusiastic talent at Göttingen under the pioneer anthropologist Blumenbach, who got across one striking lesson to his pupil: the equality of the races of mankind. But with all Europe astir over Napoleon, Maximilian could not be left to his tutors and his books, but must, by tradition, become a man of arms. In 1802, at the age of twenty, he joined the army of Prussia.

Now, Prince Max was just a petty prince in a petty principality, one of the hundreds who idled about Germany in those times. True, the dynasty of Wied was an ancient one, with even a legend of descent from the Romans whose ruins lay scattered along the Rhine. But, alas, it was not a very prosperous house. The old family castle of Altwied now stood aloof in lordly ruins among the green hills, half-embraced by the waters of the Wiedbach, while its current heirs sought refuge in more modern mansions at Neuwied and Koblenz. At the Schloss Neuwied the Prince was born, but at Koblenz his mother's family Sayn-Wittgenstein had a lovelier castle with rolling gardens and swans in the lakelet.

The homeland of Maximilian had interlocked various frontiers ever since the legions of Rome. The name *Koblenz*, in Latin *Confluentes*, commemorates these intersections, the flowing together of the Rhine, the Lahn and the Moselle. It was a land where Roman and Gothic met, a land of vineyards and castles, of healing spas and the cliffs of the Lorelei.

The dynasty had sprung from a monotonous line of Sigrids and Dietrichs until it intermarried with the Counts of Tecklenburg. Now, the Tecklenburgs were lackluster counts among the swarms of counts as they emerged from the dark Teutoberg Forest and probably more quarrelsome than many, but they had a knack for discreet marriages, one of them to a lady of the line of Charlemagne, others to brides descended from the Guelphs, from Eleanor of Aquitaine, the warlords of Aragon and Navarre and of course Robert *le Diable*. In that round about fashion they did bring some sparkle into the lineage of Wied. And from one of his mother's French lines, Prince Max seems to have been a cousin of sorts to the scientist Laplace.

Ironically though, it was against the French that Prince Max was called to arms. In 1806 he was one of the 40,000 in the Prussian army who suffered

---

[7] Some say eighth.

miserable defeat at Jena or Auerstedt. Taken captive, he was tossed into prison, then exchanged and sent home. Germany in those times was vibrant with the thought of men like Kant and Goethe, Beethoven and Humboldt, so back to the University went Prince Max (1811), then back again into the army to fight Napoleon (1813). When the Brandenburg Hussars invaded France, the prince naturalist took part in various battles, plucking reptile specimens even from the war zone and won the rank of Major and the Iron Cross. When the allied armies marched victorious into Paris, Maximilian was with them. Along the Champs Élysées they paraded, from the unfinished Arc de Triomphe to the Place de la Concorde. And how natty he looked in those green years in his bell-hop uniform and his dark little moustache! April in Paris is neither place nor season but the state of mind when all wounds heal and old grudges die, and the family of Wied acquired a home on the Champs Élysées. It was probably in Paris too, the favorite resort of Alexander von Humbolt, that Prince Max made a friend and mentor of this famous voyager.

The dreams of Maximilian were not of arms but of voyages, travel for science, and inspired no doubt by von Humboldt, he sailed away to South America. His ship was the *Janus*, a British hulk of 320 tons. Pointed out of London in May, 1815, it slipped down the Thames and out to sea. The *Janus* had trouble clearing the English coast in the English weather but at last pulled off and away, past Madeira and across the equator to Brazil. With the Prince traveled his gardener and his retainer, David Dreidoppel, expert huntsman, taxidermist and faithful companion. Off Pernambuco, the voyagers were trapped in storms. After a week they arrived at Rio de Janeiro.

In Brazil Prince Max confined his attention to the east coast. He described the Indians, the geography, the flora and fauna. This was the Brazil of King João, refugee from Portugal and Napoleon, who had fled here with his entire court of 2,000. Max could hardly have guessed that one fine day his own modest dynasty would merge with the prestigious Braganzas of Portugal and Brazil. For the present he was grateful to receive the hospitality of the Braganzas, the courtesies of the Conde de Barca and the foreign delegates. One of these was Dr. von Langsdorff, who had traveled with Rezanov in Alaska and California. Was it he perhaps who inspired Prince Max to turn eventually to the Northern Mystery? This mystique, it seems, had already appealed to Max, but the trip to Brazil was substituted because of the War of 1812. Happy substitute!

Since the Prince and his party carried recommendations from the Prince-Regent of Brazil, they were easily enabled to visit *fazendas* and missions for the Indians. So Max became a first-hand observer of the Jesuit system in South America, based theoretically on Plato's *Republic* and More's *Utopia* and later to be projected by De Smet for his missions in Montana. Prince Max always showed a special interest in communes, but even more in the under-dogs of society like the Indians and blacks of Brazil. He hated slavery and denounced the brutality of whites. Among the Botocudo Indians, naked forest dwellers and allegedly vicious cannibals, Max found people of wonder. He ransomed a black slave and a Botocudo named Quäck and in 1817 brought them to the comforts of home on the Rhine. Did he ever reflect, I wonder, that he was liberating them from one bondage only to commit them to another?

An ex-slave and a Botocudo at court may not have been such an incongruity as it appears. The rulers of Wied were notoriously hospitable to dissenters and outcasts from other lands. As far back as 1662, Friedrich III zu Wied had set the tradition of toleration by granting the town of Neuwied the privilege of welcoming refugees. Koblenz became a haven for émigrés from the French Revolution. Jews too might be held in esteem, and the Moravian Brethren established a colony of Neuwied. From the Rhine and Palatinate, many refugees eventually sailed for America, and Prince Max wondered how they fared; the mystique of North America.

Liberal as they were to outcasts, the lords of Wied like their neighboring lords were intensely male-oriented. Of the eight survivors of the House of Wied at the period we have reached, all remained unwed except the eldest brother Johann August Karl, whose poor addled wife could hardly reign at court but did at least provide her husband with a successor. This was little Hermann, only three but a prospective match for a princess from over the hills. And just over the hills up the River Lahn lay the duchy of Nassau, a refuge for Huguenots that tilted, not toward Prussia, but toward France and Austria. So too another prestigious house, Württemberg in the east. Though all three houses were Protestant, French was the language of the German courts, and royal Rhenish children were sometimes schooled in France, learning French even before they knew German.

Duke Wilhelm of Nassau was a martinet with a flare for the absurd. Already the father of quite a brood, he was still on the prowl for a new wife and on whom did his eye alight but his late wife's nubile niece, Pauline of Wurttenberg. Sweeping the frightened creature first to the altar and then into an air-tight wedding carriage, he spent two or three hours puffing smoke in her face. By such ploys did his progeny increase. From his first wife came Marie, lovely little dancing Marie, the Rhineland Fairy (or as Prince Max said, the Will-o'the-Wisp) and in any event the perfect match for little Hermann zu Wied. And by Pauline came Nicolas, who would one day grow into the most prankish prince on the Rhine.

Such was the family and the neighborhood into which Prince Max introduced the ex-slave and Quäck from Brazil. But in this land of the free, the black slave died and Quäck fell prey to drink and pneumonia. But he liked the snow and survived many years as his prince's black shadow. In their double portrait (by Max's own hand?) they appear as each other's alter ego.

Prince Max's tour to Brazil followed a trend set by von Humboldt and Louis Philippe for European aristocrats to sail to America and behold in person the Noble Red Man. So Quäck, now living in their very midst, must have been a marvel for better or worse to neighboring blue-bloods. Caught up in this wonder and wanderlust was Paul of Württemberg, another naturalist with the common touch (not to be confused with his first cousin, the father of Pauline). Paul's travels of 1822-24 are well documented, though accounts of his later jaunts are sometimes desultory. From the far Missouri, Prince Paul brought home another Quäck, none other than the son of the Shoshoni princess spirited away from the Three Forks by the Hidatsa warparty. For six years Paul and Pampi Charbonneau attended the courts of Europe, where Pampi was groomed in the language and manners of aristocrats. One cannot but wonder what consternation this handsome young *métis* spread among high-born ladies. Surely Paul and Pampi must have encountered Max and Quäck somewhere along the high line. But in 1829 Paul returned to St. Louis with his protegé, ascended the Missouri in 1830 and the Yellowstone and then went south to Mexico City. It got to be quite a pattern for naturalists: Duke Bernhard followed Prince Paul, Agassiz would follow his counsellor von Humboldt, Charles Darwin his friend Charles Waterton, the Counts de Pourtalès followed Agassiz and so on. So Prince Maximilian was falling behind and had to make haste if he expected to get back on stage.

He was already about fifty. In his times, a man of that age was entitled to his eccentricities. If we can go by the portraits and caricatures, painted perhaps by the Prince himself, Maximilian had his share. A short feisty man, he was still a bachelor and known among his familiars as *der Onkel*, everybody's archtypical uncle. By this time he had amassed a grand collection of scientific specimens from far and near and was fond also of the chase, presumably with Quäck at his elbow. A warrior no more, he was prone to melodramatic war-talk, rather stooped for a royal and military personage, and somewhat careless about his dress, his smoking habits and his duck-walk. Yet he seems to have been meticulous about shaving, affecting a trim blond beard and scimitar side-burns. Locked into a role in life based on Aristotle's dictum about master and slave, he had nevertheless cultivated liberal concepts of the Rights of Man. Having refined his sketches and reorganized his relics from Brazil, he realized it was now or never to make a similar collection from North America. So he took counsel with Duke Bernhard of Saxe-Weimar and so too, it is reported, with Paul of Württemberg. In 1831 he received a letter of advice from Bernhard, perhaps introductions to persons like William Clark in the United States as well. Certainly he consulted with his brothers and his sister Luise Philippine, who urged him to find an artist to accompany him in his new adventure.

Though Prince Max was something of an artist in his own right, he must, for this excursion, have an artist of special talents. Just such a man, half the prince's age, was at the time paying a visit to Koblenz with his elder brother. His name was Karl or Charles Bodmer. (It seems he preferred Charles.) An athletic young Swiss, born near Zurich in 1809, Charles was trained with his brother by their uncle and then pursued more advanced studies in Paris. For Bodmer, Prince Max drew up a detailed contract, and the race was on.

Race, I say, because the travelers, Max, Bodmer and Dreidoppel must have realized it was high time to be off and away, for rumors of cholera were abroad, cholera from the Far East creeping now along the green waters of the Seine or the sewers of Paris and the labyrinth of canals across the great plain of north-western Europe.

Why was Quäck not included in the trip? Perhaps he was too elderly now or already ailing. Or was the Prince, who had been so indignant at the whites' treatment of Indians in Brazil, wary of what he might find in the new jewel of democracy across the sea?

The three travelers must have descended the Rhine to Rotterdam, down past the Dom of Cologne, the never complete symbol of German unity, down past the woodlands and the windmills. It was still the age of the tall ships, the sailing ships, the grand white swans of the sea, and in one of these, an American vessel, they were swept out into the North Atlantic.

Amid the festivities of the Fourth of July, 1832, they landed in Boston. A veteran patriot himself, longing for the failed unity of his own land, Prince Max was nevertheless dismayed at the American brand of patriotism, laced as it was with racism and arrogance so obvious to foreigners, so obscure to Americans. In the cradle of liberty, one of the first sights to confront him was the Bostonian abuse of black freedmen. He thought the country was beautiful in its natural endowment but flawed by human exploitation. He thought New York was beautiful too, but not so beautiful as Paris, and he noted that people were already fleeing the city in fear of cholera. No, Max had not escaped it by coming to America. He had to move on.

He found Philadelphia rather drab, more so than New York. Accustomed to the grace of Gothic, he was dissatisfied with American architecture. In the heart of Philadelphia, he could only comment, "The country has no history like the Old World." But he was pleased with the estate of Joseph Bonaparte and happy to find many Germans in Pennsylvania, not so happy to discover that cholera had arrived before him. He made contact with the Philadelphia Academy of Sciences, with which Joseph Culbertson was involved, and probably too with the same naturalists Humboldt had consulted. At the academy he engaged in an interview regarding a new commune on the Wabash. Max was fascinated by the religious communes that were springing up in the United States, forerunners of Transcendentalism.[8] Interest in socialism was spreading among Americans, Germans and the French, often with religious overtones, and soon was to acquire a more radical slant from Prince Max's fellow Rhinelander, Karl Marx. So with one eye ever peeled on the advancing wave of cholera, Max moved on to the Moravian Brethren at Bethlehem.

Though one of his main objectives in America was the study of the Indians, this concern was now overlapped by his interest in German socialism as exemplified by the Moravians, whose communal style of life had some affinity with the Indian way. A cross-section of the Moravians may have come from Wied-Neuwied, who by tradition were missioners among the Delawares and Iroquois. Prince Max speaks well of them in his journal describing their community and their special school for girls, the Moravian Ladies Seminary. Their settlement, populated mostly by Germans, included a few English. It covered the top of a hill and sprawled down one slope to the Monocasa Brook that wended its way into the Lehigh or Lecha. The German church crowned the hill, while the "female seminary" nestled in shy retreat near a brook "where flowers of many kinds attract the little hummingbirds." The school had a well-shaded garden along the Monocasa. The inn where the Prince and his party resided stood guard over the bridge on the Lehigh, and there they kept a pet skunk in the garden. It may well have been Prince Max, in days soon to come, who passed on these favorable impressions to Alexander Culbertson. Maximilian struck up a friendship with prominent men of the colony, Dr. Saynisch, the young botanist Moser and the landlord Mr. Wohler from Westphalia, who may be identical with the administrator mentioned in the Culbertson accounts as Wohl, Wolh or Wolle.

After making extensive notes of the flora and fauna around Bethlehem, Max undertook a tour of northern Pennsylvania late in August. Wohler drove the carriage with the Prince, Bodmer and Saynisch as passengers, visiting the Alleghenies, the Poconos, Delaware Gap, the Wyoming Valley of the Susquehanna and even some coal mining country. From an old Frenchman named Dutot the Prince at last got some information about Indians, the Delawares who once inhabited Pennsylvania. He was "filled with melancholy" by the reflection that, in the whole of this extensive state of Pennsylvania, there is not a trace remaining of the aboriginal population. "O! land of liberty!"

Returning to Bethlehem at the beginning of September, Maximilian prepared to move westward. Rumors of the cholera, which happily had spared Bethlehem, were now raising fresh alarms, inducing the Prince to avoid a northerly route and attempt a trip down the Ohio River. Though Bodmer remained behind for a while because of an injury to his hand from his fowling-piece, the Prince set out to Harrisburg and Pittsburg, pausing to visit the socialist colony Economy. This was the third such colony established by Georg Rapp from Württemberg with hundreds of followers who perpetuated German (Frankish?) customs, costumes, and language under an efficient but autocratic regime. The earlier establishments were Old Harmony on the Ohio and New Harmony on the Wabash.

Since the Ohio River, at this season, was not yet navigable, Prince Max caught

[8] See Acts IV: 32-35

the stage down to Wheeling, Virginia (now West Virginia), where he boarded a steamer down the Ohio. Comparing the Ohio to the Moselle, he was fascinated at last by signs of the erstwhile Indian inhabitants in this land; the Mound Builders. But he lamented as ever the love of sheer destruction, even devastation, that seemed to obsess the pioneers of frontier America: the destruction of trees, of wild animals, of the Indians themselves and now even of the Indian remains. If he thought he was escaping the cholera by taking the southern route, he was soon disillusioned. For at Cincinnati about forty people were dying each day. Max quickly transshipped to another steamer and hurried on.

While his comments are consistently restrained, they sometimes take on a caustic tone. At Louisville, he encountered a number of merchants, who he claims were very numerous in America, the most idle of classes, contemptuous of foreigners, conceited and boorish. "This American conceit is to be attributed partly to their excessive patriotism, and partly to their ignorance . . ."

But there was panic in Louisville, and on board the steamer one of the passengers took ill of the cholera in the morning and was dead by eleven o'clock. Shortly afterwards, the Prince fled the steamer to take refuge at New Harmony on the Wabash in Indiana.

At New Harmony, Prince Max passed the winter among his scientific colleagues, from the 19th of October until the 16th of March, 1833. Charles Bodmer, who had caught up with him, made a side trip to New Orleans in December and January, off-season there for the endemic yellow fever. The Prince had read about New Harmony in the reports of Duke Bernhard, and added attractions were the fauna and flora of Indiana. He was happy with the cardinals, the blue-crested rollers and the flocks of parakeets. He was not charmed,however, by the "backwoodsmen" who overran the country, mostly Irish and English in origin, ignorant, untutored, rowdy and addicted to whiskey. He called special attention to the brutality with which American frontiersmen treated their animals and also to their indifference to religion. And though he noted many relics of both ancient and recent Indian inhabitants, he found no Indians. Lamenting that he had seen not a single one, he protested that this very winter the whites would drive the last of the Cherokees and Choctaws across the Mississippi: "What cruelty! This is the vaunted freedom of America!"[9] Only beyond the Mississippi could he expect to find the native people he had crossed the sea to learn about.

Though Prince Max especially enjoyed the companionship of the two scientists of New Harmony, Thomas Say and the globe-trotter Charles Alexandre Lesueur, he had not planned to stay there so long. But alas, it was at New Harmony, seemingly beyond reach of the cholera's octopus claw, that the cholera finally caught up with him. Or at least he came down with an unspecified illness, now regarded as probably an attenuated form of cholera. It was not easy to strike down the old warrior.

As spring came on, he improved amid rumors that the cholera was on the decline. So once more he set forth to find the Indians. Down to the mouth of the Ohio he traveled with his two comrades and then up the Mississippi to Cape Girardeau and Ste. Geneviève. Here, of course, they were running deep into territory where French was the prominent element of the population, the speech and the culture. There were lots of Germans too, relative newcomers. And at last the Indians. St. Louis, as he remarked, was "the most interesting to us . . . because we had, there, the first opportunity of becoming acquainted with the

---

[9] All quotations from Maximillian are taken from the Thwaites translation and edition unless specified as derived from the Orr version, much more recent.

Black Hawk and Five Other Sauk and Fox Prisoners, *George Catlin; National Gallery of Art, Washington; Paul Mellon Collection.*

North American Indians in all their originality."

And at St. Louis, of course, he met General William Clark, to whom he was introduced in a letter "by the kindness of Duke Bernhard of Saxe-Weimar." General Clark gave the Prince's project his official blessing and invited Maximilian and Bodmer to his own home to attend a council there with the leaders of the Sauk and Fox. A delegation of these chiefs led by Keokuk (the Watchful Fox) were gathered on behalf of Black Hawk, who was then a prisoner at Jefferson Barracks. Since the Prince wanted to see the famous political prisoner himself, the next day he and Bodmer accompanied General Clark and Keokuk's party aboard a steamer to inspect the Barracks and their inmates. Also on the tour, it seems, was the Scottish traveler, Sir William Drummond Stewart, who, like Maximilian, was a veteran of Waterloo and bound for the wild frontier of America. The Prince met all the chiefs and described them in words while Bodmer sketched their portraits. Especially impressive to them was one handsome young Sauk named Massica, the Turtle. Though Prince Max questioned the theory that American Indians came from Asia (not so widely accepted then as now), he had to admit that Black Hawk did have a somewhat Oriental physiognomy. But like George Catlin before him, Maximilian was disturbed by the cruise to Jefferson Barracks. On this, his first meeting with the Indians he had sought so long, what a shock to find them in chains and irons, in the heart of the land of the free!

One can only wonder what the Prince really thought of St. Louis. He tended to be discreet in what he committed to publication, less discreet in his field notes, but always frankly admitting his abhorrence of American racism. Regarding the conditions of life for blacks in the U.S., he had already noted in Boston that ". . .all menial offices must be performed by blacks, who though free people, are still held in contempt by the Americans (who so highly esteem the dignity of man) and form a rejected class like the Pariahs in India." And now here in St Louis, he found the blacks "numerous" but "poorly treated". Especially was he appalled to witness a slave being publicly flogged in the street. How then must he have reacted to the auction of human flesh in the shadow of the churchly domes and spires![10] Similarly, Prince Max regarded the attitude of white Americans toward the Indians: ". . .the Anglo-Americans look down on them with a certain feeling of hatred." And ". . .it is incredible how much the original American race is hated and neglected by the foreign usurpers." He does, however, cite "a few eminent men" as exceptions. Paul of Württemberg, by the way, thought there was less racism in St. Louis than farther south and that there were fewer slaves and those fewer "treated most humanely". But he, too, deplored over and over the general apartheid of the US, especially laws forbidding intermarriage of races, forseeing a time of disaster, national schism and revolt. "Nowhere is a human being so utterly despised on account of his color if it is not white as by this, in all other respects, so generous and noble race, the Anglo-Saxons." (Neither Paul nor Max seem to have detected any difference between Saxons and Celts.)

Prince Maximilian was in a quandary about where to go beyond St. Louis. He toyed with the notion of attending the summer trappers' rendezvous with his new friend Sir William Drummond Stewart, who was headed for Green River. Max was something of a pawn for the rival companies of Ashley and Chouteau. He was evidently entertained at the home and gardens of Pierre le Cadet, and also at the home of Clark's nephew Major Benjamin O'Fallon, who drove home a point by providing the Prince with a map of the Lewis and Clark route. He also showed him pictures done by George Catlin on the Missouri. Partisans of AFC advised him to go up the Missouri instead of the Platte if he wanted the best opportunity to study Indians. So Prince Max, perhaps sort of an innocent regarding American corporations, fell into the web of the American Fur Company. He presented himself for passage up the Missouri to M. Pierre Chouteau, who had so hospitably received Prince Paul.

Always a patron of the arts and sciences, Pierre le Cadet welcomed the princely naturalist with the deep courtesy of which he was the master. No doubt he turned on the Prince that special smile that could have charmed a rattlesnake. And of course he arranged Maximilian's passage to the Land of the Shining Mountains and the mysterious Blackfeet.

As Prince Maximilian was amused to recall, American Fur could hardly have refused him its hospitality since its own king of kings was the Prince's fellow countryman, John Jacob Astor. Quite a triumverate! The mightly German in New York or Europe, the French Creole at the western gates, the wily Scot beyond the frontier— and all of them under the benign, indulgent smile of General Clark. Who is to say which of the trio was the most powerful or the most imperial? But at least M. Pierre seemed the most astute and at the same time the most warmly human.

They neatly balanced each other—Pierre and Maximilian: the merchant prince with his big family and vast principality, Catholic, captalist, monopolist, and the royal prince with no family of his own, no land to rule, no people to lead, Protestant, scientist, pluralist.

---

[10] St. Louis did not have an established slave-market, but slaves there would be auctioned or sold at the court house or the sales of estates.

CHAPTER IV

Corn

This was the spring when Pierre le Cadet was sending two steamers up the Missouri. First to leave was the stern-wheeler *Assiniboin*, the larger of the pair, carrying on board a young hunter named Alexander Culbertson, his friend Edwin Denig, and evidently a hot-tempered hunk of bravado named Alexander Harvey. There was something else aboard the *Assiniboin*, something very mysterious stowed away in the dark of the hold: the prefabricated parts of a whiskey distillery. One had to be cautious about such things. Liquor had long been prohibited as an import into Indian territory, but for years the brothers Chouteau had been flavoring "brandy" with tobacco for Indian consumption. What quicker way to get customers hooked on your business? But just last summer (July, 1832), Congress had cracked down hard against the liquor traffic. McKenzie himself had gone to Washington to try, hope against hope, to save his freedom of enterprise—all in vain, and he was now returning to the frontier with hope gone but an illegal still in the hold. The master of the *Assiniboin*, Bernard Pratte, must have been aware of all this.

After the *Assiniboin* got underway, the side-wheeler *Yellowstone* would follow. Among the passengers were Maximilian, Bodmer, Dreidoppel, veteran mountain man Joshua Pilcher and assorted Indian agents. On the morning of the 10th of April, 1833, inhabitants of St. Louis crowded the shore to bid farewell (or maybe good riddance), with a flock of Sauks and Kickapoos among them. The *Yellowstone* was hardly a luxury ship. But to Prince Maximilian, who had just crossed the Atlantic under sail, it was fine enough, even crowded as it was with a hundred people, tipsy French voyageurs, a rambuctious Robidoux, a "Spaniard" named Hernández, and one or two Chippewa *métis*, all of whom caught the Prince's sharp eye. And besides, the urbane Pierre Chouteau himself came aboard with his gaggle of daughters, all no doubt very French and very charming. At eleven o'clock the cannon boomed, muskets talked back and forth between ship and shore, and the *Yellowstone* pulled away from the docks of St. Louis.

Before long, the good ship entered the mouth of the Missouri, whose "blood red flood" probably exceeded in volume that of the Mississippi. (Or in other words, maybe the geographers have got things backwards.) Next morning the voyagers reached St. Charles, where M. Pierre le Cadet and his elegant family disembarked, and Mr. Kenneth McKenzie came on board. The accounts fail to tell us whether these two lords exchanged knowing winks about the distillery on the sister vessel.

Above this point, Maximilian was concerned less with the cholera and more with the perilous snags and shoals, with the turkeys and cranes and the beautiful countryside. No, it was not the Rhine, of course, but nevertheless two great towers of rock reminded the Prince of the Castle of Heidelberg, the seat of his

George Catlin, **St. Louis from the River Below,** *1832-1833, oil on canvas, 19³/₈ x 26⁷/₈ in.
National Museum of American Art, Smithsonian Institution, Gift of Mrs. Joseph Harrison, Jr.*

ancestors, Ruperts II and III. He was delighted by the natural beauty, especially
the redbud (rosebud), "the most beautiful of native trees." Everything was
"lovely"; the woods, flowers, sunshine, birds, even the weather (with its summer thunderstorms) and the poisonous snakes. He noted the May apples, the
pawpaw trees, and already, the ominous scarcity of beaver where beaver had
once thrived. After all, he was a naturalist and alert to ecology, before that
science had even been thought of. "The beaver," said the Prince, "have given
way to European greed and destructive expertise."[11]
    At Blue Water some French Canadian engagés from upriver joined them. One
of them was an expert half-breed pilot whom McKenzie had summoned to steer
the *Yellowstone* through the watery hell that lay ahead. There were rumors of
an Iowa attack on Omahas. Progress was slow, of course, and the journey
dangerous and toilsome. Many were the accidents and the stops, sometimes
for repairs, sometimes for wood, sometimes for fueling, fowling, botanizing,
or hunting. There were occasional layover, as on one starlit night when the
engagés built a bonfire on the shore and chattered in joyous French and sang
Scottish ditties to the tune of clarinets. Bodmer and Dreidoppel were forever
running ashore to hunt game and specimens.
    But now they approached the Cantonment of Leavenworth, where the U.S.
Army must check all vessels entering Indian country. Here too were the settlements of the Kickapoos and the Delawares. Evidently the *Assiniboin* had got

[11] Orr's translation.

by with its whiskey still undiscovered by the soldiers, but the barrels hidden aboard the *Yellowstone* were ferreted out. And the inspector kicked and knocked and jabbed through bales of English blankets. He came up with eleven barrels of shrub, rum, wine, and fibe whiskey. General Clark was disposed to tolerate "medicinal liquor," but not so the Army. The Prince was allowed just enough to preserve his specimens. Kenneth McKenzie was furious. Perhaps the thing that most galled him was the thought that the law favored his rivals, the free traders, who somehow evaded his monopoly and could more easily smuggle liquor to the Indians.

At the mouth of the Kansa River they crossed the line which Maximilian called the boundary between the United States and the territory of the free Indians, and he and Bodmer, art and science hand in hand, strained eagerly on the lookout for the people they had come so far to see.

One by one, they passed the landmarks that would make their journey a memorable one. Above Leavenworth they passed the site where the Spanish had posted a few soliders at a Kansas Village. The Prince called the Indian huts "ranchos". a term he must have picked up in Brazil. The post of Joseph Robidoux was one of the first to appear, the site of the future city of St. Joseph. Well, there at last the Prince found one creature that got the benefit of his precious alcohol. When a Chippewa *métis* warned the Prince of a rattlesnake on a tree trunk, he stunned it and stuffed it into the cask of whiskey the soldiers of Leavenworth had left him.

Early in May they were at the post and farms of Fontenelle. Charles Bodmer painted the lovely landscape of Bellevue, which the Prince realized had once been the stomping ground of the pioneer fur trader, the Spaniard Manuel Lisa. In fact, he found Lisa's Omaha wife, Mitain, and their son, both wounded by Iowas but recovering. The Prince was entertained by two of Chouteau's brothers-in-law, John Sanford and the elderly French-born Jean Pierre Cabanné. At Council Bluffs, Cabanné had the Omahas perform a dance that evoked memories of Brazil. The Prince was entranced by the setting of the dance itself, the full moon and the call of a whip-poor-will. Plenty of corn and other crops were grown around Bellevue and Council Bluffs, well inside Indian territory. McKenzie had need of corn for you-know-what, and probably picked up a load of it at Council Bluffs.

Though the *Yellowstone* ran aground on the Devil's Racetrack, the delay was not serious, and on May 11th the vessel caught up with the *Assiniboin*. Maximilian visited aboard the sister ship and was well impressed with its roominess. This may have been Alexander's first chance to get a good look at the Prince, and a description of Maximilian often quoted is attributed to him. Alec, only twenty-four at this time, judged the Prince to be twenty years older than he really was, but otherwise his portrait of Maximilian probably stands true: medium in height, slender, toothless, glued to his pipe, speaking only broken English and wearing a "white slouch hat," a well-worn black velvet jacket and "probably the greasiest pair of trousers that ever encased princely legs." The Prince was easily upset by both Dreidoppel and Bodmer (something one would never guess from the Prince's own accounts), so that there was "hardly a bluff or a valley on the whole upper Missouri" that had not echoed an angry rebuke from Maximilian to his companions.

A few Ponca Indians came to visit their agent, who had previously innoculated some of them against small pox, and Kenneth McKenzie complained that the Poncas did not plant enough corn. He sent some men ashore at the mouth of the Iowa River to start a cornfield. Corn, corn! McKenzie must have corn! He ordered François Roi to start a new plantation.

From here on, after the *Assiniboin* broke loose from the strand, it was nip and tuck between the two steamers. They shifted cargoes so that both could stay afloat in the shallows. Luckily, the *Assiniboin* was accompanied by the keelboat *Maria*.

At long last, the first antelopes were sighted and then the first buffalo. With his scientist's eye, the Prince was quick to forsee the impending destruction of the wildlife of the Missouri basin. But it was still not too late for Bodmer to catch some the of the finest pictures of buffalo herds that have survived.

A "furrier," William May brought down bad news from Fort Union: three men had been killed by the Arikaras, thirteen by the Blackfeet. These two tribes were then regarded as the most formidable of the Upper Missouri, with perhaps the exception of the mighty Sioux. And they were now entering the domain of the Sioux, the Land of the Spotted Eagle, *Wambli Galeshka*, symbol of the Great Spirit. These were a people in whom Maximilian was most interested. Bodmer and one of the agents left the steamer to ride overland to the Sioux agency, where the Prince rejoined them the next day (May 25th). The artist did a specially remarkable portrait of a warrior named Big Soldier in full elegance.

At the Big Bend the two steamers followed the river for 25 miles while the distance gained across the peninsula was a mere mile and a half. They met a canoe descending the river with Major Mitchell and took him aboard back up to Fort Pierre. David Mitchell was a remarkably handsome Virginian, a gentleman and a cavalier to the bone, to whom, at present, the Company had entrusted its precarious commerce with the Blackfeet. At Fort Pierre, the *Yellowstone* reached the end of its voyage and turned back to St. Louis. Prince Maximilian and his party transferred to the *Assiniboin*. Lucky for them!

The passengers who returned downstream with the *Yellowstone* ran into a catastrophe that we cannot overlook. That ill-starred side-wheeler came bow-foremost into the wave of cholera. The pilot and many of the crew were suddenly wiped out. The captain had to go ashore to look for another crew and turned his vessel over to the youthful pilot Joseph La Barge. The Yellowstone now lay close to Missouri shores, settled by rough-and-ready individualists who wanted nothing so much as to burn the polluted steamer to the staves. La Barge, despite his inexperience, managed to get the steamer across the state line to safety from the Missourians if not from the cholera.

Meanwhile, aboard the *Assiniboin*, Alexander Culbertson came to loggerheads with the mate who had assigned him to a detail for going ashore to cut wood. "I was hired as hunter and trapper," declared Alexander, "not as a wood-chopper." He could have taken his clue from Shylock and announced: "I see it not in the bond." So the mate put him on report to Kenneth McKenzie. The great lord of the Upper Missouri may have been somewhat taken aback by this strong young upstart who wanted to stick to his bond and nothing else. He recalled Alexander from the days at Fort Snelling. He cancelled Alexander's contract (unilaterally?). Great lords can do strange things, and he gave Alec a new contract on the spot making him clerk at $2,000 for three years. In the fur trade a clerk was something of a V.I.P., and since V.I.P's can also get by with strange things, Alec promptly interceded for his friend Denig and won him the same terms.

When the *Assiniboin* pulled off from Fort Pierre with a three-gun salute and two keelboats, she carried away Alexander, the Prince, Harvey, and their comrades as well as the pieces of the whiskey still and 200 pounds of gunpowder. But she left behind McKenzie and Mitchell and another agent, who, as the Prince mused in his field notes (but not in his official report), seemed reluctant to leave

Maximilian and Bodmer welcomed by the Hidatsa as painted by Bodmer. Note that one of the Indians is identifying the Prince so that the other Indians would not mistake him for the more elegant Bodmer. Smithsonian Institution. Photo No. 43179B.

"their Indian beauties."[12] McKenzie and perhaps Mitchell caught up later on. The *Assiniboin* had considerable trouble working free of the sandbars but at last she drove past the Arikara village and reached the old headquarters of Lewis and Clark, the land of the Mandans. The Prince-naturalist was busily taking notice of new wildlife now: mule deer, Virginia deer, elk and even a white wolf. Bodmer and Harvey went hunting and almost missed the boat.

At Fort Clark among the Mandans, they were welcomed by Montrealer James Kipp, the AFC's factor or bourgeois at this fort, and also by old Toussaint Charbonneau, the one-time husband of Sacajawea, by Chief Four Bears or Matótopa, as well as by some Crows and Minnetarees (Hidatsas). Kipp's wife was the daughter (grand-daughter?) of old Matótopa, the worthy chief who had greeted Lewis and Clark. Though an unusally short and slim man, he made a specially favorable impression on Prince Maxmilian. Kipp's wife was Ipashá or Good Eagle Tail. Alexander could hardly have guessed that this was the beginning of a life-long friendship between himself and this family.

The Mandans and Hidatsas were the people who dwelt in settled villages of earth-covered houses, raising McKenzie's corn and other crops, and according to one theory, carrying on the traditions of their ancestors, the Mound Builders. The Prince declared the Hidatsas (Minnetarees) to be the "tallest and best formed Indians on the Missouri" as he gave his detailed account of their elegance of dress and bearing, and their athletic horsemanship. These people were friendly with the Crows, perhaps their remote kinsmen, and there was a Crow camp nearby. With Charbonneau as interpreter, Maximilian visited the Crows too and one night entered the tipi of their chief, Rotten Belly, a fine tall man, in the Prince's esteem.

[12] Both McKenzie and Mitchell had Indian wives.

It was here also that the travelers from the Rhine and Alexander as well made their first acquaintance with the Blackfeet. Among the Hidatsas, the Prince noticed an especially distinguished couple from the Blood branch of the Blackfeet, whom he did not name but who have been identified as Pi-inakoyim (Seen-From-Afar) and his wife, who were on a friendly visit to the People of Earth Houses. The *Assiniboin* took aboard two men of the Blackfeet tribe who sought passage home to their people. One was the husband of an Hidatsa woman, who came to see him off with their baby in her arms and many tears in her eyes. The husband's name is given as Kiasax or Awkward Bear. He played a tune of farewell on his long flute. Bodmer painted a portrait of the good-looking young fellow with his sensitive features and his ornaments of trade from New Mexico: a silver cross and a "Spanish" blanket. Prince Maximilian was happy to notice the quiet courtesy of the two Blackfeet passengers, who made a practice of bringing him plant specimens from the shore.

The mouth of the Little Missouri (the Bad Lands of North Dakota) was regarded as the milepost 1670 of the river's course. Beyond this point the steamer rounded the Grand Detour, another sweeping bend in the river. Then real trouble began for all on board. Fire broke out on the upper deck, caused by the chimney, and menacing the 200 pounds of gunpower below. All hands scrambled to put out the fire, while the boat was driven back by high winds and swift currents. Some of the lower deck was smashed. With many hands towing from shore, everyone had to pull together.

Now the first Assiniboines appeared, and their chief came aboard as a passenger to Fort Union. Delays of many sorts gave Maximilian opportunities to study the wildlife: the wolf, deer, and the many snakes, the curlew, and for the first time, the bighorn sheep.

It was not long before they reached the mouth of the great Yellowstone; Elk River to the Indians. It was the 24th of June, 1833, and the seventy-fifth day out of St. Louis. And there before them stood Fort Union, the premier post of the American Fur Company on the Upper Missouri, capital of the UMO, and headquarters for Kenneth McKenzie. A hundred engagés swarmed down to the beach to welcome them: Americans and Englishmen, Germans, Russians, Frenchmen, Italians and Spaniards, all accompanied by a flock of Indians, wives and children. McKenzie had left his key post to the management of a haughty English nobleman of mysterious origin who went by the alias of Hamilton (but whose real name was Archibald Palmer). He amazed his engagés by insisting on a daily bath, was hospitable to whites but hated Indians. Once he cast a fine silk handkerchief into the fire because an Indian had picked it up.

Maximilian spent eleven or twelve days in McKenzie's house, where life was pleasant but plain, while the *Assiniboin* loaded up for the return down the river to the States. Some Crees put in an appearance, allies of the Assiniboines but linguistic cousins to the Blackfeet. They were led by their Chief Broken Arm (Bras Cassé), alias Eyes on Each Side, who (the Prince noted) wore a medallion with the image of the U.S. President. He had been taken to Washington in 1831 to meet Jackson and was painted by Catlin at St. Louis, but he refused to be impressed and reported back to his people that Americans were an inferior lot. One of the Crees shot and killed the Blackfeet companion of Kiasax, and although other Crees came to express their regret and innocence to McKenzie, Kiasax realized the danger of attempting to go farther, simply gave up and returned on the steamer to his wife and child. The Prince observed that McKenzie was much loved by the Indians, though I suspect he did not look far below the surface for this observation. Evidently, though, Maximilian himself got along well with this magnate, who had managed to retain some semblance of refinement in the wilderness.

The routine of Fort Union which the Prince describes as plain but pleasant, sounds somewhat different in the account of Larpenteur. Under McKenzie, "who played the nabob," one dressed for dinner. No man was allowed at the dinner table without his coat, and McKenzie himself appeared in elegance. Summoned by the bell, the clerks and officers took their seats according to rank. The table was ablaze with clean white linen and fine "victuals:" fresh meats, fresh vegetables, butter, cream, milk, and biscuits. . .One or two slaves did the serving, and decorum was carefully maintained.

After sending the Prince and his party with Mitchell and Alec up the river on the keelboat, McKenzie concerned himself with his bright new distillery. He must have kept at it on and off during the summer and on into the fall— that and his little game of corn. "We want only corn to keep us going," he wrote to Pierre Chouteau. And would Pierre please send up plenty of bushels from Council Bluffs? Yes, the Mandan corn produced a sweet liquor,but it was not abundant. And yes, the still was running in grand style. And Kenneth's conscience (if he had one) was quite clear because, as he said, the law forbade the importation of alcohol into Indian country, but said nothing about its manufacture inside the boundaries.

Besides, what better way to encourage agriculture?

But, in August McKenzie had two guests, coming east from the summer rendezvous on Green River: Nathaniel Wyeth and M.S. Cerré. They were hospitably received but rather heavily charged. And on their way on down the river these two veterans of the rendezvous paused to explain things at Fort Leavenworth and left an affidavit with the U.S. Army. Their allegations were reported to William Clark (who may or may not have been altogether shocked), and Clark requested an explanation from Pierre Chouteau le Cadet. Pierre le Cadet made a protestation of innocence both for himself and for the honorable American Fur Company. Yes, it was true (he did admit); the Company had authorized experiments for making wine of wild berries and fruits, not supposing there could be any objection to something so natural, but it did not authorize commerical production. And McKenzie, magnetic as always, came forward with his excuses: the still was just being kept at Fort Union temporarily until it could be transshipped to a friend in Pembina. Meanwhile, it had been used only for a little experimentation. (Never mind, of course, that any use involved setting it up, and that Fort Union was a bit out of the way to Pembina, where the Red River of the North flows into Manitoba.)

When the charges finally reached Washington, D.C., orders from there were sent back to McKenzie to terminate the use of the distillery and ship the whole contraption back to St. Louis. McKenzie complied. But it was a hard blow and the beginning of the end of his career, though his withdrawal from the fur trade was gradual and from the whiskey trade almost nil.

Before long, there would have to be a new King of the High Missouri.

CHAPTER V

Alec in
Wonderland

The Indians of the high Missouri and beyond the Divide had different notions of the Indian Apocalypse than the tribes of the Mississippi, whose hopes had already been crushed with the defeat of Tecumseh and Black Hawk. Many of the prairie people had no dream of defeat at all. They saw themselves triumphant forever and the buffalo eternally abundant. Beyond the Divide, however, rumors of doom had already arisen. Horrible diseases, unknown in the past, had begun to devastate the western tribes.

The Kalispels had a story to explain it all, the story of Shining Shirt—perhaps a Spanish castaway from one of the galleons wrecked off the mouth of the Columbia. He taught the people about new foods and medications and the sign of the silvery cross at his breast, and he warned them to distiguish among the strange palefaces. Some would come as healers and some as spoilers. The problem was: How to tell them apart? Some raconteurs enforced the point with other details, adding, for instance, that Shining Shirt went about in quest of his dead wife, who fled to the Great Sand Hills where no river rolls. . .

Call it what you will, a variation perhaps of the Orphic myth that occurs from the Great Lakes to the Grand Canyon. But other rumors were added to it by the Iroquois and Nipissings fleeing west as free trappers, bringing rudimentary Christianity from Caughnawaga. Wherever the source, whatever the stories, a native revivalism spread over the Pacific Northwest from Alaska to California, sometimes spilling over the Divide onto the Great Plains. The Prophet Dance began. It began like the dance of the stars in the sky sweeping out of the constellation Leo. It promised a charismatic messianism: you must dance away the tired old world and revive the new one. In the years to come, the Prophet Dance would produce the Prophets Smohalla and Wavoka, the flight of the Nez Percés, the Ghost Dance and Wounded Knee. . .

While McKenzie was getting himself into all that trouble over his distillery, and the *Yellowstone* was slipping down the river into the on-rush of the cholera, Mitchell, the Prince, Alec and many another set off into Montana aboard the keelboat *Flora* on the 6th of July, with displays of gun-salutes and fireworks. The *Flora* began the trip under tow.

Sometimes towed, sometimes rowed, the keelboat was the old standby along the river. Up to 70 feet long, with a keel from stem to stern, the keelboat had a runway along each side so that it could be poled forward by two lines of men, one file in each runway, simply striding toward the stern, pushing the boat forward beneath their feet by means of their *perches*. To the commands "*A bas les perches!*" and "*Levez les perches!*" the voyageurs applied or lifted the poles. Sometimes the keelboat had to be cordelled. That is, a cordelle or line hundreds of feet long was attached to the mast and pulled from shore by crews of twenty, thirty, forty men. Or again, the men rowed and sang in tune to French-

Canadian folk-songs. But rowing, towing and poling all the way from St. Louis to the Piegan post would have taken eight months. Little wonder Pierre Chouteau dreamed of supplanting the keelboat with steamers! But the keelboat, in its turn, had supplanted craft much more primitive than itself: the old bull-boats of the Plains Indians, the canoes of the voyageurs, birch-bark rarely and more often pirogues or dug-outs with square sterns, and the flat-bottomed mackinaw, typically 50 feet long and manned by a crew of five but good only for travel downstream.

So the Prince and Alec were lucky to have got as far as they did by steamboats. Travel on this keelboat, 60 feet long and only sixteen feet in the beam, could be a tight fit. David Mitchell was captain, and with his Indian wife occupied one of the two bunks in the cabin on the stern. The other bunk was reserved for Prince Maximilian. Alec, Bodmer, and Dreidoppel probably slept on the cabin floor, while the crewmen slept on deck or ashore, when they were not needed for poling or cordelling. Altogether there were fifty-two persons on board at the start of the trip, including one other Indian woman besides Mrs. Mitchell, a carpenter, a helmsman, various hunters and the crew. One of the engagés was Deschamps, a devil-may-care Cree *métis*, probably the father of Mitchell's wife. It seems that Denig was left behind at Fort Union, while the roughneck Harvey and the interpreter Berger[13] were dispatched from Union to the Piegan post overland on horseback.

Blissfully unaware were the travelers on the *Flora* that as they progressed farther and farther into Montana, they kept moving one step ahead of the epidemic of cholera. But they had troubles of their own in the struggle for survival, though mostly derived from heat and storms, wind, dust, and whirlpools. Then too, the meals on the keelboat were not what they had been on the steamers, amounting to nothing but a wearisome round of salt pork, hardtack, pemmican, coffee and whatever came to hand for the hunters. In spite of the hardships and the sultry heat, Prince Maximilian made his own refinements just by studying the country itself, the swans and the game animals, the grizzly bears and the butterflies. He was reminded sometimes of Brazil, sometimes of the Rhine—two regions Montana is not usually compared with. On July 18th he wrote in his journal (or his notes) that today he could not avoid comparisons with Brazil, or rather contrasts. In Brazil, "where nature is so infinitely rich and grand," the rivers were lined with primeval jungles that echoed the cries of parrots, macaws and monkeys, while here the Missouri was engulfed by a "bare, dead, lonely wilderness," occasionally resounding only with the bellow of buffalo, the howl of wolves, and the scream of crows. This was more like the African deserts than the Brazilian tropics. The high plains of the Missouri no longer resembled the savannahs of the lower portions of the river. The Prince also observed similarities and contrasts among the native people. In both Brazil and North America he found one-eyed Indians, but he thought there were more cripples here in the North. He had also seen several dwarfs up here, whereas he had noted none in Brazil. Apparently, too, there was nothing in Brazil like the Plains Indian wolf dogs, often so deformed and so hungry that they could not straighten out their spines but remained humped up and grouchy.

Just as blissfully unaware were our voyagers of the mysterious epidemic that lay far ahead of them, like the second prong of a pincer movement. Rumors of this fatal malady must have begun to circulate with the trappers returning from the summer rendezvous at Green River, and not only rumors but perhaps the germs themselves. This unidentified plague, sometimes called "the

[13] Probably Bercier or Bergier.

ague," had been spreading for several years along the Columbia River and was now moving down into California, leaving in its wake deserted Indian villages full of putrid corpses too numerous for survivors to dispose of. Though both Indians and whites were afflicted, Indians were stricken the hardest, in vast numbers, sometimes writhing and shrieking in agony. The death toll is estimated at 75 percent in the Indian populations contaminated. Presumably, the fur trade was the main means of transfer. Even Prince Maximilian, alert to such menaces, never seemed to have guessed the whole truth.

Contrarily, little by little, the Prince, Bodmer and Alec began to realize that the high Missouri provided its own special kind of wonderland. Highlights of the first leg of their journey included the pyramid of elkhorns at the *Prairie à la Corne de Cerf*, supposedly built as hunters' charms, and there were hunts and science trips ashore. The Prince himself, Alec, Dreidoppel, Bodmer, Mitchell, and Deschamps all took delight in these romps through the woods and prairies. Maximilian set off to shore with Mitchell and Alex ("my American friends") who got so hot they cast themselves into the water. Maximilian observed hunters outdo Indians in stripping raw meat from fresh kills and wolfing it down on the spot. Dreidoppel preferred to roast antelope loin over a bonfire with a pair of white wolves as his complacent audience. On both the 18th and the 19th they hunted bears, probably grizzlies. Passing the mouth of Milk River and rounding another Grand Detour, the *Flora* brought its passengers to gaze dumbfounded at the strange rock and clay formations of the *Mauvaises Terres*, the badlands and the hills and cliffs that began to build higher and higher around them. The Prince was now reminded even of Switzerland, and he considered the badlands to be an extension of the Black Hills. Bodmer painted one scene and another, especially the setting of the White Castles (July 25th). Some of the wonderland that the Swiss artist reveals in his beautiful landscapes has by now been effaced by the dams of the upper Missouri.

Shortly after reaching the half-way point between Fort Union and Piegan post, they encountered a boat with three men coming down to meet them from Fort McKenzie. One of the three was the interpreter Doucette. The next day, as the keelboat pressed on upstream, the Prince himself headed a party of bear-hunters, following the boat along the shore. Evidently, Alec stayed with the boat. They sighted the Little Rockies, but it was the badlands, that continued to fascinate Maximilian and continued to occupy the brush of Charles Bodmer. From time to time they had to maneuver over rapids, towing and poling, and the Dauphin Rapids proved especially troublesome until the wind boosted their sail. ". . .we could fancy overselves now in Switzerland, now in the valley of the Rhine. . .," wrote the Prince, except that the croak of the ravens added a peculiar note of dreariness, and of course the Rhenish castles all turned out to be works of wind and water. After crossing some rapids during a terrible storm, the keelboat began to leak badly and had to be unloaded and repaired.

Though the Prince made a remark about not seeing any Indians, they presently ran into an adventure that does not square at all with that statement. It had seemed as if all humankind except themselves had fled that fantastic country, but at the mouth of the River Judith (August 5th), they met some Gros Ventres, cousins and allies of the Blackfeet. First there were just five of them, then the five were joined by some women, then a "troop" appeared, then "a number" both on foot and horseback. . . . As the *Flora* passed through the gorge of the Stone Walls, the travelers met more and ever more of the Gros Ventres until "the whole prairie was covered with Indians." Some swam out to the boat, which was saluting the encampment with cannon while Indians saluted from shore with their guns. Mitchell and Doucette the interpreter rowed ashore and brought

Bodmer's painting of the encounter with the Gros Ventres. Smithsonian Institution Photo No. 43172.

eight chiefs back to the *Flora* for a smoke. Meanwhile Indians, both men and women began to swarm about the *Flora* in their bull-boats until in reality they held the keelboat and its passengers at their mercy. Their initial friendliness seemed to turn into importunity and insolence. Doucette and companions were sent ashore to barter and there they too were altogether engulfed. But somehow (partly with the help of a little wind in the sail) the *Flora* kept moving, and even some of the Indians helped in the towing. This was not easy to do, overloaded as the keelboat was with stowaways and panhandlers. At last the travelers got rid of their unwanted guests, mostly women, who had hidden in the boat (I wonder how!) and set a watch for the night. This they passed on the right bank of the Stone Walls, which Prince Maximilian considered "the most interesting part of the whole course of the Missouri." He included similar instances in South America. Scary as their plight had been among the Gros Ventres, our adventurers soon realized that the Indians had really treated them with restraint, for otherwise they could easily have destroyed them all at will. One of Charles Bodmer's most dramatic paintings describes this incident, while others of his landscapes illustrate the Stone Walls.

The *Flora* passed around the Citadel Rocks and through a sandstone country bristling with junipers and pines and Gothic formations—like an old French garden, thought the Prince. He, and no doubt all the other tenderfeet like Alec marveled at the obelisks and the urns and the tonsured trees, the slabs and balls that perched atop their pedestals. It was cactus country too, yet at the same time the habitat of sheep and buffalo. The hunters got four buffalo to keep the travelers well fed.

On August 7th they reached the towers and the gates of the Stone Walls and took aboard two passengers, a husband and wife of the Blood tribe, the Kaina of the North and a branch of the great Blackfeet nation. They were a fine looking pair, well dressed, and the Prince remembered seeing them back down the river among the Hidatsas. What the Prince did not know, of course, was how they had wandered so far from home, which was somewhere along the Belly or Bow River in British America. This was the couple identified as Seen-From-

Afar (Pi-inakoyim) and his wife, royalty among the Kaina, for Seen-From-Afar was as true a prince as ever there was. Their story has been preserved in the oral tradition of the Kaina and runs this way:

In the spring of this same year (1833), just after the breakup of the ice, Seen-From-Afar and his wife had come down from the Blackfeet post (Fort McKenzie) on one of the boats, probably a mackinaw loaded with the winter returns. They must have continued past Fort Union and on down to somewhere around Fort Clark. This would explain how they had evaded all their potential enemies along their way. At Fort Union (according to tradition), the travelers joined some Mandans and visited their village. So cordial was their welcome that they even received a sacred pipe as a gift for Seen-From-Afar, and for his wife, a woman's buffalo headdress. It took the couple thirty-four days to make the trip back up the river.

Nothing is mentioned about how they returned nor about their hitch-hiking a ride on the *Flora*. And of course, no account mentions the reaction of Alec, for whom this meeting was something of an historic occasion, but that would be seeing into the future.

This was not the only journey of Seen-From-Afar to the Mandan people, though probably his first one. He acquired his name for his habit of making far journeys, regardless of the dangers, and in fact, his name may be more appropriately translated as "Seen-Afar". He is believed to have spent a year taking a trip all the way to Mexico, not alone, it is true, but in charge of a party. One of his war-trail partners[14] with whom he made frequent excursions was White Wolf. On one of these adventures, which may have occurred when these two were quite young because another was in charge, they attemped to raid the Crows but were trapped in a coulee, eight men against a hundred or more. They dug a pit, held out for several days and finally all escaped in the dark. One of this same party was Little Dog. Seen-From-Afar had a very lovely, and no doubt spoiled, little sister of whom he is said to have been especially fond, in the family manner of the Blood people. She must have been about eight years old in 1833. But more of her in good time. One thing is clear for now: this royal couple had somehow or other come all the way up the river from the Mandan villages, had passed unscathed through the lands of foreign tribes and had at last caught up with the keelboat.

As our travelers pulled, poled, plodded and cordelled their way up the picturesque Missouri, they came in sight of the Bear Paw Mountains and the Highwood range. These they took to be the Rockies. This was not strictly true, of course, though in those times, the term "Rockies" and its substitutes were not used with modern precision. These were parts of the "island mountains," the more or less isolated ranges of central Montana, guardians to the Shining Mountains.

From Spaniard Island the hunters returned with geese and a big rattlesnake and reports of sighting the eternal snows of the Oregon. They also brought in some chokecherries, which, if not easily digestible, were at least regarded as medicinal for dysentery. (In other words, you could not be sure which way you would go with them.) The canyon walls were now more like rainbows: orange on a blue base, reflected in the green waters of the Missouri. Presently they reached the mouth of the Marias River, which the French Canadians called *Maragnon*. Near its mouth it catches the flow of the Teton River and so drains the heart of the homeland of the Piegan or *Pikúni* branch of the Blackfeet. Fort McKenzie, Piegan post, was not far away, but twilight overtook the travelers before they could reach it.

---

[14] *nitaka* = my partner, friend, shadow, soul. It also suggests the circle or mandala which one's shadow describes.

Noticing several Indians along the shore as well as the ominous ruins of the former Fort Piegan, they grew apprehensive. They heard rumors of trouble and also perhaps a cannon shot, or at least so Deschamps reported. David Mitchell posted a watch and with four hunters, set out to reconnoiter in the moonlight. On board, a full alert was maintained. Mitchell had left orders that the boat was to fall back if he failed to return by midnight. Through the warm quiet evening those left aboard could hear the tom-toms from some Indian encampment and the howls of the wolves. Mitchell got back well before the deadline, having lost his way and collected plenty of cactus thorns in his feet. Two of his scouts were still out checking. So the *Flora* just sat in the river and waited for the dawn.

With the dawn came a hard rain, and later in the day, hordes of mosquitoes. It was hard to keep up patience. But as the travelers drew around a point, they frightened away some antelope but attracted a party of five men on horseback. With a gun salute, the five came aboard, proving to be the fort clerk and his aides welcoming the *Flora* to the Piegan post. All the fears and quivers had been for nothing. "Universal joy prevailed." As they drew closer to the fort, Indians appeared all along the bank, often shouting with delight. Horses swarmed over the prairie, guns saluted back and forth and the rain drove hard upon them all. Then, around a bend, appeared the fort itself (no great wonder compared to Fort Union) and a large camp of tipis on the flats. Eight hundred Blackfeet men formed a military battalion, while women and children covered the bottom land and the roofs of the fort, or swung from the palisades and the trees. The cannon boomed and braves war-whooped and muskets chattered and various chiefs came to greet the new arrivals, led by *Ninoh-Kyaiyo* or Bear Chief. The necessary hand-shaking was almost overwhelming.

It was now the 9th of August, thirty-four days above Fort Union. This was the end of navigation on the high Missouri. Above this point, there leaped the Great Falls, and beyond that soared the Shining Mountains, all aglow with the eternal snows of Oregon.

CHAPTER VI

Pandemonium

$\mathbf{P}$rince Maximilian had hoped to ascend the Missouri all the way to the Three Forks (the Jefferson, Madison, and Gallatin), but it soon became obvious that such a hope must go the way of all rainbows. Small parties of strangers in Blackfeet Land would probably be bushwacked.

The observations of Maximilian regarding the Blackfeet are among the earliest that survive and include even a study of the language. The Prince was perhaps the first to realize that the Blackfeet were not Siouan, though he does not seem to have recognized them for the Algonquians they are. He identified their three tribes: Piegan, Blood and North Blackfeet or *Sixika*, and suggested a total population of perhaps 20,000. In his time there seems to have remained some degree of friendship between the Piegans and the Kootenais, but not between the Kootenais and the Bloods or *Sixika*. The Bloods (*Kaina*) in particular impressed the Prince as "dangerous" and "more predatory" while the Piegans were "more moderate." Yet inside their tipis all of them were hospitable. He regarded them as a stalwart, well built people; some of the women very pretty. Their hands and feet were small and showed prominent veins like those of the Brazilians and indeed (thought Maximilian) of all American Indians. Their noses often seemed to have the Semitic crook. The Prince was impressed with the fine physiques of a gaggle of young men he observed swimming and diving in the river, their copper color redder and darker than that of the Brazilians. He noted their hazel eyes and jet-black hair. He spotted dwarfs, two and a half feet high, among the Blackfeet, as among the Sioux. The people wore beautiful shirts, dresses and robes, though boys often went naked until twelve or fourteen years old. They carried wing fans and whips and used skins of ermine and panther (cougar?). They painted their faces elaborately but did not tattoo. Their special paints or cosmetics were a vermillion and a blue obtained from the Shining Mountains, which later on, in Paris, the Prince discovered to be peroxide of iron. Women, observed Maximilian, were relatively well treated, but many had their noses cut off for adultery, and even white men did this to their Indian wives. (Perhaps the term "adultery" is rather elastic here, for as Maximilian probably did not realize, many of these women were merely victims, willy-nilly, of the increasing demands of the fur trade for slave-wives, and one can question whether a slave-wife is a wife at all. Maybe the lack of a nose merely indicated an indocile slave.) The Blackfeet were fond of their children, in the Prince's judgment, but were even more fond of whiskey and would sell wife or child for drink. Wives were shared willingly with whites. (Again, what does "wife" mean? I suspect the favorite wife, the one-who-sits-beside, was not shared with anyone.) Their medical techniques were poor but they did have some useful herbs. Their religion was then almost unknown to whites except for the sun cult. The word for "sun" was recorded by the Prince as *Natohs* or *Nantohs* and might refer just to the abode of the Deity. (Today we would spell this *natosi*, suggesting a change in pronunciation since 1833.) They traded with the Hudson's Bay in the north and with the Spanish of Santa Fe in the south, and obtained (perhaps on raids) Spanish artifacts like crosses and blankets. And among the "people of several nations" that Maximilian noticed among the 80, more or less, who populated the fort, there were two "Spaniards" from the neighborhood of Santa Fe: the hunters Sandoval and Loreto.

Loreto had just come down from the trappers' rendezvous on the Green River—also called the Verde, the Spanish River, and the Siskidee (which in Crow means "sage hen"). From him, Prince Max might have learned something about the famous annual rendezvous that he himself had missed.

The Piegan post, labeled Fort McKenzie, was a flimsy affair compared to Fort Union, temporary and overrun with mice. It was the second of the series of posts that AFC finally built near the head of navigation, shifting them about up and down the river, on one side or the other, and changing names at least as often as locations. The end result, of course, would be Fort Benton, but not for many years to come. To make things at the Piegan post a little more comfortable for royalty, David Mitchell made the Prince a gift of a pet fox as his personal mouser.

The opening of trade was always a ceremonious affair, and this time it included gun salutes, cannonades, flag-waving, songs, a parade and an exchange of gifts. Officers of the fort donned their finest uniforms and the Indians, their most elegant costumes. David Mitchell, the bourgeois in charge, singled out Bear Chief to receive a fine new uniform as a reward for boycotting the British traders. but "gauche" is the word for such a gesture because it caused Bear Chief to hang his head in shame and the other chiefs to hang theirs in sulk. Quarrels soon erupted all around. These led to bloodshed between two brother branches of the Blackfeet nation, the Piegans (*Pikuni*) and the Bloods (*Kaina*). A fight broke out also among the engagés, and liquor began to flow.

Yet not all was lost. From the third branch of the Blackfeet, the North Blackfeet (*Sixika*), came *Kutonápi* or Old Kootenai, a chief who had greeted David Thompson long ago and now bestowed his courtesy on Prince Maximilian. The Prince was pleased with the cordiality and the cleanliness of the family of *Kutonápi*, who was specially welcomed by the dignitaries of the fort (probably Mitchell and Alec!). But the good will was always being interrupted by one crisis or another. And one person who displeased Prince Maximilian was a tall half-Indian, half-Englishman named James Bird, formerly of Hudson's Bay, but now delivering letters from Fort Union. The Prince sized him up as a provocateur. When the nephew of Bear Chief was killed by Bloods, the engagés who had been sent out to work on a compound for a new fort rushed back into the territory of the old.

But in spite of all the contretemps, Bodmer kept painting and the Prince kept collecting samples of Indian languages never before recorded. The Mexican, Sandoval, served as the Prince's interpreter and informant too. One of Bodmer's prime subjects was a kindly old Kootenai with a Blackfeet wife and son, and even a Blackfeet name *Omahk-Xahkum* or Great Earth. This man provided Maximilian with a Kootenai vocabulary.

But at dawn on the 28th of August, the gates of hell burst open once more. A shot was heard and Doucette rushed in to wake up the Prince "*Levez-vous! Il faut nous battre!*" Consternation prevailed, and some men were firing from the rooftop or the palisades. It appears that the fort was under attack by some 600 Crees and Assiniboines, swarming down over the bluffs above the

The attack at Fort McKenzie by Bodmer. (Note at, not on since the attack was not directed against the fort itself.) Smithsonian Institution Photo No. 43177.

post. The Prince, veteran that he was of the Napoleonic wars, hurried to a port-hole in the upper bastion, loaded his fowling piece (not knowing it was already loaded) and fired. Back across the room he was kicked and fell sprawling over the floor.

At the gate of the fort stood thirty tipis of the band of Lame Bull, so Mitchell ordered the gates thrown open for the people to take refuge inside. Alec mann-ed the gates, trying to help everyone he could reach to safety. Surrounded as he was by Assiniboines, it was a wonder that he was not dispatched then and there. But the Assiniboines did not dispatch him. One of them, *Lunica* or Long Hair, yelled at him, "Get out of the way!," thrust him aside and killed one of the persons Alec would have rescued. It may have been *Lunica* whom the Prince describes as poised with arrow to bow shouting, "White man, I'll shoot those enemies!" Bodmer made a masterful picture of this battle at the post gates. Mitchell and his engagé Berger were also at the gates trying to drag women and children to safety, when finally Mitchell began to realize the attack was not directed aginst the fort or the whites. He gave the order "Cease fire!" Somehow, the gate was closed.

However, some firing continued. Loreto and Doucette and eight or ten other engagés joined the Blackfeet in their counterattack, and Loreto shot the nephew of the Assiniboine Left Hand.

The main Blackfeet camp lay near the *Croquant du Nez* [15] (Bridge of the Nose), a ridge several miles from the fort, dividing the Teton and Missouri Rivers. From this camp charged something like 2,000(?) warriors to the defense of their kinsmen at the fort gates, and the Assiniboine forces now discretely withdrew to the bluffs of the Marias. Mitchell and Culbertson rode after them in the lead ranks of the Blackfeet but were driven back by an Assiniboine rally. With the horses of both of them shot down, these two did not get back to the fort until about ten o'clock. In the heat of the day, the Prince stayed with others of the fort to view the engagement from afar. Perhaps getting caught in that backfire was quite enough for the old warrior for one day. Anyhow, he was absorbed by the dramatic spectacle: the throngs of Blackfeet in their war-bonnets of black and white eagle feathers, astride panther hides lined with red, and with a wolf skin across their naked shoulders, and ornamented shields grasped in their hands. "A truly original sight!" exclaimed the Prince, accompanied as it was by songs and war-whoops. Yet the Assiniboines, in the opinion of some, really outfought the Blackfeet, apparently holding their position on the Marias until nightfall.

Most reckless of the fort's defenders was Deschamps, Mitchell's father-in-law, wild and brave to the core. He had relatives among the Cree allies of the Assiniboines with whom he argued back and forth across the lines of battle.

Inside the fort walls, meanwhile, chaos reigned. Many of the engagés, it now appeared, had sold their ammunition to the Indians so that now there was a mad rush for powder. The wounded were laid beside the walls, suffering all degrees of agony. One victim was surrounded by wailing, singing, rattling attendants who poured brandy into him until he was singing with the rest. The Prince, Mitchell, and no doubt Alec and others tried to help with balsam and bandages but to no great advantage. Later, after things had quieted down a bit, they went about the tipis washing and medicating wounds, applying plaster and distributing sugar and water in place of the "brandy." Many Indians showed their gratitude and renewed trust. Bear Chief was acting like a spoiled child, rejoicing that he was unscathed because he had let Bodmer paint his picture. James Bird took off in a fit of anger.

On the 30th of August a little expedition set out from the fort for the Kootenai to trade and obtain hides of the mountain goat. Isidoro Sandoval with his Blackfeet wife, Doucette, the Kootenai Great Earth, another Kootenai and four engagés were sent out on horses with nine other animals in a pack train; they planned to follow up the Teton River and then turn north to the mountains. It would take twelve days to reach the Kootenai country. That could, of course, mean crossing the Divide into the upper Flathead or Tobacco Plains, or perhaps approaching the area of Macleod and the St. Mary Lakes. I would estimate about five days to St. Mary. At any rate, the venture would probably take them to the vicinity of Glacier National Park, but how far they got we cannot tell. Doucette was shot by a Blood, and the project ended in failure.

These days the little fort was overrun with people come to trade or make mischief. Many displayed their most elaborate costumes and were disgusted that whites appeared before them in plain clothes. A camp of 400 tipis clustered close about the fort for fear of marauding Assiniboines still perhaps behind the hills. Since the whites were so greatly outnumbered, David Mitchell put on a demonstration of skyrockets and the cannon, which failed to make the hoped-for impression because it did not out-rival similar exhibitions put on by the

---

[15] *Croquant* means gristle (of the nose). The name occurs in various forms: Cracon du Nez, Croaking Jenny, and so on.

British traders at HBC posts. When some Bloods appeared on the horizon and Bear Chief made his threats of vengeance, Mitchell sent Berger out to warn them away until the Piegans were finished trading. Such a continuous multitude of Indians amounted almost to a siege.

The Prince listed various chiefs and noted that one *Onistahna* was regarded as the head chief of all the Blackfeet tribes. He also noted that the chief of the Bloods came by, and his wife entered the fort and apologized for the hostility that had arisen between the brother tribes of the Bloods and Piegans. This incident suggests at least two things: the wife as an ambassador of reconciliation may fit into the Blood tradition of the chief-woman, and secondly, that there existed among the three Blackfeet tribes a sort of dynasty centering among the Bloods, of limited authority but considerable prestige. One wonders if Alexander Culbertson was taking due note of this because it would mean a lot to his future life. Maximilian, however, did not specify hereditary chieftainship as a factor in Blackfeet politics. I am tempted to suggest that his *Onistahna* may have been the chief later known as Manistokos, that the lady with the apologies may have been his head wife.

Charles Bodmer did a rushing business those days, because the word was getting around the camp that your portrait gave you some sort of immunity to enemy arrows and bullets. Some of the North Blackfeet were also on hand, and Mitchell made all officers share stringent guard duties, even Prince Maximilian. It seems possible that Alexander was now the second in command. There was no end of beggars, and some professional trouble-makers forced their way into the fort, distinguished by a special costume and faces painted red and black or yellow. With food running low and even the precious luxury of coffee disappearing, with no man to spare and the prairies overrun with bushwackers, Maximilian abondoned all plans of going farther west. If he was lucky, he got a bare glimpse of the true Rockies from afar, perhaps the outlying Sweet Grass Buttes, or at least something that he was satisfied to call "the eternal snows of Oregon" since in those times "Oregon" could mean what we would call the Pacific Northwest, from the Californias to Alaska and from the Rockies to the sea.

Mitchell managed to send most of the horses down to Fort Union under four engagés headed by Deschamps. He assigned Harvey with thirty men, a pirogue, and the rest of the horses to go to work on the new fort structure, and he sent others to build a mackinaw for the Prince.

Bodmer finished his portraits and his landscapes while Prince Max assembled his collection of specimens and his pages of data, his vocabularies of the Blackfeet languages from Berger and others, of the Flatheads from Bear Chief, of the Kootenais from Great Earth, of the Shoshonis from Sandoval. It is worth noting that in his Blackfeet materials Maximilian records a rare "R" where others have heard a gutteral, and yet the Prince is careful to distinguish true gutterals because of their similarity to those of German.

Forebodings of autumn were already setting in. So finally on the 14th of September, the Prince got his mackinaw loaded with his baggage, specimens, cages for the bears, and room for the pet fox—only to discover that the boat was too small and leaky. Even so, by ten o'clock he was ready to shove off. He bade a special farewell to David Mitchell and Alexander Culbertson, inviting them both to visit him in Neuwied on the Rhine and promising Mitchell a double-barreled rifle and Alexander a meerschaum pipe. Then with Bodmer, Dreidoppel and four French Canadians, the Prince departed, waving back wistfully at the men of the fort he would never meet again, exiles for the winter at the edge of the world. The cannon boomed farewell.

CHAPTER VII

The Year Of
The Falling Stars

At Fort Union Prince Maximilian, Bodmer and Dreidoppel spent four weeks with Lord Palmer and his clerks, Chardon, Moncravie and Brazeau. Of these three men, Joseph Brazeau would be the most distinguished, partly for his family back in St. Louis, partly for his career along the Yellowstone River, but mostly for his future with "The Bay" in British America; a peak in Jasper National Park is named for him. McKenzie was away at this time, so Prince Max's host was Lord Palmer, who supplied him with refreshing punch every day.

The Prince saw more of the Crees, Assiniboines, and even Chippewas, recording it all for his readers for generations to come. With Bodmer, Chardon, two *métis* and one of the black slaves, he participated in an October buffalo hunt, on horseback of course. But the Prince was not altogether comfortable to witness the "terrible slaughter." More cheerful, it seems, were the visits they made to the Opposition post, Fort Williams, conducted by the competitors of AFC, William Sublette and Robert Campbell. And with Palmer and a "circle" of companions, the Prince enjoyed fireside chats in the evenings, sometimes about the American frontier, sometimes about "our distant native land." Was Maximilian getting homesick, perhaps for his sister Luise Philippine, his brother Karl or his elder brother who was head of the House of Wied and had not much longer to live, or his nephew, Prince Hermann, now about nineteen and so soon to succeed. . .? Strange visions arise in the flames of an evening fire, especially if there's punch.

No doubt there was also talk of the Cree medicine man who was stirring up the people outside the fort gates with his feats of conjuring and his prophecies of future events. The Prince was both fascinated and amused, but he could not have guessed what lay behind these demonstrations. Anyway, Charles Bodmer made a portrait of the noted shaman, who would not stay still, and other portraits of Deschamps' Cree wife and the Cree hunter Speaking Thunder. This native engagé brought Maximilian a piece of a tooth of a "huge serpent," which the Prince happily identified as belonging rather to a fossil mastodon.

If he had been a more practical man and less of a scientist, he would have stayed with these companions for the winter, but no, down to Fort Clark he must go to make a special study of the Mandans and their neighbors, "the people of the earth lodges, the people of the First Man and the Master of Life." It turned out to be a grand plus for science but almost a disaster for Maximilian. He had the particular assistance of James Kipp, old Charbonneau and even Chief Matótopa. It is a peculiar thing that Charbonneau, whom every other journal-writer treats with contempt, the Prince speaks of gratefully. It was a tight squeeze for Max and his retainers to live in the same quarters with the family Kipp, where sanitation was minimal, at best. But when special quarters for

Prince Max had been hastily thrown together (even with glass windows), the new accommodations proved drafty and frigid and not much of an improvement. For the terribly cold weather with its high winds, the only remedy was patience. Of that commodity he must have needed a large store, for his residence in the vicinity of Fort Clark extended from November 8th until the 18th of April. When food ran low and meat was not available, there was at least corn bread and bean soup. Honoré Picotte, a top trader, supplied meat occasionally.

Hardly had Maximilian settled in at Fort Clark when it happened—the grand opportunity of his scientific career. I doubt, however, that the Prince fully appreciated his unique position. On or about the 13th of November (the date he recorded in his journal), the Leonids put on their most remarkable display in human memory. The Leonids, of course, are meteors that appear to radiate from the constellation Leo (the Lion), associated with the comet named 1866-I, and revolving around the sun in a period of slightly over 33 years. (1833 + 33 = 1866; 1833 - 33 = 1800 — actually 1799 for the record.) Indians came in to the Prince much upset by the sight of so many "stars" fleeing away into the west, and apparently too into Ursa Major, the Seven Persons. What could it all mean? What to think of it? Was it a sign of war, of death, of doom? Some people went into mourning and covered themselves with white clay. Perhaps they guessed, even then, that soon the Mandan people would be almost extinct.

But to scientists, of course, a meteoric shower is not a sign of anything except itself, and in 1833 it was hardly even that. People then knew very little about the astronomy of meteors, so that in fact the date of November 13, 1833 is said to be the birthday of that science. And no scientist had a better opportunity to observe the event than Prince Maximilian at Fort Clark.

It was an unparalleled display, that meteoric shower of 1833, something like the dragon of the Apocalypse that sweeps a third of the stars from the sky and casts them upon the earth. The study of meteors that began on that date reveals that they travel in an elongated elipse and that it takes the earth a few years to cross their path. By checking records from far corners of the world and from remote times, astronomers have found that the return of the Leonids had been sighted periodically by the Arabs, the Chinese and other peoples as far back as the 12th of October in A.D. 902. Since the period is not an even thirty-three years but a trifle more, there is naturally a variation in the date.

The phenomenon was visible in many widely scattered parts of America. At Fort McKenzie, Alec Culbertson made note of the meteors and the alarm they precipitated among the Indians, and years later reported all this to Lt. Bradley, his proto-biographer. On the Blackfeet Winter Count of Manistokos, the time is labeled ominously as "The Year of the Falling Stars." (The Blackfeet year generally began in the fall.) Far to the east and down the Missouri, young pilot Joe LaBarge, who was camping on a river island, was startled by the meteor shower that lit up the sky and drove a terrified deer right into his camp. Away in the south, in New Mexico, some people chose to see it as a warning that the secular authorities were not being nice to the churchmen. In Missouri, on the other hand, it was interpreted to mean that Gentiles should quit ill-treating the Mormons. And far to the west, a handful of mountain men from the recent rendezvous stumbled toward the little Mexican settlements around San Francisco Bay and were enabled to date their historic crossing of the Sierra Nevada by the time of the meteors. In California, too the spectacle may have seemed a sign to the Indians, a sign of doom, for that past summer 20,000 of them perished in the mysterious "ague" up and down the interior valleys.

Among the Mandans, Maximilian was more of an ethnologist than an astronomer, and there both he and Bodmer did their finest work. With old

Charbonneau, the Prince discussed the Indian tribes and such specific questions as their apparent "unpredictability", even among a relatively stable people like the Mandans. This was a question that frequently occurred to pioneer observers. The Prince was a cooly scientific inquirer. In his writings he called the Mandans a vigorous, well-built, hospitable people, very fond of sugared coffee and tea, but who as yet had evidently not obtained alcoholic drink from the traders. He declared that he found no trace of cannibalism among the tribes of the Missouri. While he regarded the Mandans as somewhat promiscuous in matters of sex, he thought the Indians in general had been judged too harshly by white writers for their moral conduct. In spite of his wild experience at Fort McKenzie, he considered the Indians to be a relatively harmonious people: "I have never observed any disputes among them, but, on the contrary, much more unity and tranquility than in civilized Europe." False is the white man's notion that whites are more intelligent than Indians: ". . .this has now been sufficiently refuted. If man, in all his varieties, has not received from the Creator equally perfect faculties, I am, at least, convinced that in this respect the (Native) Americans are not inferior to the Whites." The Prince considered taking another Native American back to Europe, but, older and wiser now, he soon dropped the idea. Since he wrote his sister Luise Philippine, we may suppose he had received news from home and knew that his protegé Quäck had died. Quäck had proved at least that he could survive 15 years in European society.

As the winter waned and spring came on, Prince Max and various others around Fort Clark were struck down by a mysterious disease. The Prince suffered "a violent fever" and his leg became alarmingly swollen. His visitors gave him but a few days to live, and he himself looked upon his condition as practically hopeless. Not so, however, the fort's black cook who had seen this sort of thing around Council Bluffs. Scurvy was his diagnosis, and his prescription was wild herbs and bulbs (wild onions probably among them). The Indian children scampered about the prairie collecting them for the Prince. And lo, it worked! By the 18th of April he was well enough to start his travels down the river once again.

Bidding goodbye to James Kipp and Matótopa, the Prince and his friends set off downstream in a mackinaw. There were sad notes in his departure, however, not the least of which was the loss of his pet fox that somehow got loose in the transition. He still had his bears, but they were hardly pets. Of the four engagés in the mackinaw, one "bad man" named Malone turned out to be a great trouble-maker, but in the end another fellow (Antoine?) Dauphin proved himself of good service.

At Leavenworth he and his party innocently presented themselves to the U.S. Army authorities, only to be placed under immediate arrest and rudely marched off to the august presence of the commandant. This dignitary presently changed his tune, treating the Prince with "tolerable politeness" if not generosity.

At St. Louis, Maximilian visited again with Pierre Chouteau le Cadet and then set off to Vincennes, a notably French town, and to Cincinnati, notably German. He took the Ohio Canal to "the little town of Cleveland: and on into Lake Erie. Near Buffalo, he paused to visit the Seneca Indians and the 'grand, sublime scene" presented by Niagara Falls, appending notes on the flora and fauna of the vicinity. In fact, the travel-wise Prince "remained long lost in admiration. . ." On Sunday he attended the Presbyterian service of the Tuscarora Indians. Catching a boat along the Erie Canal, he also visited the Oneida Indians who lived near the waterway. On his voyage down the Hudson, he was again reminded of the Rhine, especially as he swept by the academy at West Point. The Point must have looked to Maximilian much as it did to Catlin when he painted his landscape of it. After another visit to Philadelphia (and no doubt to the scientists there), the Prince, Bodmer, and Dreidoppel embarked at New York to Havre de Grace. With them sailed the two bears—which are supposed to have been grizzlies.

It is hard to know whether Prince Maximilian realized the full value of the contribution he and Charles Bodmer were making to the world of art and science. In fact, the realization is just now coming round to the rest of us at the time of this writing. But the care with which he prepared the results of his trip for public attention, both at home and in Paris, suggests that he was a good guesser. It seems clear too that he correctly surmised the ecological disaster that would result from the fur trade. But his worst expectations fell far short of the reality.

The Indians too—some of them—foresaw the doom of their world, and to counter this eventuality, one of the Iroquois employed in western Montana by David Thompson, old Ignace La Mousse, insisted that the Flatheads go to St. Louis to request the Black Robes. The Flatheads were reluctant, but Ignace and his son reached St. Louis about 1824, and General Clark placed the lad in school at Florissant. Other delegations to St. Louis, comprised of Flatheads and Nez Percés, were sent out in 1831 and 1835, yet the Black Robes were slow to come west to save the tribes from the spoilers.

So the despoilment went on. First to go were the beavers, and with them went their beaver dams and beaver ponds, and down went the water table and up went the fire hazard. Year by year, the land grew more arid, the grass less luxuriant. Next to go were the buffalo, the uncountable thousands of buffalo. Surely they would last forever. But they did not. As commerce shifted southward from the Saskatchewan to the Missouri and the American Fur Company, buffalo hides replaced beaver pelts as the chief target of the "fur" trade. The Indians, seduced by traders, learned the greed of competitive consumerism and acquired guns and more horses, They must get more and more buffalo hides! To prepare the hides for market, they must take more and more wives, even slave-wives. Coupled to all this: the ravages of bubonic plague, small pox, cholera, tularemia, tuberculosis, rabies, venereal contagions and alcoholism . . .

I wonder who started the notion that history is glorious?

CHAPTER VIII

Day of Wrath

In the Spring of 1834 David Mitchell took twenty packs of beaver furs and two hundred packs of buffalo hides[16] down to Fort Union, leaving Alexander Culbertson in charge at Fort McKenzie. His return gave clear evidence (if any was needed) of the end of the great trapping days, the end of the beaver slaughter and the beginning of the slaughter of the buffalo. Mitchell continued on down the river to St. Louis and quit his job with the Company. Alexander had only twenty men left with him at the far outpost and was soon put to the test of his command.

Three Bloods came by, with the sister of one of them. They were on their way to steal horses from the Crows. Alexander, now "Major Culbertson," urged them to give up the idea and go home. They retired to have a smoke at the *Croquant du Nez*, and there the would-be attackers were themselves attacked— and by Crows, thirty of them. Two of the Bloods were killed and the third wounded. The wounded man knocked a Crow warrior off the best horse around, jumped onto the animal himself and made a dash for the fort. Major Culbertson went back with him to the scene of the attack and had the bodies buried. The woman, who was the sister of the wounded warrior, had by this time been abducted by the Crows.

One evening not long afterwards, as Alexander was sitting at his ease in front of the fort—smoking his pipe, I suppose, since that was evidently his delight, he noticed something strange astir in the brush across the river. He took a skiff and ferried across. There was the the sister of the Blood warrior, naked except for some sagebrush tied about her, hiding away in the bushes. Her feet were cut. She was starved, bruised and depleted. Alexander, of course, carried her safely back to the fort, where she was fed and clothed and in time brought back to health. Her story was this: The Crows, as they carried her off toward their own country, had kept her under surveillance, removing her clothes at night to prevent her escape. But one stormy night she escaped anyhow and for five days struggled back toward Fort McKenzie. She also told Alec that the Crows were planning to attack the fort in great numbers and wipe it out.[17]

This message seemed corroborated when some Crows drove off all thirty of the fort's horses. Alec did not wait for disaster to strike, but had the weapons checked and a cannon of three pounds set up in each of the two bastions. He posted guards. But with no horses, it was hard to lay in a supply of meat.

In June (1834) the Crows appeared in large numbers under their famous Chief

---

[16] Ten buffalo hides to a pack, says Maximilian.

[17] For another (and I think less reliable) version of this story that places it at Fort Benton years later and portrays the captured woman as white, see the Great Falls *Tribune*, 9 April 1933, p.6.

Rotten Belly. They sent in a delegate under arms requesting admission to the fort. "You have driven off our horses," Alexander replied—in sign language. "That's what we have come to talk about," the Crows answered. "Let's have a council."

"Bring our horses to the gate and leave them there," demanded Alexander. "We must have a council first."

"Go away. If you come with guns, I'll fire. If you come unarmed, I'll let you in."

Then he had the Blood girl he had rescued appear on the walls in sight of the Crows, quite to their astonishment. The Crows were finding Alec as obdurate as McKenzie did. I wonder if that characteristic had anything to do with the big nose and the big feet in the Culbertson boast.

But the Crows were obdurate too. They did not leave. They did not bring in the horses. But neither did they again approach the fort with arms. Since the beleaguered people inside the fort dared not go to the river for water, they dug a well ten feet deep and struck water. (Fort McKenzie stood on a flood plain.) But their fresh meat soon gave out, then the dried meat was gone, then the dog meat. Then the buffalo hide of the pemmican parfleches was boiled to the consistency of glue and eaten with revulsion.

Harvey headed up a group that demanded an attack. Alec said no. Be patient. He refused to fire on unarmed men. The Crows, without arms, appeared every day within gun-shot, and it is said that some men in the fort handled their muskets nervously. Harvey the hot-head (so Alec heard) was planning to lead a party of deserters·by night and escape on a boat. Perhaps to forestall any such attempt, Alec got word to Rotten Belly to decamp by noon or expect the cannon to be fired. Rotten Belly laughed. At noon Alec fired the cannon at a tree, showering branches onto startled Crows. The camp evaporated. People fled up the river. Though some fired from the bluffs across the river, they too withdrew.

The Crows presently encountered a dozen Gros Ventres near *Bec d'Obard* (Goose Bill Hill) and wiped them out. But in the fray Rotten Belly fell too, and his dying words were: "Go back and tell our people to keep peace with the whites." So ended the siege of Piegan post. Alec admired Rotten Belly as a brave and reasonable man who had not been in favor of this siege in the first place. (The news of Rotten Belly's death was carried by William May to Fort Clark.)

Such, at least, is Alec's own version of the siege, or the version that comes down to us through Lt. Bradley's journal. The account written by Alec's friend Denig is similar and makes the siege last a month, but has it broken by the arrival of a Blackfeet contingent of 800 tipis. Also, Denig has the "great chief" Rotten Belly die in combat with the Blackfeet rather than the Gros Ventres. The time of this siege is fixed as June 1834. The lordly Englishman with the alias Hamilton, who was in charge of Fort Union, wrote to McKenzie that the men of the Piegan post lived on parfleche hide for fifteen days. Audubon's extracts from the Culbertson journal say that the siege lasted only two days, June 25th and 26th, and that the Bloods lifted the siege on the 30th, bringing meat to the beleaguered. There seems to be no way to resolve all these discrepancies.

Just in case someone did not get the message of the Leonids last November, this year on November 30th there occurred an eclipse of the sun. There is no more ominous display in the sky.[18] Alec sighted it from Fort McKenzie and years later reported it mistakenly to Lt. Bradley as occurring in 1833. Another fright appeared in the skies in 1835: Halley's Comet.

[18] Information kindly provided by Owen Gingerich of the Harvard and Smithsonian observatories. It corrects statements made by Montana historians.

McKenzie, meanwhile, left for the States this summer of 1834, utterly discouraged by the rebuff over his cherished distillery, and he did not stop eastward until he reached Europe. During the winter he came to the Rhineland, where Prince Maximilian received him with expansive hospitality. One thing they had in common was their troubles with the Army at Leavenworth, and it may well have been Max's association with McKenzie that drew down on him the Army's disfavor. But the Prince seems to have borne no grudge. He asked McKenzie whether Alec and Mitchell had ever received the gifts he had sent them. No, they had not. Presumably, the gifts had gone down in a ship or been stolen en route, just as Maximilian had lost many of his precious specimens on the *Assiniboin.* In one account we read that the Prince lived humbly with a brother (probably Karl Emil, 1785-1864), in a little stone house on the family estate (Schloss Neuwied?). In another we are told that he welcomed McKenzie "lavishly" in his palace at Koblenz (perhaps the estate of his mother's family Sayn-Wittgenstein). Believe what you like. But Prince Max must also have been busy in Paris since his return, for he submitted the Blackfeet blue paint for chemical analysis to Pierre Cordier, geologist of the Paris Museum of Natural History, and received help in preparing his journal from Achille Valenciennes, director of the Zoological Museum in Paris.

The dates of McKenzie's trip to Europe are not clear, but on May 5, 1835, someone in authority wrote from Fort Union to Alec at the Piegan post, and the letter sounds like McKenzie. It informs Alec that Kipp had arrived with cargoes from the upper post and a keelboat under J.B. Lafontaine is heading back upstream. "Mr. Harvey" is re-engaged because of his courage and integrity and his professed willingness to serve under Alec. Also, J.B. Moncravie is being sent up to Alec. He has been useful at Union and has "considerable medical and surgical skill." Also sent up are two barrels of alcohol and six barrels of wine, not a drop for "the men." If the Crows bother again, "do not spare them tooth or nail..." Better send down all extra horses, under Harvey if possible. Sell traps cheap but do not lend them. From now on the "robe trade" will apparently be "our sheet anchor"[sic]. Since the present fort will soon collapse, find a place to rebuild. Messrs. Hamilton and Kipp join in drinking your health...

About the 10th of May, 1835 (while Harvey and Moncravie were still on their way), a wrangler gave the alarm that some Bloods were making off with horses. Alec, Loreto and a French-Canadian named Hammell jumped onto a few mounts kept inside the fort for just such emergencies and scaled the bluffs. They did see about 30 Bloods but no horses. Loreto charged off in pursuit. It was foolhardy, of course, and he even fired a shot, putting a hole in a warrior's robe but not in the warrior. The Bloods fired back and rode on. Loreto turned back too, shot in the groin and upper leg. He would have fallen from his horse had not Alec jumped up behind him for support and then got him home to the fort. The horses were soon found and the affair turned out to be a false alarm. But with no way to treat Loreto's wound properly, the young Mexican grew increasingly worse.

"Why did you do it?" his friends wanted to know. Loreto replied that he did it because he did not want Harvey to call him a coward. In three weeks he died. This would be about the beginning of June 1835. The story, as I have it here, must derive from Alexander through Bradley again, but a different rumor occurs among Loreto's, or Spotted Eagle's, descendants to the effect that he survived, went over the mountains to live and later revisited his Blackfeet relations. And once again, I cannot reconcile these accounts except to suggest there may have been two Loretos, father and son, or possibly some connection between this Loreto and the other engagé called Pablo, who evidently had sons named Michel and Lorette (Miguel and Loreto).

Shortly after this episode, the engagés wanted to celebrate the Fourth of July and fired off a small cannon in one of the bastions. Gabriel Benoit was preparing the next shot when the thing blew up, destroying his right hand and his right eye, and lacerating him about the chest, face and arms. Harvey, now again at hand, came to Gabriel's rescue with a razor and a carpenter's saw, amputated his arm above the wrist, applied Peruvian bark and flagroot and saved his life. Later, Alexander had an iron hook made to replace Gabriel's hand and assigned him to light duty henceforth. It seems strange, however, that Harvey, that hotspur for every crisis, was the person to do this complicated piece of surgery when Moncravie must now have been present for emergencies of just that sort. Is there a mistake in the account by Alec or Lt. Bradley? Did both the amateur surgeons, Moncravie and Harvey, arrive too late to save Loreto?

Here is another insoluable mystery: Some time in 1835 a daughter was born to Alexander Culbertson. He named her Maria, perhaps after the river (though I have heard the name pronounced by a family member as "Maria" in the German and Spanish fashion). But who was Maria's mother? Alec must have taken a wife among the Indian women, but there is no record of the event. As simple speculation, I would suggest the Blood girl captured by the Crows and rescued by Alec. I wonder too if her brother, wounded by the Crows, was Seen-From-Afar? It was the Indian custom for a man to take sisters as his plural wives, and we shall see Alec later marrying a younger sister of this warrior. We do not know what became of Alec's first wife, but she must have given him two daughters before she left the stage.

There were battles this summer near the fort, but between various Indian factions and apparently did not involve the traders. The Crows and Gros Ventres had a fight, and off near the Sweet Grass Buttes Gros Ventres also fought Assiniboines and Crees. And it appears that the Gros Ventres had another fight with Crows at Shonkin Creek. In April Alec took the returns down to Fort Pierre coming back up to Union about the first of July.

Fort Union was McKenzie's castle, where he ruled with an ox-whip. A Mexican and a Dutchman made off with horses but came back and turned themselves in. The Dutchman's flesh was too tender to take much flogging, so the Mexican, with tough brown flesh, got extra stripes.

It was there that Alexander beheld what was one of the most appalling episodes in the history of the Upper Missouri. You will remember the rambunctious Deschamps, father of Mrs. Mitchell. He had recently been murdered in a feud with other *métis* at Fort Union and so the feud intensified, now that Mitchell was withdrawn from the scene. Deschamp's troublesome family included the mother, uncles, three sons, and two daughters, who with some other *métis* occupied a small outlying fortification close to Fort Union. In a drunken fight one of the occupants was killed and all except the Deschamps fled the building. Apparently on McKenzie's orders, about sixty men surrounded the stockade and the fight was on in full fury. McKenzie had the cannon turned on the structure. Log-chains were attached to tear the walls down, though in vain, and the fight dragged on for hours. One of the Deschamps was killed, then one of his brothers. The mother came to the gate to surrender but was shot. Two other brothers carried on the battle until twilight, when McKenzie ordered the stockade to be set aflame. Since it contained hay, it burned quickly and the brothers with it. Two persons did escape, the daughters ten and twelve years old.

This horror seems to be the crowning achievement of McKenzie's career, and in deep disgust this "greatest of the traders of AMC" resigned his post for good in 1836 and went east. I wonder if he took his half-Indian son Owen with him or left him on the river? David Mitchell took up his job again with the Company and returned up the river to Fort Union. Alexander went back to Fort McKenzie in a keelboat loaded with supplies.

Sometime about now Alexander acquired a second daughter, whom he called Janie. Again we do not know the mother, not even if she was the same person as the mother of Maria, though this seems to be the assumption. Neither do we know how Alexander managed to care for his two little girls in this rough-and-tumble world he had chosen to make his own. One story claims he divorced the mother of these two daughters. But if true, it must have been a casual divorce, Indian style. I suspect the lady concerned simply did not survive the disaster of 1837; otherwise it seems that she, not Alec, would have the care of the daughters.

For in the spring of this year a steamer, called by some the *Trapper* and by others the *St. Peter*, captained by Bernard Pratte set out from St. Louis. In its hold, it carried a bundle of dirty old clothes, supposedly planted there by some revengeful old rascal who was refused passage. This pile of rags was the suspected source of the smallpox that broke out on board. Yet the steamer continued on its way nonchalantly. and the disease might have been kept under control had not some Indian (says the white man's story) stolen a blanket from a sick watchman on the boat. The factor or bourgeois of Fort Clark, Francis Chardon, did everything he could to get the blanket back, but all to no effect. The sickness swept rampant through the Indian villages. It is, of course, impossible to get accurate figures and facts of the ensuing catastrophe, but the estimates are gruesome enough: Among the Hidatsas, one half or more perished. An Assiniboine village had but eighty survivors. The Mandan people were all but wiped out. Some people died immediately, some felt pain in the neck and back and died in a few hours. One warrior slaughtered his dogs, his horses and his family and then killed himself. Many others committed suicide. The bodies of the dead turned black and swollen. Matótopa, the grand old chief of the Mandans, who had befriended Lewis and Clark, Catlin, Prince Maximilian, and all the pale-faces he met, who gave his daughter to be the mother of the family Kipp, now saw the pale rider on the pale horse. Donning his splendid attire, he too mounted his death horse and paraded through his village to the walls of the AFC fort, shouting his challenge to Francis Chardon. "White men are black-hearted dogs!" he cried out to his people. Then he went home and died.

Alec had sent Harvey on a keelboat down to Fort Union with the seasonal returns. When the steamer of Captain Pratte reached Union on the 14th of June, one of the passengers was still afflicted. Edwin Denig caught the germ, while Harvey rushed back up the river to escape it. Too late. He had on board a Blood, a white man, and one of the Deschamps girls, all of whom came down with the smallpox. At least Harvey showed better judgment than others: he stopped the boat at the mouth of the Judith and sent word up to Alexander, who ordered him to stay there.

Meanwhile, at Fort Union, the disease had spread deceptively. It seems not quite certain how many had the smallpox on the steamer when it arrived, but both the one known passenger and Edwin Denig pulled through in fair shape. Then a project was undertaken, following some text called *Dr. Thomas' Medical Book* in which all the Indian women at the fort and some other persons were vaccinated with the virus taken from the sick passenger.[19] About thirty Indian women let this be

[19] This was probably the treatment called *variolation* (*variola*=smallpox), perhaps invented by the Chinese, introduced into Europe from the Middle East in 1718. Sometimes it worked.

done to them unsuspectingly and most of them soon died. There is another report that only four died out of twenty-seven, but it seems more likely that the figure was high, especially since Larpenteur in his account adds that some people went crazy, some were partly eaten by maggots and the stink was scarcely bearable for two weeks. From Fort Union smallpox spread to the Assiniboines. It is true that the traders tried to warn the Indians, but the historian Chittenden severely censures the Company officials involved: They seemed more concerned for business as usual than for human lives. Probably through similar negligence, thinks Chittenden, the disease also struck the Crow post Fort Van Buren and may even have worked its way up to the Blackfeet by the simple act of letting a Blackfeet board the steamer at the Little Missouri and then releasing him to go back to his people.

This Blackfeet may have been aboard Harvey's keelboat, which we left stalled at the Judith with smallpox aboard. At the Blackfeet post there were about 500 tipis of Bloods and Piegans encamped and waiting impatiently for the trade goods on the keelboat. They began to raise a clamor at the delay. The consumer mentality reigned supreme. Alec tried to explain. The Indians refusted to listen. Nothing he could say convinced them, and they threatened to go down and seize the keelboat. They believed that the story was just another white man's lie.

About the first of July Alec sent out six men in two canoes. one drowned in rapids, two reached the keelboat alive. There they found that the Deschamps girl was improving. The keelboat now continued upstream, reaching Fort McKenzie about the end of the month. Its two other sick passengers died. Even so, the Blackfeet still had no concept of the disaster that had befallen them and had evidently forgotten all their fears of the portentous meteor shower of '33 and the solar eclipse of '34. They completed their trading in about five days and took off, the Piegans toward the Three Forks, and the Kaina to the River now named St. Mary, or perhaps to the Belly River.

It seems strange that the Blackfeet disregarded the danger so carelessly. Older members of the tribes must have recalled the previous pandemic of smallpox that had swept through their country in 1781-82, when a Blackfeet warparty raided a Shoshoni village, only to find it full of dead and dying, and a-stink with both. The warparty took home not only loot but death. The epidemic flashed up through the Rockies, both east and west, leaving half the people dead and maybe many more. David Thompson recorded the catastrophe from the lips of his Cree host *Sahkúmapi*, who was in the raiding party that entered the Shoshoni village. Others must have observed too the mysterious diseases supposed to have been transmitted by the white man to the poor beasts of the forest. When caribou began to vomit blood, Indians fled to the French for refuge. From man to beast and beast to man and man to man the diseases spread...

Now, at Fort McKenzie, Alec made what seems to us at this distance another mistake: he got virus from previous cases and held a general vaccination. He fell sick himself and so did almost all the 80 or 90 persons in his fort. At first the dead were buried, but finally there were not enough people still on their feet to perform the service and they began to throw the dead into the river. Twenty-nine died: the two men from the keelboat, Antoine Dauphin and twenty-six Indian women. There is a bare possibility that this maverick vaccination or variolation saved some lives, but I would not count on it. However, a report attributed to Archibald Palmer claimed: "Mr. Culbertson appears to have acted with great energy and judgment. At one time he had fifty-one cases of small pox in the fort. The squaws nearly all died." The onslaught began with severe pains in the head and loins, and in a few hours the victim fell dead and the corpse soon grew black and appallingly swollen. But Bull's Back Fat survived and was still friendly. Did he have some immunity from 1781-82?

A great silence fell over the land. Week after week no one came to the fort. Around the first of October Alec and Isidoro Sandoval, who may now have become Alec's right-hand man, rode out to see if they could find anyone. But when Alec felt a sudden relapse, they returned home to start out another day. This time they went toward the Three Forks and after a few days reached a camp of 60 tipis. A terrible stench greeted them. The rotting bodies of people, dogs, and horses lay everywhere. The only people they found in the ghost camp were two old women, keening. Many had fled the camp only to die here and there over the land. Alec and Sandoval turned back to the fort.

In about a month, representatives of all the Blackfeet tribes appeared with their stories of horror. The disease had struck about 10 days out from Fort McKenzie after the trading was over. Many died quickly, many in sheer panic jumped into the river or stabbed themselves. Near the place that later became Whoop-Up, Alberta, so many perished that the site was now called the Graveyard: *Akai-nuskwi* or Many Dead. (At one time this seems to have been a name for St. Mary River.) About two-thirds of the three Blackfeet tribes perished, especially the young and active—about 6,000 or more. Older people generally survived. It does not seem that they blamed Alexander. He had warned them, as well they knew, and they had disregarded his admonition. But he many not have been altogether above suspicion, and some people did blame whites in general. Even today one hears the charge of germ warfare.

The Assiniboines also suffered a loss of about two-thirds of their population, but the Gros Ventres had better luck, perhaps because of some immunity acquired during a previous epidemic when they visited their Arapaho brothers in the south. The Crows were luckier still, keeping beyond the sweep of the plague. There seems to have been no attempt to hold back infected robes, though evidently such items did not carry the epidemic down to the States, where immunity was better established.

Among the victims of smallpox, one was probably the wife of David Mitchell, as recorded at Fort Clark in September 1837. She must have left him descendents, however, some of whom may still live on the Fort Peck Reservation. Another victim may have been the wife of Alexander. It is strange Alec himself tells us nothing, and it is equally strange that the Blood winter count for 1838 names that year only for the death of Calf Chief: Onistina Oxitinitahpi. In 1838 McKenzie and Mitchell met George Catlin in New York and told him about the death-toll. Catlin noted that the government had made efforts at vaccination. I do not know where or when.

Although by this time Alec was well accepted by both co-workers and Indians, there were still trouble-spots. In the spring of 1838, Alec sent Harvey down to Fort Union with the returns. Harvey came back with a passenger he had picked up along the way. This was Big Road, a large man with a reputation among his own people as a compulsive nuisance. (I wonder if Big Road was also known as Calf Chief?) On board the boat he began throwing rocks at people, and at the fort he burst into Alec's room when Alec was on his bed. They wrestled. Big Road would have won had not Harvey and Sandoval rushed in and forced him outside. Alec followed but only to find that the Indian had already been dealt a mortal wound. The standard account (by Lt. Bradley) implies that in this way Harvey settled his score for Big Road's insolence during the boat trip up the river. However this may be, the body was dragged outside the fort and the gates closed. In revenge, some fiery young braves ran off horses while the older chiefs counselled patience. Next morning tribal leaders came to the fort to parley, and Alexander put forth a claim of self-defense. The chiefs accepted his explanation but requested the customary compensation for Big Road's two brothers. Alec in turn requested the return of the horses. When the horses were brought back, Alec gave each brother a horse and other gifts, and all was settled.

At least so it seemed. Almost two months later the Bloods made camp on the Marias River about a day's ride above Fort McKenzie and sent Alec an invitation. "Don't go!" advised Harvey. Alec had his own misgivings but felt he could not refuse an invitation that came from persons he should trust. So off he rode for the acid test, up the Marias. Yes, the two brothers of Big Road were on hand, and it was plain they were still angry. In the evening they did make some attempt against Alec, only to be quickly cut off by their fellow tribesmen and kept at a safe distance. The next day, a bodyguard comprised mostly of chiefs, escorted Alexander back to the fort. Though no chiefs are named, one suspects that Seen-From-Afar had something to do with the reconciliation. Harvey was dumbfounded.

Some time thereafter, the two brothers were killed by Crows. So ended the last known hostility toward Alec among the Blood people.

In the spring of 1839, Alec himself took the returns down the river. At Fort Union he got eight mackinaws, had 300 packs loaded onto each one and in one month brought his little fleet down to St. Louis. It was the last recorded mackinaw fleet on the Missouri.

William Laidlaw, a capable Scot commonly in charge of Fort Pierre, despotic and ill-tempered, leveled a complaint against Alec (1839). He objected to Pierre le Cadet himself that Alec was out of bounds in bringing this mackinaw extravaganza down the river.

Alec must have wondered how he would be received, for he would have heard that recently Pierre le Cadet proved himself a hard man and had sued his own brother Auguste for debt. And Auguste died. And in June of last year Alec had written from Fort Union to AFC that McKenzie had offered him an interest in the UMO:

"I feel truly greatful for this mark of confidence but still I beg leave respectfully to decline expecting (sic) the terms which Mr. McKenzie stated he was authorized to make. There are many reasons for doing so but let one which is the most ergent (sic) suffice. It is simply the fear of having someone placed over me under whom I might be unwilling to act."

He adds that Mitchell understands and has power of attorney to act for him. So who is the "someone?" McKenzie? Lord Palmer?

How would the enigmatic Pierre respond?

CHAPTER IX

West Point

By the late 1830's Mitchell Simpson Culbertson, a fledgling missionary only in the fond eye of his mother, was headed anywhere except the foreign missions. An old friend of Frances Stuart, Judge and Congressman Chambers, won Michael Simpson an appointment to the U.S. Military Academy. True enough, the Judge had a touch of misgiving about this, fearful that he was running contrary to the long-held hopes of Frances Stuart, but he argued that if God had work for Michael Simpson in the foreign missions, surely He would bring him into them as well from West Point as from anywhere else.

So off to West Point, high above the Hudson, marched young Culbertson at the golden age of sixteen and a half. As the rawest of raw recruits, he entered the Class of 1839 on July 1st, 1835. This was pretty much the Academy as George Catlin had painted it, as Prince Maximilian had glimpsed it, and as Sylvanus Thayer had reformed it. Unfortunately, we cannot learn what was in Michael Simpson's thoughts as he began his new adventure. Articulate as he was in later life, he left us no record from his youngest days. He almost seems like a different person in youth than in maturity, and as a matter of fact, he called himself by a different name. At West Point he was Michael. In later years he called himself Simpson, or M. Simpson.

For him as for all the beginners, probation lasted from June until the oral exams of January. After the orals, the students (who survived) became warrented cadets and would prepare for the orals of June and then the second camp. Military studies were inculcated during these summer encampments, which replaced vacations. This, of course, meant that Michael would not be going home to Culbertson's Row for a long time. He would never again be under the careful tutelage of his mother. Perhaps it was a relief. But no vacation?

The academic courses for the plebes included algebra, geometry, trigonometry and French. The French language received emphasis in early days at West Point, maybe because of the Napoleonic influence of the times. One of the most prominent professors from 1815 to 1848 was Claude Berard, librarian and teacher of French Grammar. The math teacher, Charles Davies, 1823-1844, also wrote his own text-books. The math and French classes were generally restricted to about a dozen men in each class, certainly an ideal situation for both teacher and pupil. During the second year, Voltaire with all his enigmatic wit was added to the French classes and a course in drawing to the curriculum. Sometimes even the math was taught in French. The third year brought on both landscape and topographical drawing as well as chemistry and physics (then called "natural philosophy" and subdivided into statics, dynamics, hydrostatics, hydrodynamics, electricity, galvanism, magnetism, electromagnetism and optics). Astronomy was introduced with the use of an observatory in what later became the library building, which even had a tower with a revolving dome and included pioneering ventures in the use of photography for astronomical studies. A great deal of the scientific material, like so many other things at that time, seems to have been derived from French sources. After this came the third summer encampment followed of course by the fourth year—which was the so-called "first class." Now the academics turned to engineering and once again French textbooks, sometimes in translation. Mineralogy and rhetoric were added as well as moral and political philosophy that stressed the utilitarianism then in vogue.

Utilitarianism may account for the doctrine of "war is hell" of certain famous graduates of the Academy, and though it seems to make a strange bed-fellow with Christianity, it was evidently taught by the chaplain. Equally incompatible with Utilitariansim was the ordeal of two-hour church services to which all cadets had to wear side-arms (unloaded, I hope) and where they sat squeezed together on backless benches like nesting snakes. Lessons from the fencing master and, in summertime, from a dancing master kept up the tradition of the officer and the gentleman.

How different was young Michael's education from Alec's! And Michael seems never to have forgotten much that he learned at the Point. Certainly, throughout his life he was the officer and gentleman, even after he became the ex-officer. And the things he learned in engineering would one day stand him in good stead in far-off China. Whether the brand of militant religion he might have learned from the West Point chaplain remained with him is more questionable.

It should be borne in mind that in these times West Point was not only the national military academy, but also the national school of civil engineering, and the young nation was in dire need of engineers, especially when the railroad industry began to expand after 1827. Engineering was presented in distinctly French overtones, since the course was established at the Point by Claude Crozet from France's famous École Polytechnique. And one other technological innovation was pioneered at West Point, for the benefit of American education generally, the blackboard.

In case the reader of these lines is as surprised as the writer of them by two things: 1) why was Michael Culbertson selected for West Point in the first place? and 2) why all the emphasis on French, let's not overlook an apparent coincidence. The supervisor of the engineering department of West Point was Brigadier General Charles Gratiot of Missouri (1786-1855), the son of the Huguenot of the same name (1752-1817) who cooperated during the Revolution in Illinois with George Rogers Clark, Father Gibault and Jean Gabriel Cerré. Charles Senior finally wed the sister of Pierre Chouteau le Cadet and, becoming a personal friend of John Jacob Astor, traveled about the U.S. and Europe in the commercial interests of his in-laws, the family Chouteau. In 1804, when Lewis and Clark were camped outside St. Louis waiting to move in, the Spanish flag was withdrawn on March 9th, the *fleur de lis* was unfurled throughout the night out of deference to the French population, and the next day, with Gratiot as interpreter, the ceremony of raising the U.S. flag and conveying Upper Louisiana to the United States was performed on the porch of the Gratiot home. That same year Jefferson appointed Charles Jr. to the Academy. Gaining fame in the war of 1812 and building the forts at Hampton Roads, Charles Jr. rose to his present status. Not the least of his distinctions was the fact that his daughter married the son of. . .yes, you guessed it. . .Pierre Chouteau le Cadet, and the son was Charles, heir to AFC. Though General Gratiot left West Point under controversy, he was in authority there during all but the last months of Michael's attendance. And of course we cannot forget that John Craighead Culbertson was also a friend of Pierre le Cadet.

I regret to say that the menu at West Point in those days does not sound very well balanced; pieces of meat in potatoes with lots of gravy for breakfast, along with bread, butter, and coffee; roast beef and boiled potatoes for dinner with butterless bread; and for "tea" there was tea, of course, with bread and butter. You had to wolf it all down fast. Taps sounded and lights went out at 10:00 p.m. For recreation there were concerts and Saturday "rambles" and, naturally, illicit escapades. The tales we read of duels among the students cannot be accepted without question. Perhaps such stories refer to bare-knuckle fights which were organized with seconds. Both these contests and the hazing sometimes did get out of hand, and the arguments of North versus South increased tensions even at this early period.

Among Michael's classmates were Edward Canby, Henry Halleck, Robert Lawton, Henry J. Hunt, Edward Cresap Ord, James B. Ricketts and—never to be overlooked—Isaac Ingalls Stevens. Ord, of course, was one of the brothers noted in the history of Maryland, Michigan, California, etc., reputed to be grandsons of George IV of Great Britain by his morganatic marriage.

Among Michael's other associates at the Point were Pierre Beauregard of New Orleans, Braxton Bragg of North Carolina, Winfield Scott Hancock "the Superb," as well as an ill-starred cadet named Egbert Malcolm Clarke. Malcolm was the son, of Lt. Nathan Clarke, formerly of Fort Snelling, Minnesota.

For reasons I cannot imagine, Michael S. Culbertson is said also to have been associated with John B. Magruder of Virginia at West Point, and in fact a story, circulated years later claimed that he had stood as a second for Magruder but managed to reconcile Magruder and his opponent and so prevent the duel. But Magruder belonged to the Class of 1830 and could hardly have been a schoolmate of Michael. There was a challenge of some sort during Michael's career at the Point involving Malcolm Clarke, not Magruder, and there is the barest possibility that this was the source of confusion. However, I have already remarked about the dubious authenticity of stories about duels at the Academy. In one story, Malcolm Clarke, a true firebrand, once challenged another student and pummeled him with a rawhide in front of his classmates. For this, Malcolm was dismissed and took off for Texas.

Another feisty cadet was Isaac Stevens of Massachusetss, nicknamed "the Yankee" and even "the Animal". His father was something of a maverick and took part in the underground railroad, and young Isaac was a maverick too. He proved it by disagreeing with his father and the abolitionists. He opposed slavery but for reasons pragmatic rather than moral. Bullied by upper classmen for his short stature, he grew quick to resent insults, even took it as a personal insult when Southern cadets referred to Yankee farmers as "slaves" and pledged himself to "act accordingly". He got his share of demerits but, as far as we know, he never had any duels. Like Michael, he was a whiz at math.

Michael was singled out at the Point and offered the opportunity to go to France for special military training but he declined the honor. He was also given the distinction of an appointment as drill-master, and at this point in his story, his biographer in the Presbytery annals grows eloquent: "Fancy the future missionary instructing the leaders of the two great armies of the North and the South in the arts of attack and defense. . ." The generals-to-be whom he is said to have trained were Towar, Van Vliet, George Henry Thomas, William Starke Rosecrans and John Newton. Oh yes, and evidently there was a red-headed collector of demerits called "Cump," which was short for Tecumseh, his father's hero. This young roughneck had once hanged the same cat nine times and even dyed his hateful hair green. William Tecumseh Sherman was a buddy of Malcolm Clarke, and in a way they were two of a kind.

At graduation for the Class of '39, on the first of July, Michael is said to have ranked third for scholarship, though the record in the archives of the Academy shows him ranking sixth out of a class of thirty-one. At the top of the class in academics but not in conduct was Isaac Ingalls Stevens (or at least according to his son Hazard, who is not shy in the praise of his father). Michael carried away with him his dress sword and a commission as second lieutenant of First Artillery. At this juncture, the graduates switched from their gray uniforms that the cadets had worn at the Academy ever since the War of 1812, to the flashy new blues with the yellow trim of Army Officers, which some would one day exchange once more for Confederate grays. Did Alec attend his brother's graduation? We cannot tell, though we have seen him come down the river this season. He was at Union in June, but I question that he could have been at West Point by the 1st of July.

In 1839 and 1840 Michael served on the Canadian border during the boundary dispute and the ethnic conflict in Canada. He was at Rouse's Point and Plattsburg, New York, in the latter half of '39 but was recalled to West Point about the first of the year. Then until the 4th of February he served at the Academy as assistant instructor of mathematics. No doubt he was filling in for some emergency, but even so this was no trivial assignment and carried with it the pro-tem rank of Captain. One of his math pupils is said to have been Ulysses Simpson Grant. Later in 1840 Michael Simpson Culbertson was back again in the Disputed Territory presumably with the rank of second lieutenant. He served at Houlton, Maine, and in 1840 and 1841 at Fort Preble.

But as it turned out, Judge Chambers was right after all. The Lord did come to fetch Michael away from the trivialities of border squabbles and the petty affairs of nations. At Plattsburg Lt. Michael Simpson Culbertson stepped forward in church to make a public confession of faith. Just picture the scene with Michael in his bright blue uniform with gold trim and maybe even the dress sword. How ladies' hearts must have fluttered! On the 15th of April, 1841, he resigned his commission to enter the theological seminary at Princeton.

Ah, but life is an hour-glass. You win one, you lose one. And so it was for Michael's erstwhile fellow student at the Point. Expelled from the Academy, Malcolm Clarke took passage for Texas and aboard ship involved himself in a mutiny. In Texas he joined up with Sam Houston, friend of Auguste Chouteau, and (according to his adoring sister) served "faithfully" in the insurrection. To this add the strange story that once when he was riding through some desolate borderland, Clarke ran head-on into his old enemy, the very man he had challenged at the Point. Neither man paused. Neither veered from the road. Neither fired. They just swept on past each other. Later, the enemy was supposed to have been killed in a drunken free-for-all. (Do with that story whatever you like.) But from Texas, Malcolm went up to Cincinnati and won a commendation from his father's old friend John Craighead Culbertson to M. Pierre Chouteau le Cadet. So he was assigned to accompany Alec Culbertson up the Missouri in 1839.

CHAPTER X

Queen of the High Missouri

Everybody scoffs at the idea of an "Indian princess", but that in fact is just what Audubon called her. Her name was Natawista, or some people said Natawista Iksana (or Iskana). In any case, it was a contrived name, not an authentic one, an adaptation from the original Blackfeet term for Medicine (Holy) Snake Woman, a name which suggests an influence from far off Mexico, even on the Canadian prairies. James Willard Schultz gives Natawista's original name as *Natoap Tsis-Tsek-sin*, applying it to Janet Lake in Glacier National Park. Canadian archives record her name as *Natúyi-tsíxina*. We can easily see why historians have settled for "Natawista," which may be the invention of Alexander Culbertson.[20]

Early accounts, call her the daughter of Manistokos (Men-Es-To-Kos), the Father of All Children and head chief of the Kaina or Blood branch of the Blackfeet alliance with probable ties to head chiefs of the other two branches. However, this claim is not corroborated by Kaina tradition. Schultz says her father was Two Suns, and a man of that name was chief of the Fish Eater band while Manistokos led a rival band called the Buffalo Followers. And someone named Manistokos also carried the name Bad Head (*Pakap-otokan*), perhaps late in life. He was a large man, acquainted with both John Palliser and John Healy (both of later times). He was tribal chronologist or calendar-maker, that is, he kept the Winter Count, painted on a tanned hide, recording a principal event for each year. One of his wives was reported as a daughter of Bull's Back Fat who was painted by George Catlin. The term *manistokos* is now obsolete but was used either as a personal name or as a title, an honorific for a chief and perhaps implying some dynastic prestige. Its meaning is variously given as "Father of All Children:", "Father of Many Children", "Children Everywhere", and "All Are His Children." We shall come upon the Manistokos quite frequently in this narrative.

Similiar confusion reigns regarding Natawista's other relations, partly because old-timers had a habit of referring carelessly to Blood leaders as "Mr. Culbertson's brothers-in-law". Her brothers probably included Seen-From-Afar, Big Plume, Black Bear and Scalp Robe, with Seen-From-Afar the most certain. Others sometimes counted among her relatives (Eagles Ribs, Calf Shirt, Gray Eyes, and Little Dog of the Piegans) were perhaps brothers-in-law, uncles or cousins. Red Crow, chief of the Kaina in later years, was her nephew (though even then sometimes called her brother), and Crowfoot of the North Blackfeet was Red

---

[20] I suggest *natoap-* as an optional alternate for *natúyi-* (holy) and *xíxina* for *zixina* (snake). Sometimes TS or Z is pronounced like X, and W may interchange with Y. Hence the variation. To say Holy Snake *Woman*, add *-aki*.

Crow's brother-in-law. It is not easy to do the genealogy of families with multiple wives.[21]

Call her what you will, *Natúyi-zixina*, Natawista, or just plain Natty, she was a rare beauty, talented and sprightly as she was beautiful. Travelers agreed on that. One or two even noted her sharp flare for sarcasm. She was probably born about 1825, but whether in Alberta, Saskatchewan or Montana, no one knows, especially since the borders did not then exist. I suggest she may have been among the Bloods who visited Fort McKenzie in the mid-thirties. But when we meet her again in 1840, she is about fifteen years old, half the age of Alexander Culbertson.

There are two or three main versions of the courtship of Alec and Natawista. James Willard Schultz, in his story of applying Alec's Indian name of Beaver Child to Mt. Clements in Glacier Park, gives us a detailed account of the matter as a big event at Fort McKenzie: Beaver Child longs to speak to the lovely Natawista but seldom finds her unchaperoned. One day, he manages it at last and speaks of marriage. (To the point.) She is pleased. He invites her parents for a smoke. To put to the test the sincerity of Beaver Child, the great chief Two Suns insists that they wait one year. Alec pleads in vain, but the year is spent in the elaborate preparations appropriate for the wedding of such a high-born lady: the crafting of many rich garments and household goods for the bride. When the year is up, all 4,000 of the Kaina tribe parade to the fort in their finest attire with Natawista herself astride a black buffalo runner with a dozen white horses packed with wedding gifts. Alexander, on his part, has a room full of lavish gifts for his bride and her people. The marriage is on.

Now, I do not think that is how it happended. I would opt for the rival version given by Lewis Henry Morgan, the "father of American anthropology," and similar to what appears to be a Culbertson family tradition. But we must wait a page or so since I think some mishaps happened first.

Alec, by this time, had passed scrutiny at AFC headquarters, where no doubt all the evidence about him from Hamilton, McKenzie, Laidlaw and Mitchell was duely reviewed. McKenzie and Mitchell retired and Denig was appointed to the command of Fort Union. Alec was made a partner in the Company with special charge over the Blackfeet trade. And it may be that Pierre le Cadet whispered into his ear the advantages of taking another bride among the Blackfeet people.

As he contemplated the theater of his activities in perspective, Alec saw the dividing line in its chronology as the plague of small pox. He realized that never again would the tribes he knew best be the same as they were before the epidemic. Now, alas, they were broken in health and physique. Broken too were their family bonds. Some survivors no longer knew even their own kinsmen, and inbreeding, perhaps incest, would be a likely consequence. The Mandans, in fact, were practically wiped out. There was the small comfort that Maximilian and Bodmer had recorded the old days and the old ways just before the end. And when the news of the epidemic reached Maximilian himself, at least through newspapers, he made forlorn reference to it in the forthcoming book of his travels. His English translator had details by letter and deplored the fact that while the eastern U.S. was protected by vaccination, the western frontiers

---

[21] Hugh A. Dempsey, in consultation with Blood tribal members and especially the Red Crow family, has probed this question and kindly provided me with material on which I have based this summary. From this source we derive the information that the later Bull's Back Fat was a grandson of Bad Head.

were left unguarded with their thousands of people abandoned to death. (Actually, Montana would not be adequately protected till the next century.) The sequence of events at this juncture is hard to follow, but according to Lt. Bradley, Alec drove a hundred horses down to Fort Union in January, 1840, taking Sandoval with him and leaving Harvey in command at McKenzie. Then he sent Isidoro back up the river with eight men to bring down still more horses. Sandoval returned in March with 50 head and bad news: A one-eyed Piegan named Weasel had called for whiskey at night. When the Scottish clerk Andrew Potts answered the call at the little window in the main gate, he was shot in the face. The Piegans executed Weasel, and Harvey, in his noble streak, adopted Potts' little half-Indian son called Jerry.

When Alec at last went back up to McKenzie in November, he got more bad news: Some Gros Ventres had got hold of some whiskey (probablly through the same small window), had gone on a fancy drunk that ended up with one dead chief and one wounded bootlegger. There had also been trouble between Harvey and Sandoval. (One account dates it in 1841, but I would think 1839 more credible.) There was a rumor of a plot to assassinate Harvey during a trip he and Sandoval took down to Fort Pierre with a load of furs. But the trip came off without any occurance, and both men returned on the steamer. But back up at Fort McKenzie, Harvey had trouble with a Gros Ventre chief. Harvey and Malcolm Clarke followed with Gros Ventre (so the story goes) and killed him near the mouth of Shonkin Creek.

Alexander kept Isidoro Sandoval under his wing at Fort Union. But in May, Harvey brought the yearly returns down on a keelboat and according to one account, Isidoro made some sort of threat against Harvey. The next day Harvey, in company with Alec himself, found Sandoval in the retail store behind the counter, challenged him to come outside and fight. Isidoro did not budge. But suddenly, as he turned his head, Harvey shot him between the eyes.

"I've killed the Spaniard! I've killed the Spaniard!" shouted Harvey over and over, daring any and all who would defy him to take revenge for Sandoval. Alexander, a brave man as men go, gave the priority to discretion. More bluntly, oral tradition claims that Alec was afraid of Harvey.[22] Strange to tell, Sandoval lived for about twenty-four hours, but that was all. Harvey calmly returned to the Piegan post on his keelboat.

It seems impossible to date this famous occurrence with precision, but it must have happened in either 1840 or 1841. It was not the end of the Sandoval story. Isidoro had a Blackfeet wife, Catch for Nothing. And he also had at least two children, an older girl and a little boy, from whom we shall hear later.

When Alec got back to Fort McKenzie in November, he made a complaint to the Company against the crime. But it is not clear which crime: the killing of Sandoval or the murder of the Gros Ventre chief. But major corporations often seem unimpressed with crime,and apparently nothing was done about either of these murders.

The trade in robes at the Piegan post after the epidemic became greater than ever. This was clear in the winter and spring. Perhaps Alec's marriage to Natawista had something to do with it, but Denig noted that after the epidemic, the population increased rapidly as if to compensate for the loss. The white savants who were piously theorizing that smallpox was the scourge of Providence to rid the land of the Indians and make it safe for whites, would now have to think again.

Alec brought the returns down to Fort Union himself, twenty-four packs of

[22] Plassmann: Forsythe *Independent*.

buffalo robes and four packs of beaver pelts loaded onto four mackinaws. There he received orders to remain for the time being, not to return to Fort McKenzie. In his place, Francis A. Chardon was appointed to the Piegan post and so took over the trip up the river. Alec was not happy with this change. He was in charge of Union for a while, for at some time not specified, the word came that a government inspector would tour the river visiting the posts of the American Fur Company to check for contraband liquor. Fort Union had thirty barrels for Alec to dispose of. Perhaps because of the Scotch-Irish thirst attributed to Alec, he could not bring himself to pour all the alcohol out onto the ground. So he had the barrels taken across the river and sunk in a lake about four miles away. No matter how they were weighted down, those bedeviled barrels kept popping back up to surface. Finally Alec ordered them buried in the ground. The inspector, of course, never showed up, and in good time, the hoops rusted, the staves split and the alcohol vanished into the ground anyhow.

Now somewhere in this sequence, the courtship of Natawista broke the monotony. One of her great-grandchildren sets the date in the autumn of 1840, when Manistokos brought his people in to Fort Union (not Fort McKenzie) en route from their summer resort in Canada to a winter resort on the Yellowstone. (I must admit I have some problem with Bloods in such a number coming so far outside their own domain and into the territory of their enemies, Assiniboines, Crees and Crows, and nonchalantly setting up camp. But let's go on.) Alec was watching them approach, we are told, through his telescope from one of the bastions. With no hesitation, he dispatched one of his clerks to the tipi of Manistokos or, in another version, of Seen-From-Afar, the bride's elder brother, with a trifling gift of nine horses.[23] Next day, nine horses were left at Alec's door. Natawista herself, clad no doubt in her regal best, came to him. There were smokes and speeches, and presto, the knot was tied. As the voyageurs would have put it: *Voilà! C'est le mariage à la façon du pays.*

The story, more or less, is the one that Alec himself confided to the ethnologist and which his descendants passed down. The mention of the elder brother, Seen-From-Afar, adds a note of plausibility because of the intimate regard between sister and brother that is supposed to be traditional among the Blood people.

It is said that Natawista regularly accompanied her husband on his many rounds. Unluckily, it is not possible to verify this statement in most instances, but it is clear that she was with him at Fort Union, settling comfortably and graciously into her new life as the wife of the post factor or bourgeois. She now became "Mrs. Culberton," "Mrs. C.," "Madame Culbertson," "The First Lady of the Upper Missouri," "The Princess," and, since Alec as factor of the fort automatically acquired the honorary title of Major, Natawista was now "the Major's Lady." Though other factors had their Indian wives, it was Natawista, by her beauty and talent, who created the role described by her titles, her role as wife (not slave-wife or mere sex partner) of the factor, her role as hostess of the multitude of visitors. And at Fort Union, so much more accessible to visitors than the Piegan post, she soon had a chance to star in her new role. In due time she also became the mother of Alec's first son, Jack (John A.), and probably the step-mother of the two little daughters, Maria and Jane, unless Alec placed one of them in school in the east. She was noted for her skill in porcupine quill embroidery, one of the special art forms of her people, and sometimes at beadwork and paintings that were made with dyes from clay and organic materials. An especially elaborate beaded saddle that came down in the family of later years may have represented her handiwork.

[23] Lewis Henry Morgan (p.145), Leslie White's edition.

The dining hall at Fort Union was the social center of the frontier, with Major Culbertson and his lady presiding at the head of the table and the clerks and guests seated around it by rank. This custom, of course, was simply a continuation of the routine made sacred by McKenzie. Evidently the menu too was similar to the one established by Alec's autocratic predecessor, and venison, milk and butter are mentioned specifically.

The political advantages of the match between Alec and Natawista can hardly have escaped the notice of anyone. Alec, of course, was eager to capture the trade of the powerful Bloods away from Hudson's Bay Company. He had recently returned from his profitable mackinaw trip to St. Louis (1839), and the Company officials were losing their best men and looking for better.

So far, Alec had not been particularly concerned with the Crow trade on the Yellowstone, but now he would be since the trade with the Crows also depended on Fort Union. None of the Crow posts seems to have been much more than make-shift, but it was the Crow trade that first attracted Lisa, Ménard and Benito Vásquez to the Montana country in 1807-1809. Their original Fort Ramón was supplanted by a series of posts in the vicinity of Forsyth, the Rosebud country and the lower Big Horn. One among the Absaroka posts was named Fort Benton after the senator who promoted private enterprise versus federal control, and it was built by Joshua Pilcher in 1821. Another was Fort Van Buren, which Larpenteur burned down in 1842 and rebuilt as Fort Alexander. It lasted six years to be replaced by Fort Sarpy, which was sometimes also called Fort Alexander. The name itself suggests who was gaining prestige.

The chief figure of the Yellowstone trade was a sturdy Scot, Robert Meldrum, who would have been one of Alec's rivals for preference in the Company. There were also some spectacular extras on the Yellowstone stage. One, with whom Alec must have crossed paths either on the Yellowstone or at Laramie, was Marcelino Baca (Vaca) from Taos, New Mexico. Still another spectacular character of the Crow country was Pegleg Smith, notorious for his recent raid on California (1841), but that's another story.

1843 was a year of distinguished visitors to the frontier, especially Sir William Drummond Stewart (returning) and John James Audubon. The steamer for Audubon's cruise up the Missouri was the *Omega*, with Captain Sire, pilot La Barge and guide Provost. The mercurial artist-naturalist made himself charming and exasperating by turns and kept his trip one of the liveliest on the Missouri run. He annoyed Joseph La Barge especially. Joseph was now 28 and Jean-Jacques Audubon 30 years older, born in Haiti of a French Lieutenant, raised in Nantes, Paris and Pennsylvania. Both men were friends of Daniel Boone if not exactly each other, and Audubon was a colleague ornithologist to Charles Waterton, who in turn, was a friend of Darwin.

The *Omega* left St. Louis on April 25th and at Glasgow overtook the steamer of Sir William who was conducting a huge hunting expedition assembling doctors, lawyers and botanists from Paris, London, Luxembourg, Scotland and the U.S., as well as scions of the families Kennerly, Ménard, Chouteau, Radford, even William Clark's son Jeff and foster son Pampi Charbonneau as carter. Father DeSmet was accompanying Sir William as far as the Shawnee Mission. When some of these adventurers heard that Audubon was aboard the *Omega*, they hurried to meet him, while Audubon in turn was most interested in DeSmet.

Then the two travelers and their parties parted company, Audubon for the new upper Missouri, Sir William for the Platte. At Bellevue, the *Omega* was inspected for liquor, unloaded its freight and got back underweigh. Then a shot crossed the bow. Dragoons marched aboard for a closer look. Audubon (in one account) managed to keep the U.S. Army distracted, giving Captain Sire the chance to hide the liquor below decks. He visited ashore, charmed everyone, went bird-hunting, and entertained the Army captain at luncheon. Captain Sire then boldly insisted on escorting the inspector into the black hole below, where of course no one saw anything.

The tremendous number of drowned buffalo along the river may have given Audubon some discomfort, but though he was the top naturalist of his day, he was not yet a real ecologist. He liked to pose, gun in hand, as much a hunter as a nature-lover. But he was learning. . .

On one occasion some Santee Sioux fired on the steamer from the shore, sending bullets through the cabins and pilot-house, but hitting no one. The two pilots on duty at the time were Joseph La Barge and Black Dave Desiré.

The *Omega* reached Fort Pierre May 31st, and Fort Union on the 12th of June. That was a good time on the upper river, but it was a rainy, windy day, and seven o'clock before the boat pulled in. It was saluted and returned six guns. A "cavalcade" led by Alexander Culbertson swept down to the shore, and after proper introductions, everyone who counted walked up to the post for some good sport. In a couple of days Alec gave Audubon a demonstration of his idea of a good sport: wolf hunting. Dashing off on horseback, he rode down a wolf, killed it for sheer fun and theatrics, snatching it up while he was riding at full speed. Now this display evidently delighted both Audubon and Natawista, but I must confess, leaves me utterly appalled.

One evening, when Audubon and his party of Bell, Squires, Sprague and Harris[24] were already retired for the night, the merry strains of music came drifting up from the dining hall with an invitation to the ball. So up they got and joined what Audubon slyly dubbed "the beau monde of these parts:" clerks, guests, engagés, and various Indian ladies. Alec played the violin, M. Guépe the clarinet, and Auguste Chouteau the drum. Reels and cotillions went swirling on until one o'clock.

On June 20th Audubon got the story of the recent smallpox epidemic from Chardon. He reported the overall mortality for the Blackfeet, Sioux, Mandans, and Arikaras at 150,000, according to the calculation of David Mitchell. The Mandans had been reduced to a mere twenty-seven persons. However, in the last six years they had increased to ten or twelve tipis. (Lesson One in demography for M. Audubon.)

The naturalist was delighted with the larks, lazuli finches and Arctic bluebirds, but he did not appreciate the scalp dance of the black-painted war party which was given lodging in the special "Indian house" in the fort. He worked on a portrait of Natawista and another of Alexander, thinking of them both as very restless models. (Sprague, evidently, did some part of both portraits.)

One day the cook, "an old Spaniard," started a turmoil by roping the horns of the fort's yearling buffalo bull, which kicked and snorted and pawed and broke loose. The chase was on. The yearling was brought under control.

Another diversion at Fort Union included something like a mock hunt or a mock warpath (it is hard to tell from Audubon's description whether it had any ulterior intent.) But everyone dressed up like Indians. Even the Indians dressed like Indians in an exaggerated style. Owen McKenzie, Kenneth's half-Indian son, wore a native costume that belonged to Alexander, and Squires donned one that belonged to Audubon. Natawista had her own, which Audubon called "superb," while the cook's wife wore another that came from Natawista. and "Mrs. Culbertson" took special pains to daub war paint on Owen and Squires

---

[24] John G. Bell, Lewis Squires, Isaac Sprague and Edward Harris.

These portraits of Major Alexander Culbertson (top) and Natawista, (bottom), are attributed to Audubon and Sprague. They were made on ticking. But there are problems with the one supposed to be Natawista, no two of whose alleged portraits resemble each other. Is this a girl of 19? Is this a child of one year? Perhaps this portrait was made later in New York? Thanks to Alice Ford for comments on these pictures. Photos courtesy of Kerrigan Family Trust.

to make them as grostesque as possible or what was labeled "awful" and "infernal." It was all great fun. The women loosened their hair and let it stream out behind them as they rode at top speed, Natawista and her maid whipping their mounts faster and faster. (Maybe the maid is the same as the cook's wife.) Audubon took particular notice that they rode astride like men, and he regarded Natawista as a wonderful equestrienne, strong and graceful, while he was pleased also to find his friend Squires as good a rider as any of the other men. To prove their male mettle, the men brought down another poor wolf. One Sunday a couple of Audubon's party joined Owen in a buffalo hunt; another day they joined the mulatto Lafleur hunting antelope. One of Audubon's hunting companions was Moncravie, who also proved himself to be a great mimic and actor (in Audubon's eye) in the shows they gave at the fort. The naturalist was already having misgivings about all the slaughter of these hunts, especially when only the tongues were brought in from the buffalo: "What a terrible destruction of life. . ." He noted that the prairie was strewn with the skulls of the victims.

One Sunday a party of Crees appeared from the Saskatchewan. They complained to Alexander that the HBC provided liquor and the AFC did not, so they would trade with the English. Audubon thought the matter should be one for international concern. The British, he thought, were solicitous for the emancipation of blacks but careless about the welfare of Indians. Again there was a buffalo chase. Again Audubon knew Alexander would surely get his prey. Again he began to have misgivings. And he noted that wolves in this country had never been known to attack men or horses.

Audubon paid special attention to the American bison, both in his art and in writing of his visit to Fort Union. Though his tour with Larpenteur in search of geological specimens was a failure, it ended in an up-beat note on buffalo, when he discovered that his "remonstrances about useless slaughter" were having an apparent effect. It seemed that Owen, probably under orders from Alexander, had restricted his hunting to "three fat cows but no more. . ." The ordinary menu, of course, required buffalo meat aplenty. A typical good dinner was made up of that, plus fresh green peas (that Audubon himself might help to shell) plus a pudding. James Kipp told him of traveling in a cart for six days in a row "through masses of buffaloes," and Audubon added it was impossible to conceive of the "vast multitudes" that even yet roamed the land.

One day, on a visit to the opposition Fort Mortimer nearby, Alexander shot off a gun. It backfired and he nearly killed both himself and Audubon at his side. On the whole, however, these two men, one younger, one older, made excellent companions in the chase and adventure of frontier life. Natawista, the "Indian princess—for that is Mrs. Culbertson's rank," attracted much of Audubon's attention. Though an excellent swimmer himself and displeased with the lack of swimming prowess among the local Indians, he marvelled at the exploits of Natawista in the Missouri River. One day she captured several mallards in the water by her own hand and made them a present, alive, to Audubon. He commented, ". . .she is a most expert and graceful swimmer. . ." adding that she could stay under water a long time and that all the Blackfeet were "proud and wonderful swimmers."

Audubon was delighted to behold Natawista and "another squaw" in high-style tribal gowns giving an equestrian exhibition of "fine evolutions at full speed" with as much ease as Alex and the other men both of the fort and his own party. And quite as much did he wonder too at her elegant gowns, her "fine shawl," her courteous manners in receiving guests, whether outdoorsmen like himself or ladies of the country speaking French and Cree. But he wondered too—and with less delight—at her preference for eating raw liver, roasted puppy or fresh brains right out of the broken skull of a buffalo. However, he found that he could relish roasted puppy almost as much as Natawista, and he describes white hunters killing a buffalo and then with their bloody, filthy fingers, tearing apart and devouring a good share of the corpse right on the spot, hot brains, liver, even the cud. (Harris found an excuse for not tasting the puppy.)

Although it is usually reported that Natawista could not (or would not) speak English, she must have spoken a little to Audubon. Since she was so proud of herself as a full blood, he quotes her stereotype of mixed bloods: ". . .all such no-color fellows are lazy." (She would have reason to change this opinion when her own children matured.)

On August 16th, Audubon, Alexander and Natawista with her baby in her arms (this must be Jack) set out down the Missouri in a mackinaw to Fort Pierre. There were 14 or 15 persons aboard including Audubon's party, Moncravie, four boatmen and two voyageurs. At Fort Pierre, the artist and his friends parted from the Culbertsons. Alexander had, against his will, been transferred to Fort Laramie.

Well, so far it had been great fun, and the Queen of the High Missouri was slated to become Queen of the upper Platte. But could she have entertained one or two misgivings as she and her baby sailed off into a strange new world? Could "Madame Culbertson" have wondered if, after all, she was really the Major's Lady or just another "country wife'— *à la façon du pays*?

CHAPTER XI

Beaver Child

Alec tried to persuade his bosses not to send him to Laramie, but the corporate heads reasoned that with the Blackfeet trade in their pockets, they needed Alec's expertise on another front. So off to Fort Laramie and the River Platte went Alec, with twenty wagons, eight carts and I suppose his wife and child. This trip probably took place in the fall of 1843, leading the Culbertsons through some of the Bad Lands of present South Dakota. During this trip or that of the year following, Alec was accompanied by Captain Stewart Van Vliet and began to gather prehistoric fossils. Captain Van Vliet was a class-mate of Michael Simpson at West Point, so he and Alec must have had plenty to talk about.

Laramie had been a center of attraction lately, and that may have had something to do with sending Alec there. Many of the best known scouts and guides and mountain men operated in and out of Laramie, among them Marcelino Baca, Baptiste Charbonneau, and many another. It is conceivable that Alec met them all. Sir William Drummond Stuart was back on the frontier again, this time with his grandiose hunting expedition along the Platte and the Oregon Trail, the one in which Baptiste served as carter and the young cousins "Jeff" Clark and "Clark" Kennerly tagged along. The Indians rejoiced at Jeff's red hair, so like his father's, and everyone agreed it was fitting that just as Pampi's mother had once gone with Clark the Red Head Chief into the wilderness, now her son Pampi came with Clark's son Jeff and his nephew Kennerly.

So much for the amenities of the season. They were only half the story. What went on behind Alec's back at the old Piegan post on the Marias is quite another story. The two chief actors in the drama at Fort McKenzie were now Chardon and Harvey, and perhaps because of the distraction of alcohol, Chardon let the reins of power slip into the hands of Harvey, little by little or by default. So the trouble started . . .

One story says an Indian stole a milch cow, and Harvey killed the Indian. Another story claims an Indian killed a pig, so Harvey, Chardon and a slave set out after the Indian and fell into an ambush. The black man was slain. Whatever the provocations really were, if any, when the Blackfeet assembled at the gate to trade, a cannon, loaded perhaps with nails, was trained on them unsuspecting as they were: men, women, and children. It mowed them down. One account claims that then the white men rushed out the gates and dispatched survivors. How many were slaughtered? The versions vary from four to thirty. It is also said that at night the whites held a scalpdance and forced the wives of victims to take part in the dance. Obviously, with so many variants in the reports, we can hardly be certain of the details, but at least we know it was a disaster and that it ruined the Blackfeet trade. At this one stroke, friendship turned to hate. Chardon burned Fort McKenzie and moved down to the mouth of the Judith. There he built a stockade, flatteringly dubbed Fort Chardon or F.A.C. but since the Blackfeet, were now on the war-path, the engagés hardly dared leave the stockade to go hunting and so passed the winter in misery. The date of this horror is still in dispute. Elliott Coues dated it 1843-44, while another editor of Larpenteur thought it might have occurred in 1844.[25]

At any rate, Harvey was summoned to St. Louis. With only his pack dog, he hiked all the way down the river during the winter. So impressed was Pierre Chouteau that he rehired Harvey and sent him back up the river in the relative comfort of the *Trapper* and in the company of that disgruntled Parisian, Charles Larpenteur. "I never forgive or forget," Harvey told Larpenteur, "and I have some old scores to settle." At Fort Clark Harvey beat up one of his adversaries and began to count: "That's number one." At Fort Union he beat up some more.

If we could date these events in sequence, we would be in a better position to understand the movements of the Culbertson family. According to Larpenteur's chronology, he himself was recalled from Fort Alexander on the Yellowstone to Fort Union late in 1842. When he arrived at night, he found a great drunk in progress, evidently with Alec and the clerks participating. "We're having a hot time, and I'm tired of it," quoth Alec to Larpenteur, who, as a non-drinker, was now appointed to supervise "the grog department." (We have to remember that Larpenteur rarely has a kind word for anyone except himself, but also that he does give us a picture of the fur trade that is more realistic than romantic.) Larpenteur soon learned that he had been recalled to Union to aid Alec against the Opposition post that had recently sprung up nearby, Fort Williams (or Mortimer). The factor at Fort Williams tried to win over a top Assiniboine named Crazy Bear with a gift of a beautiful uniform and a keg of whiskey. But Crazy Bear, with all his gala attire and fire-water, presented himself to Alec,tore off his finery and declared he would not foresake Fort Union. Alec, of course, laid the evidence before his competitor.[26]

Near the end of January (1844, according to Larpenteur's editor), Alec suddenly assigned the poor Parisian a most miserable job: to accompany Denig about a hundred miles over the frozen prairies north to Wood Mountain (in southernmost Saskatchewan), to trade alcohol and whatnot to the Crees and Chippewas. It was terribly cold, terribly stormy, in fact a world filled with snow and wind. Denig went only part-way, to a point where he was able to make a liquor trade, and Larpenteur had to push on without him, confident that Denig could not freeze to death because "he was too full of alcohol." Larpenteur, with two companions, his mules and sleds, plowed on through ice and snow to the camp of the Cree chief Broken Arm, fulfilled his mandated liquor trade, got just about everybody drunk and had both his mules frozen dead. Though he portrays himself as very nervy, his story does little credit to Alec or anyone else and certainly none to the fur trade in general. On his return, another keg was broken out to celebrate, and "a certain Indian named The Hand, the greatest rascal in the tribe," made himself so obnoxious to his own people that Alec and Larpenteur restrained him inside the fort in protective custody. But when The Hand became intolerable, they released him. In the morning an Indian

[25] Larpenteur or his editor dates the trip on the *Trapper* in 1840 (so that it would precede the massacre at Fort McKenzie of the Piegans). He suggests that Harvey killed Isidoro Sandoval in 1841 and places his own assignment to the Yellowstone post and his recall to Fort Union both in 1842.

[26] It is not clear what—if anything—Alec was doing at Fort Union, in Larpenteur's account, when he had been assigned to Laramie.

knocked on the gate and dumped a bundle at Larpenteur's feet. "I killed a dog last night," he declared. Inside the bundle was the corpse of The Hand. So much for happy days at Fort Union.

In 1844, times were different at St. Louis as well. It was the year of the great flood that inundated the St. Louis waterfront. But AFC was not going to let a flood wipe it out and Pierre le Cadet sent the *Nimrod* up the Missouri under Captain Sire and pilot La Barge as if times were normal. Among the passengers were two French noblemen, traveling separately from each other. One was the Count d'Otranto, the cheerful son of a tyrant father (Napoleon's Gestapo-style agent Fouché), and a strange loner listed as the "Count de Peindry." Otranto lingered on the Missouri maybe a year or so with his happy entourage, but "Peindry" went to California the next year and was later assassinated. Such is the story as told in the history of the upper Missouri. I suspect, however, that "Peindry" was really the Marquis Charles de Pindray, who was involved in the California gold rush.[27]

Alec may not have had to cruise the river this year. Since William Laidlaw (according to Larpenteur) was in charge at Union, Alec must have gone to Laramie. But the corporate heads were having second thoughts. They generally agreed he ought to go back to the Blackfeet trade. Alec, however, was in no mood for games (or at least not other people's games, though he could have been playing one of his own). When he brought his wagon from Laramie to Fort Pierre, the district bosses tried to insist that he replace Harvey and Chardon among the Blackfeet. Alec saw it not in the bond. But at last he got a letter from Pierre le Cadet: "Meet me in New York."

American Fur was moving up in the world. M. Pierre Chouteau was no longer stuck in those offices on the Mississippi waterfront (perhaps the recent floods had something to do with that), but was now ensconced in offices that overlooked the waterfronts of the world—in plush offices (says Mildred Schemm) and I suppose in some sort of high-rise that would command a view of his new empire. And M. Pierre's son Charles, who was being groomed as the imperial heir, had been sent to the office in London and on to continental Europe. Charles came home in 1845, married his cousin, General Gratiot's daughter Julie, and prepared to await the crown of AFC.

So it was to New York that Alexander Culbertson had now to wend his way. There are still problems with the chronology of this trip, however. Several significant events took place about this time, none of them well recorded nor clearly dated. But the date appears to be June 1845. There is some reason to think that Alec made trips to the East coast in both 1845 and 1846, though he may have made only one such trip, during which all these things occurred. The simplest explanation is that he made one trip to the East coast in 1845 and the next year went only as far as St. Louis. But simplest, like Descartes' "clear and dinstinct," is not always true.

At any rate, he went to New York. Perhaps he brought Natawista and Jack with him (as both Mildred Schemm and Alec's great granddaughter Dabney Taylor think he did.)

To appreciate the quandary in which AFC found itself, we should recall that Fort Laramie (Fort John) and the ill-starred outpost at the top of the Missouri were both peculiarly strategic. Laramie was AFC's toe-hold on the Platte, which otherwise might easily slip into the control of the rival Creole trading family, the Robidoux. The brothers Robidoux were rapidly expanding their interests all over the west, along both the Oregon and Santa Fe trails. In Santa Fe,

[27] See Notes.

members of the family were already well established, intermarried with Hispanic families and spreading out over the old Spanish Trail to California. There was even a connection to the pirate Jean Lafitte and the New Orleans slave-trade. But the Blackfeet trade of the upper Missouri, on the other hand, was about to slip into the hands of the Hudson's Bay unless Alexander Culbertson could retrieve it at this last moment.

Be that as it may, M. Pierre le Cadet in New York must have turned on all his charisma, which could be a good deal. Alec complained that the Piegan post was now a perilous assignment, with the peril created not by him but by others. It was hardly fair to expect him to risk his scalp to save someone else's. Then, too, Alec was now a family man with wife and child and maybe another child on the way.[28]

Pierre pleaded. He offered Alec any compensation he wanted. Let him name his terms. Pierre le Cadet was irresistible. Aha, but Alec knew how to be noble in times of trial. He would require no compensation other than a brief vacation in New York and a chance to return to Laramie first. Voilà! It was all agreed. (And if you find that denouement a little incredible, you have my sympathy.)

Alec spent his vacation (and Natawista's?) at the estate of John James Audubon at Harlem-on-the-Hudson. This was Minnie's Land, thirty or forty richly wooded acres between 155th and 156th Streets. The Audubon family had a fine colonial mansion with a colonnaded portico overlooking the river. They were quite a clan: John James himself, his wife Minnie, his two sons and their wives, all living in the grand style. Alec fairly burst with admiration, especially at the mounted specimens of American quadrupeds that Audubon had collected along the Missouri. He enjoyed the sons too, who were nearer his own age, and especially for fishing jaunts along the Hudson. Sometimes Alec rode into the city. As a souvenir of their two worlds, Audubon gave Alec the three-volume set of his *Quadrupeds of North America*.

It is possible too that Alec and Natawista visited Alec's family in Chambersburg this same summer. It may be that they were there either in 1845 or 1846, for their daughter Julia was allegedly born there. Such, at least, is the family recollection, though the date sounds more like 1846.[29] However, '45 has much to recommend it too. Alec is said to have brought, in 1845, his fossils of extinct ruminants from the Bad Lands to his father and perhaps his uncle, Dr. Samuel Duncan Culbertson—relics that eventually found their way into the Academy of Sciences in Philadelphia and stirred the curiosity of scientists at the Smithsonian Institution.

These years of 1844, '45, and '46 when the Culbertsons *seem* to have been spending much time in the east, remain confusing after all. Perhaps one motive for Alec's visit or visits was his brother's wedding and departure for China. At Princeton, Michael Simpson graduated with a D.D. in 1844, and on the 29th of May of that year he was ordained by the Presbytery of Carlisle.[30] Since it was deemed proper for a young missionary to have a wife, Michael took one at once. She was Mary Dunlap of Salem, New York, a residence that suggests she and Michael had known each other since his tour of military duty in that region. Michael was handsome young fellow, darker than Alec as it seems from his

[28] To keep the record straight, we should note that the families Chouteau and Robidoux were not always rivals, and could sometimes act in partnership.

[29] I am not convinced Alec ever took Natawista east of St. Louis and Peoria.

[30] At Carlisle there was an important church that dated from the 1750's, but this must not be confused with the famous Indian school at Carlisle, which was not established until 1879.

Michael Culbertson, Shanghai, China. Presbyterian Historical Society photo.

portrait, but evidently endowed with the traditional big Culbertson nose and ears. His portrait tells us nothing about his feet. He and Mary were allowed a few weeks leeway after his ordination, and then in June they bravely set off from New York to China.

Since both Michael and Alec had connections in New York, made either by correspondence or in person, this seems to be the period in which they were developed. And both had ties to the Presbyterian Board of Missions, which in turn drew them into the orbit of two Scottish families of New York, the Lowries and the Olyphants.

To explain the Culbertson's involvement with these families, I suspect we must refer again to Frances Stuart Culbertson and the royal Stuarts. The family Olyphant came of nobles devoted to the old Jacobite cause, the restoration of the Stuarts to the British throne. When the Jacobites lost out to the Georgians, the House of Stuart to the House of Hanover, David Olyphant switched his enthusiasm to the China trade and built a mercantile house in New York and Canton. He also joined the executive committee of the American Board of Foreign Missions. He operated at least two ships in the China trade, which were among the first American vessels to penetrate to northern China and Japan. As early as 1807 he had taken a Scot named Robert Morrison of the London Missionary Society, to China and now he sponsored the American missioner Elijah Bridgman. In Canton, Olyphant established his go-down called Zion Corners, a name that might have referred to his entire enterprise, devoted as it was to opposition to the opium trade.

First secretary of the Presbyterian Board was Olyphant's co-worker, Walter Lowrie, a native of Edinburgh but now a U.S. Senator, an exacting and tight-fisted Scot, who, however, was generous about giving his sons to the Lord. One son was Walter Macon Lowrie, who would be Michael's companion. Another was John Cameron, a missionary in India, and a later son was Reuben Post. All three appear to have met ultimely deaths overseas. Such were the families with which the Culbertsons would now share their destiny.

Whether Michael and Mary traveled to China on Olyphant's line is not certain, but they were reported to be members of the first contingent of Presbyterian missionaries to the Middle Kingdom, sailing away on June 22nd, 1844, and reaching China four months to the day from their departure. In Michael's letter to the Reverend John Lowrie of New York, we learn that they sailed by way of Cape Horn. They were, as it turns out, following in the wake of other missioners, Father De Smet and his recruits, both parties crossing the equator about the same time, one moving south, the other north. Bursting with enthusiasm, Michael Simpson assured John Lowrie, "I enjoyed our ocean voyage exceedingly. The novelty seemed never to wear off. . ." With fair weather, even the rough waters around the notorious Cape were but "a pleasing variety." From Anguar (which Michael called Angor) in the Palau Islands, the missionaries were able to send mail home. But thereafter they encountered doldrums, and Mary had dysentery crossing the China Sea. Michael made a try at converting the sailors, but alas they seemed more concerned about their "incessant" song at the yards. Michael was sympathetic: "Poor fellows, they seemed to be almost worn out." Struck by a strong gale near a spot where Walter (Macon Lowrie?) had once been wrecked, their ship was swept into the port of Macao (Aomen) on October 22, 122 days out of New York.

In the meanwhile, after Alec's visit to Pierre Chouteau in New York and his idyllic vacation with the Audubons, he headed back to the frontier, first to Fort Laramie to set his house in order there, then to Fort Pierre. He sent a keelboat up-stream with provisions, catching up with it himself at Poplar River. There is some evidence that Natawista went with him on this treacherous venture.

Harvey came down to meet him fifteen or twenty miles, short of the Piegan post, perhaps to offer some sort of amends, but aboard the keelboat were Harvey's old friend and new enemy Malcolm Clarke and also Jim Lee and one or two others. They plunged after Harvey with tomahawks and whatever else came to hand. In one account Alec intervened; in another Harvey escaped back to the stockade at the Judith. There he and a comrade took to a canoe and headed down the river, passing the keelboat under cover of night. He was bound to St. Louis to sue the Company.

At the Judith stockade, nicknamed Fort F.A.C. for Chardon, Alec singled out the men responsible for the massacre of the Blackfeet and sent them packing downstream with Chardon himself. Then loading what he could onto the keelboat and leaving Malcolm at the Judith with five men, Alec kept on up the Missouri, deep into Blackfeet country. He headed for the approximate site of an early Opposition post called Fort Cotton. (The term "fort" need not be taken literally for most of these establishments.)

Past the site of the burned out Fort McKenzie (now nicknamed Fort Brulé), past the site of modern Fort Benton, Alexander plied his way upward almost to Pablo's island. (Probably the island had not yet been so named, and in fact the New Mexican engagé named Pablo may have been with Alec at this time since he had a Blackfeet wife.) About the first of September, Alec began to build a new stockade on the south side of the Missouri, thus putting the river between his new fort and the main body of the Blackfeet. To avoid hunting, the crew had to live for a while mostly on dog meat. By the turn of the year they had a stockade about 150 feet square with the usual pair of double-storied bastions, probably on opposite corners. Alec called it Fort Lewis, in honor of the explorer.

About New Year's some Crows ran off ten horses. These animals were promptly repossessed by a party of Bloods and, wonder of wonders, were politely returned to Alec. This event certainly suggests that the Blackfeet had been watching Alec from afar for a long while back and knew just whom and what they were dealing with. Soon after that, an old man appeared and told Alec the Blackfeet were up on Belly River—far away. Alec sent him off with a present of tobacco to invite the people to Fort Lewis. In due time, they came riding in, about fifty of them with the old man too and under the head chief Big Swan (perhaps *Imahkaii*). Alec went out to greet them with handshakes all around and brought them into the stockade. He made them a speech about the anger the head traders had felt over the killing of their people, assuring them that the guilty had been sent away and that he was here to make peace.

Big Swan responded, addressing his own people: "If there are any among you here who have lost friends in this massacre, you must now hold no grudge. You must steal no horses, kill no white man. Beaver Child (Alec) has returned to us and made the earth clean once more. Let not the first to spill blood upon it be the Blackfeet." And he must have closed with *Kyene*.[31]

Alexander presented rifles to the six chiefs, adding gifts of tobacco and blankets. And so, Lt. Bradley, Alec's first biographer who jotted things down from Alex himself and filtered them through his own military bias, tells us that public hostility from the Blackfeet in this area came to an end. In any case, the reconciliation is remarkable. What becomes of the stereotype of the vindictive Indian? Let me suggest a new stereotype to replace the old: the existentialist approach of the Indians in contrast to the essentialist stance of the whites.

In the next four months trade boomed. Then Alec himself took the triumphal returns down to Fort Union, pausing at the Judith to burn "Fort F.A.C" and rid the land forever of that symbol of treachery. Since Chardon had died of scurvy, Alec conveyed his body to Fort Pierre for burial and then continued on down to St. Louis.

Harvey was filing suit against AFC and was also forming an opposition company of his own with the backing of formidable veterans of the fur trade, Joseph Picotte, Charles Primeau, and Robert Campbell. Already last year the bond of American Fur had been put in suit when Harvey revealed the whiskey trade still going on in defiance of the Intercourse Law (as if everyone didn't know!), and there was a possibility that AFC would be dissolved. At this point, however, Senator Thomas Hart Benton of Missouri, father-in-law of Frémont and

---

[31] It was customary to close a discussion with *Kyene*, or some equivalent expression meaning: The End. That's All. Amen.

personal friend of Pierre le Cadet and of Alexander Culbertson, intervened politically. In the settlement, the Company would pay $12,000 and cease all importation of liquor. Since the Hudson's Bay Company also suspended their liquor trade about this time, AFC would suffer no real loss from British competition.

But what about Harvey's opposition? Harvey brought up 15 men and a keelboat and built Fort Campbell, first across the river from Alec's new post and then, about 1847, rebuilt it of adobe on Alec's site..Though his men may have kept close to home in fear of their customers, they did cut into Alec's trade. There is no record of conflict between the two rival posts at the top of the Missouri, though once, when a keelboat caught fire, Harvey's outfit was suspected of arson. It would have been an uncomfortable situation, in any event. Alec must have had butterflies in his stomach whenever he thought about Harvey, and is said to have deliberately kept Malcolm Clarke posted well out of Harvey's reach. The oral tradition is that Harvey had his gang and Malcolm his, with no love lost between them and Alec caught in the middle but leaning toward Malcolm.[32]

In the meanwhile, another settlement had popped up in Montana, across the Divide in the Bitterroot valley: the Jesuit Mission of St. Mary. In 1839 a couple of Iroquois named Pierre Casaveta and Young Ignace joined some men of "The Bay" for a canoe voyage down the Yellowstone and Missouri and met Pierre-Jean De Smet at Council Bluffs. The Black Robe was a bit short, a bit stout, had a fine round face a-sparkle with wit, enthusiasm and occasional satire. He had left his twin sister, his brothers and all his fond family in Belgium in 1821, and come to complete his training at Florissant. He would eventually spend much of his life in travel, around the Americas with nineteen trips back and forth to Europe. Now he was busy operating a mission for the Potawatomis and discovering the realities of the frontier and the fur trade: drunken orgies, mayhem, murder, child-abuse, all under the agent's nose and promoted by whiskey peddlers on AFC boats. In April, Father De Smet had gone on a peace mission up the river to the Yankton Sioux with two scientists, Joseph Nicolas Nicollet (an old friend of De Smet), Charles Geyer the botanist, and their escorts John Charles Frémont, Etienne Provost, James Kipp and Jospeh La Barge. On his return, De Smet met the Iroquois envoys.

Next spring he answered their call, proceeding up the Platte to the rendzvous near the Grand Tetons. In 1841 he came west again, over the Oregon Trail into the Bitterroot and north, as far as Flathead Lake probably on his famous mule Lizette.

Returning to Europe, he rounded up missionaries for the "Oregon missions" and brought them to America. In 1845 he made a futile attempt to contact the Blackfeet, circling far up into the Canadian Rockies and down to the "Mountain of Quilloux." In 1846 he tried again accompanied by the French Jesuit Nicolas Point, who had come out onto the plains in '42 with the Mexican guide Manuel Martín. Now, traveling with the buffalo camps, the two Jesuits arrived at Fort Lewis (Maragnon to De Smet), where the French and "Spanish" engagés welcomed them by ringing the great bell (September 24th). Four days later De Smet boarded a skiff with Malcolm Clarke and two others, bound for St. Louis. He is said to have baptized Maria Culbertson, aged eleven, at Fort Lookout (1846) or on November 5, 1846, at Fort Union. There must be some error here. De Smet was at Union in October and on November 5 he baptized "thirteen little half breeds" at Fort Bouis.

[32] Plessmann: Forsythe *Independent*.

Father Point stayed on at Fort Lewis, and being more of a rigorist than De Smet, began some abrasive reforms on the high Missouri: no violations of the "Sabbath," no cussing, no pagan rites, and either get married or get out! Apparently, some of his doctrine was taking effect among the engagés, for when the Culbertsons returned to Fort Lewis about the first of December, they found it a utopia of clean living or at least a mission in the wilderness. Alec, a trader and not a missionary like his brother and little more than a casual Presbyterian, may not have been altogether delighted. But as a natural ecumenist, he made himself conspicuous at services. This degree of rectitude, however, hardly satisfied Father Point and did not save Alec from a chiding on the question of Sunday labor. I must confess that Point seems more Calvinist than Alec, in fact, something of a Jansenist. One Sunday, during a freshet when Alec had engagés cover the packs of robes, Point protested."Major, I thought you were a Christian, and here you are working on a Sunday and making your employees work on a Sunday too!"

Alec kept on with what he was doing, and the preacher kept on preaching. Finally, Alec could bite his tongue no longer and told his chaplain, "Go to your room and read your Bible, and then you won't see what is going on."

When Natawista's child (presumably baby Julia, but just possibly Jack) was sick with the "croup" and standy-by remedies seemed ineffectual, Alec sent for an old Kaina medicine woman. She heated stones, prepared herbs, and throwing water on the stones, gave the child a steam-bath accompanied by the usual chant. Downstairs at the breakfast table with Alec, Point heard the chanting. Up the stairs he rushed and put the old lady out. Then he had some blunt words for Alec who paid them no heed. And Natawista had blunt words for Point: "Go mind your own business!" or something to that effect, since Natawista's English was always put into her own idiom. She summoned the old lady back, and the child recovered, whether because of the treatment or in spite of it.

We do not have Point's side of the story, even though he did write an account of his life at Fort Lewis and his temporary mission there. But the fact that neither Alec nor Natawista was Catholic and that Point did not legalize their marriage as he was doing for others suggests something amiss about these details or something impertinent about Point's behavior. It is said, however, that Point baptized one of Alec's children, but on what evidence I do not discover. Despite these contretemps, his stay at Fort Lewis seems generally to have been a happy one. He had a good sense of humor and the heart of an artist, forever painting pictures in an untrained folkish style, even portraits of both Alec and Natawista, of Malcolm Clarke and others. He describes the routine of the fort: employees are paid $150 or more per year without board or lodging; skilled workers are paid better. The clerks, head interpreter and traders eat at the captain's table (Point might well have said the "Major's table") and there are two meals. Women, children, visitors and the sick are provided for. Prices are high, though gifts are sometimes presented to visiting chiefs and warriors. In general, Point notes, the routine at this and the other forts is "very pleasant" and the work moderate.

Alexander realized that Fort Lewis was situated on the right side of the river for security but on the wrong side for trade. Ice-floes and floods made the river hard to cross or impassable in some seasons. The Indians preferred to camp near the Teton or Marias. So he selected still another site, where Fort Benton stands today. He had the stockade and the houses taken apart and the timbers floated downstream and across to the opposite bank. On the new site they were promptly reassembled. In about a month supplies were sent down by mackinaw and formal possession was taken. Bradley says, "It had been rebuilt, almost to a timber, as it stood before and was therefore not a new post, but simply Fort Lewis transferred to a new site..." But it seems to have been called Fort Clay, and/or Fort Honoré with its "auxiliary" post, Fort Campbell.

Father Point tells us that he left Fort Lewis on the 19th of March 1847, the very date on which the fort was dismantled piece by piece and moved down to the more suitable spot to be reconstructed. (We can hardly suppose that all this took place on a single day, and Bradley gives different dates, though I should think Point would be more reliable on this detail.) He must have passed two or three days at the new site, because he left the area on the 21st. It gave his heart a wrench to depart, but he seems to have enjoyed his scenic cruise down the Missouri by barge. The Culbertsons accompanied him on this trip—at least for a while. Alexander left James Kelly and ten others to complete the reconstruction of Fort Lewis and was now escorting the yearly returns to Fort Union. From there he continued on down to St. Louis (perhaps) with Father Point and with his family.

There, Jim Lee and Malcolm Clarke were to appear in court, but since Harvey did not show up, the charges were dropped.

CHAPTER XII

Intermezzo

To tell the truth, the next few years in the story of the upper Missouri and the Shining Mountains are something of a mystery, not because we lack records, but because we have so many records that do not jibe. We may call it an Intermezzo of discrepancies. Most of the recorded events seem clear enough, but their sequence is often impossible to make out. Probably the confusion that resulted from the war in Mexico and the Southwest had something to do with it, even so far away, as well as the discovery of gold in California.

There is nothing that I have unearthed to tell us how Alec Culbertson reacted to the war in Mexico. He would probably have followed the lead of Stephan Douglas, Thomas Benton or even Democrat Benton's Republican son-in-law Fremont. Alec tended toward jingoism as evinced in the report he wrote about old Fort McKenzie, closing in a sentimental paean of "Old Glory." So he probably was swept along in the popular cause labeled "Manifest Destiny," which of course has overtones of Calvinist predestinarianism. On other more specific issues of the period he might not have so easily agreed: that is, the "All Mexico" policy (the U.S. should swallow up the whole or best parts of Mexico), the policy of taking over Mexico but not its inhabitants, or the crusading policy of "rescuing" the Mexicans from their Hispanic culture and Catholic religion.

A number of Alec's associates were drawn into the dispute much more deeply than Alec and even set off southward. There was Seen-From-Afar, for example, who is said (by Schultz) to have made a trip to the Southwest or Mexico. James Bird and Mad Wolf, the son of Lame Bull, went along. However, Schultz, who recorded this story, was more of a raconteur than a historian, and it is hard to distinguish his fiction from fact. Schultz's identification of Seen-From-Afar is never certain.

But another person close to Alec who was swept away toward Mexico was David Mitchell. Off he rode as a Lieutenant Colonel of the Second Missouri Regiment over the trail to Santa Fe. Poor David was hardly at home in Latin New Mexico, especially not when he ran low on funds for his troops. Imagine his chagrin when he had to borrow money from the "banker of Sante Fe," the beautiful monte dealter known as "La Tules." For her part of the bargain, this noted or notorious lady insisted that the handsome Virginian aristocrat escort her to the gala ball in honor of General Kearny. And to make things all the more embarrassing for poor David, representatives of the best old families of both Virginia and St. Louis were on hand: Meriwether Lewis Clark (William's son), Clark Kennerly (William's nephew) and Lt. "Giesso" Chouteau. Clark Kennerly, I must add, found La Tules to be quite a charmer. But Colonel Mitchell finally got away from the dancehall and off to the war, leading his troopers (fortified, no doubt, from the coffers of La Tules) into the capital city of Chihuahua. From

Clark Kennerly's account, we gather that the troopers were more tourists than warriors, attending cock-fights, bull-fights, Mass and fandangos, even rescuing Mexican children from Comanches.

Kearney, of course, headed instead for California. So did Clark Kennerly, his cousin John Radford, Edward Cresap Ord and Pampi (Baptiste) Charbonneau. Pampi was assigned to guide the Mormon Battalion and seems to have been joined by an other guide, Manuel the one-eyed mestizo. These guides took the Battalion via Mission San Xavier, Tucson and Yuma to Temécula and San Diego. Pampi was appointed alcalde for the Indians of Mission San Luis Rey but after the war, took off for the Mother Lode. In California, ironically, there occurred the great falling-out among the scions and in-laws of the grand families of St. Louis: Kearny and Frémont and the brothers Robidoux, perhaps even Bentons and Kennerlys.

Another acquaintance of ours who headed south was Isaac Ingalls Stevens, who you will recall at West Point as head of the Class of '39 in academics, but only so-so in conduct. Stevens' career got its send-off in Mexico, where a lot of things happened to him which shed light on his controversial behavior in later years in the Northwest and beyond. A truly complex man, he stirs, both then and now, admiration and antagonism. Though a New Englander, he favored Andrew Jackson, Jacksonian democracy, Manifest Destiny and the war against Mexico. True, he did attend lectures by Transcendentalists Emerson and Channing, but he also studied Napoleon and Machiavelli. Bullied by upper classmen at the Point because of his short stature, he learned a thing or two about the *lex talionis*. And perhaps because he was clever at mathematics, he seems to have thought that the universe was one big equation, in which all he had to do was discover the factors that worked out.

The call to Mexico caught Stevens in Maine on Christmas, 1846. He had to hop a sleigh to catch his ship at Boston. Landing at Vera Cruz in 1847 with the troops of Old Fuss and Feathers (General Scott), Stevens led in preparations to lay siege to that city of 12,000. Among his comrades in arms were Beauregard, McClellan, Robert E. Lee, William Harney and Lt. U.S. Grant. Lt. Stevens wrote reassuring letters to his wife Meg and his family, in one of which, after the bombardment of the city and the fall of the Castle of San Juan de Ulúa, he revealed an emotional mix that we rarely find in him again. Appalled at the destruction of the "many inoffensive people" who had perished miserably, he discovered the survivors to be impoverished but "mild and courteous." Wandering about the streets at night, he marveled at the "Moorish" city, like something out of the Arabian Nights. In Vera Cruz Stevens was billeted with Robert E. Lee in the government *palacio*. When they moved out into the country, they marveled at the beauty of the lush tropics under the snowy crater of Orizaba.

Stevens was with Scott's forces during the long, toilsome march through Xalapa (which he labeled "the Eden of Mexico") through Perote, Puebla and over the pass to Churubusco. He was with them too in the assault on the boys' academy of Chapultepec in the ancient groves of Montezuma. While he was scouting the suburb of San Cosme, Stevens was wounded in the foot and soon contracted blood poisoning. As he lay shattered in health, who should take care of him but Don Juan el Diablo, and with singular devotion! El Diablo was a brigand chief, one of the guerrillas with the priest Jarauta who beset the road from Vera Cruz. Disgusted with the debauchery of the U.S. troops in Mexico City, Stevens still never seems to have questioned their right to be there, to invade other people's countries. When he was sent home, he who was already so touchy about his short stature had to wear a special shoe for years to come.

At the end of the war, among the thousands who joined the stampede to

Isaac I. Stevens. Photo courtesy of Montana Historical Society, Helena.

California gold, we find a few Culbertsons. The California census for 1850 lists Lewis Culbertson, age 32, from Ohio; J.S. Culbertson, age 30, from Ohio with his wife Rosetta in Yuba County. Perhaps Lewis was the physician of Zanesville who prepared the Culbertson genealogy, but otherwise it seems impossible to make identifications. There is a story (from Charles Kessler) that Alec's nephew Cyrus J., son of James of Cincinnati, went up the Missouri at a date unknown and spent some time with Alec, maybe on buffalo hunt. There is supposed to have existed a portrait of Cyrus in his hunting attire. After this adventure, Cyrus went on to California, where he died in 1851. I have found no evidence to corroborate or refute this story. A few of the Álvarez familiy of Missouri are also found in the California census of 1850: Gregory and Robert, both 25, were in Yuba County and perhaps Eugene, age 28, in El Dorado County. From western Montana came a few French-Indian settlers around Flathead Lake: Brun,

Launcelot, LaPlante, Benetsee, perhaps with their wives and families. But they all returned north in short order, wiser if not richer, and Benetsee brought back the expertise to find placer gold. He found some near Deer Lodge in 1852.

In such waves and counter-waves of humanity, disaster was inevitable. On the night of the 17th of May, 1849, the Great Fire struck St. Louis, devastating the business section and the waterfront. Cholera swept Missouri and Kansas leaving a frightful number of victims at St. Louis alone. During all this turbulence, Joseph LaBarge kept plying his way up and down the river to transport more and more people toward their goals in hope, or back from their goals in frustration. Many were the notables that crossed the Captain's path—or more likely—his decks: Senator Benton, many times; Fremont again and again, Brigham Young, who became LaBarge's friend; Joseph Smith, who did not; Army brass that would eventually include Harney and Sherman, Lee and Grant and so on and on. About 1848 Joseph brought his wife Pélagie up to Fort Union as the first white woman to penetrate so far into the high Missouri. To the Indians, she was a living marvel, and she made many friends among them.

At the top of the Missouri, Alexander Culbertson was building his new Piegan post. But even in such a simple matter as the name of the new post we are led into confusion by the sources. Was it Fort Lewis, Fort Honoré, Fort Clay or Fort Benton? Whatever people called it, the post was a busy place during the trading season of 1846-1847, with the supplies all traded off by spring. We have seen that Alec left there with Father Point, perhaps to travel all the way to St. Louis. Though after taking the returns to Union, he is said to have continued to Council Bluffs to meet the up-river steamer *Martha*, captained by Joseph LaBarge but under charter to AFC. In any event, he must have hastened back to Fort Union. The *Martha* was bringing the government agent and the annuities to the Yankton Sioux, who were so incensed at the inadequacy of the goods that they dumped them into the river and opened fire. A boathand was killed. Sobered by this casualty, the Yanktons presented three horses and twenty-five robes as compensation for the crewman's family, offering them not through the agent, but through Alexander. (Existentialists will recognize their forerunners.)

From Fort Union Alec sent a mackinaw with Charles Larpenteur up to Fort Lewis (Honoré, Clay, Benton), while he himself escorted the Crow agent and Robert Meldrum up the Yellowstone with two boats loaded with annuities. The Yellowstone was more of a problem to navigate than the Missouri. Especially toilsome was the cordelling, and especially treacherous, the quicksand. There a black engagé sank before he could be rescued. Near the mouth of the Powder River, the agent Colonel Redfield fell ill and had to return to Union with Alec. Meldrum went on with the annuities up to Fort Alexander, where he was very efficient in charge. Redfield had recovered and, with Alec, caught up in about five days overland. In late August Alec returned to Fort Union, and leaving Denig in command there, got back to Fort Lewis about the first of October. This was not the first time that Alexander would be imposed upon to help a government agent do his job. It was the beginning of a pattern that would soon become a burden, and probably all without compensation.

Fort Lewis had by now been rebuilt. But lo and behold! Major Culbertson was still not satisfied. Nothing, nothing would do but to rebuild once more, and this time with adobe bricks. In his experience at Fort Laramie, which had been reconstructed in adobe in the manner of the Southwest to become the best built of all the AFC posts, Alec had discovered his ideal of fort architecture. He seems to have been determined that his own new post would not be outdone by any other.

Not only this, but with the recent growth in trade, Alexander set up three

Pi-inakoyim, a sketch by Gustav Sohon. Photo courtesy of Glenbow Archives, Calgary, Alberta.

outposts of Fort Lewis (Benton) to be opened seasonally between October and March for the winter run: one post at Milk River Crossing under Michel Champagne, one at Willow Round on the Marias under Hammell, and one at Flatwood, thirty miles farther up the Marias, under Malcolm Clarke. These outposts were all established in the fall of 1848, according to Bradley's chronology. Alec (says Bradley) visited Flatwood in '48, so it may be that he had surveyed the sites earlier in the year.

On the Flatwood tour, Alec came across his brother-in-law *Pi-inakoyim* or Seen-From-Afar, whom Alec regarded as the greatest Blackfeet chief he knew. Seen-From-Afar had ten wives and a hundred horses, the symbols if not the substance of greatness, though everything we know about this chief suggests the substance as well. Whereas the ordinary tipi was made of poles 15 to 25 feet long and covered with eight or twelve (occasionally twenty) hides, the lodge of

Pi-inakoyim used 30 poles, 35 feet long, covered with 40 skins and contained two fireplaces. According to Schultz, Pi-inakoyim was a medicine man, and it may be that this is simply a reference to the fact that he was the owner of the Different People's Pipe, which he had brought back from the Mandans.

In the Spring of 1848 Alexander is said to have gone down to Fort Union, and of course this report conflicts with the one I have just mentioned regarding his visit with Seen-From-Afar. (But I warned you at the beginning of the chapter! No doubt dates, etc. will have to be re-adjusted.) At any rate, from Union, he sent Kipp's nephew, Jacques Brughière (Bruyère) up to Lewis-Benton with a load of provisions and then he went eastward "to visit friends." He reached St. Louis on July 19th on the *Wyandotte* accompanied by 70 Company men. The branch of the Company known as the UMO was now to be reorganized. Of the Company's twelve shares, six now went to Chouteau and one each to Alexander Culbertson, Kipp, Laidlaw, Drips, and Labone.

Meanwhile, the *Martha* under Joseph La Barge left Union about June 29th with Alec's cousin Ferdinand C. Culbertson "from Fort Benton." Also aboard was the famous Irish explorer and sportsman, John Palliser.

On his way back west, Alec was side-tracked to deliver supplies from Bellevue to Fort Laramie with 23 ox-drawn wagons along the north side of the Platte as far as Fort Kearny. Nearly a week's journey above Kearny, he fell sick and turned back to the fort in a buggy, only to be waylaid by Pawnees. Though he was robbed, he was left with both horses and rifles. As he and his two companions were driving away, Alec paused, fired back and then tore off in the buggy. Reaching the Platte in the dark, the three refugees saw the welcome lights of the fort, plunged into the river and made it to safety. (Still, there is something a bit disturbing about Alec's behavior lately. Power rarely improves character—rarely, perhaps never.) After about ten days of recuperation, Alec set out again westward, running into 300 Cheyennes in pursuit of Pawnees. The Cheyennes probably recognized him and provided him with meat. He overtook his wagon train at the forks of the Platte. But the Pawnees struck again and this time made off with ten yoke of oxen, and the train did not reach Laramie until the end of October.

In his hurry to get back to Fort Pierre (where I suppose he had left his family), Alexander was caught in the early snows and took another month to conclude his trip. With James Kipp and others, he pressed on up to Union. But at the Arikara village, he was called to a feast. It turned out not to be a celebration of joy, for the Arikaras were angry over the death of a chief whom they thought the Company should have protected. Alec became his old self again, went among them unarmed and paid them two horses. He reached Fort Union for the New Year, but it would be a long time before he would see his home at Fort Benton again. At Poplar River he was sick and had to turn back to Union. We have no clue as to what was causing his periodic relapses.

What of Natawista and her children during all this era of confusion? I wish I knew. There is nothing on record, unless we credit the single remark of a passenger on an up-river cruise in the summer of 1849 to the effect that Natawista was a "happy influence" on the upper Missouri.

As for others in Alec's world, we know almost as little. from Charles Larpenteur, the Parisian who writes as if he had chronic dyspepsia from every cuisine not Parisian, we learn that after a vain attempt to cross the Rockies with his guide Satá, he spent the winter of 1848-1849 at Fort Benton, sick but well treated by Alexander Culbertson. Coming from Larpenteur, that comment is score one for Alec. But it is hard or impossible to reconcile with the other details

I have just mentioned, unless Alec had learned to bilocate. Dates, however, are the hardest part of our memories to bring into recall. Larpenteur goes on to tell us that early in the spring of 1849, he and Alec set out in a mackinaw, taking twenty days to reach Fort Union and fighting ice to boot. Larpenteur kept on down to the Vermillion Post, where he again met Alec, who was now planning to take the steamer. But there was a rumor of cholera once again, cholera aboard the steamer. Alec cancelled his plans and turned back to Fort Pierre.

Apparently, Pierre was the place he spent the summer, and perhaps with Natawista, Jack and Julia. But about the first of December (1849) he started eastward again, and this time it seems clear that Natawista was not with him. Was it a lingering fear of the cholera that prompted him to leave her behind? Or was it fear of his family's reception of her? At any rate, he continued eastward to visit his family in Pennsylvania.

CHAPTER XIII

Brother Thaddeus

Back at home in Pennsylvania, Alec had a half-brother, somewhat more like Michael Simpson than himself, and also the product of Frances Stuart's pious tutelage. This was a brother who wanted to become both a naturalist and a divinity student. Born at Chambersburg, February 18, 1823, Thaddeus Ainsworth Culbertson was much younger than Alec, in precarious health, and knew nothing of the great wide West except through books or family reports. So the relationship between the two was bound to assume the nature of protector and protegé. Thad was much better schooled than Alec, first at the Chambersburg Academy and beginning in 1844, as a sophomore at Princeton. Three years later he graduated with a Bachelor of Arts and undertook to teach school in Virginia, probably at Clifton in what is now West Virginia. At one point he made a botany field trip to the James River, which must have taken him on quite an arduous adventure through Virginia, the Blue Ridge, the Piedmont, perhaps even the Tidewater. After these experiences, he returned to Princeton and spent perhaps one year (1849) at the Theological Seminary that Michael had attended. It must have been at this time that his health began to give way under the strain, and he thought of substituting travel for school.

We can see in this program that Thaddeus had not been much at home lately and so may never have met or heard of Natawista or any of Alec's children. This would perhaps explain why there is no notice of them in his journal. Specifically, he must have been away from home when Julia was born at Chambersburg, *if she really was*. It is possible too that he did make references to them in his original journal or his notes which were crossed out in later years by someone at the Smithsonian Insitution as unscientific digressions. His text was much altered there and portions of the original destroyed.

If Thaddeus' interest in theology evinces his kinship with Michael, his knack for science marks his affinity to Alec, who as we have seen, had begun to collect fossils from the Bad Lands of South Dakota. This gave Alec a bright idea. Since Thaddeus was not a healthy man, Alec suggested that he travel with him to "the mountains," that is, the upper Missouri. In those days, of course, travel was often thought of as the panacea when all else failed, and so perhaps travel would restore strength to Thaddeus and at the same time serve the interests of the Smithsonian. In fact, the Smithsonian liked the idea too and contributed about two hundred dollars for Thad's trip, while Alexander paid another portion. Thaddeus in return would collect fossils and other specimens. It seems possible that Thaddeus was tubercular, but whether it was obvious to Alec we can only guess. At any rate, in February of 1850 Alec and Thad set out from Chambersburg.

It must have been a bizarre experience for Thaddeus to travel, slowly dying, expecting any moment to be his last, balancing his young life constantly on the brink of death and yet loving life deeply, even with a mystique incommunicable to Alec. For though Alec was certainly a man inured to danger, he seems to have taken life for granted. That was something Thaddeus could not afford to do. Cheerful, resigned, devout, courageous, Thaddeus was one of those rare beings whom cynics like to call too good for this world. To Thad, as for De Smet, God was love.

At St. Louis, Alec began to introduce his young brother to the life of the frontier he himself knew so well and Thad knew so little. They took passage on the *Mary Blane*, along with a couple of French Canadian voyageurs named Nerselle[33] and Antoine, two Italian voyageurs Vincent and Angelo, Jim the black cook for their little private party and a "fine little dog" named Carlo. They also had thirty horses on board, apparently all belonging to Alec. Just to travel with such comrades and with that livestock must have been something of a revelation to Thaddeus. And sometimes the departure of a steamboat for "the mountain run" could also be a real-life drama: the booming of the cannon, the salutes of muskets to and fro, the raucous blast of the calliope or perhaps the rhythm of a local band striking up the latest hits from Stephan Foster or some other minstrel. There was the mingling of Indians, mountain men and fashionable citizens of the St. Louis establishment, perhaps too some of the elegant Chouteau family with their slaves in attendance.

But for this trip the *Mary Blane* was a floating hell. Built for 100 passengers, she was now overcrowded and overloaded, with nearly five times her quota of passengers in cabins and on the decks. Alexander's party was berthed in the pilot room. The throng of passengers, perhaps many of them greedy for the California gold fields, seemed rowdy, reckless gamesters with little concern for either science or divinity. The steamer pulled out of St. Louis at noon on the 19th of March, 1850, bound for St. Joseph. It was a rough job to fight the mob for the dining area, so Jim brought meals into the cabin for Alec's party, happily sitting about on trunks and berths. With delays caused by snags and sand bars, the trip proved something of a bore even to the good-natured Thaddeus, but he kept working at his French Bible, his diary and his meditations. And though he does not seem to have learned much French from his Bible, his meditations were very meaningful to him, especially one on *the great dignity of being a child of God*. Thaddeus had the harmonious mind, unfragmented, that saw nothing amiss about including remarks on the God-given dignity of man in his scientific treatise for the Smithsonian.

The travelers reached St. Joseph about midnight, March 25th. Here they disembarked, horses and all, and took lodging at the Mansion House. Alexander went on a shopping tour and bought more horses from Joseph Robidoux (though I must add that some of Alec's horses turned out to be mules). Joseph Robidoux, was the founder of St. Joseph in some sense or other, and the town was named for his patron saint since old Joe himself was not what most people would call a saint. He was the brother of Louis and Antoine (who had gone to New Mexico and California) and dealt for slaves with Lafitte. Once the partner of the Chouteaus, he was now a major part of their Opposition. Thaddeus was surprised to hear so much French spoken at St. Joseph. And he was delighted and grateful for his brother Alec's constant generosity. No one enjoyed this world so happily, no observer was more alert and appreciative of everything in it than this young man who knew he was about to leave it forever. The sunshine, the

[33] Perhaps this was Paul Narcelle, who married a daughter of Thomas L. Sarpy (Peter Sarpy's brother) by his Sioux wife.

light clouds, the farmlands, the birdsong—all held Thaddeus spellbound. On Sunday, March 31, he kept the Sabbath in meditation. Alexander must surely have wondered.

As they traveled along, they would stop at night at the homes of settlers, perhaps persons well known to Alec. One of these hosts was Peter Sarpy, the fur trader near Council Bluffs, but others were much less elite. Though somtimes Thaddeus was repelled by their filth, he did not lose his appetite, and even while he was not edified by whiskey traders, he still relished the food they offered. At the Big Sioux river, their host was Théophile Brughière, who married two or three daughters of the Yankton Chief War Eagle. Passing no overt judgement on their life-style, Thaddeus thought their cooking was fine and the Sioux language sounded very sweet. He was acquiring a taste for "corn bangs" (*beignes*); fried cakes or fritters served with honey and coffee. He said nothing about predestination.

Crossing the Big Sioux with their buggy, horses, mules, dogs and maybe a wagon to boot, they left the "States" and entered Indian territory. Alexander decreed a rest of two days at Vermillion Post, and keeping a critical eye on his brother's condition, tried talking him into feeling more healthy.

"Your shoulders are three inches broader!" declared Alec. And indeed Thaddeus was feeling stronger than he had for years. Now he could put up with the wind and the cold and the fatigue, and he still had his wonderful appetite.

But Thaddus was happy to have April 14th as a restful Sabbath for a change. He regarded the New Testament as more fruitful reading than the biographies of pious men which lead readers to imitate their eccentricities. However, he liked such reading too, in its place, or as he said, "to have my sluggish soul fired by their burning zeal." Thad would even read an occasional novel. He thought fondly of home and his friends in Virginia and his old classmates at Princeton.

"Alexander and I frequently speak of Simpson," he wrote, referring of course to Michael Simpson Culbertson in China. "Will we ever see him again?" Both brothers were wondering about this as they relaxed by the River Vermillion. Thaddeus was wishing too for "Simpson's" good counsel, but he could not even hope for that now. "But Simpson is right," he mused, and "May God bless him and his. . ."

The Vermillion was in flood, and Alexander commented, "You can't see the river for the water." At last the travelers made it across. Thaddeus had to admit to himself that his mind did not really feel exalted at the sight of flat prairies far and wide. Less so, when they came upon a prairie fire. But their voyageur Nerselle (Narcelle) led them through safely. On the other side they met some Indians in two tipis, and Thaddeus spent his "first night in an Indian lodge." It began to snow, and the lodge was crammed with children, dogs, and smoke. But at night, a stormy night, he dreamed happily of home. Next day the Indians joined them on their journey.

It was not long before they encountered buffalo, but also snow, fierce winds and more spring floods. Thaddeus often mentioned his physical weariness in his journal but he found the tipi warm and the buggy comfortable for sleeping. A large white wolf drew near enough to stir his wonderment, but not near enough (luckily) for Alec's gun. Thaddeus was much impressed by the Indians as fellow children of God—the Indians who came to trade, travel, feast or have fun. He was impressed with their intelligence and particularly with one thoughtful, retiring young man. He studied his brother's way with these people, once describing Alexander at Yankton Post giving a feast and making a speech. Alec just sat back on a bench as he talked with his pipe in his mouth and his hat perched casually on his head.

Starting each day's travel very early in the morning, they came opposite Fort Pierre on May 4th and were ferried across to the post about noon.

While Alexander remained at the fort, Thaddeus set out for a scientific visit of the Bad Lands, the *Mauvaises Terres*, accompanied by an engagé and also by Owen McKenzie. Two years before, Owen had won the admiration of John Palliser, and now he won Thad's. It is hard to say what these young men found in each other: the pious, sickly scholar and the half-Indian son of a dynamic, unscrupulous tycoon, but they became good friends. Every thesis seeks its antithesis so that life can go on. Owen explained to Thaddeus that the Indians worshipped the Great Spirit and often something besides. What Owen probably should have said was that since the Great Spirit was regarded as transcendent and ineffable, the common suppliant often sought an intermediary, but I suppose such an explanation would have been much more meaningful to Thad than to Owen.

Setting out on the 7th of May, they reached the White River Bad Lands on the 11th. Thaddeus compared them to a city of palaces for a race of giants. For a few days he filled his buggy with specimens for the Smithsonian, and in spite of the heat, was still enjoying the Gothic formations, the towers on the Rhine and the far view of "the Black Hills." Fortunately, they came upon some traders with carts who agreed to carry in their heavy load of specimens. Thaddeus was now close to exhaustion. On the 17th at sunset they got back to Fort Pierre, but Sunday evening Thad had a fit of vomiting. The crisis passed once more, and gradually he recovered with the help of short rides by Alec's side, with some botanizing, bird watching, visiting the Indians, playing bandy ball and reading the Bible and Schiller.

What, I wonder, was the affinity Thad found in Schiller at a time like that? Why had he carried Schiller's poems to the wild Missouri? Perhaps he found his theme in the "An die Freude," where the poet turns the trochaic measure of the *Dies irae*, that medieval song of death and doom, into a paean of joy and renascence as in Beethoven's symphony:

"Day of Wrath, that final day, When earth to ash dissolves away..."

now replaced by:

"Prince and beggar, brothers all, Responding to God's joyous call..."[34]

That sounds like Thad, once again he was in high spirit. When the Indians came to dance, he had to confess he found the performance more of a curiosity than a total delight, but he wrote a long piece on Indian customs, gleaning his information no doubt from both Alec and Owen.

On the 5th of June the steamer *El Paso* rounded the bend and lay to below the fort. Thad and Alec went aboard for Fort Union, and Thad declared this part of the trip was the happiest traveling he had ever done. It was now the heart of the buffalo country. Thad began to ask pointed questions about the accumulated packs of buffalo robes, ten robes to a pack. From Honoré Picotte, he came up with some ominous statistics: About 100,000 robes would be shipped to St. Louis this one season from all the posts together. The Indians and other inhabitants would use and waste more, for each Indian needed two robes a year for himself and others for tipis, etc. In all, an estimated 400,000 buffalo were killed annually.

On June 12 they reached Fort Clark and the Arikaras. Alexander, Thaddeus and Picotte visited the village of earth lodges and in spite of the contretemps of a year ago, were now welcomed hospitably. Thad was well impressed with the cleanliness and orderliness of the earth lodge, regardless of the chicken coop

[34] My own paraphrase.

Thaddeus saw them as fellow children of God. Kurz drawing of Gros Ventres or Herantsa. Smithsonian Institution Photo No. 2856-16.

in the corner. He also liked the crops of corn, squash and pumpkins and the appearance of the people. He noted that women suckled their children sometimes to the age of four or five, and so too little animals, like an antelope or grizzly cub. They visited the fort but did not linger, for having taken on a load of "Ree corn," the *El Paso* kept its way. In about sixty miles it reached Fort Berthold and the Hidatsas, but again did not dilly-dally except to let some Hidatsas aboard for a feast and some presents. A few stayed on as passengers.

As they passed the mouth of the Little Missouri, Honoré Picotte explained to Thaddeus that the Indians who live in fixed villages, Arikaras, Hidatsas, Mandans, Pawness, Otoes, Omahas, etc., ran greater risks from disease and attack than did the nomadic tribes and also experienced population slumps. His theory was that sedentary life was less healthy, less safe than the roaming life.

Bad Land formations soon appeared, and a violent storm broke over the steamer. A skiff from Fort Union came down to meet the *El Paso* in charge of Malcolm Clarke. Then Alexander and Joseph Howard took off from the steamer to get to Union ahead of it by land. Even that short separation reminded Thaddeus that he must soon part from his kindly brother for good. On the 16th of June, the steamboat reached Fort Union, welcomed by the Assiniboines, Denig and Ferdinand Culbertson of Chambersburg, first cousin of Alec and Thad. Since there were two Crow passengers aboard, the Assiniboines wanted to kill them at once, but "the gentlemen" intervened. Fort Union was four miles above the mouth of the Yellowstone, and the Opposition fort of Harvey and Honoré's nephew Joe Picotte was just below the mouth. But the *El Paso* was heading farther up into Montana, and Thaddeus stayed on board as it pulled away up into the Missouri. Clarke, Picotte and cousin Ferdinand were now also aboard.

When they reached the celebrated pyramid of elk horns, the *El Paso* stopped to let them all take a closer look. No one seemed to know when or why this mysterious monument had been erected. As another diversion, Malcolm Clarke gave Thaddeus a lesson on sign-talk. Then they passed a herd of swimming elk and mustered an attack. But when they passed a herd of swimming buffalo calves, Picotte forbade any shooting. Some attempted to lasso calves, but in vain. On June 20th the *El Paso* reached a point a little above Milk River. A sign to commemorate the event was nailed to a cottonwood, the freight for Fort Benton was put ashore and the steamer turned back. This was then the highest point on the Missouri yet gained by any steamboat. Piously, Thaddeus declared:

"I really feel very thankful that my life and health have been spared me during my journey. I have reached a point to which few, except traders, have attained...But it is a long distance, nearly four thousand miles to my home, and no one can tell what may befall me..."

On the evening of the 21st the *El Paso* was back at Fort Union. As Thaddeus reflected on the departure early tomorrow morning, he felt both happy to go homeward and sad to leave Alexander, probably for the last time: "I feel sad at heart to part with my brother, and I know that I shall be lonely tomorrow without him. May all his kindness be returned to him tenfold."

And the next day, off they went, firing a salute. Thaddeus caught a last glimpse of Alexander standing in a boat that was just pushing off.

He would not be altogether lonely, however, as it seems that Malcolm Clarke, James Kipp and Ferdinand Culbertson all accompanied him down the river. Honoré Picotte was also aboard, but when the steamer reached Fort Pierre on the 28th, he bade farewell to Thad and went ashore. Nevertheless, Thad seems to have had a chance to greet Owen McKenzie and other friends. At Vermillion Post on July 2nd the steamer was welcomed by Larpenteur. On Saturday, the 6th of July, 1850, it landed Thaddeus safely in St. Louis as he quietly gave praise to God.

And now the question that must gnaw at us: Where was Natawista and where were her children all this while? Why do they not appear in Thad's journal? Should Thad not have known his nephew and nieces? And, what seems to me equally strange is that no editor or commentator that I recall has ever asked these questions. There is no reply to them that I can give except to point out a few probabilities. Surely, Alec must have left Natawista for this period at some post with proper conveniences, presumably Fort Union. And at Fort Union Alec himself seems to fade strangely out of the picture in Thad's journal, almost as if he were acting as a screen between his brother and his wife.

So I must conclude my story of Brother Thaddeus, not only with a note of caution, but also with a note of sorrow. Yes, Thad did see his home again, though for some reason it took him a long time to get there. He reached Chambersburg in August. And on the 28th day of August he died. The Smithsonian Institution accepted his collection and published his journal.

Thaddeus had walked in beauty.

CHAPTER XIV

Freedom of
the Will

While Thaddeus was wending his way to home and death, Alec was accompanying Robert Meldrum and a party of seventeen up the Yellowstone in a mackinaw to replace Fort Alexander with a new post for the Crows below the Rosebud. This new station was named Fort Sarpy but sometimes was still called after Alexander. When Alec rode back to Union, he was free at last to go home to Fort Benton, and probably with Natawista. In 1850, Jack must have been about seven but whether he was still with his parents or in some boarding school we have no word. We can presume that Julia was still with her parents, and I suppose that Janie and Maria were at the Moravian Seminary in Bethlehem, though no record of their presence there has been found. Efforts to keep track of the children usually demands some conjecture.

At Fort Benton Alec had the work started (or perhaps continued) on his project of rebuilding the fort in adobe bricks. Since the fall of 1850 was a warm one, it was quite right for the manufacture of adobes, which were made and sun-dried on the spot and nicknamed "doughboys"—and other things—by the engagés. They were fashioned in the style of the Hispanic Southwest with a mixture of local mud and wild grass and about 6x4x15 inches in size.

There were several engagés of Mexican origin, though some were already of the second generation in the Northwest and may not have known adobe architecture from first hand experience. We may notice that across the Divide at St. Mary in the Bitterroot, John Owen was building Fort Owen of adobe bricks with the help of Mexican laborers, so we can only wonder if there was some sharing of ideas and even workers between these two establishments, perhaps via the Jesuits who passed between them.

As the autumn advanced and the temperature fell below freezing at night, the adobe bricks froze too, but even when they were set into the walls still moist, they dried without cracking. So progress continued until Alec's own residence of two stories was one of the first adobe constructions completed, shortly before Christmas, 1850. It would take another decade to rebuild the rest of the fort. Evidently the log structures were replaced by adobe walls little by litte, with some original log walls retained.

Though the name "Fort Benton" appears on AFC ledgers from 1848 onwards, the tradition claims that on Christmas night, 1850, the Culbertsons held a grand ball at their new adobe home. There were several fiddles in action (with Alec probably at one of them) and maybe more orchestra besides. Natawista dazzled everyone in her famous red gown with the buttoned bodice. I would also suggest a hoop-skirt but would be somewhat doubtful that she could have at this date been sporting the emeralds and rubies that she later became famous for. The engagés skipped and swung with their Indian ladies, some of whom wore hoop-skirts for this gala occasion, and that strange custom must have created an hysterical sensation at Fort Benton. (One wonders if the Blackfeet "Spanish Owl Dance" had its origin here.) All in all, it proved to be a happy affair—with punch at least, and perhaps a little too much of other things. Alec climaxed the occasion by the announcement (or proposal, in one version) that in honor of Senator Thomas Benton, friend of American Fur, the Piegan post would henceforth be known as Fort Benton. The assembly applauded.

Come spring, Alec went down to Fort Union and took a herd of horses on to Pierre. From there he joined Honoré Picotte for a mackinaw trip farther down to meet the up-river steamer, the *St. Ange*. Little did they guess what they were getting into!

The St. Ange had left St. Louis under charter to AFC but owned and commanded by Joseph LaBarge. By one account, the Captain's wife Pélagie and their family were aboard for this cruise, perhaps to evade the cholera that was spreading over the land. Also on board were the two Jesuits, Pierre-Jean DeSmet and Christian Hoecken, as well as Dr. John Evans, a geologist who had been on the river with Thaddeus last year. There were many AFC employees: Irish, Germans, Italians, Swiss, Americans, Frenchmen, but mostly French Canadians—and, it is said, everyone was ominously silent. The trip was toilsome with the river now in high flood, and suddenly became a horror. According to DeSmet, the boat turned into a floating hospital when about a dozen people were stricken with cholera. Captain LaBarge dared not put ashore and passed St. Joseph by, leaving unanswered the signals of Alec and Picotte. Alec got a horse and Honoré a wagon. They raced the steamer thirty miles up the river. Finally, LaBarge let them aboard. At Bellevue Alec got off, while the artist Rudolph Friedrich Kurz came on.

Kurz has left us a remarkable journal and some of his pictures were eventually published by the Smithsonian. He was born in Berne, Switzerland (1818) and there he would die (1871): a man of special discernment, disturbed—perhaps tormented—by religious and philosophical tensions, not always in the best humor, not well impressed by Americans but favorable to the Indians. In fact, he was another one of the long series of talented Europeans drawn to the Great Plains by a fascination with the "American Red Skins." Once he tried married life with the daughter of an Iowa chief, but with the coming of spring, she vanished. Rudolph knew Maximilian, either personally or indirectly, and spoke of him as the "Prince von New Wied, alias Baron von Berneberg." [35] Charles Bodmer was Kurz's own friend, the one who probably passed him the torch that lit his way to the western frontier. Bodmer, after his tour with Prince Max, had settled in France: Compiègne, Paris, Barbizon, an art colony near Paris in the forest of Fontainebleu. There he continued his career without adding to his fame. But he created his own art work and taught and aided other artists. No doubt Kurz was one of those who came under his tutelage, while another was Jean Franszçois Millet.

Rudolph Kurz had set out from LeHavre and reached New Orleans on Christmas Eve, 1846, hoping to go to Mexico, but found his way blocked by the war unless he volunteered for the U.S. Army. This he refused to do and regarded the U.S. as an unjust agressor. Outraged by the invasion of Mexico and by the enslavement and abuse of blacks, disgusted further by the segregation of sexes, the greed of goldrushers and traders, intolerance, jingoism and many other American quirks, Kurz at last betook himself to the Indians of the far Missouri. To do this, of course, he had to submit himself to the good

---

[35] Braunsberg, the name under which Maximilian traveled.

will and authority of the American Fur Company. However, he could always confide his frustrations to his journal, and fortunately for us, he did.

Kurz was above all an artist and a philosopher of art. He was unhappy to discover that in the U.S. he had no hope of earning his livelihood by art since Americans generally had no taste for art and regarded the artist as a charlatan. They were put off by his preference for nudity in art. His special gift was the expression of the natural grace and dignity of the human body—and, he hoped, also of the human spirit. To portray the human spirit on canvas is no easy matter. In Kurz's eye, even a Christus or Madonna of the Italian master (Raphael) lacked soul if it failed to reveal the freedom of the will. That was a key term in Kurz's equation—the freedom of the will, creativity. He placed himself at the opposite end of the scale from the Greek master (Phidias) with his "classic repose." To Kurz, it was free will that gave Man his dignity as the child and image of God, and it was precisely that which he tried to put into the men and women he portrayed. How far was he from Calvin, his fellow countryman! How far from the Calvinists and predestinarians all around him! His existentialism might have disturbed Thaddeus or Michael, but Rudolph Kurz, like Thoreau, had his own way to walk in beauty.

Yet, when he stepped aboard the *St. Ange*, he suddenly realized he walked in woe. He had been staying with Peter Sarpy in Bellevue, had met Alec and Honoré Picotte on their way down the river and had been invited by them to catch the up-river boat. On June 16, 1851, that turned out to be the *St. Ange*. Bidding farewell to his friend, young Decatur, he wondered to himself, "Shall I risk it?" But the boat was already underway and he was in the midst of the sick and dying. There was no physician on board. Dr. Evans was a geology professor, but he had Kurz pass around meal mixed with whiskey, while Father Hoecken passed out "spiritual consolation." Then on the 21st, Father Hoecken died, stricken down in two hours. It was Kurz who found him in convulsions and called Father DeSmet. When Picotte's clerk died, Kurz got his job. DeSmet too was sick, but recovered. When relief finally came, people attributed it to the "purer air." Below Sioux City, the boat was fumigated and the ordeal ended.

From Bellevue, meanwhile, Alec traveled by land to Fort Pierre, intercepted en route by a messenger from the Superintendent of Indian Affairs requesting him to gather delegates of all tribes on the upper Missouri for a grand council at Fort Laramie in August. And so began the great wave of treaty-making which would solve all problems by contract. Both DeSmet and Hoecken had been summoned for the same end by David Mitchell, and that was why they were on the *St. Ange*. Missionaries and traders were alike regarded as servants at the beck and call, it seems, of government officials. Concepts of the separation of church and state, or government and the "private sector" that are current today, were less prevalent then. You were expected to serve both God and Mammon. So of course as any good "Good Citizen" would do, Alec dropped everything and went about rounding up delegates: Four Bears of the Hidatsas, Fool Bear of the Assiniboines, Iron Bear of the Arikaras...There was not enough time to recruit any of the leaders from the Blackfeet or the Gros Ventres (expect one Blackfeet hunter). Some Crows joined the delegation, bringing the total number of envoys to thirty-two.

DeSmet rode from one camp to another seeking emmissaries to the council, evidently without adverting to the incongruity, the conflict of interest inherent in his role. As he traveled through the country, he was enraptured by the beauty of it all, much like Thaddeus, on his way rejoicing. The woods and prairies, the rivers and deserts and the Rockies—all were a marvel to DeSmet. There was even some sort of celebration aboard the tragic *St. Ange*, for at the mouth of the Platte, which now marked the boundary between the lower and upper Missouri, DeSmet noted that "the Neptunian tribute was exacted of all 'pork eaters.' " He foresaw great states about to emerge from the wilderness, cities out of parklands, and the ecstacy turned to ashes in his records. But what of the Indians? What would become of them? He hoped they would "be incorporated with all the rights of citizens into the Union," but he feared they faced genocide instead.

Among the Yanktons he found smallpox on the rage again and DeSmet went about helping the sick. When he met a sick little orphan, cast out into the rainy night, he prevailed on a French Canadian to nurse him back to health. At Pierre, where influenza had recently appeared, the new threat of small pox and cholera created panic. And on the 14th of July, cholera, sweeping up the river, hit Fort Union.

Yet the council must go forward, and DeSmet wrote of his project:

"Mr. Culbertson, superintendent of the forts on the Missouri and Yellowstone rivers, is a distinguished man, endowed with a mild, benevolent and charitable temper... If need be he could be intrepid and courageous. He has always given me marks of kindness and friendship, but most particularly in this last hour. Being at the head of our troop, he was able to aid me in my project."

One of the many baptized by DeSmet during his tour in 1851 was Nancy Culbertson at Fort Union in July. She had been born there in 1848.

On the 31st of July, the delegation crossed the river and headed up the Yellowstone through a storm of thunder and a swarm of mosquitoes so thick that the travelers pulled gauze sacks over their heads. When the hunter brought in bear, antelope and skunk for supper, DeSmet observed that though skunk had an odor intolerable to white people, Indians found the meat very tasty. (Frémont, Washington Irving and others support the Indian viewpoint. DeSmet merely adds *De Gustibus non disputandum.*)

The Jesuit traveled in one "ambulance," while Alec used another. There were two carts of baggage, and most of the Indians walked. Crossing the watershed between the Missouri and Yellowstone, they saw thousands of buffalo that drew off the mosquitoes. On a sage-covered desert they found petrified trees and shell heaps. DeSmet gives us one of the most competent early descriptions of the area of Yellowstone Park, and he adds an account of a lunar halo: four circles around a glaring moon—azure, purple, white, and black. The Indians were alarmed.

After several days at Fort Sarpy, they followed the Rosebud to its source, crossed to the Tongue and then to a lake Alec named for DeSmet. On the 27th they reached Powder River with great labor for the waggoners. When three young Crows pointed out a short-cut that was never intended for wagons, they named it the Valley of a Thousand Miseries. DeSmet suspected that the three Crows were enjoying a good laugh. But on September 2nd they emerged onto the Oregon Trail, the Great Medicine Road, which DeSmet described as "smooth as a barn floor," very wide and littered with white man's junk. One man's trash is another man's treasure, so the Indians went treasure hunting. In another week they reached Fort Laramie where a few days later, Meldrum arrived with forty Crows.

Since the council ground was 35 miles down the Platte from the fort, DeSmet drove there in a carriage with Robert Campbell and was greeted by David Mitchell, still the chivalrous Virginian. An alleged ten thousand Indians of various tribes were already in camp. The council lasted eighteen days and the assembly twenty-three. Peace reigned supreme, much to DeSmet's delight: "Implacable hatreds, hereditary enmities, cruel and bloody encounters, with

Return from the Dobies' Ball, a Kurz drawing. Smithsonia Institution Photo No. 2856-11.[36]

the whole past, in fine, were forgotten." Feasts and gifts, peace-pipes and adoptions were the order of the day. The treaty included a guarantee of peace, reparations and indemnities for both Indians and whites, the government's right to establish roads and forts. A second treaty granted rights to half-breeds and resident whites. Several tipis were arranged as a chapel, and DeSmet offered Mass. When he went about visiting, instructing, baptizing, he explained the Ten Commandments to the Oglalas and created quite a stir. The head chief replied: "We hear you. We did not know the words of the Great Spirit...We have done all the things the Great Spirit forbids. Help us try to do better."

During his trip, says DeSmet, he baptized 1,586 persons, many of whom later died of disease. None knew better than DeSmet, a proponent of free will like Kurz, that from font to grave slips many a knave. So he was filled with both euphoria and foreboding, with euphoria on top. He rejoiced at a peace ceremony between Shoshonis, and Cheyennes, including a feast of corn (no dog for Shoshonies), gifts and adoptions, songs and dances. "These amusements among the Indians are perfectly innocent..." wrote DeSmet, the Northwest counterpart of the Southwestern Garcés. (Some of his colleagues in St. Louis must have winced to read that.) DeSmet was edified by the well-kept order of the camps, the mutual courtesy among all tribes, the smoking of the calumet.

But the assembly dragged on too long. Food ran low, and for dogs this was

[36] On pages 126-7 of the Ye Galleon Press edition of his *Journal*, Kurz explains this picture: "It is approaching midnight, but the moonlight is beautiful and the party as merry as possible without 'love and wine.'" The rider in the lead with the pistol is labeled simply "Morgan." Then follows "Mac" (Owen McKenzie) on Toku, "his superb courses" with his wife behind him and hanging onto him. Kurz is following them and talking to the two women on another horse who are trying to coax him into a race. These two women are Denig's younger wife (probably Deer Little Woman) and the wife of (Jeff?) Smith.

not a happy season. DeSmet found dog meat "delicate," but he relished plum stew with more gusto. When buffalo were reported nearby, the council was over. Mitchell gathered DeSmet and others at Robidoux's post near Chimney Rock. DeSmet met Prince Paul of Württemburg, and returned to St. Louis. Alec went back to Fort Sarpy and Fort Union. According to Lt. Bradley, he never received any compensation from the government for his role in the Treaty of Laramie.

While Alec was away at Laramie, Kurz had many petty adventures at Union that he turned into colorful vignettes in his journal: word pictures and brush pictures of life at Fort Union and its neighbor Fort William, the adobe post of the Opposition, nicknamed the "Dobies." One of his happiest subjects is his moonlight ride home from the "Dobies Ball" with Owen McKenzie and their friends. One of his most suspenseful is his story of engagé Cadotte, whose lovely Assiniboine wife was lured away to the Dobies by the factor Harvey. Cadotte boldly marched into the "the Tiger's lair" and took his wife back. Harvey might have shot him on the spot had not others intervened. Kurz, who had done profiles of "Pere DeSmet" and Joseph LaBarge, now got around to portraits of Edwin Denig, his dog Natoh (the Bear) and Opposition trader Joe Picotte. Happiest with the Indians, he put more emphasis on their nudity, grace and spriteliness than other artists had done. Among the people he tells of are Fool Bear, Owen McKenzie, Paquinaud, Bruyère, Ramsey the hunter, Joe Dolores the horse guard. Kurz was sensitive to the various castes he found in the camp: some women he regarded as "riffraff," others as aristocrats: "half-breed children of clerks and traders are a credit to the white race." One supposes he may be thinking of the Culbertsons and Denigs, but not all the frontier folk were such a delight to Rudolph Kurz. "The worst Indians I have seen in my travels are the white people who live on the borders." This witticism Kurz attributes to President Monroe, but he likes to quote it for himself. His relations with Denig, both his boss and his host, were variable. Once Denig gave a cotillion ball, played the fiddle himself, while Kurz beat the drum.

When Alec got back from the Laramie council, his assessment (at least as recorded by Kurz) was much less positive than DeSmet's "You should be glad you did not go," he told Kurz, adding that although he would have seen over 2,000 warriors in gala costume, no dancing was permitted(!). (Perhaps this means no dancing that would disturb the fragile peace.) Kurz remarks that Mr. Culbertson has now been named colonel by Mitchell. "Colonel of what?... Oh, the passion for titles among these republican Americans!" On one occassion Denig woke Kurz up late at night "to keep Mr. Culbertson company." So they smoked, sipped whiskey and talked of God. It sounds too as if Kurz got in a few pointers on free will to counter Alec's early background in predestinarianism. At any rate, the upshot of it all was that Alec engaged Rudolph Kurz to work at Fort Union and to paint portraits of Alec and Natawista and also one of the dog Natoh. Soon afterwards (November 5th) Kurz started the portrait of Alec, handicapped as he was by inadequate paints and brushes. Unluckily, he was unable (at that time at least) to paint the picture of Natawista, because she had cut her hair short in mourning for her younger brother who had just been shot by an Assiniboine. Otherwise, remarked the gallant Rudolph, "I should have had a chance to study one of the most beautiful Indian women... She would be an excellent model for a Venus...!"

Soon after that, on a Sunday, Alec and his family left for Fort Benton. This was the first wagon trip through that country. They were accompanied by LaBombarde, an engagé who was supposed to drive horses back down to Union on his return. The trip overland took twenty-four days.

Sketches made in October and November, 1851 by Kurz. Alec Culbertson appears at the top, probably in 3 different poses. The Indian is Ours Fou (Fool Bear). Below and a bit to the right is Domicila La Bombarde. Smithsonian Institution Photo No. 2856-13

Kurz evidently got along well with most of the people around him but endeared himself to no one. He regarded the traders as no worse than other American businessmen, basically immoral. Curiously, he noted that Denig contended that alcohol did the Indians no harm! Missionaries were not his favorite people, and he specifically disclaimed being either a "Romanist" on the one hand or a Freemason on the other. He had run-ins with Father Scanlon of St. Joseph, Missouri, and with Father Lacombe, whom he met among the métis on a visit to the Kipp family (though he mistakes the names of both these priests). With Father DeSmet, however, he seems to have gotten along well enough, though he refused to believe a popular tale that DeSmet's prayers had once calmed a storm at sea off San Francisco. As the gloomy winter of 1851-1852 passed over him, he hoped Alec would take him back down the river in the spring.

In March (1852) he spent some of his last days of adventure in the west in a horse camp on the Yellowstone, in the company of Morgan the Scot, Joe Dolores, Cadotte and various other engagés and their Indian wives. However pleased he may have been to get away from the fort for a while, by the middle of April he was glad to be back. So when Alec came down from Fort Benton, Rudolph Kurz was prepared to return to civilization. "Adieu, Fort Union! Farewell, ye red men! Farewell, ye wild beasts of primeval woods!"

On April 19th he set out on the keelboat captained by Alec and accompanied by Morgan, Cadotte, Joe Dolores, Baptiste Champagne and an unnamed young Blackfeet who is identified in the records only as Alec's brother-in-law. In the tradition of the Blood people, however, he is identified as Seen-From-

Afar.[37] In that case, the persistence of Seen-From-Afar for travel with Alec seems quite remarkable. How far he continued down the river or how he returned we are never told. Everyone was expected to do some of the rowing, while Alec was sometimes at an oar, sometimes at the wheel. Joe Dolores probably with his Mandan wife and other women, disembarked at Fort Berthold, leaving the boat less crowded. On May 3rd, it reached Fort Pierre. On May 11th, at Bellevue, Kurz dined once more with his old friends Decatur, LaFleche and others. On the 21st they were at St. Joseph and on the 25th, at St. Louis. For some reason, Alec was trying to catch up with Harvey, who was ahead of them in a skiff, but Kurz does not tell us why.

In poor health now, Kurz was not especially happy to leave America, nor happy to get home. But he certainly left behind him a trail of beauty in his pictures. Even his horses have free will!

[37] Information from Hugh A. Dempsey.

CHAPTER XV

Rhine Gold, Seine Silver, Missouri Mud

Do you ever think how wonderful to be born a prince or a duchess or even a court jester? Then you should read some of the memoirs of such people and especially those written from the distaff side. And in this instance, I mean the distaff side quite literally, for the niece of Prince Maximilian wielded the pen and the distaff with equal dexterity. In the intertwined families of Wied and Nassau, it was sometimes a major problem for the women and children just getting from one day to the next. Discipline, in the words of one who endured it, amounted to "Draconian penalties attached to every trifling misdeed." This from Carmen Sylva, the grand-niece of old Maximilian and the grand-daughter of autocratic Duke Wilhelm of Nassau. Her small brother Wilhelm was once incarcerated for three weeks on bread and water (though a kindly servant slipped in occasional goodies, and poor little Willi did escape to the roof).

Women were required to be elegant and obedient, to remain standing for hours on end, begowned and bejewelled and rapt in adoration of their godly males playing at billiards. Ladies must never lean or lounge. If allowed to be seated, they must sit upright and perhaps be strapped to a piece of iron that forced them upright. Carmen Sylva was even obliged to walk about with this "odious device," and her great-aunt (a sister of Prince Max?) had to wear a spiked collar to keep her head erect. Carmen Sylva blamed the ancient Romans for such male dominance lest the women of the world gain the upper hand by their greater cleverness. Most terrible of her relatives in her view was Prince Paul of Württemberg, not the Prince Paul who educated Sacajawea's son in Europe, but rather his first cousin.

And yet, even in such households, there were light-hearted moments: frolics in the woods, vacations in Paris, family concerts and theatricals. Carmen Sylva, tutored by Madame Schumann herself, would star at the piano or in some stage role, and her musical fame has been enhanced by the "Carmen Sylva Waltz," composed for her by Rumania's waltz-king Jon Ivanovici. (Perhaps you would recognize it.) There were also delightful cruises on the Rhineboats—though ladies on board might be forbidden to join in the hearty chorus. And in the fine displays of horsemanship, blue-blooded women were required to be perfect equestriennes—but not just for fun.

The dynasty of Wied was once described by an intimate (Marie of Rumania) as "somewhat improverished but very ancient and blue-blooded." Although *der Onkel* Maximilian, an inveterate bachelor like his mentor von Humboldt, had done nothing to enrich the blue blood, his nephew Prince Hermann did it for him and in 1842 married Marie of Nassau, thereby probably enriching even the coffers of Wied. Marie descended from the Houses of Orange, Hanover,

Stuart and Castille, and what fresh charm and gaiety she bestowed on the staid old House of Wied! Like the Rhineland Fairy she danced, or so the family said, leading everyone in merriment, in woodland romps, songs, and theatricals.

Old Prince Max, in these later days, could hardly have joined in woodland frivolities. Though he made tours about Europe, he never returned to his globe-trotting career after his epic trip to the high Missouri. Much of this long later life he spent puttering with the materials he brought home, cataloguing and clarifying and publishing his reports, his journal, his notes on the mammals and reptiles and flora of North America. To many species, he assigned scientific names. In Paris he consulted with his colleagues, perhaps with Bodmer. In Koblenz (1838-41) he issued two volumes of his *Reise durch Nordamerika,* containing eighty-one copper engravings of Bodmer's wonderful art. The work was a triumph of partnership between art and science. There remained in Maximilian something of the romantic. In this, as in other respects, he resembled his grand-niece. Still, being a royal male, he could be difficult. When Marie of Nassau, Carmen Sylva's mother the Rhineland Fairy, first came to Neuwied as a dancing bride, she was shocked and frightened by Uncle Max, who: ''. . .related how he had ridden about on the field of Waterloo, in the hope of finding Napoleon and making an end of him. 'That fellow Bonaparte! If I could but have got at him!' Uncle Max would say, clenching his fist; and my mother turned away in horror at such savage sentiments.''

One suspects, of course, that *der Onkel* was putting on his own palace theatrical, tongue-in-cheek. No doubt he relished Beethoven's cancelled dedication of the ''Eroica'' (Carmen Sylva's favorite), and he probably kept a low key about his own fiasco with the cannon of the Piegan post. But he had his occasional royal caprice, as Carmen Sylva recalled: ''Our great uncle, the traveller, whose delight it was to give nicknames to everyone, amused himself with twisting and turning the servants' names.'' The valiant and faithful Dreidoppel was ''King David.'' A retainer named Long he dubbed ''Short'' (Kurz), Shepherd (Schafer) he turned into ''Hare,'' and one poor fellow named Corcilius was re-christened by the cosmopolitan Prince as ''Garcilaso de la Vega,'' for the Spanish poet or the Inca historian. (You must remember, of course, that servants were treated as members of the royal families they served from generation to generation.) Carmen Sylva was ''Lisi'' (for Elizabeth) and seems to have caught the contagion of nicknaming for she and her two brothers, Wilhelm the strong and Otto the sickly, styled themselves the 'shamrock of ill luck'' or WOE (OWEH). But what did der Onkel call Carmen Sylva? Indeed, ''a Whirl of the Wind, a Will-o'-the-Wisp, a Flibertigibbet.''[38]

One of the great diversions of lowland Europe in the 1840's—and one which surely must have caught the eye of Maximilian—was the residence of George Catlin in Paris and his tours with his paintings (almost the rivals of Bodmer's) and his troupe of American Indians. In June 1845 Catlin met von Humboldt in Paris. Catlin had some Iowa Indians with him, exhibiting a tipi set up in the Louvre itself. And though Victoria had scorned Catlin, Louis Philippe received him regally, and Victor Hugo offered his admiration. We have no record of Prince Max's activities, but he could hardly have missed the show, especially since it was so closely linked to his own book recently off the press. But when Catlin

---

[38] In *The Sound of Music,* Maria is described in song as ''a will-o'-the-wisp, a flibertigibbet, a clown!'' Coincidence?

took a party of Chippewas on tour through Belgium, they were struck down by smallpox.

Around 1847, sickness also began to stalk the House of Wied-Nassau. Uncle Max, of course, seemed to live forever, but not so his relatives. The widow of his brother (probably Johann August Karl), had been out of her wits for years and shut away from the world. Hermann, the son of Johann and successor to the rule of Wied, became a sickly, pensive man, slowly succumbing to some mysterious affliction. His dancing wife Marie sank crippled into a wheelchair, wracked by frequent and horrible convulsions. She would be taken to England and immersed by the servants in the waves at the shore, writhing in paroxysms on the sand as the English crowd gathered about to gawk at the royal foreign lady in a fit. The Rhineland Fairy danced no more. Of the three children of Hermann and Marie, the mischievous Willi turned out to be the healthy ox, the baby Otto the chronic invalid, deformed perhaps but very bright, and Carmen Sylva became Elizabeth of Wied, bursting with health, vitality and romantic imagination.

Just as these were turbulent years in America, so too were they troubled times in Europe with the revolutions of 1848. Karl Marx emerged in Cologne and Paris and, with Engels, issued the *Communist Manifesto*. Insurgents in Paris slashed the paintings in Catlin's apartment, and King Louis Philippe took flight. The royal families of Wied and Nassau were seeking relief up and down the Rhine and were caught by the revolution in Heidelberg, where they had gone to consult doctors for convulsive Marie. Their children, even little Otto, cheered at the colorful revolutionaries marching under their balcony with red liberty caps and flashing scythes—young, eager revolutionaries singing their hearts out. The family applauded, then fled. At Nassau mobs surrounded the palace as if to burn it down with the family inside. Duke Wilhelm, the smoker, was not at hand, so his teenaged son Nicolas Wilhelm met the wrathful throng face to face, promising them concessions. It was Nicolas too who had to sign the constitution.[39]

And who was this bold young Nicolas? The uncle and also cousin of Carmen Sylva, the godson of Czar Nicolas of Russia. Well liked by the people of Wiesbaden, he was called in their dialect *unser Nicläsche* (our little Nicki). Even though raised by a governess and a Nassovian captain, he nevertheless grew into a light-hearted young man, laughing aloud at the smells of chloroform and ether that permeated everything and everybody in the royal household. He was not depressed by the strict economizing, the short funds, the cut in servants. He helped reconcile the people with his less-loved step-brother. And he took up the new fad for hypnotism (then called mesmerism). He became the family poltergeist, reducing even the most staid ladies to un-genteel fits of hilarity. That is, those of them who were not the victims of his pranks, for even if he never blew smoke in their faces, as his father had to his mother, Nicolas had his own brand of chauvinism. And he must have had a special grudge against the governess of his sister, perhaps for her severity. He simply hypnotized her into a chair and left her there helpless and incapable of severity to anyone. Once at a state dinner, he made her stick out her tongue in front of *tout le beau monde*.

Perhaps it was for his proclivity to fun that Nicolas was chosen as the last hope for the life of Prince Hermann of Wied. About 1852 the doctors put their wagging heads together and decreed that Hermann must be separated for a year from

[39] See page 17.

his melancholy family. Travel, that panacea of the age, would carry him far from the convulsions of poor Marie, far from stink of ether and chloroform. And Prince Nicolas, his happy, healthy brother-in-law, the young man with *panache*, was just the right person to accompany Hermann and bring a little fun and caprice into the older Prince's waning life. But in the leave-taking there was no fun or caprice. What tears were shed—family tears, never seen in public! Discipline, discipline, you know, and never any vulgar displays of sentiment. . .

And where would they travel? Why, to the American frontier, of course, so often the mecca of royal tourists. To the far Missouri, in the very footsteps of Prince Max, who seemed to have found in those mysterious climes a veritable Shangri-La, a Fountain of Youth. No doubt *der Onkel* was duly consulted and gave good advice. At the very least he could have provided introductions and most particularly to M. Pierre Chouteau. It may be that this was the origin of the letter which, years later, researcher Kessler found at an auction, the letter which alluded to Alexander Culbertson, the letter now lost again. So away they sailed—Hermann and Nicolas. We know only that they reached Havana en route to New Orleans. They appear to have eluded the notice of the U.S. State Department.

Meanwhile, Alexander Culbertson was moving in the opposite direction, from Fort Benton by land to Fort Union and then by mackinaw to St. Louis. This time, luckily, we have it on record that he brought Natawista with him, and that on their arrival in St. Louis, in May, they were accompanied by Colin Campbell, half Sioux, and his Indian wife. They had a sad story to tell of the fierce winter just past on the upper Missouri, where even mules froze to death. In St. Louis, Alec met an old classmate of his brother Michael Simpson from West Point. Now the Governor of Oregon country, newly appointed by his good friend Franklin Pierce, to make preparations for a transcontinental railroad. This man, of course, was Isaac Stevens, veteran of Vera Cruz and points inland. It was an easy thing for him and Alec to strike up a friendship and almost inevitable that Alec be attached to Stevens' expedition to the upper Missouri, at least as an agent of Pierre Chouteau and Company.

Now it happened that the Smithsonian Institution was once again looking to the Bad Lands as a treasure-trove of prehistory. Recently, it had received some Eocene fossils from Alec himself. The Institution proposed to sponsor an expedition by Fielding Bradford Meek and Ferdinand Vandeveer Hayden, a medical student at Albany. Pierre Chouteau, as usual, promised the aid of AFC, and Alec was cooperative. But alas, Governor Stevens had two other scientists of his own in tow: geologist Dr. John Evans, and fellow geologist Benjamin F. Shumard. Since Stevens resented what he viewed as the intrusion of the Smithsonian, Meek and Hayden turned to seek the support of a scientist more noted than any of them: Jean Louis Agassiz of Harvard, who at this juncture happened to be on a lecture tour to St. Louis. Since Agassiz, like Maximilian and Paul of Württemberg, was one of the scientists of the day tutored or at least deeply influenced by Baron von Humboldt, one wonders if his lectures attracted Maximilian's relatives. At any rate, Agassiz did appeal to Stevens on behalf of his Smithsonian colleagues, but the Governor was intransigent. So Hayden and Meek were reduced to pursuing their project without government support. Alec, as agent for AFC and personal friend of Stevens, was caught in the middle.

Since neither of Maximilian's relatives, Hermann and Nicolas, have left us any journal of their travels in North America, we are at a loss to learn the details. Prince Hermann was known to be quite meticulous about keeping records of family adventures, but if he kept any about this adventure, they have not been found. Perhaps ill health prevented him from recording the trip. Even if he was not a scientist like his Uncle Max, he had something of the same inquiring mind and was regarded in the family as a kind of philospher or metaphysician. But both he and Nicolas did write letters home. The letter from Nicolas we learn about through Carmen Sylva, but the letter from Hermann we have intact (or almost) in the private archives of the House of Luxembourg. Hermann addressed this letter to Duke Adolph of Nassau, from somewhere in America. The letter carries a date of the 2nd of June, 1853. In it Hermann says that he left Nicolas in Havana and has not heard from him since. But Nicolas was planning on traveling up the Mississippi in April and in the middle of May to join the steamer of the American Fur Company to go up the Missouri. Nicolas wanted to learn about the great western wilderness and the Indians who lived there. Hermann adds that everyone he has discussed the matter with has said such a trip was relatively safe but very tiring and that no regular mail passes beyond St. Louis. Nicolas will then have to learn to live in utter isolation, and that may bring him to a more serious view of life. Hermann hopes that Nicolas' health will be none the worse for his experience, but his own health has not been helped by the climate of Havana. He has suffered much from the heat, but since he has moved to a cooler zone he has improved somewhat and would do better were he not buffeted by daily tribulations.

The letter from Nicolas told about a seance he had witnessed during his trip, and—marvel of marvels—a table was actually made to move about, as if the ghosts had nothing better to do with their non-life than disturb the furniture. At least it seems clear that in Nicolas there still lurked some of the Old Nick, and the ladies left forlorn in Bonn were amused to read about it. But Hermann said "Humbug!"

In May of 1853 Prince Nicolas was in St. Louis and booked for the *Robert Campbell*, which was then under lease to the American Fur Company. He was not, as Hermann had described him, abiding in miserable loneliness, but was accompanied by a "suite of four." Somehow his name had been reversed in American records to "William Nicholas," thereby concealing his identity from American historians. Also booked for passage on the *Campbell* were the members of one contingent of Stevens' expedition, in particular, six soldiers and two lieutenants, Andrew Donelson and John Mullan. Donelson had been obliged to attend a preliminary errand: a special mission to Montreal to solicit the aid of Sir George Simpson of the Hudson's Bay Company, which was still a very powerful corporation in the Oregon country. Stevens himself traveled by way of St. Paul to organize his overland contingent from there, the group he would accompany in person. All four of the geologists, both Stevens' team and the Smithsonian pair, would go aboard the *Campbell*, along with the astronomer W.N. Graham, Indian Agent Alfred J. Vaughan and the representatives of AFC for this cruise, Jean Baptiste Sarpy and Alexander Culbertson. It was the custom of le Cadet, as you recall, to play host to scientists, artists, missionaries and royalty on board the steamers owned or chartered by him, where they would travel gratis or with a discount. Though documents are not in evidence, we have to suppose these usual privileges were extended to the dignitaries on board the *Campbell*, and also that Sarpy, Alec and Natawista would act as delegate hosts and hostess.

In spite of the many gaps in the records of this very important cruise, we have more details on some aspects of the trip than need concern us. The *Robert*

Campbell pulled away from St. Louis on May 21, 1853, sporting a banner with Chouteau's name on it—misspelled. The vessel was crowded, with 170 passengers. The river was in flood and the packet in labor. On the 24th a fire broke out on the bow, driving the frightened passengers into the stern ready to jump ship. But Sarpy (single-handed?) got the flames under control.

By the time the *Campbell* reached St. Joseph, life aboard seems to have subsided to normal. The reporter for the St. Joseph *Gazette* was impressed with some of the passengers, noting that the vessel, bound for the mouth of the Yellowstone, had passed St. Joseph Sunday last, carrying "a number of highly distinguished and scientific gentlemen." And he enumerated some of them: A.J. Vaughan, Indian Agent for the tribes of the upper Missouri, for whom he was carrying on board some $30,000 worth of commodities to be issued as presents. Then there was "Mr. Culverson, an old and gentlemanly trader among the Indians for many years." Alec, old at 43? Well, there is some evidence that he may have looked older than he was, rugged perhaps from so much adventure out of doors. There was a physician aboard, the surgeon Dr. Treedman "of extensive information and long experience." And of course there was the Prince of Nassau and his retainers, a young fellow, "free and easy and unostentatious in his manners, liberal and democratic in his views." And the reporter went on to name others, including the scientists Meek and Hayden. Hayden, however, was less impressed with his fellow passengers for he sniffed that no one seemed much concerned for science. He does, however, acknowledge much assistance from Alexander Culbertson. Though Alec's role on this trip must have been important, no details are revealed to us. Surely he should have recognized the young relative of his old friend Prince Maximilian, especially as they traveled together so many days. Stevens refers to Alec as some sort of special "Indian agent." If true, Alec was wearing two hats, and that can be a treacherous business. The regular Indian agent, of course, was Vaughan, one of the most efficient men in such a position. It is not clear whether Vaughan's Indian wife accompanied him on this trip. But on the whole, everyone seemed to enjoy good health and high spirits during the balance of the cruise.

The Captain for this trip was John Gunsollis, a man who was accorded a good rating, but said to be illiterate, quarrelsome and dangerous when drunk. The *Robert Campbell* was a double-engined packet with a tonnage of three hundred, drawing five feet and usually making around five miles per hour upstream.

The reports of this trip tend to be either military or scientific and tell us but little about people except in the abstract, a condition, I believe, in which no person has ever been found. But then to the Army, people *in concreto* are expendable. Lt. Donelson, in his reports to Stevens, carefully records the topography, the soundings and astronomical observations taken by himself, Lt. Mullan, Sergeant Collins and astronomer Graham. He tells a lot about the geography, the rivers, sand-bars and many shifts in current and the erosion of banks, but very little about human beings. Curiously enough, he mentions the surveys made by Nicollet and previous scientists on the Missouri yet seems utterly ignorant of the monumental work of Maximilian and Bodmer, even with Uncle Max's younger generation represented at his elbow.

Travel was impeded by snags and sand-bars so that above St. Joseph his packet stopped each night. The scientists had many opportunities to go ashore for specimens. There is no record that Prince Nicolas made any display on board of his hypnotic pranks, but his desire to behold at first hand the American Red Men of the Far West must have been adequately satisified, for in general the

Indians were friendly during this cruise and the passengers responsive. The Prince saw the Indians as Maximilian and Bodmer had portrayed them twenty years ago, not so elegant nor so invincible, but still a fulfillment of Continental fantasies. Food for the Indians was thrown ashore by the passengers or presented more formally by Agent Vaughan at Vermillion.

Below Fort Pierre, a tornado or some other freakish blast almost made a wreck of everything, but the *Campbell* struggled on to her refuge. Two hundred Sioux thronged aboard for a big feed and a palaver with Vaughan. The feast was mostly a success, for though some of the Indians were angry, none of them carried out their threats. At Fort Pierre the four paleontologists disembarked, though apparently still not reconciled. Nevertheless, their surveys added to science and to their own reputations.

The *Campbell* chugged on up the river. Early on June 29th, it reached Fort Clark and the land of the Mandans, the very place where Uncle Max and Bodmer had done so much of their finest work. At one o'clock the next day the travelers were at Fort Berthold. On July first they passed the Little Missouri, on the third they reached the Yellowstone and, that evening, were at Fort Union.

It was here that most freight and many passengers were put ashore, the Culbertsons apparently among them. Sarpy, however, and Lt. Donelson continued up the river, and we are left to suppose that the Prince and his party did so too. (No one mentions them.) On the 6th of July, the *Campbell* swung past Poplar River but about seven miles farther was stopped by sand-bars. So the freight for Benton was set ashore for the keelboats. The steamer turned back to Union on the 9th, making a speed about three times that of the ascent. It had taken forty-two days from St. Louis to Fort Union and seventeen to return. Whether Prince Nicolas went back with the *Campbell* is a matter for conjecture. If he took this down-river voyage in July, he had, as his fellow passenger, Maximilian's old host, James Kipp. It may be that Nicolas disembarked somewhere along the route, for the next place we catch up to him is along the Oregon Trail.

And it appears that somewhere, somehow, he again rejoined Prince Hermann. As summer faded into fall, 1853, we find them both, the "Prince de Viede" and the Prince of Nassau, at the Lost Sandy "returning from a pleasure trip through this country," So reported another traveler (unnamed), in an account published in the New York *Tribune*, November 14. This caused some speculation and more confusion; Nicolas was thought to be a grandson of Prince Paul of Württemberg who had died in Paris, but this is simply mistaken identity. It was the elder Paul (the one Carmen Sylva called "the terrible"), the grandfather of Nicolas who died in 1852. The younger Paul, a cousin of Nicolas, and once the guardian of Pampi, was at this point still traveling: Mexico, California, New Orleans, St. Louis, Utah, around South America and back to New Orleans—certainly very much alive. Meanwhile, shortly after the adventure on the Lost Sandy, "two German noblemen" and their retainers were reported camped along Walnut Creek near the Santa Fe Trail hunting buffalo. This was on the 15th of October. It seems strange indeed that the sickly Hermann would be on a buffalo hunt. I am wondering if the hunting companion of Nicolas may have been his cousin Paul, the details of whose itinerary are not available (at least not in English). For Paul, New Orleans was the Paris of the New World, his favorite refuge again and again. He spent the winter there, 1853-1854. Nicolas and Hermann may have done the same for we do learn that, at an unknown time during his trip, Hermann was stricken with an ear infection which left him temporarily deaf and stranded in New Orleans. One wonders too if this might have been the daily tribulations of which he wrote to Adolph of Nassau. A letter from America did in fact, reach the ladies left at home, who were having a dreary Christmas until the letter arrived in time to get pinned onto their Christmas tree. Though it has been supposed in Germany that Hermann came home leaving Nicolas in America, it appears now that no German scholar has been aware of the reference to the "Prince de Viede" on the Oregon Trail.

On their way home, Hermann and Nicolas—or just Hermann if he went on ahead—paused in Paris to consult a Hungarian count noted for his skills at mesmerism and well known too as a charismatic faith-healer. The call was made evidently not so much for Hermann's sake as for his wife's. At Bonn the family had a sad home-coming and reunion, for it was obvious to everyone that the year of separation had done nothing to heal anybody of anything. It had perhaps wrought even further havoc.

The Hungarian count promptly moved the family to Paris, though the train trip threatened to push the Princess to the very point of death. In Paris, at least, the family was together again and free from the chloroform and the ether. On the Champs Élysées they settled into a two story house. Little Carmen Sylva loved Paris, a city where she would return again and again throughout her lifetime. She learned all the streets round about, befriended the family Valette and the stern French Huguenots, and attended the Saturday classes for little girls of quality in the Rue des Saints Pères. It was there that she proved a little German Protestant girl could rise and shine under the tutelage of the Abbé Gaultier. But regarding the treatments her mother had to undergo she was never able to discover much, for one did not discuss such matters with the children. In six months, however, she did see the first signs of improvement. Slowly, very slowly and with much help, Marie took one step. Then two steps. . . The convulsions ceased. And one glorious day she walked. She walked to her three children in the garden. Marie, the dancing Rhineland fairy, walked at last. No date is given, but surely it must have been in April in Paris.

The skeptical Hermann declared, "I have not the dogmatic arrogance to deny the existence of phenomena just because I do not understand them." And with that he proceeded to write another book.

It was part of the Count's plan that the healed become the healer for another, and so it was with Marie of Nassau. In good time she would fill her house with the deaf, halt and blind, and rumors spread around her that she fell into ecstasies, rose in levitations and even floated downstairs. But her daughter Carmen Sylva was more guarded in her comments.[40]

Prince Hermann lived on for another ten years, so maybe the American trip did him some good after all. His Uncle Maximilian lived longer yet, and Princess Marie had another half-century on this earth.

But their poor little son Otto! Subjected to one round after another of painful medical and surgical procedures, he could not be healed, not even by his own mother. All Marie could do for him was to feed him the laudanum prescribed by the doctors and to cry Halleujah when he died. In his few short years Otto had been a little saint—witty, intelligent and forever reminding stiff-necked grown-ups about God.

And what of maverick Prince Nicolas? So far as I can discover, he never returned to the high Missouri, but he did retain his flare for romanticism. At

[40] See the Notes

first, though, he consented to play his proper role as part of the royal establishment, was appointed to government in 1856 and took part in 1865 as a major general of infantry in the Prussian War. Then, two or three years later in London, he defied his peers to marry Natalia, a Russian beauty and daughter of Pushkin of ancient Boyar and Abyssinian descent. After some travel, Nicolas and Natalia settled in a summer villa at Wiesbaden and a winter villa at Cannes and established a family and a line of nobility of their own. He gave up all ambition in politics or the military. He became instead a long-time president of the Wiesbaden Red Cross. He preferred to mingle with the people of the street and the country-side, the strollers and the tennis-players. At the age of seventy, he was described as tall, grey-bearded and still much admired.

CHAPTER XVI

Peacemakers?

$\mathbf{D}$oves do not come in the feathers of hawks, but often enough, hawks sport the guise of doves. It is a pretty-ticklish business telling these birds apart.

We have seen Governor Isaac I. Stevens off to St. Paul, and there we shall now catch up with him. We noticed before that the new Governor was a personable, handsome man with an undercurrent of insecurity that did not immediately surface. It would have been easier to notice these traits after the wound in the foot that Stevens endured in Mexico and which may have still been perceptible in his gait. Not that a man is necessarily insecure because of his wounds, but he certainly is not easily reconciled to his deformities, no matter how slight. Then too, Stevens could not have felt altogether secure in his hopes for the Northern Pacific Railroad since he had a rival—and a vigorous one—in the quest for a railway route across the continent, namely John Charles Frémont, who this very year of 1853 was busy seeking a southern passage for a railroad. This was, in fact, Frémont's fifth expedition.[41] Stevens must have known that a southern route would be much more acceptable to Jefferson Davis, who would ultimately make the final choice.

But Stevens was not a man to be outdone. At St. Paul he continued his preparations for the overland contingent of his expedition, enlisting the help of Governor Doty of Wisconsin, who was perhaps an old friend. The special help that he enlisted turned out to be the Governor's son, Lieutenant James Doty, a most loyal and persistent young man, though just a little straight-laced. All-in-all a good example of the curious paradox the Germans noticed about U.S. Army officers: they were more Prussian than the Prussians.

Stevens was a man who had goals for everything, and the goal for his expedition of '53 was Fort Benton, selected perhaps with a prod from Alec. According to Stevens, Alec was in charge of Forts Benton, Union and Pierre. And, in spite of Alec's apparent skepticism, the Blackfeet people would be a crucial element of Stevens' plan. So upon the Blackfeet post Stevens' forces would converge from three directions: up the Missouri River, cross-country from St. Paul and over the Rockies from Washington Territory. There would be other branch trips as well.

Governor Stevens arrived overland at Fort Union on the first of August, well after the departure of the *Campbell* on its return downriver. He was welcomed by Edwin Denig with an offering of champagne.

While Alec had been commuting up and down the river, the eternal river,

---

[41] 1) 1842: on the Oregon Trail. 2) 1843-44: to Oregon and California. 3) 1845-47: to California before and during the war until the treaty of Cahuenga. 4) 1848: to California via Taos and the Gila. 5) 1853.

"Fort Union and Distribution of Goods to the Assinniboines," a John Mix Stanley color lithograph. Courtesy Amon Carter Museum, Fort Worth, Texas.

Denig had stayed behind to guard the walls. He was the man of no-nonsense needed on the frontier. He learned to understand the Indian tribes and married two of their daughters, by whom he had four children. The better known of his wives was the Assiniboine Deer Little Woman, to whom he was eventually married by a priest (though Denig himself was a persistent follower of Swedenborg and the Freemasons). Like Alec, he seems to have reasoned that Protestantism was the religion best suited to whites and Catholicism to Indians. Yet for a man who cared so faithfully for his wives and children, Denig surprises us with his commentary on Love (as recorded by Rudolph Kurz): "Love—damn the word!—is a madness of the brain: a contagious disease, like smallpox or measles. . ." But love, or some close facsimile, prompted Denig to take his wife east and introduce her to his family. The reception was cool; Denig vowed never again to go where his wife was not welcome.

Alec and Natawista joined Stevens at Fort Union and accompanied him with a party of Blackfeet from Union to Benton. En route, near the Little Muddy, a confrontation arose with the Indians, which Natawista brought to a peaceful solution. Stevens recorded: "On this, as on previous occasions, Mrs. Culbertson, a native of the Blood tribe of the Blackfeet, was unwearied and efficient in her good offices." He also noted with approval that Natawista's children had been sent to the States to be educated in "our best schools." The appearance of a comet and an aurora borealis broke the monotony of this trip, but may not have allayed the wariness of the Indians. On the first of September the Governor arrived at Fort Benton amid the boom of guns. (Nothing is said about the great bell that welcomed DeSmet, but this may indicate nothing more than that the present arrivals were more attuned to guns.)

The detachment of forty came over the Rockies from Fort Vancouver via St.

Mary Mission (Fort Owen) under command of Lt. Rufus Saxton and guided by Antoine LaPlante.

It must be conceded that it was risky business to round up so many different tribes. Alec had his misgivings, but in his office as perpetual intermediary, he sent out messages and presents to various chiefs of the Blackfeet alliance inviting them to come to Fort Benton and meet Governor Stevens. This too had seemed to Alec a risky business. He had proposed leaving Natawista safely in residence at Fort Union. But Natawista declared:

> My people are a good people, but they are jealous and vindictive. I am afraid that they and the whites will not understand each other; but if I go, I may be able to explain things to them. I know there is danger, but, my husband, where you go I will go, and where you die I will die.

At least these are the words Stevens puts into her mouth. How much of this eloquence is hers and how much Stevens' and how much comes from Ruth of Moab, I leave everyone who reads it to decide. Stevens seems to have been quite unabashed about using the Culbertsons or anyone else as chessmen in his railroad game, admitting frankly that he relied on Alec because his wife was a full-blooded Blackfeet. However, to judge by what Stevens wrote in his "reports from the field" to the Secretary of War, Jefferson Davis, we may think that he had other reasons for depending on Alec:

> Whilst at St. Louis I secured the services of Alexander Culbertson, Esq., as a special agent among the Blackfeet Indians. He has lived in the country twenty years, and knows by name every adult male in each tribe. He estimates the number to be from fifteen hundred to eighteen hundred lodges.[42] I found him to be a reliable, steadfast, calm man.

And he continues optimistically, ". . . Mr. Culbertson assures me that we shall have no difficulty in securing the confidence of, and controlling the Blackfeet. With vigilance and firmness, I entertain no apprehensions whatever." These remarks were penned from a steamer on May 27. From Fort Benton on September 8th, Stevens, wrote that though his funds were running low, he was:

> . . .on the eve of complete success. My parties are now exploring the passes of the mountains. My intercourse with the Indians has been of the most satisfactory character. The Blackfeet Indians have sent their chiefs and braves to invite me to their camps; not a horse has been stolen, not a man touched; no private article has been missed. They have brought our disabled animals into camp, and acted as guides and guards."

He adds that today he and Alexander were to leave for a large Piegan camp in the Cypress Hills (which lie just north of the border on the line between Alberta and Saskatchewan). It is not clear that Stevens and Alec actually made the trip, but on the 21st of September, thirty Blackfeet chiefs of all three tribes answered the invitation to come to Fort Benton. Natawista went along for the peace talks, for after all, her own father and brothers may well have been among the talkers. She had a wonderful time and kept her people laughing, "inspiring them with perfect confidence" (as Stevens puts it). In camp, her tent was pitched "beyond the line of sentinels" to render her easily available to her people. Little

---

[42] Compare these statistics with those cited from Alec ahead on page 111.

wonder then that men and women gathered about to hear her tell of sights she had beheld in the inscrutable east: the circus, the fat lady, the social queens of St. Louis. Hiliarity prevailed. There may have been much more talk of funny whites than of Stevens' ambitious plans. Though Stevens claimed she gave "the highest service to the expedition," she did it with laughter.

It is also commonly thought that it was Natawista who won the cooperation of Little Dog, a high chief of the Piegans, evidently her cousin or some other relative. This figure of Little Dog or *Imitáikoan*, who now moves front and center in our story, is generally recognized as one of the grandest of the Blackfeet chiefs. His name can also be translated "puppy." Not very dramatic for such a chief, but of course he did belong to the aristocracy of the high plains. Though a chief of the Piegans, he must have been partly Blood or Kaina and was sometimes referred to rather loosely as "the brother-in-law of Mr. Culbertson." Tall, statuesque, handsome, he made too great an impression on white people for his own good. His "devotion" to white people was probably good politics rather than any special admiration for those pale-faced creatures swarming out of the east. He was giving the devil his due, recognizing the ugly fact that the whites inevitably had the upper hand. But there was more to Little Dog than *Realpolitik*. He had a genuine sense of justice and cherished the ideal that a promise made is a promise kept.

So now Little Dog undertook to assist his cousins (or whatever) the Culbertsons for the sake of peace. He escorted the artist of Stevens' expedition, John Mix Stanley, to the Cypress Hills inviting the chiefs to Fort Benton. The artist won over the chiefs by making their daguerreotypes, which the Indians regarded as a demonstration of "sun power:" *natósini*. Little Dog is always said to have been the source of Stevens' notion of Marias Pass as a suitable route for a railroad, and for that reason a prominent peak overlooking the pass today bears the name of Little Dog. But of course, the old chief, wise as he may have been, can hardly have known what a railroad was. Although he may well have indicated where the lowest pass led across the Shining Mountains, it was easily sighted from the prairies anyway. Along with Lt. James Doty, Stevens' right-or left-hand man, Little Dog rounded up stolen horses and returned them. (This may be the episode referred to in Stevens' letter.) But Doty was not the only one who rode with Little Dog. There was also The Fringe, son of Little Dog and his father's constant shadow and support. A very handsome young fellow, says Hamilton, who with his classical flare, goes on to describe the Fringe: handsome as Apollo and proud as Lucifer. (Since the peak named Little Dog in Glacier National Park is one of a pair, it would seem fitting that the twin peak be named for the son.) At any rate, as a result of his contacts with Little Dog, Natawista, Jim Delaware and so on, Stevens had been mollifying his stereotypical notions of "the blood-thirsty" Indians of the high Missouri.

Among others who served Stevens were Hugh Monroe and Sata', both as guides, the Mexican hunter Pete Martínez (more noted for his white buffalo), and one of Stevens' own men, Frederick Landers, who was sent to find Marias Pass. Landers failed. It is difficult today to appreciate the old mystery that used to hover about Marias Pass. Probably the most famous of Stevens' followers was his artist Stanley, and that of course, because of the pictorial records he left us of the high Missouri. Although not on a par with Bodmer's, they are excellent in their own way.

When Stevens left Fort Benton to return west over the Rockies to Washington Territory, he detached Lt. Doty to stay with the Blackfeet and prepare them for the great inter-tribal council yet to come. He also arranged with Alec, as his "special Indian agent" to go as his emissary to Washington, D.C. So on the

22nd of September, before the sun was up, Stevens bade adieu to Alec, Lt. Saxton and some soldiers as they shoved off in a keelboat for the east. Then Stevens turned westward and crossed the Divide into the Bitterroot Valley with Hugh Monroe as his guide. From there he sent A.W. Tinkham and a young Flathead Indian to approach the Divide from the west side. Up the Middle Fork of the Flathead they struggled, up Nyack Creek, around Mt. Stimson (Flint Lodge, home of Thunder) and across Cut Bank Pass to Fort Benton.

Toward the end of December 1853, as Doty reported, some Crees and Assiniboines attacked the camp of Little Dog, wounding both the chief himself and one other. Little Dog, however, declined to seek revenge, declaring that he would wait for the peace council.

Some time, at a date unknown but possibly on the trip Alec made down the Missouri in 1853 or even earlier, his little daughter Nancy fell into the river at Fort Union and was drowned. Whenever it happened, Alec was still haunted by it at this period. He could never quite forgive his old friend the River—the River that had so long been his life and his livelihood and had finally, in exchange, exacted this ghastly tribute. He made up his mind to quit the River. Natawista's reactions are nowhere mentioned, but we know that she generally suffered miseries when her children were torn away from her. Gone was the light-hearted lady of the summer camps. telling stories to her people of circus and society! In her own culture, she probably would have been consulted about important decisions. But in Alec's?

In spite of the late season and the menace of ice-jams. Alec got his keelboat down to Leavenworth and spent a couple of weeks in St. Louis. Then he was off to Washington for his winter's task. He had been made a special agent, not only for Stevens, but for American Fur also, and with that, $5,000 a year ($2,000 more than had ever been paid to his predecessors). Yet during the winter of 1853-1854 he was working in large measure for Stevens, performing as a lobbyist on the Potomac. He hated it. It does not seem quite like Alec to take such a negative attitude toward an abstraction, but for the sake of his friend Stevens and for the peace of the tribes on the upper Missouri, he did his job as best he could.

Where or how he lived during the dull winter we are not told, whether or not with his family, whether in Washington itself, in Arlington or another suburb, or even whether his family would have been socially acceptable anywhere—none of these matters are of record. What we are told is simply that he interceded with members of Congress, one after another, to help fund the Blackfeet treaty. To Achison of Missouri he made his way, to Dodge of Iowa and Dodge of Wisconsin, to Chandler of Michigan, Butler of Georgia, Chase of Ohio, Steele of Illinois and of course Cooper of Pennsylvania, who was the chairman of the Senate committee on Indian affairs. In the House, Alec waited upon Speaker Orr of South Carolina, Phelps of Missouri, Sebastian of Arkansas. These were the men he seemed to win over to his cause, but probably he went to others with whom he failed. We notice that he typically mixed Northerners with Southerners. He even went to President Franklin Pierce, although Pierce as a friend of Stevens would hardly have been hostile to Stevens' project. In spite of Alec's efforts, the bill for the Blackfeet treaty did not pass.

Alec was a persistent fellow, as we know, and he turned about and started over at the job he detested and kept at it like Bruce and the spider. The bill was presented once more. Once more the dispute went on: Who were those Blackfeet anyway? What were they like? Why should tax-payers let their money be appropriated for a treaty with a tribe of nomads no one ever heard of? Alec was often called in to confer with members of Congress.

Finally, the bill did pass. The money was appropriated.

How many days Alec must have watched the stately Potomac flow serene between the capitol dome and the green shores of Virginia, as if nothing on either shore ever mattered a ripple. In later years, Alec confided to his first biographer, Lt. Bradley, that the job of lobbying during that winter on the Potomac was "the most distasteful proceeding of his life." One grows weary of being someone else's alter ego.

About 1854 and probably in Washington, D.C., Alec penned a report either to Stevens personally or to the Bureau of Indian Affairs about "The Blackfoot nation." It must have answered many of the questions put to him at this period. In his paper Alec estimated the Blackfeet population at about 400 tipis in each of the three divisions (Piegan, Blood, Northern Blackfoot), "each about eaqual (sic)," or 1,200 tipis altogether. With eight "souls" to each tipi, that would be a total of 9,600 persons, of whom he thought 2,700 can be regarded as warriors of age fifteen and up. The Piegans were the group that lived in the upper Missouri country. "The Blackfeet and Blood Indians" traded with the Hudson's Bay Company but came to the Missouri around Fort Benton in fall and winter. The Gros Ventre allies lived mostly on Milk River and near the Bear Paw Mountains. The entire Blackfeet country Alec considered "perhaps the best buffalo country in the N.W. Territory." So of course there were many horses in it, averaging fifteen to a tipi. The grass was especially nutritious and land well adapted to raising stock (a point Stevens might like to stress). Alec also mentioned the smallpox epidemic, remarking that the Blackfeet had not yet "recovered from its effects although no contagious disease has appeared among them" since 1838. (This point may require a little closer scrutiny.) He reported the Blackfeet as evidently "the most warlike" of all western Indians, especially their young men. "Polygamy is general." Men had from two to ten wives, who formed part of their wealth. He pointed out that before the Treaty of Laramie of 1851 other tribes were similarly warlike but were subdued by the treaty, and that therefore similar results should be expected from a treaty with the Blackfeet. As the techniques that should be effective in Indian-white diplomacy, Alec recommended annuities of ten or twelve thousand dollars in goods, wisely conferred, trips sponsored for tribal leaders to Washington and the east, and councils for dialogue. He did not recommend agriculture.

I find no mention that friend Thomas Hart Benton aided Alec during this session in Washington. Nevertheless, there was a precarious element in any alliance with Benton, famous for his controversies, his love-hate relationship with Andrew Jackson and his duels which created tensions among some of the St. Louis aristocracy. But since Alec was now turning his attentions from the far west, he began to involve himself in mid-western politics and finances. By August of 1854 he was still staying in St. Louis, probably with Natawista. It was late in the season for them to linger there, but Alec seems to have become involved in the affairs of both Senators Benton and Stephan Douglas, more deeply than wisely. It may be coincidental that his long-term partner Pierre Chouteau was tied into railroad development west of the Appalachians, especially in the Illinois Central, the railway for which old Pierre Ménard eventually became a director. Trade in furs and hides had always been connected to transportation, so the link between the decline of the one industry and the rise of the other was yet another example of life's hourglass effects. Such were some of the lures that must have beckoned Alexander Culbertson, wealthy and still vigorous.

Besides, some of Alec's relatives were now residents of Illinois and Ohio, and to this part of the country he now wended his way. With a forward look at his gradual retirement, he purchased 160 acres from William Archdale of Peoria for $3,500 on the 14th of August. The property lay in Limestone Township outside Peoria, perhaps near the farm of his uncle Dr. Samuel D. Culbertson. Alec's niece Anna would live with Alec and Natawista and care for the children when the parents were heading up and down the river.

What great decisions we make for a future we can never foresee!

CHAPTER XVII

The Judith
Council

So up the river Alec must go, this time in the company of a Scot named Andrew Dawson, who would one day become his successor. Yet, though Dawson claimed descent from the kings of Scotland, he could never really fill Alec's place as king of the high Missouri. Times were changing too fast for that, even though Alec was engineering his retirement to be slow and gradual.

About this time, he had charge of forts Union, Benton, and Sarpy on the Yellowstone.[43] At Union Denig was still the factor, although like Alec, he was on the verge of retirement and would take his Indian family to Canada and good schools. At Fort Sarpy, James Chambers was the bourgeois. This post had been reestablished by Alec but was only a simple affair of cottonwood uprights with none of the prestige of the other two posts. At Fort Benton, Alec, presumably with Natawista, was welcomed September 28th with a grand salute and a ball, at which only two of the guests made fools of themselves.

Govenor Stevens authorized Alec to purhcase $1,000 worth of merchandise from the Company and distribute it to the Piegans and Gros Ventres in order to soften these tribes up for the grand council to come. So he bought a lot of flour, rice, tobacco, coffee and sugar (all of it "unreal food" to the Indians) and in late October went by carriage to Milk River. As he passed out his presents, he warned the people to prepare the edibles well. But many either did not understand or disregarded his admonitions, ate the foods raw and came down with the "colic." Several died.

Natawista is said to have made tours to her people, in a buggy, accompanied only by her maid, and more and more often as time went on. This may have been the period referred to in the oral report that in their travels Alec and Natawista met a young slave-wife somewhere above Chinook who was being abused by the "sits-beside" wife of a chief. (The chief must have been their mutual husband and the sits-beside wife perhaps the slave-wife's own sister. Sibling rivalry seems to have been a frequent cause of domestic disorders.) The slave-wife hoped for deliverance, but Natawista told her, "I cannot take you with us because your husband is a chief." so the poor girl ran off and hid herself in some spot where her sisters-in-law smuggled pemmican and moccasins to her at night. When the Culbertsons drove away, she and a sister of hers followed their tracks, overtaking them at the Big Bend. But once again Natawista said, "I cannot take you." She left them food, however, and also a fire banked against the chill of autumn. But at night the two girls continued to follow the Culbertsons, all the way to the mouth of the Milk River. There, at last, the reluctant

---

[43] Obviously, there are differences in the statements about Alec's jurisdiction over one fort or another. I cannot solve this problem.

Culbertsons received them into the wagon and kept them in custody until the treaty.

Alec distributed some of the food to the Piegans at Fort Benton and took some of it to the Bloods during the first week in December. He may have dropped off the rest at Milk River during his return trip to the east. One wonders if he took the two escaped slave-girls to Peoria.

In the meanwhile, Governor Stevens was still driving for his golden goals. And on Stevens' behalf, Lt. James Doty was driving for them too. In the spring of 1854 Doty, accompanied by Hugh Monroe and others, almost found one of these goals: a prospective railroad pass across the Divide.[44] At any rate, they skirted the eastern base of the Rockies up to Chief Mountain on the Canadian line, then dropped back to Marias Pass. Hugh was wary of the pass, but Doty entered it. Even so, Stevens' hopes for a northern transcontinental railroad were crushed by Jefferson Davis. Stevens had to shift gears.

He brought his wife Meg and their children around through Panama to Olympia, Washington. After a worrisome trip across the Isthmus and a bout with yellow fever in San Francisco, Meg found relief at Olympia. She was smugly complacent that her husband held the Indians "under his thumb" by fear unto death. But Stevens' biographer Richards is less complacent about this "cocksureness," which indicated that Stevens did not realize that his apparent success, with the Blackfeet especially, "resulted in a large measure from the excellent liaison work of Alexander Culbertson. Stevens exaggerated his own role. . ."A man cursed with goals can be a curse to all around him, and poor Stevens was plagued by the demons or idols we like to call goals. In spite of his charisma, he became high-handed, stubborn and temperamental, the classic dissenter intolerant of dissent in others. Even as a civilian, he liked to sign himself "Commander-in-Chief." Yet in his favor, we must point out that he had an impossible job in which he wore three hats as explorer, governor, and Indian superintendent and was subject to three different departments of the federal government: War, Interior, and State. A conflict of interest was inevitable. But he hoped to solve his dilemmas in 1855 by three grand councils: one at Walla Walla, one at Hellgate, one at Fort Benton.

This new goal required a lot of preparation besides that which Alec had engaged in at Washington, D.C. Stevens' over-all scheme was to clear the Northwest of Indian title to the land, then to enclose the Indians into restricted enclaves and throw open both the coast and the interior to white settlement. To this end, he had first secured the western coastal areas by a series of treaties and would now gain the interior by his three grand councils. The process would neatly package the entire Northwest for white development (or exploitation) and at the same time turn Indian warriors into "good citizens." His technique for achieving this end would run something like this: Act One—courtesy with a flourish of paternalism. If that did not work, then Act Two—firmness *d' la militaire.* And if that failed, Act Three—guile and browbeating. This, after all, is the classic pattern of land condemnation. But here the land to be condemned encompassed one fourth of the continent! It may help to remember that Stevens reflected the prejudices then current in the white population of this territory: prejudices against Indians, halfbreeds, Catholics—often the same person in real life. (Richards, pg. 273, suggests that there was an unorganized influence of the Know Nothings even in the Northwest.)

The technique would be infallible, of course. When he said, "Come!" all must

---

[44] Maybe I should drop the word "almost," but we must be careful not to disturb the legend carefully created by the Great Northern Railroad.

come, and when he said, "Go!" all must scurry off. His treaty plan was a military objective and civilians were his troops. A white man with an Indian wife would serve his purpose, as Alec had done to date, but if he resisted, perhaps as Louis Brun and other French Canadians were doing, he was subject to arrest. No interference, no deviation could be tolerated, and even neutrality was suspect. Special bugbears to Stevens were French half-breeds, "squaw men," the Jesuits and the Hudson's Bay Company. At Cataldo Mission, he initiated foreign-born Jesuits into U.S. citizenship, but he did not win allies. "Catholic missionaries," quoth he, were nominally neutrals but really partisans of the Indians against him so that their influence was "most baneful and pernicious." Neither could he expect the support of "the Bay," since he specifically wanted to break HBC's hold on the Indians and clear it out of Washington Territory. Angus MacDonald, HBC's man at Fort Colville and Alec's counterpart west of the Divide, had tried to promote good relations with the U.S. government as represetned by Stevens and Captain George McClellan (General-to-be). So he had invited them both to a spree with fifty Imperial gallons in his stock. Stevens was the first to go under. Next McClellan slipped from sofa to floor. Angus stayed on his feet, wobbling. Ah, Manifest Destiny!

To understand the Indian attitude at Stevens' treaty councils of 1855, we should perhaps recall the Prophet Dance with its messianism and warnings of doom. Did Stevens represent the healers or the spoilers? What were his relations with the Black Robes? Was he offering renewal or disaster? The Blackfeet were outside the main sphere of the Prophet Dance, though not altogether beyond its influence.

The council at Walla Walla was a rough affair. The Indians of the interior were not easy to bamboozle, and the tensions springing from the Whitman massacre were still a-throb. Instead of mollifying them, the council made them more intense and perhaps marked the inception of the Yakima war. Not too much was demanded there of the Nez Percés, traditional friends of Americans. Some were compliant like Lawyer, others recalcitrant with Looking Glass. A Nez Perce' delegation prepared to attend the councils at Hellgate and Fort Benton: Looking Glass, Spotted Eagle, White Bird, Eagle From the Light (mostly in-laws of Angus MacDonald). And as usual at major functions of Stevens', the faithful James Doty was secretary and recording angel.

The second council was held at *la Porte de L'Enfer* (the Gate of Hell, because it was the entrance-way for Blackfeet war parties near present day Missoula). Here the goals of Stevens and the non-goals of the Salish did not mesh. It was Stevens' aim to include the Salish groups (Flatheads and Kalispels) and the non-Salish Kootenais in one confederation assigned to one reservation, and so to open all the rest of the interior to white occupation. Such a plan required drastic cessions of territory. Chief Victor's Flatheads wanted to keep the Bitterroot country around St. Mary Mission. Chief Alexander's Kalispels preferred to remain in the ronde where St. Ignatius Mission had just been established (1854). The Kootenais under Michel held the territory from upper Flathead Lake far up into the Tobacco Plains to the headwaters of the Rivers Kootenay and Columbia in British America and saw no reason to move south into the domain of others. None the less, Stevens requested the missionary of St. Ignatius to come to Hellgate. This was Father Adrian Hoecken, brother to the cholera victim on the *St. Ange*, who was now coping with cholera among the Indians at St. Ignatius and was reluctant to leave them and come to the council. He regarded the council as none of his business. But Stevens insisted, "requiring" the Jesuit to come. Hoecken surmised that only one-tenth of the proceedings was understandable to the Indians. The interpreters included Ben Kiser, (a

Soey-te-sum 'hi, or Bear Track, a chief and one of the pure Flathead Indians. He is said to be a very brave and daring man. Sketch by Sohon. Smithsonian Institution Photo No. 37417-D.

Shawnee or Delaware), Mary Lumphrey, (a Shoshoni), and Gustav Sohon, (a German!) The presence of some Nez Percés may have added to the tensions that already existed between Victor and Alexander. Victor was an hereditary chief who remembered Lewis and Clark. Alexander of the Kalispels was half Shoshoni, a friend of DeSmet and was named No Horses because he had so many. Such was the cast, so how was the play? Stevens put on his full repertoire:

Act I: The Governor addresses his children. He hints the Black Robes are nice to have around, but have no real authority. Alexander counters politely. Stevens promises a school, a blacksmith, a hospital, mills, farming equipment. Wouldn't the Kalispels like to have all these things? "No," replies Alexander. "We already have them at the Mission." Both Alexander and Victor disconcertingly talk about their people going to heaven. Stevens suggests that the way to go to heaven is to sign his treaty.

Act II: Arguments grow more murky. Big Canoe declares: "Why talk of treaties when there is no war? We have our land. You have yours. Go back to it!" The Kootenais say, "We are a different people. We are only here as onlookers. That's why we don't talk." Which Stevens translates to mean: "The Kootenais will agree to whatever the others agree to."

Act III: Stevens accuses Alexander of crooked talk. Alexander declares Stevens has two mouths: "At first you spoke well. Now you talk sharp—like a Blackfeet." Victor tries to intervene, but Stevens brushes him off. Finally Stevens loses his temper. He calls the royal Victor a son of a bitch. Victor withdraws.

And in spite of all these cross words and cross purposes, and for reasons that quite escape me, most of the leaders signed the treaty. Did they really understand what they were doing? Victor made a last-minute statement to this effect: Let the President of the United States come here and I will deal with him. Evidently, Victor signed something that he thought represented this proposal. But Moses, the second chief in the Flathead echelon, refused to sign at all. His name was added by another's hand. Stevens blamed the Jesuits for the split between the Salish chiefs, and as Father Hoecken hurried to return to St. Ignatius, Stevens said to him: "Father. . . it is on your account that the savages cling to their lands." The Kootenais went home in disgust.

Such was the background for the crucial Blackfeet council.

At the third council, Stevens would be required to share the leadership with Colonel Alfred Cumming, Superintendent of Indian Affairs at St. Louis. Cumming was a true Southerner—all 300 or 350 pounds of him, a son of the slave states with notions of the racial inferiority of non-whites, partisan of AFC, disinclined to rush things, oriented to different goals, obsessed by different demons, quite a contrast to his short, slender, authoritarian, bustling Northern colleague. They had one thing in common. They both thought there were two kinds of people in the world. Cumming used Aristotle's distinction: some are born to be masters; some are born to be slaves. Stevens thought some were born to command and others to obey. Not much difference. And yet their relationship turned out to be a preview of coming distractions, namely the Civil War. It got off to a bad start with Stevens specifically (and maybe wisely) insisting that the federal government send its own boat of treaty goods up the Missouri to expedite negotiations, whereas Cumming turned the job over to AFC instead. This move put Alexander Culbertson in the middle once again, entertaining Northern sympathies but representing American Fur. Alec always had trouble fitting himself into other people's dichotomies.

Colonel Cumming and his party came up on the *St. Mary* with the brother Captains Joseph and Jean LaBarge and Pierre's son Charles. The party included Alec, the Virginian Vaughan and his son, and young Henry Kennerly as attaché, a nephew of William Clark, a grandson of old Pierre Ménard, and part of St. Louis' *beau monde.* At Fort Union, Cumming and his party disembarked and continued their trip by land, accompanied by Baptiste Champagne and various other hunters, herders and carters. Chief Little Dog and probably his son The Fringe had driven horses down from Fort Sarpy with two "Spaniards" and now joined the overland party up the river for safety in numbers. The treaty goods were to be brought up in two or three keelboats under Andrew Dawson.

Meanwhile, Stevens and his personal party were on their way over from Hellgate with Stevens' young son Hazard, his guide Delaware Jim, and of course, Lt. Doty. Still another of the parties converging on Fort Benton was made up of the guide Ben Kiser, Agent Thomas Adams, Chief Victor with some Flatheads

Fort Benton, a John Mix Stanley color lithograph. From the U.S. Government's Railway Survey.

and Chief Alexander with some Kalispels. Among the last to arrive was Father Hoecken with his party, complying with Stevens' request to attend the Blackfeet council too, in spite of the minor hell the Governor had given him at Hellgate. Stevens had tried to gain the support and even the presence of Father DeSmet, but DeSmet wisely declined. The Governor arrived from the west at Fort Benton on the 26th of July and since Cumming was not there yet, continued down the Missouri to meet him at Milk River Crossing.

Immediately, the two Commissioners discovered that the chasm of disharmony between them would be harder to bridge than the wide Missouri. Cumming was the "senior commissioner," so Stevens had to yield him priority on that point. But discord penetrated their objectives and their very cosmologies. Alec stood back in some sort of disgust. Had he become skeptical of treaties? Of Stevens? The Governor retaliated by accusing his old friend of "serving other gods" (revealing metaphor!) and treating him "with great coolness." Alec felt he was obligated to Cumming through AFC. Hurt by Stevens' charge, he refused to assist in the council as an interpreter. And after so many months of dedicated service to the cause! (There must be a lot here that was not recorded.)

When the combined forces reached Fort Benton on August 17, Cumming took quarters inside the walls as became his Southern dignity, while Stevens camped at the gates like Homer's sulking Achilles. People snickered. Even so, a salute was fired, flags were unfurled, much liquor was passed around, and several persons made a "beautiful display" of themselves.

On August 27, Hugh Monroe guided a party out of Benton to contact the Gros Ventres and Blackfeet. He carried a letter from Cumming and Benjamin de Roche, factor of Fort Campbell (the Opposition post near Benton) and met a large Blood camp on the move. About the same time four Kalispels came in with a complaint from Chief Alexander that four horses had been stolen by Northern Blackfeet boys—not an auspicious way to start peace talks. Stevens sent Little Dog to recover them but without success. Then he sent Lt. Doty with Little Dog and "Jackson," who traveled 50 miles a day some 200 miles up into the forks of the Saskatchewan to a camp on Bow River. There Doty got three of the horses. Turning them over to Little Dog, he took off after the fourth 70 miles farther to the Elk Fork. He got it. So all four animals were returned to the Kalispels.

Henry Kennerly tells us in his memoirs that he and Baptiste Champagne rode off into the paling summer via Sweet Grass Buttes to Canada, then west of Cypress Hills to the camp of Lame Bull. He circled back by way of Chief Mountain and St. Mary Lakes. It is possible that both he and Hugh Monroe were traveling together for a while on this return, in company with a band of Indians and *métis*, because later both claimed to have witnessed the formal naming of St. Mary Lakes and River (*Lacs et Rivière de Ste. Marie*), which Henry says occurred at this time. On the 21st of September, Alec set out from Fort Benton with two wagons for meat. He seems to have crossed paths with Kennerly and Wilson (?) at Lame Bull's camp on the Marias on September 29. Kennerly got back to Benton on the 30th and Alec on October 1.[45]

Now it was fall and still no treaty goods. So Alec with a son of Vaughan and others went down the river to find them. And find them they did at Arnell Island. On the return, at Dauphin's Rapids, they encountered a small hostile party of Crows. When one of them grabbed Vaughan's coffee cup, the young greenhorn would have killed him on the spot had not Alec intervened. Then came 40 Gros Ventres who ran down the Crows and killed them all. They would have spared the Crow woman at Alec's request, but she got in the way. Peace does not come easily.

When Alec reported back to Fort Benton, there turned out to be one thing at least that everybody could agree on: moving the council grounds downriver to a point which supply boats could reach in time. So everybody moved down to the mouth of the Judith to a cottonwood grove already shedding its autumn leaves. There the tribes gathered, and there the business of the council consumed ten days. Indians strolled about the camps afoot or on horseback singing their hearts out. The repartee in council was not nearly so dramatic as it had been at Hellgate, for luckily, both Stevens and Cummings behaved themselves rather well. They even pretended to be brothers of some sort and addressed the Indians as their "children." Stevens could hardly get away with his routine in three acts without his "senior commissioner" getting into one of the acts.

The interpreting, which had been so faulty at Hellgate, may have improved at the Judith. To take Alec's place, Stevens chose the controversial James Bird (the same James Bird who had deserted DeSmet in the snowy fall of '45 and who disgusted Maximilian in '33). Alec, however, was finally and officially listed among the interpreters for the Blackfeet, so he may have condescended to participate after all, though I must confess some skepticism about Alec's skills as a linguist. The third interpreter for the Blackfeet was Benjamin de Roche (Durocher) of Fort Campbell, who was married into the Blackfeet tribe. He must have been a cousin to the brothers LaBarge since his mother also was of the old Spanish family Álvarez Ortiz.

The interpreters for the Nez Percés were William Craig and Delaware Jim or Jim Delaware. Whichever way you say his name, he turns out to be one of the most interesting figures at the council. Sometimes called "Mr. Owen's man" because he lived at Fort Owen/St. Mary, he was truly no one's man but his own. The son of a white mother and a Delaware (Leni-Lenape) chief, he was credited with having spent a lifetime "hunting and traveling over all parts of the country, from the Mississippi to the Pacific. . ." Tall, slender, intelligent, reserved

[45] See notes.

and sharp of eye, he earned Stevens' admiration. Jim and his brother Ben Sim-
monds are both reputed to have explored with Frémont. In a party of Delawares
and probably Shawnees, Jim traded pelts all the way to California and may have
joined his people who were engaged by Don Juan Bandini during the political
turbulance of 1837 around San Diego. Jim and Tom Hill lived with the Shoshonis
and the Nez Perces.

For the Flatheads, the interpreters were Ben Kiser and the German trooper
Sohon, who also sketched the participants at the council. The Gros Ventres,
Kootenais and Crees had no official interpreters, but there was only one Cree
in attendance, Broken Arm, now under the personal protection of Little Dog.
Among the estimated 3,000 Indians present, we find Lame Bull, Mountain Chief,
Kihzip-Onista (*Satá?*), *Manistokos, Onistai-sainakoyim* (evidently Seen-From-Afar
by an alternate name), *Natosi-Onista*, Calf Shirt, even *Kutonápi* of the North
Blackfeet. Representing the Nez Percés were Spotted Eagle, Looking Glass, Eagle
From the Light, White Bird; while from the Salish came Victor, Alexander,
Moses, Big Canoe, Bear Track and Little Michel. Lt. James Doty was the
secretary and Little Dog the champion orator. He lectured his people six hours
on end. Imagine the relief with which they must have greeted his final *Kyéne!*

The main business of the council took place on October 16th and 17th, 1855.
The terms guaranteed to the Blackfeet and the Gros Ventres all the present state
of Montana north of the Missouri and east of the Continental Divide. A Common Hunting Ground for various tribes including the Blackfeet was reserved
west of the Musselshell and enclosed much of southwest Montana. Provisions
were made for annuities, roads, military posts and so on, while certain northern
passes were declared off limits to western tribes. Seen-From-Afar pinpointed
one big flaw in the arrangements: the absence of the Crows. He, as head of
the Fish Eater band, promised to try to restrain his young braves but doubted
that he could. Especially important were the legal implications of this treaty,
the Laramie treaty and many another, which probably no participant fully
realized but which were foreseen by Chief Justice John Marshall and maybe
few after him: the relationship forged by these covenants between Indian tribes
and the U.S. Government was unique under the Constitution, not shared by
any other citizens or residents of the land. This special status guarantees that
Indian tribes in perpetuity have an "internal sovereignty" of their own, under
which each member of the tribe retains the right to participate in self-
determination. (In other words, when the U.S. citizenship of Indians was finally
acknowledged in 1924, each Indian was also implicitly acknowledged to have
a kind of dual citizenship.)[46]

When the deed was done, Stevens approached Alec and said he wanted to
part friends. Alec was only too happy to make up, and if they seem like a couple
of boys, well, so be it. The Governor and his entourage returned westward over
the Great Divide to Washington Territory. Colonel Cumming wanted a sight-
seeing tour of the Bad Lands between the Judith and Arrow Creek and arranged
for a cruise with Vaughan and Kennerly (who tells the story). The Indians
gathered on shore to watch the white men have fun. All went well when the
two guests climbed aboard, but when Cumming got in, the boat sank. With
one grand guffaw the Indians had the last laugh. By a quirk of history, the Treaty
of 1855 prepared at the Judith Council, written by white men to promote the
interests of white men, legalized the Blackfeet claim over a vast territory in

---

[46] Consult the U.S. Constitution, Article I, Section 8, and Article VI.

Montana in the white man's own system. It was ratified by the U.S. Senate on April 15, 1856 and proclaimed by the President soon afterwards. One thing no one seems to have explained to the Blackfeet was that what the President proclaimed, he could also disclaim by a device called an "executive order."

It turned out as Colonel Cumming had feared. October frosts had already touched the leaves, and ice was forming on the river. Then the river froze over, and Sioux braves made off with the mules. (The Sioux, after all, had not been on hand for the Judith Treaty.) Cumming, the man who had created delays in the first place, now accused Stevens of dilly-dallying. But at last he managed to get away in a special mackinaw with three of his men and even his ambulance on board—this time the boat did not sink. Alec and Ferdinand Hayden went with him, and perhaps Natawista too.

At Fort Pierre they appealed to General Harney for transportation. The General replied in his own magnanimous manner: "I only regret that when the Indians got your mules, they didn't get your scalp also... You have been patching up another of your sham treaties to be broken tomorrow and give us more work." In the end, Alec got the mules that Cumming needed from the American Fur Company.

In the euphoria of the new era of potential stability, Fort Benton itself was physically stabilized by a new north bastion of adobes (1855-56). The east bastion and other adobe stuctures would take another four or five years.

But stability proved something of an illusion, and the aftermath of the treaty entailed tragedy. In Washington Territory Stevens proclaimed martial law, the suspension of civil liberties, and was rebuked for that act by the President himself, his old friend Pierce. And having promoted 28-year old James Doty to Lieutenant Colonel, Stevens assigned him to check on half-breeds, probably the relations of French "squaw men" with their Indian wives, something which had long been a bugbear to the Governor. It may have been at this time that the Bruns fled back to Montana. Stevens ordered all persons near Olympia suspected of communicating with Indians to be taken into custody by Lt. Colonel Doty. Instead of carrying out this impossible task, Doty got drunk. Promptly and curtly, Stevens dismissed him. Yet Doty, Stevens' latest alter ego, lingered pathetically on the horizon until Stevens relented a little and made him a clerk. Then James Doty got drunk again and shot himself (1857).

Alas, Stevens could only pay him "humble tribute" in words, as usual, spoken too late, too late: "He is now no more; but he was my friend and companion... Twice did he traverse the country with me from the Pacific to the Missouri. Unwearied, indefatigable, and able..."

Such a denouement lends a special meaning to the story about Doty's old trail-mate Little Dog, who celebrated the Judith peace by making a personal visit across the Divide to the Salish people and their mission at St. Ignatius (1856). He brought his followers with him, leading them up to the mission with flag unfurled as the traditional symbol of peace and taking a special delight in "martial music," presumably performed by the mission band. Deep down in his vision Little Dog knew that something was missing. To the Jesuit missionary he confided:

"The traders never speak to us of God."

CHAPTER XVIII

Zion Corners to the Great Falls

"There are two kinds of people in the world," declares Chairman Mao, "those who believe in God and those who do not." His dichotomy proves at least that the mania for dichotomizing the human race is not peculiar to the Occident. It ignores the vacillators, the temporizers and the sort of God they toy with. This book is a saga of vacillators.

Alec's vacillations are tedious and bewildering. He who began as the in-between brother, spent his life in between polarities he could never learn to synthesize. Go east, go west, retire, not to retire, marry, not to marry. Up the river, down the river, year in, year out. He dabbles in farming, politics, and now even church.

The first home the Culbertsons had at Peoria was a brick structure in what later became Madison Park golf course. In these affluent days they could afford to educate their children in style: son Jack at a military academy (so it is said without any proof I know) and the girls at "ladies' seminaries." Vigorously did Natawista protest the surrender of her children. But Alec was adamant. There may have been a scene—perhaps a long series of scenes. Alec took stubborn pride in the education of his children, perhaps to compensate for his own minimal schooling. From the confused reports that have come down to us, we would suppose that all his daughters attended the Moravian Seminary for Young Ladies at Bethlehem. Perhaps the traditional bond between the Moravians and the Indians had something to do with Alec's choice. Curiously, about this same time, Freemason Edwin Denig moved to Canada to send his children to Catholic schools where he could live near them. Alec made no move to live near his children that we know of. But the Moravian Archives at Bethlehem have records today of only two daughters of "Major Alexander Culbertson:" Julia and Fanny. Julia was enrolled there "from Fort Union at the mouth of the Yellowstone" in 1850, but Fanny not until 1859 and 1865. Julia must have entered at the age of four or five, and indeed her grand-daughter tells of her being committed there as a tiny girl, so alienated from her parents that she knew them only as "Natty" and "the major." It was the school superintendent, Rev. Wolle, and his wife, whom she called "Papa and Mamma Wolle." No wonder Natawista hated that kind of education! Family recollections add that Julia, poor little Julia, spent many summers there, sad and lonely, with her soft gray eyes full of question marks. Why did her grandparents not take her home for the summers to Chambersburg or Palmyra? Did they think of her as just a little savage? We'll never know. We are told, however, that Alec and Natty often left their children in the care of Anna Culbertson and visited them in the east every year. The vignette of lonely little Julia, torn from her mother to wait out her time in Bethlehem is one that will haunt most of us long after we have forgotten the rest of this story.

At least we see that Peoria had become a sort of middle ground to the Culbertsons from which Alec left to go east and west. He may have been in New York in 1855 or 1856 conferring with Senator Walter Lowrie, Secretary of the Board of Foreign Missions. Now that peace reigned along the upper Missouri in the aftermath of the Stevens treaty, Alec thought it was a strategic time to establish a mission among the Blackfeet. If this notion seems a bit out of character for Alexander Culbertson, it may simply show how little we really know him. According to Lowrie himself, it was Alec who proposed the Blackfeet mission to the executive committee of the Board. It may not be wholly coincidental that this was about the time when Michael Simpson was returning from China, and it is a matter of conjecture whether Michael was in some way a catalyst for the Blackfeet project and also whether Alec was on the dock when his brother arrived.

The Culbertsons had spent six years at Ningpo as part of a missionary team that included young Walter Lowrie. There, in 1845, Michael had become the first pastor of their first church in China, while Walter had to take boat trips across Hangchow Bay to Shanghai as delegate to the Convention for Translating the Scriptures. On one of his returns, his boat was assaulted by pirates and Walter himself cast into the sea. Not long after that, Michael's son died. In 1851 Michael was appointed as Walter's successor and had to move his family to Shanghai, where the Tai Pings, in revolt against their Manchu oppressors, kept the entire region in turmoil for years on end. In this chaos, the Culbertsons may have lost another child. With the arrival of Reuben Lowrie, Michael was relieved to take a vacation in the States.

The Culbertsons, on board the *Cathay* out of Shanghai, reached New York on the 11th or 12th of January, 1856. Their voyage had been fair until they approached their home coasts, where the weather was horrible. The *Cathay* ran aground on Long Island and had to be towed into port. Among the seven on the passenger manifest, five were Culbertsons' M.S., age 35; Mary D., age 32; H.O. (Helen), age 10(?); an illegible, age 8; and Mary, age 3. As usual, Michael's health was improved by the voyage. He reported directly to the Board, assuring the directors that the translation of the New Testament was now completed and the two day-schools of Senator Lowrie's daughter-in-law were in operation. Less optimistically, he had to admit that in China the Gospel was usually received with "perfect indifference" and even with the retort: "We have enough to do attending to the necessities of this life. How can we look after the world to come?" (Michael did not add that it might be the preachers' fault for preaching a dualism of two worlds, mutually irrelevant.)

The Board had no intention of turning Alec Culbertson into a missionary or of sending Michael Simpson among the Blackfeet. But they would dispatch a couple with the proper credentials to evangelize western tribes. This they would do with Alec's cooperation, especially since Alec evidently felt responsibility for the project. The new couple chosen by the Board: The Rev. Elkanah D. Mackey and his fragile and pregnant young wife Sarah. Mrs. Mackey would probably be the first white woman to reach Fort Benton. What she lacked in stamina, her husband made up in zeal. The Board's mission would reach from Zion Corners to the falls of the Missouri.

On the 8th of April, 1856, Rev. Mackey wrote from Dover, Delaware, to Walter Lowrie asking how to get in touch with "Mr. Culbertson." He made this contact in St. Louis, if not before, and there Alec showed the Mackeys every possible courtesy. When Lowrie reported, he must have meant that Alec showed the Mackeys all the courtesies the Company of Pierre le Cadet traditionally bestowed on missionaries. From St. Louis the Mackeys moved on up to Bellevue,

Nebraska, perhaps with Senator Lowrie himself. On the 4th of June Elkanah wrote the Senator that he was still awaiting a boat for the upper river.

The whereabouts of Alec and Natawista, meanwhile, is not easy to determine. We have a letter that Alec wrote to Julia, dated June 9, 1856, but the letter seems far out of joint with all the other documentary evidence we have of this period. I am disposed to think that it may be mis-dated "56" either by Alec himself or a copyist. It was addressed from Sioux City and the steamer *Robert Campbell.* "My dear daughter," Alec began. He reminded Julia that from his last letter she must have thought he was coming home to Peoria, but now he was headed once more "to the Mountains." When the steamer had reached "St. Jo." Alec met Colonel Vaughan and other friends who prevailed on him to join them on their cruise up the river. Apparently, Natawista was with him. When the captain offered them free passage to Fort Benton, they could not resist. So Alec tells Julia that she and Fannie must not be disappointed but must "bear up and endeavor to pass (the time) usefully and as pleasantly as circumstances will permit until I return. . ." He will be back in the fall and would then go to Palmyra. Alec cannot help falling into his stilted style even when he is writing to his children. If his mask begins to slip, he quickly readjusts it: ". . . in the mean spare no pains. . . to facilitate the Education of Fannie(?)," but he hastens to add, "I want you to be careful of her health as you know she is not over strong." He urges Julia to keep writing to Janie and to pass on the news of this letter, adding, "your mother says tell Jane she must keep that little girl go(ing) constantly to school." Alec promises to write often before they reach Fort Benton. "Give your kind Regards to Uncle and Aunt. Yourself and Fanny Accept our Affection." He closes, "Your Affectionate Father Alex Culbertson."

This seems a strange letter to write to a little girl of ten or eleven. (Another reason for thinking the date may be off.) And who are "Uncle and Aunt?" Perhaps Dr. Samuel Culbertson and Nancy.

Alec seems to have been delayed in St. Louis waiting for the government annuities, which of course would be necessary to keep the upriver tribes in a receptive mood. He must have come up the Missouri, either on the *Robert Campbell,* the *St. Mary,* or some other vessel, in company with Jean (John) Sarpy, Ferdinand Hayden of the Smithsonian and perhaps John Purviance Culbertson, Alec's cousin, brother of Ferdinand Culbertson and the son of Dr. Samuel and his wife Nancy Purviance. The Mackeys caught the *St. Mary* at Bellevue, and at Fort Pierre Natawista came aboard with little Fanny, then judged to be five years old. It was at Fort Pierre that Natty promised to be Mrs. Mackey's friend in need. At Fort Clark Andrew Dawson came on board too, and solid Scot that he was, beamed a happy eye on the Presbyterian missionaries. When he found so many women and children on the boat, he brought along his own five-year-old son, half Arikara. The *St. Mary* reached Fort Union and kept on for another ninety miles into Montana to unload the merchanise and probably the annuities for Fort Benton, then returned to Union, with both the Culbertsons and the Mackeys evidently still aboard. On July 22nd (whether on his first or second arrival) Elkanah addressed Walter Lowrie from Fort Union, assuring him that he was expecting to leave for Benton on the 25th but that meanwhile he and his wife were "comfortable" where they were. He has some kind remarks about the Culbertsons and seems to have been quite delighted with the Indians:

> Mr. Culbertson and Mrs. Culbertson too do all they can to make it pleasant for us. I think she is a very remarkable woman, considering the opportunities she has had. Her influence over him seems to be of the most favorable kind. She is very prudent and has the most deepseated and perserving opposition to the use of liquor.

And Elkanah went on to explain something about the Assiniboines. On Wednesday, said he, Agent Vaughan held a council of chiefs in a tipi, accompanied by the Culbertsons and the Mackeys. Though there had been some "variance with the Blackfeet," some of the young men and chiefs planned to "bury the tomahawk and smoke the pipe of peace" with them, while the rest of the Assiniboines went off to their hunting grounds. Elkanah made a particular friend of Fool Bear, "a noble, fine-looking man" of extensive influence. Fool Bear affirmed that indeed his people believed in God and prayed to him. "They were sure there must be a God, for what would be the use of praying to God if there was none?" Elkanah declared his logic irrefutable and invited him to come and read the Bible. Already one can see that Elkanah's heart is aching for the Assiniboines, whose population he estimates at three to four thousand.

Their journey from Union to Benton took three weeks and evidently all by land, for Elkanah later described it by the remark, "During this time we were dwellers in tents. . ." Their companions were Alexander "and his family," his cousin John Culbertson of Cincinnati, S.A. Bennett of St. Louis, the various teamsters and a peacemaking contingent of 15 or 20 Assiniboines. Up the Missouri they trekked to the mouth of Milk River. Another report mentions Alec at Milk River and Cow Island. Elkanah says they passed "the Bear's Paw Mountains" and then crossed a wide prairie to Fort Benton. He was fascinated by the multitudes of buffalo, by the sprightliness of the antlered elk and the curiosity of the antelopes, but a little depressed by the howling of wolves. At Poplar River they were held up two days by a flood, and one night the wind blew down the Mackey's tent. They hurried into the Culbertson's tent, which they had to tie to the wagons. In the morning, alas, the young Reverend's hat was gone. Hunt and pry as they might across the prairie, they could not track down the precious hat until Natawista found it two miles from camp. Bennett's hat was never found, but they had a good laugh at their vexations. Remarkably enough, they met many Indians along the way, Gros Ventres and Piegans, of whom "all greeted us with a hearty welcome." The Indians were somewhat flabbergasted to see a white woman, as none had yet come farther than the mouth of Milk River, but they "treated her with the greatest respect and kindness." For Elkanah the trip was "invigorating." For his wife it was a disaster.

In the journal of Indian Agent E. Alward Hatch we learn that the Culbertsons and the Mackeys arrived at Fort Benton on the 16th of August, 1856. The Agent scrutinized the Mackeys with a cynical eye, noting that on their arrival "the Priest and his wife" seemed pleased for now but "will probably get enough of it before spring." They did. Long before spring. In two days, Sarah took to her bed and "continued very weak and nervous." Yet her husband was all the while bursting with vitality and good cheer, holding services every Sunday "in Mr. Culbertson's Room," instructing Indians, exploring the wilderness for potential mission sites. In the valleys of the Teton and Marias he made a reconnaisance, and up into the valley of the Highwood. With Choquette he took a tour to the Great Falls.

The Mackeys were not the only novelty that summer of '56. This was the time when the monotony at Benton was broken by contacts with emissaries from west of the Divide. Satá, son of the late Nicolas, brought over a letter from John Owen of the Bitterroot. Satá's little boy died during his visit. And a packer for Owen named John Silverthorne brought gold dust for $1,000 in trade. (The value varies a good deal from one version of this story to another.) Young Silverthorne would not reveal the source of his gold, it is said he acquired it from old friend Benetsee as something to shop with at Benton. Benetsee, you will recall, had gone to California with the Bruns, LaPlantes and others and on his return to Montana (1852) had discovered gold at Gold Creek. Some of this he took to Angus MacDonald at Fort Connah near St. Ignatius for verification. But what proof had Alec? What to do? Trust Silverthorne? Call it a hoax? Alec consulted with one of his employees, perhaps his relative, Ray or Wray, and then obliged Silverthorne from his personal account. Ultimately, the mint repaid Alec $1,525. (But at least one version reduces the trade value of the dust to $12 or less and Alec's return to $15.) This event is dated October 1856, but that is not possible for Alec was gone by that time. Either month or year or event must be wrong. More certain is that John Owen himself came over to Fort Benton with a few of his west-side associates, among them Jim Delaware and Pierre Lafontaine. That was in September. Other western visitors may have been the family of Angus MacDonald, who is reported to have sent them as refugees to "the buffalo plains of Montana." The Plains were peaceful at this period compared to the farther Northwest where the Yakima war raged (1855-56), and a gold rush boomed in lower British Columbia. Angus' wife Catherine Baptiste, a cousin to Eagle-From-the-Light, had as a girl in 1841 made the fantastic trek to "Coyoterra" (Arizona and California) as a protogée of "the Spaniard Manuel." The lack of details leaves the story of Catherine's visit to Benton in limbo, but if true, this would be the only occasion when the two families could have met— the families of the king of the high Missouri and the king of the high Columbia.

Another vague story of this summer comes from J. W. Schultz and tells of trips to the Southwest by Seen-From-Afar. It includes a romantic bit that sounds remarkably like the story of Marcelino Baca[47] and, all in all, has to be taken with a sack of salt. I think it is probable Seen-From-Afar went to the Southwest, but I do not know what to make of Schultz's use of his name. It is curious to note, by the way, the Canadian tradition that links the fame of Seen-From-Afar and the fame of Alec directly together: they were men who made each other prominent through Natawista, rising, revolving like binary stars.

There was a smallpox epidemic in 1856, which during the following winter spread even among the métis.

As the time approached for the Culbertsons to go back down the river to their home in Peoria, the Mackeys suffered through "a violent inward struggle." One thing was clear: there was no medical care available in Fort Benton for Mrs. Mackey. So after many prayers, tears and consultations, Elkanah felt obliged to abandon his fond dreams of a Blackfeet mission. At some time in September the Mackeys set out with the Culbertsons in two wagons and a buggy for the first lap of their trip east. The date of their departure traditionally is given as September 15th, but Elkanah's report suggests September 23.

This was not the end of the adventure, however, for about four weeks after the arrival of the Mackeys and the Culbertsons at Fort Benton, the Piegans and Gros Ventres gathered at the mouth of the Judith River to collect their annuities, the Piegans on the southern bank, the Gros Ventres on the northern. On their way down the river, the Culbertsons and Mackeys camped with them for awhile on the north shore. On a date given by Elkanah as the 19th, Lame Bull and Spotted Cow of the Piegans crossed over to confer with them. Elkanah, in his report to Walter Lowrie, quoted a long speech by Lame Bull approving the coming of missionaries. He had been obliged to consult with his fellow chiefs overnight before he could give his concession, but now he compared the missionary process to the taming of wild pets. "We have been running wild on the prairie and now we want the white sons and daughters of our Great Father to come to our country and tame us." And he went on "We have been like crying

[47] See Notes, page 212

children . . ."When a child cries, you tell it *maupit* (*amaupit* = shut up!). Now the Piegans wanted the missionaries to tell them *maupit* so that they would be good children. And so on. What portion of this speech is Lame Bull's and how much Elkanah's? That is anybody's guess. But no doubt Lame Bull was very cordial in the customary Indian tradition of hospitality that had not the historian's advantage of hind-sight. On September 21st Elkanah got similar results on a visit with Gros Ventre chiefs in the tipi of Bear Shirt. Probably the chiefs agreed that the occasion called for courtesy, not wisdom. (And perhaps tongue-in-cheek.)

Anyhow, down the river they all went eventually, Elkanah implies that they traveled together at least part of the way. But at Fort Union Alec ran into a problem which I would think Elkanah might have mentioned had he witnessed it. The problem was Sir St. George Gore, "the Irish Nimrod." He had been busily ravashing the prairies with his train of forty-odd men, slaughtering the four-footed creatures of the Great Spirit on a grand scale that fulfilled old Indian prophecies of doom. Along the Platte and the Tongue, Gore had left the country littered with rotting meat. Rarely has a man been so properly named. The Crows protested. Agent Vaughan protested. Some Indians drove off Gore's horses, and a Blood war party attacked him—among them Big Plume, "Mr. Culbertson's brother-in-law." Now at Fort Union, Gore built himself a grand mackinaw. When confronted in person by Alec and Vaughan, he turned belligerent and with outraged dignity burned his own wagons and took off to winter at Fort Berthold. There the Indians got away with the rest of his horses, small compensation, probably, for the ecological ruin he had wrought in their country.

In October Alec went on down the river in a keelboat, accompanying Pike Vásquez to St. Joseph and probably taking Natawista to Peoria. There seems to be some discrepancy between this report and the accounts of Elkanah, who is not mentioned further in the traditional versions.

At any rate, Elkanah wrote a letter (probably to Lowrie) from a "Mackinaw Boat" above St. Joseph on November 5th, explaining his return with his ailing wife, and from St. Joseph on November 13th he addressed his lengthy report to Walter Lowrie and the Board of Foreign Missions in New York. He wanted to make it clear that his view of the enterprise was optimistic in spite of its collapse and that he hoped to renew the adventure when his wife was well again. The Indians of the high Missouri were wonderful, and "The climate is without doubt one of the most healthy in the world." What concerns us most, however, are his comments on Alec and Natawista, about whom no other traveler I know of made such detailed appraisals:

> But with reference to Mrs. Culbertson we can speak more particularly, as we have been in close contact with her at Fort Pierre on our way up the River and have had an opportunity of seeing her under a variety of circumstances. If her character may be taken as an index to the character of the nation, our impressions are of the most favorable kind. She has at all times been to us a fine and firm friend and has fully redeemed the promise she voluntarily made when we first met her that she would be Mrs. Mackey's friend when we got to the country of the Blackfeet. She has a noble, kind and generous heart, quick to detect the wants of those around her and prompt to relieve them. We have contracted for her a strong and we trust a lasting personal friendship, and attachment.

Elkanah goes on to mention "the kindnesses which under all circumstances Mr. Culbertson has shown us . . ." and especially the sympathy he always evinced towards Mrs. Mackey. He had given them a ten percent discount on their freight to Fort Benton (about $32.00 altogether) and had offered to store their goods for free until the following spring. He had paid for the Mackey's board and transportation from Fort Union on the trip up-river in July until "we left the Mackinaw Boat a few days ago." And in spite of the high cost of living of the upper Missouri, "For all this he charges us nothing."

You could get the impression that Elkanah's praises of Natawista were a bit more spontaneous than his plaudits for Alec.

Elkanah found a physician at Fort Pierre who gave Sarah some medicine that helped a little, and all in all, she did get stronger as they drew nearer home. On November 19 they were approaching St. Louis aboard the *St. Mary.*

But poor Elkanah never fulfilled his hopes of returning to the high Missouri. He and Sarah went on to Maryland, where in spite of his youth and apparent vigor, he died quite suddenly on the 6th of September 1858. A few hours later, or perhaps the next day, his baby son followed him into death. Father and son were both interred in the churchyard.

CHAPTER XIX

A Wee Voice in Alec's Ear

Alec's dream was focused now on his retirement, yet even so he could not resist the yearly temptation to ascend the River. In April of 1856 or 1857 Michael Simpson made a remark to Walter Lowrie that Alec was expecting to depart from St. Louis on the 5th of May "for the return." This casual remark does not help us to track Alec's itinerary, but it does suggest that the trails of the two brothers had crossed. We have no way to tell where "the return" is to, or where from.

It is true that the disastrous mission of the Mackey's was not the only missionary venture at this period into the Blackfeet country. We have no certain dates or details, except that we learn that Benton's opposition post, Fort Campbell, was once used as a Catholic mission. Father Jeremiah Trecy visited the high Missouri and had some sort of mission station at Fort Benton from about 1855 onward. Father Scanlon also came up the river and went down again. Otherwise, it appears that the legions of the Lord had to beat a graceless retreat from this rough-and-tumble frontier.

There is another point about Fort Campbell we should not pass up. In the spring of 1857 the Opposition company of Robert Campbell, John B. Todd (cousin to Mrs. Lincoln) and other eager entrepreneurs ran supplies up the river to their posts, Fort Williams near Union and Fort Campbell near Benton. And who should be in charge of Campbell (succeeding Benjamin de Roche?) but old friend and ally Malcolm Clarke. His reason for quitting AFC and Alec is not known. But it was quite a game—that hide and fur trade! AFC countered this effrontery by sending the *Spread Eagle* up-river under Jean LaBarge, Charles Chouteau and Alec Culbertson, and they did themselves proud at least by making the trip in a month and a half, both ways. They also brought back a meteorite. This may be the trip Michael mentioned to Lowrie, and that one brief statement about it is the only evidence I know of that Alec went up the river at all in 1857.

In New York, on May 3rd, 1857, Michael Simpson delivered a lecture titled "The Religious Condition of the Chinese, and Their Claims on the Church: A Sermon Preached for the Board of Foreign Missions of the Presbyterian Church..." Since this seems to be his first wide-spread pronouncement after his return to the U.S., he may have been allowed a year for recuperation. Also in 1857 this lecture was published in New York and so too was his book, *Darkness in the Flowery Land; or, Religious Notions and Superstitions in North China.* (Today we would call it "East China.") The Preface of his book was initialed "M.S.C." at "Chambersburg, Pa., Sept. 7th, 1857." Most of this work is not remarkable but repeats the hum-drum stereotypes about the Chinese. Superficially, even prejudicially, it summarized the Taoist, Buddhist and Confucianist traditions, sometimes quite missing their main thrust. But here, as in his earlier work on the Tai Pings, Michael reveals his sympathy for their movement. Both in his book and his lecture, his remarks might well have sent some jitters through the halls of the State Department or up and down Wall Street. After all, how can you reconcile such talk with Manifest Destiny? Michael concludes his book with a special chapter on the Tai Pings and their "remarkable revolution," calling it "undoubtedly one of the most wonderful among the many wonderful events of the present age," and even adding, "Must we not bid them God speed in such a work?" True, he does acknowledge that there is "doubtless, much fanaticism connected with this movement." But in the long run, says he, "We cannot but recognize in this strange revolution the power of God." Similar remarks appear in his "Sermon," with a note dear to the hearts of Calvinists: "The idols they have utterly abolished." And he confides to his co-religionists that he prefers the Tai Ping doctrine, not only to the Chinese traditions, but also to Islam and "Romanism." Complacently, he relates in his book that during the capture of Nanking the insurgents destroyed the temples of the idolaters and also "domolished the Romish churches and their idols along with the rest . . . It was certainly a very natural, and very pardonable mistake."

On the day after his lecture, he attended the meeting of the Board and was put on a committee to make reports on "missions to the Indian tribes." Perhaps the Board members reasoned that he might lean on the expertise of his brother. Whatever became of this project is not clear. In the long run, however, the Board made no effective attempt to pursue the course set by the tragic Mackeys.

Something else Michael must have discussed with the Board was the Term Question, the dispute over the name of God in the General Convention for Translating the Scriptures. The Senator's son Walter had been regarded as a special expert in this matter. Of the five delegates to the Convention, the two British members of the London Society preferred the ancient Chinese term *Shang Ti* (Lord Above), and Dr. Bridgman, musing over Matthew I:23, offered the term *Shin* (currently spelled (*shen* and meaning deity, spirit, divine). The rivalry between the two factions, British and American, grew to fever pitch, based less perhaps on linguistics than on nationalism. The Americans accused the British of deploring all things American as "colonial" or "provincial," and when one of the London members at last agreed to *Shen* his learned colleague retorted, "You shall not do it! You shall not use that American term!" But Michael, it seems, tended to side with the Tai Pings who preferred *Shang Ti*.

During Michael's stay in the U.S., he surely must have visited his brothers, whether in Pennsylvania, Cincinnati or Peoria, Ohio or Indiana. Since he was in this country seeking improved health, it is reasonable to suppose he would consult his own uncle, Dr. Samuel Duncan Culbertson, a well known and skilled physician and surgeon, though a specialist in obstetrics. Or he might have consulted his brother William, also a doctor, living in Logansport, Indiana, and married to Nancy McCulloh (a Purviance on her mother's side). However, William died this very year.

At any rate, the missionary reports for 1857 reveal that the Culbertson's were expecting to set out once more for China in a few months. Michael seemed recovered.

Curiously, we never hear of the Alec Culbertsons running off to Chicago, so near Peoria, whereas we often find them enjoying the delights of St. Louis, particularly their regular stand-by, the old Palmer Hotel. No doubt the lure of Creole gumbo with venison and eggnog had something to do with it. Alec's long connection with the Creole and Virginia families of St. Louis (Clarks, Kennerlys, Chouteaus, Robidoux, and perhaps the Radfords and Ménards) must surely have left an imprint on his set of values, for better or worse. One impression concerned slavery. It could no longer be taken for granted. Perhaps it had never been as brutal an institution among the Creoles as among other Southern populations. In St. Louis the aristocracy often cared for slaves as for members of the family. A master might cane his slave for drunkenness today and tomorrow spend hundreds to ransom his slave's children. St. Louis was the encapsulation of the many tensions, ethical and political, that were beginning to tear the nation apart.

So it was on a trip to St. Louis for the New Year of 1858 that Alec revealed his new plans. It now seemed to him a proper time for a courtly wedding. Wedding? For whom? Why, for himself and Natawista, of course. After all, the children must be legitimized and their legal interests protected. So too the property rights of Natawista. Father DeSmet, who held both Alec and friend Denig in high esteem, addressed a letter to Denig, who had now retired to the Red River of the North with his family. The letter was dated from the University of St. Louis, January 13, 1858:

> About a fortnight ago I received a visit from Major Culbertson: he is now settled with his family near Peoria, Illinois; he requested me to visit him and to remain some days with him, to enable him to arrange matters... I think he intends to marry his wife and have her instructed and baptized. I intend to visit him soon. He placed his daughters at a convent in St. Louis.

The date of Natawista's baptism is not known, but her records in Canada refer to the event as taking place in the United States and give her name as Nellie. But "Natty" was the nickname the family used—at least in later times. It is fair to assume the baptism preceded the wedding. I am puzzled about the daughters at the convent.

One is tempted to suppose that it was Michael who had influenced Alec to step at long last into canonical matrimony, but if so, then why is Alec preparing for a wedding ceremony by someone else rather than his brother, and a Catholic ceremony at that? Perhaps Father DeSmet is doing some wishful thinking, but in any event his letter is the only evidence we have on this point. As if to compound the riddle, at some time in 1858 Alec made contact with Walter Lowrie in New York regarding business with the Board of Missions about the conversion of the Blackfeet to Presbyterianism. One thing is sure; no one can accuse Alec of consistency or denominationalism. He's a tough nut to crack.

If this discussion with Walter Lowrie occurred on a trip to see Michael and his family off to China, it must have taken place early in the year. For within a month, or thereabouts, after Father DeSmet's letter, Michael set sail via a route from west to east. The Culbertsons must have left New York in February because on April 24, 1858, Michael sent a letter from Java, and in May other letters from Hong Kong. He was at Hong Kong at least from May 21st to the 29th and on the latter date declared they had experienced a prosperous voyage of one hundred days. Michael, like Thaddeus and Elkanah, is the eternal positive thinker when a little negativism might have been more realistic. In June the Culbertsons were back in Shanghai.

After Michael's departure, Alec seems to have lost interest in wedding ceremonies of any sort or at least to have postponed once more the legalizing of his own marital status. But he had not lost interest in home-making, for on March 16th, he bought 160 more acres next to his other holdings near Peoria from a certain Southworth Shaw, at the total price of $1,600. This tract was in Limestone Township overlooking the Illinois River.

Natawista (according to a family tradition).
Photo courtesy of Mollie F. Culbertson Sedgwick.

But in spite of all these new concerns for a home in the east, quite typically Alec set everything aside to make the annual cruise up the Missouri. This time he and Natawista traveled on the *Spread Eagle* with Charles Chouteau, Jean La Barge, James Kipp, Andrew Dawson, the naturalist Thomas Kennard, some Yankton Sioux returning from Washington, D.C., and Father Thomas Scanlon. (Doesn't it seem that whichever way Alec turned, there was always someone at hand with a wee voice for his big ear?) Evidently, the *Spread Eagle* was representing AFC.

This was not the only cruise of the season, for the *Twilight* set out in May as a neutral ship or perhaps representing the Opposition. On board the *Twilight* was Henry Boller, who wrote a description of the leave-taking that may stand

Father De Smet & Indian Chiefs at close of Oregon War, 1857. This was a peace delegation conducted by Fr. De Smet for General Harney. Photo courtesy of Montana Historical Society, Helena.

as typical for the cruises of this period. Throngs of common folk swarmed aboard the steamer, which was delivering rolls of black pollution into the atmosphere along with a booming burst of steam. Robert Campbell was on hand for the send-off. He was titled now as "Colonel," more or less retired like Alec but still representing the Opposition. He was bidding farewell to Agent Vaughan and Malcolm Clarke, now a Campbell man as you recall. Malcolm was robed in a blue blanket capote and carried a tobacco sack of scarlet cloth delicately beaded by his Blackfeet wife.

Suddenly, there rang out the call to clear the decks. People scurried to and fro, on and off, in a chaos of adieux. Captain Shaw stood aloft on his hurricane deck taking the roll-call of his voyageurs, who in turn were intoning the boisterous Canadian boat-songs. The calliope played "Oh! Susanna." To veteran travelers it must have seemed like old times, now quickly coming to an end.

Back aboard the *Spread Eagle*, we catch up with Alec and the AFC people. They too should have seen the signs that the good old days were numbered. They began to meet starving Indians along the way. The Great Plains, Land of Bounty, were bountiful no longer. But in times of stress, people often learn to share, and at Fort Union, traditional enemies gathered together: Blackfeet, Crees, Assiniboines, Hidatsas. This was an explosive mixture, to be sure, as well as an acid test for recent treaties. But the traders, with the help of Natawista, persuaded the motley throng to keep the peace. (At least, such is the story in the accounts of the times.) Charles Chouteau celebrated with a feast for all.

The Culbertsons must have continued up to Fort Benton. There, on August 29, Alec met John Owen, who came over from St. Mary or Fort Owen in the

Bitterroot, and in September, Delaware Jim also reached Fort Benton.

Another who came over from the Flathead to the Blackfeet country (or at least claimed he did) was William T. Hamilton, that fair-haired boy of historians and—according to himself—of Army officers and officers' wives. He would become a founder of Missoula, and the namesake of a town in the Bitterroot. His story would be one we could pass up except that it concerns relatives of Natawista.

In 1858 Hamilton, in his own account, was sent by Colonel George Wright as a scout and spy from Walla Walla to determine the mood of the Blackfeet. With a "one-eyed half breed," he reaches the Flatheads in late September and crosses to Sun River and Agent Vaughan. (No explanation is given why Wright should thus be intruding on a military department not his own, especially since the Plains tribes seem to have been pretty calm this season.) From Sun River, Hamilton proceeds to the Piegan camp where he meets Little Dog and his son, the handsomest Indians he knows and the only ones he calls friends. The Fringe is now nineteen. But finding the Piegans encamped near some Crows and engaged with them in horse-racing, Hamilton manipulates the occasion to pro-voke tensions. (He is supposed to be on a peace mission.) Next day he goes to trade with (and spy on) a camp of what appear to be Bloods on the North Fork of the Milk River, provided by Little Dog with a passport of three arrows and escorted by The Fringe.

Even so, they are icily received by the Father of All Children and by Calf Shirt, who apparently had had a previous encounter with Hamilton somewhere in the south. So once more tensions are near the kindling point when The Fringe manages to get Hamilton safely out of the Blood camp and over the Hudson Bay Divide to the Kootenai camp of Black Bear on St. Mary Lake. But then, lo! The Bloods pursue and attack the Kootenais, driving the entire camp up the Red Eagle Valley and over the pass into Nyack, all during a running battle and much bravado from Hamilton. So instead of a peacemaker, Hamilton turns out to be a provocateur. But of course he is the hero of his own account, laced as it is with braggadoccio. At least one historian, Robert Burns, S.J., treats his story with caution since it has "such errors of detail, as to make it difficult to accept."

There is another point, however, that we should not overlook. The Father of All Children sometimes is identified with Bad Head, and this is one detail that fits into Hamilton's story. According to John Healy, the whiskey-trader who dealt with the Bloods from 1869 to 1874, Bad Head's band normally kept south of the border, and in 1860 John Palliser encountered Bad Head in the Cypress Hills seeking the body of a son killed by Crees.

Well, whether his tongue is straight or forked, Hamilton is always the perfect English gentleman. His golden rule: Never scalp an Indian in the presence of a lady.

The Culbertsons must by this time have returned to their home near Peoria. Nothing appears about further plans for their wedding. But Alec was still somewhat implicated in transactions regarding the Presbyterian mission to the Blackfeet, which Senator Lowrie reminded him about by letter, April 19, 1859. Lowrie admitted the mission project had "reluctantly" been shelved "at least for the present." Alec replied from Peoria on the 23rd that he was leaving for St. Louis on the 26th and would attend to business matters, adding "I am sorry you (have) given up the establishment of a Mission amongst the Blackfeet all tho I scarcely ever expect to visit them again I still feel an interest in their future welfare."

Never return to the Blackfeet? From St. Louis, Alec and Natawista continued right on up the river as if to have their honeymoon before their wedding. In 1859 they traveled on the *Spread Eagle*, which was accompanied by the stern-wheeler *Chippewa*. Their captain was Jean La Barge, their director Charles Chouteau and their fellow passengers Hayden, the German artist Karl Wimar (Weimar?), a young nobleman named Lord Richard De Aquila Grosvenor, Dr. Elias J. Marsh and later on, Jim Bridger and Agent Vaughan. This must have been the trip recorded by Henry Boller during which Natawista's brother Seen-From-Afar came down the Missouri to greet the Culbertsons as they came up the river. Boller names this chief "White-calf-that-disappears." In Blackfeet this would be *Ap-unista-sai-nakoyim*, the same name (minus the *Ap-*) by which he signed the treaty in 1855. (John Ewers identifies him as Seen-From-Afar.) Says Boller: "He was splendidly dressed, and had a magnificent bonnet of war-eagle feathers, falling to his feet. . ." His handsome wife, as usual, came with him. They had planned to wait at Fort Union for the arrival of the up-river steamer, but since some Crows were camped nearby, James Kipp discreetly sent them on down to Fort Berthold. Even so, the passage of this elegant chief through the country evidently stirred some panic: horse-rustling probably by Crows and Sioux, reinforcement of the guards and a dangerous prairie fire. In a more peaceful mood, when everyone got back up to Fort Union, Natawista presented Indian artifacts to Dr. Marsh, and Jean La Barge shifted to the *Chippewa* to take that vessel all the way up to the Marias. Whether the Culbertsons and Seen-From-Afar accompanied Captain Jean on this first steamboat cruise that far upstream we can only conjecture.

On the 19th of August, 1859, the Peoria press announced grandly that Major Culbertson would return home to Peoria the next day, Saturday, from the Upper Missouri, where he had now retired from his partnership in AFC, and would withdraw to the quiet of his estate. The announcement seems a bit premature because Alec probably retained some bond to the Company until 1861.

Anyhow, he was coming home to get married.

CHAPTER XX

Locust Grove

Alec's new home near Peoria was set in a lush green setting, enhanced by two elegant gates and a picket fence. Alec called his estate Locust Grove or Grove Mont. It was dominated by a gabled mansion with a grand mirror in the reception hall. A portrait of Natawista painted by John Mix Stanley was hung in the drawing room. The handsome grounds were landscaped by an English gardener but included paddocks of elk, antelope and buffalo as well as stables of fine eastern horses. All this, of course, required grooms and servants and who knows how much money for the upkeep.[48]

In summer, or Indian summer, Natawista in tribal dress retired to a tipi set up on the lawn. She was fond of emeralds and rubies but not of diamonds (fortunately!), fond also of wearing rings on every finger. Some of her gems eventually went to daughter Julia. With or without her jewelry, Natty preferred the tipi in summer because it was cooler there than in the house—though one must wonder how often she spent the summers at Locust Grove since she and Alec were so often on the river. White curiosity-seekers would ride by the estate just to marvel at the sight of an Indian lady bedecked with rubies and emeralds and living in an Indian lodge from the wild and mythical upper Missouri.

Once during these tipi days Natty emerged from her retreat to witness her horses wreck a carriage. She clapped with glee. There are two versions of this story. In one version she herself has a team of colts hitched to a brand-new carriage and then turned loose to smash it to smithereens. The other version, perhaps more plausible, has a team of high-steppers shy by accident and kick to pieces a fine English carriage. In both versions Natty laughs and applauds—a reaction you might expect of persons who are trying to make themselves immune to the pain of disaster. The Culbertson horses at Locust Grove were hot-blooded, but usually behaved themselves with better manners, or at least with dignity enough to carry off blue ribbons at county fairs and the horse show at Cincinnati.

The mansion at Locust Grove contained velvet floral carpets and imported wall-paper, original paintings and gilt-rimmed mirrors. Nothing is on record concerning the chandeliers, but certainly there must have been some fancy ones. Sofas and chairs were of rosewood, upholstered in velvet. All this extravagance offered son Jack his own special kind of fun. He liked to ride his horse up the mansion steps, and once brought in his pet goat, let it butt its reflection in the prize hall mirror and smash it to pieces—not altogether unlike Natty's carriage. How to pay for all this nice, clean fun? Well, there were rumors of sacks or

---

[48] Quaife, in his edition of Henry Boller, p. 306, says Alec's farm was 300 acres 6 miles west of Peoria, and that later he moved to a mansion on a bluff overlooking the city and only one mile from Peoria.

casks of gold coins in the basement. Guests were even allowed to dip their fingers into this treasure for the sake of hospitality, and Alec amused himself by tossing coins at turtles in the stream.

And this was the setting for the nuptials. It was quite a wedding! The Peoria journalists hardly knew how to handle it but managed to be discreet. The *Daily Transcript* labeled it "An Interesting Marriage Ceremony" and also "A marriage ceremony of a peculiar and interesting character. . ." Many must have held their tongues in their cheeks, particularly two or three of Alec's older children. Julia's granddaughter of later years liked to recall how Julia's eyes sparkled with delight when she would tell about that wedding day. It was Friday the 9th of September, 1859, when Alec and Nellie were united in holy wedlock at their own elegant "mansion house" with their four children in attendance and no one knows how many bemused guests. The vows were witnessed, not by DeSmet, but by Father Thomas Scanlon of St. Joseph. Old colleague James Kipp was on hand and the only guest mentioned by name in the news, though the guests were numerous. One would suppose Anna, who lived on the estate part-time, maybe the physician brother Samuel, Cyrus the pork-packer and James. . . The Peoria paper added that Mrs. Culbertson "is said to have rendered great service to Governor Stevens and Major Cummings"(sic), who was now Governor of Utah. The marriage license and certificates were both issued the same date as the ceremony was performed, and the license called Natawista by still another name: "Miss Natowiska—of the Blackfoot tribe. . ." The press commented that the bride was "a lady of fine talent" and took note of her "three very interesting children." (Interesting indeed! The reporters seem to have been at a loss for a non-commital term.)

Of the children, of course, four were Natty's and probably all four were on hand. Maria, the oldest of Alec's, was married to Samuel Kipp, probably a son of James by his "French wife" and residing at the Kipp farm in Missouri. Alec's other daughter Janie was also married about this time (1858 or 1859) but died in 1860. Son Jack was sixteen now, born at Union about 1843, and I wonder how he kept out of mischief during all this ritual (if he did). Julia was thirteen (by a family estimate) and Frances perhaps nine. Then there was the new one, baby Joe, born the 31st of January, probably 1859, in Peoria. His nurse held him up to witness the solemnities.

Both Julia and Fannie specialized in piano, and Julia even had a teacher named Pauling in residence at Locust Grove. (Later, it is said, he taught the children of Brigham Young.) Fannie was at the Moravian College in 1859, perhaps in the fall semester because we must suppose it was to her and to Julia that DeSmet refers when he mentions the convent at St. Louis in 1858. Fannie is also said (probably on her own testimony) to have put in a year at Maplewood near St. Louis majoring in piano. During her course there she spent week-ends at the Chouteau's and wondered about the slaves. Isaac Stevens held a reception for her aboard a river boat, presenting her with a loving cup inscribed "To the Second Pocahontas." (To date this reception we must recall that Stevens died in 1862.) The cup was destroyed in a warehouse fire in St. Louis along with other family treasures.

So the Culbertsons were perched at last on the top of the social escalator. Of course they became the object of gossip, always the fate of people on pedestals. There were the usual racist innuedoes, sly hints of alcoholism and heavy debts. Alec himself committed the *faux pas* of confiding to a friend that the reason behind the wedding was to keep the neighbors from gossiping about Natawista.

For the time being, the Culbertsons maintained their social status. We have a picture of life at Locust Grove while Joe was still an infant, and it comes from the recollections of a relative, Robert McCulloh, in later years a resident of Great Falls, a friend of Granville Stuart and a miner in the Sweet Grass Hills. (One of Robert's aunts married Alec's brother Cyrus, while another had been married to Alec's brother William.) Robert spoke of "Uncle Aleck," evidently a favorite family way of referring to Alexander. "Uncle Aleck," would visit Robert and his widowed mother in St. Louis just about every year, sometimes accompanied by his son Jack, who was around Robert's age. So the boys became pals. Mother would let him go to the estate seven miles from Peoria. Robert thought he was about eleven that "delightful summer" that he spent at Locust Grove. Long did he remember the paintings on the mansion walls, particularly the one of Fort Union, perhaps also one of Alec in hunting garb with Cyrus, John, Ferdinand or some other family visitor to the west. There was also an Indian boy named Kisenaw from Fort Union staying at the farm that summer. Kisenaw and Jack filled poor Robert's head with such tales of the west that he longed to be off. Julia and Fanny were at hand too, but perhaps there was some childish squabble between Robert and Julia. What summer vacation would be complete without that?

The presence of the Indian boy Kisenaw at Locust Grove or Grove Mont need not surprise us. There is evidence that the Culbertsons often took youngsters under wing. We shall notice later that Alec had a trading associate named Kisenar who had an Indian wife. Perhaps this lad was a son and his mother a Cree, because in Cree *kisinaw* means "(it's) cold weather." When James Kipp withdrew from the frontier to his farm and "French wife" in Missouri, he seems to have left his son Joe and Joe's mother Ipasha' in the custody of Alec and Natawista, returning up-river from time to time to visit them. Similarly, in the testimony of Julia Schultz, granddaughter of Standing Bull and daughter of a Frenchman, we are given a few private revelations: 1) Alec "always routed the women folks up to Benton" while he went to St. Louis on business; 2) Julia's mother Mary (Standing Bull) was raised with the four Culbertson children since about the age of seven (in the west?, in the east?); 3) the Culbertsons also took care of the two nieces of Natawista or other Blackfeet relatives, in particular, Louise and Melinda Chouquette. It is fair to point out that much of this oral testimony is unclear. Another interview, conducted for the National Park Service in 1982 with Selina Monroe, a daughter of Melinda, tells us that Melinda was educated at Peoria for nine years under the care of her aunt, Mrs. Culbertson. It also mentions the trips up and down the Missouri river. It is true that Melinda was educated well enough to become an official government interpreter. Selina's daughter adds a note to the interview: "She (Melinda) was in the audience when Lincoln was assassinated." Well, it is a long way from Peoria to the Ford Theater, D.C. But with Alec's involvement in politics, it is possible that the Culbertsons might have taken their little protegée, who was then 11 to 14 years old, to see the capital city. If so, it is odd we have no further evidence on the point. One cannot help but wonder whether Natawista, deprived of her own children, sought compensation in these foster daughters. A family report claims that she made tours among her own people in the west, so perhaps this was the occasion for contacting these youngsters. And we do get the impression that by the time they got their marriage finally formalized, both Alec and Natawista had grown accustomed to some independence from each other.

Alec once took pains to point out to Lt. Bradley that his colleagues in the fur trade usually provided their Indian offspring with a good education. Apparently, to Alec, "good education" meant sending your children away to boarding schools where they could learn to become good citizens for the white man's world.

Senator Benton was not Alec's only political friend. So too was Stephan A. Douglas. From this combination we can form some notion of Alec's political stance: Democratic, probably somewhat sympathetic toward the South but not "secesh" (Secessionist). The Democratic Party was now a house divided on the slavery issue, about which there is no evidence that Alec had any strong opinions. Surely, he must have followed the Lincoln-Douglas debates and attended some of them as they shifted about the state of Illinois. Douglas, though a Vermonter, was the chief proponent of the Kansas-Nebraska Bill of 1854 as a compromise between the pro- and anti-slavery forces. He had been a judge of the Illinois Supreme Court, then a Congressman, then a Senator. After the debates, he was re-elected over Lincoln, though in both 1852 and 1856 he failed to win the Democratic candidacy for president. In 1856 Frémont, the Republican candidate, lost the election to Buchanan (Scotch-Irish Presbyterian, born at Chambersburg, Pa., alleged descendent of the Stuarts, friend to AFC). In 1860 Douglas presented himself for nomination once again and this time with the support of Alec. In June of that year the press reported that "Colonel Culbertson" was on his way to Baltimore to help his old friend Douglas at the Democratic national convention.

In Baltimore, Alec probably encountered other old friends: John Mullan and Isaac Stevens. After the fiasco with martial law in Washington Territory, Stevens had become a territorial delegate to Congress and now threw himself with his usual wholeheartedness into the struggles of the national convention. And though an old friend of Douglas, Stevens now opposed him and played an energetic role in sundering the Democratic Party. Stevens, regardless of his public image, had never been much of a reconciler. When the Democratic Party split in two, both halves lost to Lincoln. Alexander Culbertson, in his customary roles of pragmatist and loyalist, was once again planting himself in the middle of conflicting interests. That is not the Golden Mean.

On February 2nd, 1860, the Peoria press reported that a home owned by "Maj. Culbertson" and rented to tenants, was set afire by some defect in the stovepipe and burned to the loss of $1,500. It had stood about five miles from town. It was not a good time for Alec to be losing $1,500.

Having never completely severed his connection with the old dominion on the high Missouri, Alec was still running up and down the river in 1860, this time for the historic first trip all the way to Fort Benton, the unique inland voyage of 3,000 miles. A veritable flotilla set out: the *Spread Eagle* under Jean La Barge, the *Chippewa* and the *Key West II*, carrying 300 soldiers to the frontier. It was quite a triumph! Though the *Spread Eagle* had to stop near El Paso Point, the other two vessels did reach Fort Benton. The dream of thirty years or so had at last been fulfilled.

But the very next year the *Chippewa* exploded, blew up the treaty goods solemnly guaranteed to the Blackfeet, and so precipitated a chain-reaction of problems.

And on December 20th, 1860, South Carolina seceded from the Union.

CHAPTER XXI

The View From the Towers of China

Where the River Huangpu,[49] emptying the westward lakes into the estuary of the Yangtze, is intercepted by Suchow Creek, there you find Shanghai. You may prefer to call these intersecting creeks and rivers mere sloughs or bayous, for this is the tidal delta of the Son of the Sea, flat as a griddle and wide as the sky. But if you took no caution with the tides, you might have found your craft fatefully trapped among pirate junks. So it had been for countless generations, and so it would be for a few years more. Shanghai itself was walled against the pirates, enclosing the Blue Willow Teahouse so often pictured on English china. At the end of the Opium Wars, the British were allowed a concession outside the walls, which soon became the hub of international trade, intrigue and imperialism. The French and Americans followed the British into the International Settlement and between the old walled "Chinese City" and Suchow Creek. With twenty ships or more in port, Shanghai seemed like a haven of security: "quite a European city" declared Michael, adding incongruously, "Like a New England country town."

"Glance at the country around Shanghai and Ningpo," Michael advises. "The land teems with inhabitants." He goes on to describe a wayfarer in his sedan chair, or another in a wheelbarrow, or even a pedestrian treading the narrow pathways between the rice paddies. Other travelers cruise on the canals or rivers, "one of which is always near" in this rich land by the sea. The two cities he knows best, Shanghai and Ningpo, each have a population of "some three hundred thousand," and he believes there must be many cities practically unknown to foreigners. In such vast multitutudes, Michael finds much to disturb him: their ignorance of God's unity and of "the turpitude of sin." He is distressed to see a beggar left to die naked and hungry in the street, and in the rhetoric of his age, he enumerates "the superstititions by which Satan maintains his hold upon the minds of this people." Yet he seems not to reflect that his own position in China is reinforced by the opium trade thrust upon the Chinese people by American and European hookers during the infamous Opium Wars, much the same as his brother Alec's position among the American Indians is supported by rot-gut hookers and corporate prostitution.

To illustrate his point, he tells us about the towers of China. Subtle influences, says he, whether benign or malevolent, are thought to be everywhere in China, and "elevated objects possess great efficacy in collecting and spreading them." Towers of five, seven, even nine stories are erected to safeguard the people from "noxious influences." These Buddhist pagodas are costly to build and necessary for the sake of *fēng-shŭi* (wind-water, that is, geomancy, enviro-

---

[49] Traditional spelling of Chinese terms will be used in the text. The official spelling now used by the government of the People's Republic appears in the Index.

Lúng Lúa Temple near Shanghai. Photo by the author.

ment). Shanghai has its pagoda of *Lúng-Húa* (Dragon Flower), and built orginally in the Sung Dynasty and set in a peach orchard near the winding Huang-pu a site with ideal *fēng-shŭi*. Michael recalls a belfry in Ningpo that was thought to spread malignant radiations onto the parade ground, and a street that so resembled a centipede that it was subject to the malicious spell of that insect.

To protect the street an arch was erected surmounted by a rooster in effigy. But alas, near that very street the Presbyterians built a church with a high tower, higher by a few feet than the arch of the rooster. To counteract this Presbyterian curse, the people placed fierce images of tigers on top of the buildings round about, but to little avail, for a conflagration wiped out portions of Centipede Street. The only solution was to build a Chinese tower taller even than the church tower and topped off by the figure of a catamount (presumably the stylized "lion"or "dog of Buddha"). The power of the catamount was clearly demonstrated when the "Papists" came along to build a cathedral. All in a single night, the "papal walls" came tumbling down!

In Shanghai, Michael saw the game of the towers begin all over. Here it was the Baptist Church that terrorized a Chinese neighborhood with its offensive tower, believed to have caused the death of a local mandarin. Not only the tower, but even the color of the church was blameworthy, like the color of the Anglican church. The resident protested the missionaries' use of the color red, begging the American consul to intervene. Red, of course, is the color of fire—a perpetual menace in the Far East. So the *tao-tai* (magistrate) complained to the consul that the *fēng-shǔi* must be favorable: For south of the building stood the temple of the god of fire, facing north in accordance with the diagrams for fire and water. Therefore, water controlled fire and prosperity reigned. But should the Presbyterians have constructed high walls or an obnoxious tower toward the west, the direction related to metal, they would bring into conflict metal and fire and so precipitate a chain-disaster of fire, disease, and who-knows-what.

Michael had good reason to learn everything that went on in the American consulate. The U.S. government was not behindhand in discovering his talents and his West Point training and decided that he must serve two masters and render unto Caesar some of the expertise he was dedicating to God (very much as it had done with both Alec and DeSmet). So even while Michael was engaged in the redaction of the Bible into Chinese, the U.S. State Department put him to work as secretary and interpreter at the American legation in Shanghai. The stamina which enabled him to undertake these diversified obligations was attributed by Michael himself to the discipline instilled into him at West Point. As it turned out, he was speaking prematurely. In any case, he served at the legation during the tenure of U.S. envoys Marshall, Ward, McLane and Burlingame.

But if Shanghai was ever really the peaceful place it sounds like from Michael's comparisons with a city of Europe or New England, that serenity was soon shattered by conflict much more vicious than the petty squabbling over the height of towers. That was the Tai Ping Rebellion. It began in Canton, in an area where the Manchu overlords had massacred thousands and from which other thousands were escaping to California, the Old Gold Hill. It spread northward to engulf the lower Yangtze Chiang and lasted from approximately 1848 to 1866. Though its name means "the Great Peace," it was in fact an incredibly bloody civil war. In some ways it resembles the Prophet Dance movement among the Northwest Indians—though of course on the much larger scale of everything in China. Both were nativistic reactions against imperialism. Inspired by a Hakka prophet named Hung Hsiu-chuan, who blended Christian and ancient Chinese ideas, the original Tai Pings taught the fatherhood of God (Shang-Ti) and the brotherhood of mankind, as implied in the ancient and most succinct formula of the doctrine ever devised: *Tiān hsia, Yī chīa* (under Heaven, one family). The proverb is still esteemed in China today, altogether destructive of all the dichotomies I have so doggedly enumerated in the course of this narrative. Hung was also following the Confucian theory of *Tiān ming,* "the mandate of Heaven." The early Tai Pings called themselves the Worshippers of God, included Chinese Muslims into their ranks, but allied themselves with non-worshippers among the fanatical tongs. The British, French and American merchants made some early pretense of neutrality.

In 1853 the Tai Pings had captured Nanking and made it their capital. The first hard news of the idol-smashing insurgents was brought down the river in May by the British steamer *Hermes*. Michael was happy to learn the inconoclasts had let their hair grow long in defiance of the Manchu decree that Hans must shave their heads leaving only the single queue. But the war unleashed forces beyond restraint: robber bands, secret societies, terrorists generally. They captured Amoy, and on the 7th of September a terrorist gang called the Red-Headed Rebels (not Tai Pings), occupied Shanghai itself. Shutting the South Gate, they manned the walls of the old fishing village and blocked out the missionaries. Imperialist forces of the Manchus were crowding in to strike back, catching the missionaries in a pincer movement. Though the Manchus recovered Amoy, they failed at Shanghai, where the walls were held by insurgents of one sort or another until February 1855, while the suburbs were reduced to wreckage. Throngs of refugees flooded the foreign concessions as the Tai Pings continued to advance on Peking. In December the French streamer *Cassini* reached Nanking and brought word back to Michael, reassuring him that the Tai Pings were sincere about their reforms. As proof, they exposed the heads of opium-eaters. Michael's government boss, Frederick Townsend Ward, a veteran filibuster in Central America, took a warlike stance of his own, siding first with the Tai Pings, then, privately with the Imperialists.

An equal vexation to Michael must have been his break with the London Missionary Society, by order of its directors in London: "We shall not consider ourselves represented in any Committee of delegates for the work of translating the Old Testament into Chinese, who have been appointed by agents of any other society."

In October and November, 1854, Legate McLane sent Michael on the *Powhatan* to Hong Kong. Arriving there December 1st, Michael went promptly up to Canton and no doubt Zion Corners and he ultimately returned to Shanghai with his own health improved, but with Shanghai in worse straits than ever. In April, 1855, the foreigners retaliated against the Manchu forces and drove them out. So poorly were the troops controlled that had it not been for the ships in port—U.S., French, British—the international settlement might not have survived. In May, Michael was off again, this time with McLane, on a cruise up the Yangtze to Nanking. Though he was not able to confer with the insurgent "kings," he did learn a lot about the revolution. It was at this juncture that he took his trip back to the States with his family.

When the Culbertsons returned from the U.S. to their home at Hong-chew, they must have found things but little improved. In the interval, missionaries had come and gone, chapels and schools had been established, tracts and linguistic studies put into print, but few converts were made. One who did convert was Ve Nae-kwae who had gone to the U.S. with a missionary couple. He seemed hopelessly unimpressed by New York or anything else in America, except the grass. But on his return to China, he converted to please Reuben Lowrie, devoted more to persons that to abstractions. Reuben died in Shanghai in 1860, leaving a four-year old son James, who was taken to America by his mother. It would be many years before James would return to China to make himself the most noted of the Lowrie clan, fulfilling in Peking what neither Lowries or Culbertsons would accomplish in Shanghai. Michael could not have foreseen this result,but he must have realized by now that his own task was to lay a foundation on which the next generation could build. He went back to work translating the Bible and preaching on Sundays both in English and Chinese. He took part in interdenominational affairs, even with the London Missionary Society. So much the better, for the Society included among its members the most distinguished Protestants in China, men like James Legge, John Chalmers and Hung Jen-kan, the cousin of the Prophet and an exceptional scholar. The Society provided sensible scholarship to replace the pioneer propaganda that had misfired in the Prophet Hung.

But already in February, 1860, we find Mary Culbertson departed for Japan along with eldest daughter Helen. Mary had been sick with diarrhea since the return to China and Dr. Burton advised Michael to send her on a health-quest aboard Olyphant's freighter *Celestial*. The accommodations were good, and the supercargo, Chun Lai-sun, was a personal friend. Though the elder Olyphant was deceased, he had left a son to carry on his commercial and missionary concerns. Mary was to spend two months in Kanazawa, a village sandwiched in between Yokohama and the ancient temple city of Kamakura. With Fuji aglow on the horizon, this country is one of the most picturesque and traditional corners of Japan, bristling with Buddhist temples and Shinto shrines; a center for Zen. Mary must have been amazed and shocked, especially by the magnificent *Daibutsu*, the giant bronze Amida Buddha. She was, however, still at Kanazawa in March, and poor Michael had been left home to mother the other daughters and was blue already on February 18th.

But Michael was again caught up in the turmoil of the Tai Pings. The effort to maintain a neutrality zone of one hundred *li* (about 30 miles) around Shanghai was not a success, and the merchant princes of the world must keep up the opium traffic. If the Tai Pings claimed the Mandate of Heaven, so did the Manchus; and the British, who have never been much concerned about mandates from Heaven, behaved as a "nation of shopkeepers" normally would. They swung toward favor with the Imperialists, and the French followed suit. Admiral Hope joined his forces to the French and to the "Ever Victorious" mercenaries of Ward in onslaughts against the Tai Pings that resulted in horrible atrocities. Eventually, Ward was killed and bequeathed his command to the pious and eccentric "Chinese" Gordon. The cause of the Tai Pings was doomed, but died slowly. Hung would soon perish of disease (cholera?) while his compassionate general Lu, his learned cousin Jen-kan and his teen-age son would all be executed. The British and French invaded Peking and burned the summer palace.

Michael's role in the military activities is hard to assess. the one-time drillmaster at West Point was put to the task of drilling civilians and sailors by day and touring the outposts by night—as military commander. I presume the "outposts" must have meant terrain between Suchow Creek, the Lung Hua pagoda and the Bund on the waterfront. I would hazard the guess that the "civilians and sailors" meant foreigners in Shanghai and the ships in port: British, French, Portuguese, Americans, Filipinos, Sikhs and some Chinese as well. At his side once again, Michael swung the old dress sword he had worn at West Point, as he now marched his troops on his big Culbertson feet. If he seems out of joint as a missionary doing military duty, I can only comment that the times were a bit out of joint too.

He must have been at hand at the legation to greet some of the prestigious visitors heading that way to assess the revolution, if not to endorse it. In 1860 William Radford (Admiral-to-be) sailed a U.S. Navy sloop up the Yangtze to the city of Hankow. Radford, of course, was the son of Harriet Kennerly, cousin to Henry Kennerly of Fort Benton, brother-in-law to the late Kearny and stepson to William Clark. Another caller of these times was Thomas Blakiston, who had broken with Palliser during their exploration of western Canada and their side-trip into Natawista's homeland. He named Waterton Lakes for the naturalist and explored the Kootenay pass and the northern fringe of Glacier National Park on the border (1858). In early 1861 he appeared on the Yangtze. On February 11 he found Shanghai soaked in rain and deep mud. Except for an occasional coolie, the Bund was deserted and the "Chinese city" only "dimly visible." Next day, the squadron of Admiral Hope, of which Blakiston was a member, sailed out via Wusung into the Yangtze estuary to behold the sweeping devastation caused by both the Imperialists and insurgents. Hope conducted his forces beyond the Grand Canal, beyond Nanking, then turned back, leaving a detachment under Blakiston with a few Chinese, Europeans and Sikh sepoys to plough their way upstream on a Chinese junk, through rapids and mighty gorges, to a point 1,800 miles above the sea. It was a remarkable trip, but Blakiston had to admit that a few Catholic missionaries had got there before him, in disguise.

The Culbertsons sold their house at Hong-chew for taels 6750 (evidently Mexican dollars), which went into the missionary coffers, and moved to a new house facing the river in the devastated area. Nearby stood buildings for the press, chapel and other quarters. One of the missionaries invented a system of printing in the thousands of Chinese characters or types and "a new method of making the type matrix." By this time, the missionaries had gained more freedom of travel and were able to spread out northward into China, all perhaps because the Manchu Emperor issued an edict of toleration toward Christians. Nevertheless, many Confucian patricians continued bitter opposition to Christianity. Since Christianity and Confucianism have so much on common, this hostility seems peculiarly ironic. Michael reasoned it was directed more against foreigners and foreign influence "than against Christ. Religious rancour seems not to be one of the traits of Chinese character." One special problem the Chinese had with Christians was the Christian preoccupation with rescuing castaway children, especially unwanted baby girls. In March of 1862 riots destroyed a Catholic church and orphanage, and though Bishop Navarro went in person to Peking seeking justice, the tensions increased. Presbyterian orphanages, however, seem to have weathered the storm.

Shanghai, during these turbulent times, was a strange place to raise a gaggle of American daughters. If I have failed to tell you much about the Culbertson children, it is because the references about them are full of discrepancies and illegibles. In 1861 the oldest daughter Helen must have been "sixteen going on seventeen" or certainly of a marriageable age. Interracial marriage was often abhorrent to the churchly establishment (reflect on Alec's apparent duplicity). So it must have been a monumental worry for the father of delightful daughters in a land almost devoid of young white bachelors. French or Portuguese "Romanists" would never do, and a white Presbyterian girl growing up in the midst of Oriental males would naturally develop an Oriental sense of masculine beauty. But alas, the Presbyterian annals tell us little or nothing of such problems. Yet we can hardly assume that therefore the problems did not exist. But. . .well it is obviously bad taste to bring the matter up.

Here are the few simple facts the sources reveal about the daughters of Michael and Mary. The Snively genealogy mentions three of them, all born in China: Helen, Josephine and Cornelia; then as if by after-thought, it adds Alice. Both Helen and Alice married missionaries: Helen married Rev. Mr. Kipp and Alice, Rev. Van Dyke. Josephine and Cornelia eventually moved to the U.S. Michael wrote Lowrie in late October, 1861, that Helen was expected to marry

Rev. Leonard W. Kip (sic) of the Dutch Board of Missions when she should become eighteen in a little over a year. He was happy for this but sad to report the death of his youngest daughter, Alice Julia at eighteen months of age in April. "This is the fourth time we have been thus smitten." And again on August 17th he reported ". . .it has pleased our Heavenly Father again to lay his hand heavily upon us." This time it was "dear Lilly" who was taken, the youngest after Alice Julia. He attributed her death to the extreme heat, adding that Mrs. Culbertson was also very feeble. A letter in the archives at West Point, written from Shanghai in 1946 describes the Culbertson gravestone in the Shantung Road Cemetery. Though the markings were then barely discernible, they did mention four daughters buried there: Alice Julia, Emma Fitch, Laura, and Lilly. Both Alice Julia and Laura are recorded as dying in 1861,(a mis-reading?). Whatever became of Mary who went to America in 1856? Did she stay there in school?

In spite of these catastrophic losses, Michael Simpson plodded on through his duties. For a relief, Mr. Olyphant offered to pay his passage to Japan or Shantung. So, to escape the heat and fevers, he took passage on a Siamese ship with all Siamese and Malay crewmen and a German captain and mate. With his two younger children and wife Mary he came aboard early in September, but when they put to sea the ship was nearly wrecked and had to "run for Amoy" instead Shantung. Writing from Amoy to Senator Lowrie in October, Michael relates their great enjoyment of a month at that port, but he expects a rough passage home to Shanghai because of the northeast monsoon. The current monsoon season is one of the worst in years, but one blessing has come out of it for it has brought Helen and Kipp together.

Amid all these distractions, even with the guns of battle booming in his ears, Michael Simpson toiled on with his work on the Scriptures. Though it is stated that he translated the Bible into Chinese, with little or no mention of his collaborators, he himself straightens the story out. Besides the two Chinese scribes, one at his right hand, one at his left, he had special co-workers, among them Dr. Boone the Episcopalian Bishop of China and Dr. Bridgman, the pioneer of 1830. For fifteen years the delegates had been occupied with his tremendous opus, but in 1861 Dr. Bridgman was cut off by death, and Michael had to struggle on without him. Even as the insurgents were capturing Hangchow and closing in ever tighter on Shanghai, Michael concluded his task:

> On the 17th of March, 1851, our Committee, consisting of five members, began their work. On the 27th of March 1862, I brought it to a close, having been left single-handed by the lamented death of my only remaining colleague, Dr. Bridgman, in November last. The translation of the New Testament, and of the Old as far as *Isaiah*, is the joint work of Dr. Bridgman and myself. From *Isaiah* to *Malachi* I translated alone, though most of it was done prior to Dr. Bridgman's death. I have found it a delightful work...

He goes on to say he hopes to see the whole book in a uniform edition, of which 1,500 copies have already been started. "Our new cylinder press, so long detained,. . . has just arrived. . ." But in the same letter he strikes a forboding note: "The smallpox is very prevalent among the Chinese and large numbers have died from it." He himself had a mild case but was pleased he apparently did not pass it on.

It is interesting to notice Michael's other collaborators: Walter Medhurst of London, a Congregationalist; Dr. William Martin, Presbyterian from Indiana who would become President of the Imperial University in Peking. And in civil affairs, Michael's boss at the legation, Anson Burlingame, the man for whom the city in California was named, amiable and easy to get along with—so much so that he squirmed his way into the confidence of the Empress Dowager.

The *Biblical Repertory* gives us a portrait of Michael: a man of vigorous constitution and rare good sense, a cheerful companion, kind, considerate, a reverent Christian, methodical but buoyant in spirit. Someone has proposed that Michael saw himself as a Christian soldier, though this concept is likely to be controversial. More to the point is the series of vignettes Dr. Martin drew from the story of Michael's life: as a lad with his playmates on the banks of the Susquehanna (perhaps he refers to the Huling home at the mouth of the blue Juniata), as a cadet among his fellow cadets in bright, trim uniforms on the heights above the Hudson. There too were Halleck, McDowell and Beauregard... But Michael, instead, must serve Christ in China, where in his "quiet laboratory," his eye bright but his hair beginning to gray, seated with his Chinese scribes he stayed busy at the mighty translation, preparing it for the revolving cylinder press which will send it all over China...

In January 1862, probably, Michael addressed Walter Lowrie to describe the terrors that began to close in on Shanghai:

> The rebels have again become very troublesome. They are advancing upon us from all sides, probably in very large force. The English and French are resolved to hold the city against them... We can muster, all told, about 3,000 men...

There was always the threat of a cut-off of supplies. And at Wusung the French had driven back the rebels with much bloodshed. "What the result will be no man can tell...Our trust is in God, and we hope these days of trial may be shortened." People were pouring in from the country round about Shanghai to seek refuge in the International Settlement. But the health of the missionaries was fairly good.

On June 3rd, 1862, Michael wrote again to up-date his report: "The rebels are surrounding us in immense numbers, bent on mischief." British forces have been withdrawn from elsewhere to concentrate on Shanghai, and "We are so well fortified and have so large a force that no alarm is felt. Reinforcements have been sent for from Tientsing and Saigon." And Michael had heard that 10,000 men had been summoned from India. What he added must have tasted like bile:

> All hope for any direct and immediate good from this rebellion I confess is now taken away. They are carrying on a war of extermination against the peaceful inhabitants of the country around us. They murder in cold blood all they meet, young and old, unless they can use them for their own hellish purposes. Thousands are now flocking in from the country who have fled for their lives leaving everything behind them. They are lying about the city dying of disease and starvation. May God have mercy on poor China.

Disturbing too was the news about the War Between the States that filtered to China through California with "conflicting" reports of battles and horrible "carnage."

With the concentration of the dead and dying, little wonder that a wave of cholera swept over the land and struck down its victims indiscriminately. In July, one victim was the missionary who had just opened a station in Shantung. Then another was Michael Simpson. This occurred on a Sunday near the end of summer, when he preached three sermons.

In his last days he was visited by Anson Burlingame, perhaps on his way to or from Peking, and Burlingame as well as Dr. Martin reminded Michael that if he had remained in the U.S.Army he might now be one of the great generals of the Civil War in America. Michael ran over the list of his old school-mates at West Point,some of them now fighting for the North, some for the South, while he alone struggled with the civil war in China. Yes, it was a distinguished roll-call: Ord, Canby, Halleck, VanVliet, Hancock, Beauregard, Grant and Sherman. Perhaps on his death-bed Michael even recalled Malcolm Clarke and Isaac Stevens.

"Yes," Michael conceded. "But there is not one among them with whom I would change places. No task in all the world could be better than giving the Word of God to four hundred million Chinese."

Soon after that, on August 25, 1862, the Lord came for Michael Simpson once again—this time for keeps.

CHAPTER XXII

Civil War, West

The War Between the States spelled the doom of the hide and fur trade and precipitated the Indian Wars along the frontier. It drove westward many people whose wills had been forged in the furnace of fratricidal strife. Missouri was a state with Southern bonds, where most of the river folk were Southern sympathizers. Its Creole families were steeped in Southern tradition and held many slaves, whereas recent German immigrants had no use for slavery. Yet the population was often dependent on the Union Army and its local investments, while the Army was dependent on the river boats. Traffic was on the increase on the Missouri as AFC tried to push its steamers all the way to Fort Benton. In Montana the gold rush, started by the Stuart brothers of Virginia, offered gold and escape for men who wanted to avoid the warfare. Wagon trains competed with river boats to reach the upper Missouri, and James Fisk brought 52 wagons from Minnesota. This invasion did nothing to guarantee Indian treaty rights, and a climax came with the Sioux uprising in Minnesota in 1862. The river would never be the same.

Typical of the war years along the Missouri was the dilemma of Joseph LaBarge. Having met Lincoln on the tour of 1859, he declared at once that the days of slaves were gone for good. Sadly, he released his slaves and took the oath of loyalty to the Union with his heart still in the South. LaBarge's powerful rival, the family Chouteau, was Southern to the core, and their premier post, Fort Union, was reputed to be a hot-bed of secessionists.

Pierre le Cadet was going blind, but his son and heir Charles swore allegiance to the Union. Most steamers on the Missouri were owned by Northerners, piloted by Southerners and manned by crewmen of every persuasion under the stars. Senator Benton, champion of the Chouteaus, opposed secession but not salvery, while his son-in-law Frémont, commander of the Union Army of the West, forthrightly decreed that the slaves were free (1861). Lincoln, not to be pre-empted, cancelled his decree. David Mitchell of Virginia hated slavery, though his beloved white wife kept a slave girl, whom David bluntly refused to discipline. Western governors became generals: Isaac Stevens for the Union, Alfred Cumming of Utah for the Confederacy. In Montana ex-Virginians, like the Stuarts, rooted for "secesh"at a safe distance. Then there was the enigmatic Alexander Culbertson of Peoria, believed to favor the North but opposed to Lincoln, friendly to Douglas and to Rebels (openly or cryptically) and notoriously influential with the Indians of the high Missouri. The Buchanan administration had contracted AFC to continue transporting annuities to the Indians, but the Lincoln administration limited the contract to 1861 and sent soldiers aboard Company boats to make sure the annuities went to Indians and not Confederates. Lincoln also started a big turn-over in appointees to the Indian service, introducing adversaries of AFC.

The Civil War on the Missouri amounted to much more than a bureaucratic fuss. It broke out in bloodshed and massive destruction. Bands of guerrillas swarmed along the southern river banks between St. Louis and Kansas City, firing upon steamers and commandeering cargoes. Union troops stationed onboard set up barricades of cotton bales and iron shields, especially around the wheel-house. Throngs of passengers poured onto the streamers to flee the war or to seek the "New El Dorado" in the gold fields of Montana, Idaho and British Columbia. Once or twice Joseph LaBarge came near being lynched and took the precaution of anchoring his vessels at night in midstream. In 1861, when he picked up some Rebel sympathizers on the *Emilie*, the colonel at Leavenworth wanted to hang him. As he started to land, a friend leapt aboard and tipped him off in the nick of time. And when Confederate General Marmaduke commandeered his steamer, Union forces placed LaBarge under arrest. The city of St. Joseph was half reduced to ashes or rubble and presented a somber spectacle to river travelers.And the *Sam Gaty* was ambushed by guerrillas who pulled off paroled soldiers and "contrabands" (ex-slaves) and massacred them on shore.

During the winter of 1861-1862 Joseph LaBarge, his brother Jean, Eugene Jaccard, James Harkness and William and/or Charles E. Galpin each contributed $10,000 to form a corporation for trade in Montana, an operation which once more put LaBarge into opposition to AFC. In the spring of 1862 the new company's two steamers, the *Emilie* (named for Joseph's daughter) and the *Shreveport* were sent together with freight and passengers to Fort Benton. Even though he had never before gone so far into Montana, Joseph himself commanded the *Emilie*, while Jean probably was captain of the *Shreveport*. It was to be one of the most memorable of all the runs in the history of the river, for the American Fur Company was also sending two steamers to Fort Benton: The *Spread Eagle*, a side-wheeler in command of Robert Bailey, and the *Key West*, another side-wheeler under William Humphreys. (Note that both rival companies had boats with Southern names and involved reluctant allegiance to the North.) The *Spread Eagle* was a luxurious queen of the waters, well equipped for pleasure cruising in war time. And at the AFC offices, two blocks from the Mississippi, old Pierre le Cadet arrived in his private coach with his black coachman to aid him in his blindness as he came to bid *adieu* to his son Charles, ready to embark on the *Spread Eagle*. On May 10th the steamer pulled out, perhaps to the boom of guns and the tunes of the calliope. Also on board was a colorful array of passengers: the Rev. H.W. Reed, Methodist clergyman appointed as agent for the Blackfeet in accord with Lincoln's policy of putting clergy in charge of Indians; Father DeSmet bringing supplies up to Benton to be transshipped to his Oregon missions; Malcolm Clarke, returning to his Piegan family; Andrew Dawson, the new king of the Upper Missouri, accompanying his half-Indian son home from school in Scotland; young Joe Kipp, the son of James by his Mandan wife; Charles Chouteau now in charge; Lewis Henry Morgan, "the father of American anthropology" recording the adventure in his *Indian Journals*; and of course, a couple whom Morgan found most informative, Colonel and Mrs. Alexander Culbertson of Peoria with their two handsome children (probably Jack and Fannie). Natawista showed Morgan a picture of another daughter, Julia, probably 16 or so and staying at home. You might have thought people like the Culbertsons and LaBarges would be bored to Sheol by the annual trips on the river or else scared away by the risks from guerrillas. At least so for Alec, who had abdicated his kingship, accumulating from 1839 to 1861 what was called a fortune in those days and calculated at $300,000. But still they came. They couldn't miss this one.

Natawista answered Morgan's queries about her people. Other informants for Morgan were Joe Kipp and Father DeSmet, so that in this way, these three made their contributions to science. Lewis Henry Morgan knew, either personally or by correspondence, just about every notable anthropologist of his day as well as many other scientists, writers, sociologists in this country and abroad. Examples: Eli Parker, Longfellow, Herbert Spencer, Charles Darwin, Thomas Huxley, Francis Parkman, Henry Adams. To such men as these he passed on his information and his theories on cultural evolution and communal property among American Indians. Especially impressed, it seems, were Friedrich Engels and Karl Marx (albeit Morgan was a good Presbyterian). It would be curious to know how many of these men were getting the message from Natawista. Morgan also picked up a few tidbits from Alex: the story of his courtship of Natawista and his opinion that among the Indians neither men nor women felt any passion of love![50] What an ominous hint about his own married life, a dreary notion for such a happy cruise, and a theory reminiscent of Denig's.

And a happy cruise it was proving to be. Charles Chouteau provided his old teacher Father DeSmet with a special chapel aboard the *Spread Eagle* for daily Mass. And for the less pious, there was plenty of drinking and gambling, but nothing to excess. At landings Indians sometimes danced to entertain the tourists and generally evinced no hostility. For the military-minded, there were drills on deck conducted by John Mason Brown. And, in the evening at dinner, there were concerts by the minstrels. The food was good too, and better when you dined to music.

Indians occasionally came aboard as passengers. But there were little problems. Above Fort Pierre the Sioux were in a belligerent mood, held a council with Charles Chouteau and Agent Latta and roundly scolded them both. Chouteau finally made them some gifts and shoved off quickly while the chance was still good. And so the *Spread Eagle* churned grandly up the river in the lead, when lo and behold, near Fort Berthold she was overtaken by an opposition boat, the *Emilie*, under Joseph LaBarge. The race was on: AFC versus the monopoly-breakers. When the *Emilie* took advantage of a side channel to steal the lead from Charles Chouteau, Captain Bailey deliberately crashed the bow of the *Spread Eagle* into the starboard side of poor *Emilie* opposite her boilers. Captain LaBarge in his pilot house threatened to shoot but was restrained, it is said, by his son, though some of his passengers made similar challenges. Finally Captain Bailey dropped back. The *Emilie* reached Fort Benton four days ahead, along with the *Shreveport,*, on the 17th of June, 1862. Chouteau had to resort to cordelling over some of the rapids.

Back in St. Louis, Bailey was brought to trial and his license revoked. Since he had a large family, he gulped down his pride and pleaded with Joseph LaBarge, putting the blame on AFC agents and asking Joseph to intercede for him. Joseph did, and Bailey got his license restored.

From Fort Benton ethnologist Morgan returned down-river with the *Spread Eagle* while Alec and presumably Natawista went on to the Blackfeet agency on Sun River with the Rev. Reed. The *Shreveport* and probably Jean LaBarge remained on the upper Missouri for the season since this vessel was of lighter draft for these shallower waters. Partner Harkness remained in Montana too, supervising the construction of the Opposition's new post, Fort LaBarge, made of logs and adobes on approximately the site of the present Grand Union Hotel

---

[50] This is, of course, another controversial stereotype. Too bad we have no replies from the various wives of Alec and Denig.

in Fort Benton. A tourist party took off to visit the Great Falls of the Missouri between Benton and the Sun. The tourists included Madame Jean LaBarge, Tom LaBarge, Margaret Harkness, Father DeSmet, Natawista and son Jack and perhaps Fannie. Most of them traveled by ambulance, camping overnight and dining on antelope. Though their guide was Cadotte, one of the most experienced of guides, they did encounter a party of Bloods. Father DeSmet and Natawista saved everyone a little embarrasment on the occasion—and maybe a little more.

This was the year the Missouri flooded, high enough at Benton to wash the lower portion of Alexander's adobe walls at the old fort. This caused some damage but no disaster, since the walls were three feet thick. It was also the summer that Andrew Dawson got a package of sand from a supposed priest who lived among the Bloods and Blackfeet. Dawson washed the sand and out came gold. The pretended priest is called La Rue in the annals of Fort Benton and in a story of J.W. Schultz, but probably he was Jean L'Heureux, a well-known imposter. He promised to reveal the source of the gold to those who came seeking it. And though a number did go seeking, from the Marias almost to Edmonton, (and probably illegally) they found neither the gold nor the "priest."

This is also the summer when the town of Deer Lodge is supposed to have put down roots, as a sort of off-spring of Fort Benton beyond the Divide. A few Bentonites or other old engagés of Mexican origin and Indian families (the brothers Lavatta, Joe Hill, Joe Pizanthy, Pete Martínez and others) had already moved over to the Deer Lodge valley and started a village called Spanish Fork in their honor or Cottonwood in nobody's honor. Now, after the *Shreveport* departed down the river, Harkness got together an ox train and brought over provisions for the mines around Deer Lodge. He is said to have reached there on July 23 and at Spanish Fork laid out the new LaBarge City.

In August, Alec Culbertson bought a mackinaw from Andrew Dawson, his own successor as King of the Golden River (so called with apologies to Ruskin). Dawson was also in partnership with twenty-four war-dodgers from Missouri. In September they all set out down the river, presumably with Natty, Jack and Fanny. At Milk River they were intercepted by an Assiniboine war-party. But as we would expect, when the warriors recognized Alec, they let his party pass in peace. In compensation, however, they pillaged the next boat. This was but an inkling of more desperate times to come in the wake of the "great Sioux uprising" in Minnesota.

The Civil War did nothing to alleviate the financial problems that began to plague Alec. But it brought much worse trouble to other players on the stage of this story. Father DeSmet, a friend of Lincoln, was in Washington, D.C. to witness the "fatal consequences" both of Bull Run (1861) and of Antietam (1862), and reported them in his letters. In 1862 Marcelino Baca, who had joined the New Mexico Volunteers, was shot in the head by Texans at Valverde. And General Isaac Stevens, by the very qualities that had made him so controversial as a governor of civilians, won notable success back in the Army. His son Hazard was now his adjutant. But at Chantilly, Virginia, during action in the midst of a mighty thunderstorm, Stevens seized a fallen flag, desperately led the charge and fell. The total hero. Perhaps I should say, sadly recalling the matter of James Doty, the total tragic hero.

Alec's nephew, Robert Simpson Culbertson of Cincinnati, was drawn deeply into the war on the Northern side. He joined the Regular Ohio infantry and spent the rest of the war in the Army of Tennessee, often in action at Lookout Mountain and Chicamauga. He was wounded but survived the war. William Radford, no longer touring the Yangtze, was now in command of ironclads for the Union, while his cousin Clark Kennerly, now a Confederate major, was wounded in the South.

But we are concerned not only with the effects of the war on the Culbertsons, their friends and relations, but also on their home town, Chambersburg. As early as 1859, Chambersburg had given shelter to John Brown as he prepared for his raid on Shenandoah Falls (Harper's Ferry). Perhaps there was a motive for revenge in what befell Chambersburg after that. Anyway, it was used as a sort of spring-board in 1863 for General Lee's advance on Gettysburg. And the next year the fate of the town was sealed.

At the end of July, 1864, General Jubal Early approached Chambersburg from the south and southwest with a force estimated at 3,000, and set up two batteries to dominate the town. At four in the morning they opened fire with no serious effect except to signal the invasion. Presently, they began to pour through the streets, followed by 800 cavalry men commanded by Generals McCausland and Johnson with Major Harry Gilmore as their right-hand man. Or should I say left-hand? Perhaps so, for their troops set about robbing citizens they caught on the streets. McCausland announced that the townsfolk of Chambersburg had a half-hour to turn over $500,000 in greenbacks or $100,000 in gold, or else their town would be put to the torch. He began to toll the bell in the Court House, and arrested eight leading citizens as hostages for the ransom. His men went about setting fire to Chambersburg. No respite was allowed to get the women, children, and invalids out of danger. In minutes the center of town was consumed by fire. A tally of buildings burned shows 559. Among the losers were the two sons of Dr. Samuel Culbertson, the Duncans, Chambers, and McCulloh. The bank was gone, the Mansion House, the Court House, the lovely McClure estate. . . It is said too that the old home of the Culbertson family went up in flames. With it went family heirlooms, perhaps precious old paintings that would have given evidence for this present story. Alec's father Joseph had departed this world, but his widow Frances Stuart was still alive to suffer through these losses, though where she was at the time of the conflagration, I cannot tell.

Alec himself, safe at Peoria, was hardly the warrior type (in spite of his titles of Major and Colonel), and he was no longer young. According to Kessler's researches, however, he joined the Eleventh Volunteer Cavalry Regiment of Illinois, commanded by ''the great agnostic,'' Colonel Robert Green Ingersoll. It is not clear whether Alec saw any action with this outfit, at Shiloh, for instance, nor whether he ever heard Ingersoll's famous denunciations of the Bible. In fact, I do not find any military record for Alec. Natawista caught the fever of the times and became chairperson of the Ladies Soldier Aid Society of the Second Presbyterian Church of Peoria, no doubt lending her talent for handicraft to the cause of the soldier boys. All during the war she may also have been foster mother to her nieces Melinda and Louise.[51]

But if the war swept some of our cast of characters right off the boards, it promptly replaced them with new cast members we hardly know. First, let me introduce you to George H. Roberts. Sometime during the war era he became a suitor for the hand of Julia Culbertson. We have no clue whatever as to how this came about, except that he too was a Pennyslvanian, in fact a descendent of the original Quakers. A good-looking ''blond young man,'' he was 22 and attending the University of Pennsylvania when the war called him. He spent four years in the war, partly as a staff officer to General Hooker. Wounded at

---

[51] Her real relationship to these two girls is not clear, but she is said to have been their aunt.

the battle of Gettysburg, he managed to make his way through an apple orchard with a boot full of blood, taking refuge in the farm house of two "Dutch" girls. The girls cleaned up the blood, helped him to recover, and just possibly both fell in love. "I'll come back," he promised. But George was taken captive and eventually paroled. Even so, he was back in action again and wounded twice more.

And there was James H. Bradley. We could hardly have got far with the story of Alexander Culbertson were it not for Lt. Bradley (1844-1877). Born in Ohio, James enlisted in 1861 in the 14th Ohio Volunteers. He was a short, wiry, young eager-beaver whose father was a colonel in an Ohio regiment, disabled and pensioned off from the war in Mexico and unwilling for his son to get involved in this new calamity. But James slipped in via a different regiment, and he was small enough so that his own father did not detect his presence in the ranks until it was too late. After action at Philippi, Laurel Hill and Carrick's Ford in Virginia, he re-enlisted in '62 in the 45th Ohio Volunteers and was engaged at Somers, Monticello and West Farms, Kentucky, and at Philadelphia, Tennessee. In October of 1863 he was made prisoner and eventually did time at Andersonville but was exchanged in the following March in time to participate in the action at Kenesaw Mountains, Peach Tree Creek, Jonesboro, Franklin, Nashville and even at the siege of Atlanta. The curious thing about Atlanta is that his bride-to-be may well have been among the besieged, whether or not young James realized it at the time. It is typical of romantic stories that the lovers represent opposing factions, like Romeo and Juliet. The irrepressible James Bradley was discharged as a sergeant in 1865. He would have been well advised at that point to stay out of the Army, but of course he did not.

No matter how Alec may have projected the image of retired prosperity in the midst of woe, in reality the war years brought him financial ruin. The burning of Chambersburg may not have had much immediate effect on his personal fortune (things like that we have no way of knowing), but at least it cut him off from any hopes he may have nourished of family relief or family backing. The management of Locust Grove was getting out of hand. It is said that even the cook had a hard time collecting her wages. There is the possibility that both Alec and Natawista were drinking beyond their capacity as the price to pay for those years on the frontier, and it is not surprising how many of the old fur and whiskey trading people went down with alcoholism. Actually, the evidence regarding Alec and Natty does not amount to much. Less shaky, however, is the likelihood that Alexander Culbertson, who had proved himself a genius for the American Fur Company, simply did not know how to take care of his own investments. Perhaps he let his heart run away with his purse. That would be a kindly explanation, but it has some basis in the fact that he tried to bolster the interests of his old friend Senator Benton.

Ultimately, his finances went the way of his wife's runaway carriage, from bad to worse and from worse to disaster. Historian Quaife blames Alec's downfall on an addiction to drink and the "misconduct" of his business agent.[52]

He set up a trust for one Thomas B. McCollock, a relative of sorts, to supervise his Peoria properties, paying the net to himself (Alec), after Alec's death to Natawista, after her death to Fannie and Joe. (Strangely, neither Jack nor Julia are mentioned in this story.) Creditors including the seminary in Bethlehem, filed claims against him. But before we accept this account, let me

---

[52] Quaife in his edition of the book of Henry Boller, page 306, suggests Alec developed a drinking problem at his Peoria home or earlier. I would think it was an almost universal malady of fur traders.

This is evidently the family photo which was Joe's favorite in his mature years. Once he loaned it to Kessler and was on pins and needles until he got it back. Montana Historical Society photo.

point out a few problems. "McCollock" maybe a mistake for "McCulloh." Julia (by one account) thought that Robert McCulloh, also a relative of sorts as we have seen, was appointed to act as Alec's business manager. That she was not satisified with McCulloh's management is implied, though not stated specifically. Could this displeasure have anything to do with the omission of her name and Jack's among the beneficiaries?

But with all the troubles of war and finance, Alec and Natawista did not abandon the River. Life on the Missouri was hardly less precarious than life ashore. The war fever seems to have communicated itself to the Indians of the high Missouri, while the corruption prevalent at Washington was spreading westward. Captain Joseph LaBarge considered venal government officials responsible for the disaster at Tobacco Gardens. This is how Tobacco Gardens came about and how Alec and Natawista got involved in it:

They still kept coming up the river, year in, year out, even though the fur trade was approaching its demise, and Fort Benton was no longer just a trading post for the Indians, but an outfitting depot for the military, the squatters and the gold-seekers. So in 1863 Alec and Natty brought little Joe to introduce him to the wild ways of the west. It was a trip Joe would never forget, even though he was still too young to recall it clearly. And on this trip the Culbertsons traveled on the Opposition steamer of LaBarge, Harkness and Company.

For this trip Joseph LaBarge was again using the *Shreveport* and also chartering the *Robert Campbell*, which would convoy the annuities for the Sioux, Assiniboines, Crows and Blackfeet. It is possible that Captain Joseph's trips to see Lincoln in Washington had paid off in winning him this contract for the transportation of Indian treaty goods. But alas, the annuities were delayed by the government, so maybe the prize was not worth winning after all. And with the annuities delayed, so too was the *Campbell,* on which the Culbertsons had passage. the *Shreveport,* under Jean LaBarge, went on ahead on April 20th. The river was low, terribly low this spring and very troublesome. Indians who were not angry at whites were nervous anyhow about the Sioux. Above the Yellowstone, the *Shreveport* picked up Owen McKenzie and his engagés, who during the last winter, had suffered an attack from the Sioux. Unable to proceed much farther because of the low water, the *Shreveport* was forced to set its passengers ashore to continue by mackinaw and wagon 250 miles to Fort LaBarge at Benton. Then Captain Jean turned back down the river to look for brother Joseph on the *Campbell.*

The *Robert Campbell* pulled out of St. Louis on May 13th at last. The passengers included the Culbertsons, Indian agents Latta and Reed, and thirty troopers to guard the vessel against guerrillas. The water was so low that sometimes the steamer had to be cordelled, while at other times, on high ground, push came to shove and to bump. There were two hostile attempts, evidently by Confederates, to board the *Campbell* but both in vain. At St. Joseph, however, the symbol of desolation, the troopers were withdrawn, and the steamer was obliged to continue on, unguarded, into Sioux territory. At Fort Pierre the Indians were already angry over the killing of eight of their people by some soldiers. When (according to Joseph LaBarge) Agent Latta released to them only about two-thirds of their treaty rations, they were furious. They did not like Latta anyway and last year had told him never to come back. Though they complained to LaBarge, he, of course had no authority over annuities. He managed to maneuver his vessel out into the stream, but the Indians massed on the shore and began to follow the *Campbell* up the river, firing into the steamer and creating many hazards for engagés trying to get ashore to gather wood or hunt for food. For an estimated six hundred miles, the Indians continued to follow the *Campbell* and when the *Campbell* met the *Shreveport* on July 2, they followed them both. Joseph LaBarge had his vessel barricaded. The hunter of the *Shreveport,* Louis Dauphin, was able to slip ashore to do the hunting necessary for both boats, leaving his kills along the banks to be picked up. But at last, as the danger finally closed in on him, he ducked into the river, letting his hat float on top of the water for one of the captains to catch sight of. As the *Campbell* drew near, Louis emerged under the hat and climbed aboard. "There'll be trouble," he warned, "at Tobacco Gardens."

There was trouble even before that. While some friendly Hidatsas were trading with the *Campbell,* they were attacked by the Sioux. The steamer managed to ferry part of the Hidatsas and their horses to safety across the river. A Sioux war-party fired upon the *Shreveport* and almost hit Captain Jean with an arrow, but the cannon of the *Campbell* dispersed the attackers. Finally,the boats reached Tobacco Gardens Creek. Here the channel forced the steamers close to the south shore, with the *Shreveport* in the lead and the *Campbell* close behind. Soon enough the shore was thronged with Indians on horseback, calling for Latta and the balance of their annuities. The Indian agents wanted to bring some chiefs in for a palaver, and Latta was persistent even though Joseph LaBarge refused to order anyone to go ashore. Natawista overheard the Sioux and knew well enough what they were about, perhaps even catching sight of warriors hidden in the shrubbery. She and Alexander gave warning. Even so, Latta was not swayed, but their caution may have kept LaBarge on the alert. The Indians continued coaxing and the agents still insisted. Finally some men volunteered, though it is curious to notice that neither Latta nor Reed was among the volunteers. A yawl set out for shore with those who wanted to risk their scalps and promptly came under attack. At least three men were killed. Then both steamers turned their howitzers on the attackers and forced their way through Tobacco Gardens.

As the sister vessels approached Fort Union, a new problem began. The low water detained the *Campbell* below the fort and made it clear that neither steamer could get up to Fort Benton that season. Agent Reed had the Blackfeet annuities placed in storage at Fort Union. Though Joseph LaBarge did not like this arrangement, as always distrusting AFC, there was no other way. So began a long controversy over the responsibility for the incident at Tobacco Gardens and also over the Blackfeet annuities. In later years Joe Culbertson read of the part his mother had played at Tobacco Gardens and his eyes welled with tears. Hers may have been a very minor part. Or it may have saved the two vessels from a massacre.

On their way back down the river, the brothers LaBarge were intercepted by General Sully, who demanded the use of one of their boats. Captain Jean refused, but Captain Joseph was forced to comply, transferring to the *Shreveport* which was "impressed" into service for the Union. Sully was on his campaign against the "hostile Sioux."

Another disturbance of that season on the river occurred on the *Nellie Rogers*, under Captain Charles Chouteau who picked up Owen McKenzie as a passenger from Milk River. Also aboard was Malcolm Clarke. For reasons unknown, Malcolm shot three times, killed Owen and then disappeared upstream. Chouteau buried Owen at Fort Union, where many years later Joe Culbertson identified the grave and brought the matter to light.[53]

Even Father DeSmet met problems on the river this year. Gone were the days when he could go ashore to palaver with a Blackfeet warparty (despite the pleas of Joseph LaBarge to stay aboard). In a past instance the "hostile" Blackfeet had listened well, then gently lifted De Smet into a blanket and carried him back onto the boat. DeSmet, in turn, had been protective of Indian interests. For instance; Though he had known about gold in the Rockies, specifically in the land of the Kootenais, he refused to reveal its precise location. He also protested to the government against the mass execution of the 39 Indians condemned to hang in Minnesota, foretelling retaliations and suggesting it would be more expedient to hold them hostage. But the Indians were hanged regardless. By the summer of 1863 the Sioux were up in arms in such wrath that even DeSmet dared not venture needlessly on the river. Even the ransoming of the Shetak captives by the Teton Fool Soldiers did not allay tensions, but highlighted the Army's inadequacy.[54] DeSmet had come up earlier in the season safe and sound, bringing supplies to his fellow Jesuits and noting that Father Imoda and Giorda had set up a mission station at Fort Benton (probably at the adobe opposition post) and during the winter of 1862-1863 had baptized 700 persons. He remarks, "I married Clark to his young wife." This is, of course, a reference to Malcolm Clarke and the daughter of Isidoro Sandoval.

But when it came time for him to go home, he played it safe and chose the long way around: to St. Ignatius, Cataldo Mission, Fort Vancouver, Portland, Vancouver Island, San Francisco and Santa Clara. There he visited the Jesuit College at the old mission. On the ferryboat over San Francisco Bay he had a happy chat with a Spanish naturalist, Martínez y Saez, who had come to California with a scientific expedition from Spain. Of course DeSmet had to treat his new friend to his typical appraisal of the much maligned northwestern Indians: good people so long as they are not contaminated by "whites who teach

[53] See notes.
[54] See notes.

Rev. P.J. DeSmet, made at Sohon's studio in San Francisco, 1863. Photo courtesy of Montana Historical Society, Helena.

them to be drunks and thieves." The missions and storehouses, explained DeSmet, were left open for the neophytes to help themselves to what they needed and to leave compensation. The scientist recorded the conversation in his diary. From San Francisco, DeSmet traveled on to Panama, New York, and St. Louis.

But next year DeSmet could not avoid coming up the Missouri again, this time dispatched there on a peace mission to calm the "hostile Sioux." He came by rail to Omaha, caught the remodeled steamer *Yellowstone* for Fort Berthold. His worse misgivings were fulfilled when he learned that General Sully was determined to carry on the war in spite of his efforts for peace. Rather than compromise his own standing with the Indians, DeSmet turned back to St. Louis and then to Rome.

Another person who was using his wits (and probably his cash) as a go-between for the government and the Indians was Joseph LaBarge. He made trips to Washington to talk to Lincoln and trips up the river on business of his own. When he came up on the *Effie Deans* in 1864 for the Blackfeet annuities that had been left in storage at Fort Union by Agent Latta or Reed, he discovered that a large share of them had vanished. Joseph suspected they had been traded off by the AFC employees. It was a loss, of course, for the Blackfeet, but also for LaBarge himself (to the tune of $20,000 by his calculations). Both Joseph and Jean were in Montana this season, so Jean took the *Effie Deans* back down the river, while Joseph hired wagons and did some trading at Benton, Virginia City and probably Deer Lodge. On his return to the east, he avoided descending the river in an open boat. Fort Union itself was under intermittent siege. He traveled instead by way of Salt Lake, where he was entertained by Brigham Young in a private box at the theater.

Joseph LaBarge visited Lincoln three times during the war. The first time was to present the President with a beaver-skin robe in lieu of the buffalo robe he had once promised. Lincoln seemed pleased, draping it over his long figure, hopping and clowning about to imitate his own notion of an Indian dance. On the second visit LaBarge exposed to Lincoln the manner in which the Indians were being systematically cheated out of their annuities, and on the third trip he tried to collect on his government contracts. When Secretary Chase informed him the payments were not made because all Missourians were Rebels, Joseph complained personally to Lincoln and got at least partial satisfaction. Again he addressed the President on the thorny question of Indian annuities, specifically the Blackfeet annuities that had disappeared so mysteriously at Fort Union. He declared the AFC receipts to be forgeries. In the evening poor Joseph tried to relax at Ford Theater, but when he was recognized from the audience and people began to call for him to stand up and take a bow, he froze in terror. The anecdotes of visits to Lincoln derive from LaBarge himself, of course, but seem more substantial than the story of the Culbertsons and/or their niece witnessing the shooting of Lincoln.

Like Alec and many another, LaBarge ended the Civil War in financial distress. Through mismanagement by his agents, his trading company collapsed and Fort LaBarge at Benton was put up for a sheriff's sale—and sold to AFC! The LaBarge Company was dissolved but managed to pay off its liabilities. Then came the double irony: the American Fur Company collapsed. Having failed to renew its license for trade with the Indians, perhaps because he was suspected of Confederate sympathy, Charles Chouteau sold out the upper Missouri posts to J.B. Hubbell and partners. In 1865 he took his *Yellowstone* for a wistful farewell tour up the river. When the news of Lincoln's assassination hit the river ports, Charles was nearly executed by a Union colonel who yearned for revenge on somebody.

Joseph LaBarge and his son, learning of the news, stayed in Montana, traded in Helena and again returned via Salt Lake.

In September , 1865, M. Pierre Chouteau le Cadet departed this ravished world forever.

CHAPTER XXIII

The New El Dorado

The Civil War released an avalanche of disasters, not only in the south and the east, but also in the west. And in the west this aftermath was something like a succession of forest giants falling one against the other. . . (Some people prefer the metaphor of cards or dominoes.) This was the era of the Indian wars. On the high Missouri hostility was fast becoming a way of life—hostility between Indians and whites, hostility of whites among themselves, and among Indians with one another. Fort Benton was a hot-bed of conflict, and just when the Lincoln administration had replaced a relatively competent Indian agent, Alfred Vaughan, with such incompetents as Reed and Upson. The water in the Missouri had been running low and so failed to carry steamers above Fort Union, leaving the Blackfeet without their annuities promised by the treaty. The one man who was trying to prevent an explosion was Little Dog.

Yet in 1865 a war-party led by Calf Shirt killed ten woodcutters near Benton. Governor Edgerton called for troops and the "extinguishment of Indian title in this territory." Acting Governor Meagher, a veteran of the Civil War and the Irish revolution, came to Fort Benton to negotiate a new treaty, aided by Upson and by William T. Hamilton. By this time Hamilton was an innkeeper at Benton, sheriff of Chouteau County, U.S. Marshall and only God knows how many other wonderful things. He and Meagher must have made the ideal couple: Englishman and Irishman. The Irishman persuaded the Englishman (by the Englishman's own account) to abandon everything and undertake an errand to the Crows and Gros Ventres, summoning them to the treaty council. Hamilton asked Little Dog for a scout named Eagle Eye[55] (who would happily die for Hamilton if need be), and off they rode on a fearfully dangerous mission into the Judith country and beyond. First they went to the Crows, who politely refused to attend the council, then to the Gros Ventres, who agreed to come. Four thousand or more assembled on Benton Bottom: Piegans and Bloods and Gros Ventres were now at odds among themselves. Little Dog was there and the Father of All Children, and of course Marshall Hamilton. The treaty was signed about the 20th of September, 1865, depriving the Blackfeet of their lands south of the Teton (much desired by the cattle kings) and providing for payments. Curiously, Hamilton says the Small Robes renounced their claim to the land south of the Missouri to the Musselshell. Little Dog signed this treaty. It really does not matter, though, because the thing was never ratified.

But Meagher's meddlesome "peace" treaty boomeranged. If we can accept

---

[55] Since Eagle Eye of the second account fills the same role as The Fringe of the first story, playing Tonto to Hamilton's Lone Ranger, one suspects these two figures may be identical.

Hamilton's account, the aftermath went like this: When everything seemed concluded, in walked Little Dog, now chief of the South Piegans on the demise of old Lame Bull. He was determined as before to preserve the peace with the whites, simply as a matter of good politics. He had, says Hamilton, executed four sub-chiefs for making war on whites. At this juncture, there was a rupture, not only between the Blackfeet and the Gros Ventres, but also between the North and the South Piegans. It was expected that Bloods and other northern Blackfeet would line up against Gros Ventres, South Piegans and the town and fort of Benton. The men of the Northwest Fur Company shut themselves up tight in the fort, and forty-five settlers manned rifle pits around the town. Little Dog, Hamilton and Eagle Eye rode around the camps, particularly those of the Gros Ventres and South Piegans preparing for the onslaught, which promised to be the biggest thing since 1833 at old Fort McKenzie. Warriors on both sides stripped for action. Some 500 hostiles began to circle the Gros Ventre camp, whooping and challenging, while Little Dog deployed his sixty South Piegans at the edge of town. Over 1,000 northern challengers put on a grand display, tying bolts of calico they had received for the treaty to the tails of their horses. Then they galloped about with the colorful streamers flapping behind them, each rider trying to have his steed stomp on the streamer just in front.

During the winter, if not sooner, rumors of gold in the Sun River valley drew whites into the country south of the Teton not yet actually ceded to them. This "Sun River stampede" involved around 500 argonauts, some without adequate supplies and clothing and even afoot. Lt. Bradley says they overran the Jesuit Mission of St. Peter. But it was a false alarm; no gold. And when the snows descended on Sun River, would-be miners began to starve.The vigilante F.X. Beidler was one of these forlorn gold-rushers, who told Bradley that it was Little Dog who helped pull them through. Almost daily, the stalwart chief went out hunting antelope and donated some of it to the marooned miners. But over near the Marias, Bloods killed nine whites and one black, and then some prospectors hanged or shot four Piegans. Indians of some sort made an attack on both the Sun River mission and agency, but evidently it was only a half-hearted venture.

Little Dog was determined to keep his word and check the horse-stealing and the guerrilla warfare. It is very likely that he foresaw that any general "Piegan War" could only end in total disaster for his people. Not all his people understood his policy, and a nativist faction began to conspire against him. There are so many versions of the consequences that I can give only a tentative reconstruction. It happened in May 1866. Little Dog caught a horse-stealer, and with his flashy-eyed son The Fringe and some of his Piegans he brought the culprit into Fort Benton and turned him over to the agent. He may also have restored a couple of kidnapped Gros Ventre children. As they left town to cross the Croquant du Nez for home camp, some of the party secured whiskey, even though Little Dog lingered behind to cut off possible bootleggers. When the Chief and his son finally caught up with the others on the ridge, the drinking must have already started. But The Fringe wanted to go for a swim—"just a body" (as the Blackfeet say): naked and unarmed. While he was gone, a quarrel broke out and Little Dog kicked three men into the river. The Fringe came running out of the water. But it was too late. Some had turned their guns on Little Dog and now shot down The Fringe on top of him. Four times (the holy number) The Fringe rose and fell back, sprawling over the body of his father. It was the end of an era.

I find no evidence that Alec and Natawista came west at all during the last years of the war, nor for the first two summers thereafter. Perhaps the war had taught them to count their pennies. But at least they had one happy respite from the sorrows of those years in the wedding of their oldest daughter. On May 9th, 1865, at Locust Grove, Julia Culbertson became the bride of George H. Roberts. George's ancestor was Thomas Roberts, Lord High Sheriff of Wales, a friend of William Penn, and convert to the Quaker faith, who had come to America at Penn's urging and bought up a huge tract of land that became part of Philadelphia.

How does a young conscientious Quaker respond to the call of war? Many Quakers of the time reasoned that of the two great evils in the land, war and slavery, the worst was slavery. Therefore, in a war against slavery, they could conscientiously partcipate. Specious or simplistic as this argument may seem now, it evidently had a strong appeal at the time, and perhaps proved presuasive to young George. At the close of the war, he was breveted a brigadier general, supposedly the youngest general in the Union Army. So it said in the newspapers. Whether official records, if available, would bear all this out is another matter.

Natawista found that she could treat her son-in-law with a good deal of confidence, and that may explain why, through the Roberts family, we derive a better understanding of "Natty" (as they called her). Once she confided to George a certain feeling of contempt for both Lincoln and Queen Victoria. They were both, said she, way behind "my back side." This little gem has been interpreted as a disparagement of their lineages as compared with her own. Perhaps she was thinking of herself as the *nina-aki* (chief woman), a role assigned by some of her people to Victoria as well as to some of their own women. Or she may have heard that Lincoln, like Washington, was distantly related to the British royal family. I suspect, however, that her disgust stemmed from her disillusionment with Lincoln's Indian program, the loss of Blackfeet annuities, the erratic behavior at least of the two Lincoln appointees she knew personally (Agents Reed and Latta), and the disaster they helped to precipitate at Tobacco Gardens. And whatever else it may evince, her attitude also reveals Natty's growing alienation from the white American way of life. Although Governor Stevens had once claimed she had "fully adopted the manners, costume and deportment of the whites," there were many things Stevens overlooked. Natty reminds me of Matótopa . . .

Some time after the wedding, the Quaker General and his amazingly beautiful bride set out for Montana. This unruly land hardly seemed a proper place for honeymooning, but George had a job waiting for him. They came up on the *Benton* in 1865, although the *Benton* probably did not reach all the way to the fort of the same name. The water was low this year, a number of trips had to be aborted, much freight had to be transshipped, and the Sioux were on the warpath, firing on several boats. The pilot house of the *Benton* was barricaded with hewn logs: Our evidence of Julia and George on this steamer comes from someone we may call "a hostile witness" (at least unsympathetic), C.J.Atkins.[56] If "hostile"seems too strong a term, at least the testimony gives us a notion of the prejudices the newlyweds would have to cope with. Admittedly, Julia and George must have seemed an unlikely pair to the frontier folk. Not only was George too young to fill the popular image of a general, but out in the west, generals were supposed to kill Indians, not marry them. Julia was snidely described as "the halfbreed daughter of Alexander Culbertson" and George was "a white man who called himself 'Gen. Roberts'!" Well, at least the General had one of those Henry rifles, the first one Atkins had seen.

---

[56] Probably the captain on this cruise.

*The caption labels this a photo of "Fannie or Janie Culbertson, 1866
aged 15 or 16." Janie died in 1860, Fannie was about 16 in 1866, but is
this a 16-year old girl? However Maria would be about the right age
for this picture. "Presented by Mrs. Esther C. Casey 11-27-33." Photo
courtesy of Montana Historical Society, Helena.*

On Wednesday, the 19th of July, 1865, the river was falling a little, but the
rain began early in the morning. About 8:00 a.m. the steamer was approaching
the notorious Tobacco Gardens, where the boat might easily have been caught
in shallow water and where some Sioux were lying in ambush. Apparently,
Atkins managed to avoid this trap, but the war-party began to fire away hitting
the steamer three times. The howitzer fired back from the steamer, but all to
no effect at that distance. The Indians were delighted to collect the spent balls

of lead that were sent their way, waving back at the boat people mockingly. When the exchange began, George simply turned his rifle over to the steward and went to his cabin to take care of his bride. In the cabin, testified Mrs. Atkins, the "halfbreed wife" was stalking up and down with a butcher knife, "determined to give any Sioux a warm reception." (No one explains where Julia could get a butcher knife in a passenger's cabin, but apparently it made a good story.) The attack never really developed, however, and the *Benton* reached Fort Union on the 21st. On the 23rd, despite the objections of many on board, the steamer continued up the river for perhaps another seventy miles, met the *Deer Lodge* aground, gave assistance and probably turned back. And that is all we learn of the honeymoon cruise. Nothing is said about landing passengers, but George and Julia must have transferred to another craft of some sort or continued in an overland party to Fort Benton. Not all travel on the river was as troublesome as this brief account suggests.[57]

The newlyweds did not stop at Fort Benton, for their destination was the mining country. Presumably, they got there by way of some portion of the Mullan Road, over the Sun, perhaps over Mullan Pass. George was superintendent of a mining company—or at least so said newspapers. But he was also credited with setting up the first quartz mill in Montana, and that certainly is not a valid claim. I would suppose that the most likely place for Julia and George to settle was either Helena or Virginia City, but we are never told where it was. Wherever, the youthful retired general and his lovely Indian bride were not likely to be appreciated by many settlers at the mines, where both Indians and Union veterans were often despised. They arrived at a time when a new burst of gold-lust was springing up around Bear Gulch and Deer Lodge. Swarms of newcomers were pouring in from the east or the south. Many were coming up from California, including Hispanics native to that state and others from Mexico and Chile.

Perhaps this is what gave George a new idea, for after about a year in the Montana mining country he and Julia pulled out for California. This was a bold move. As yet the railroad had not been completed and the common roads were exposed to highwaymen. At least there were the Concord coaches. Somehow or other they did get to San Francisco. (Curiously enough, about this very time, Pampi Charbonneau was making the reverse journey, from California to Montana, and—according to one opinion—died along the way.) George and Julia may have crossed the Sierra Nevada to Marysville, which was an outfitting center, and then gone on through Sacramento. Whatever the route, it must have been a very trying trip, but they were still very young. We have no way of knowing how long they remained in San Francisco, but from there they took a steamer for Panama.

Though it is not possible to discover their ship, we get some notions of the trip between California and New York from the writings of other travelers, from Isaac Stevens, for example, or from DeSmet or Bancroft the historian, both of whom give details relevant to the period we are concerned with. Bancroft gives data for travel in the opposite direction via the Pacific Mail Steamship Company with a travel time of ten and a half days from New York to Aspinwall (today Colón) and a day longer with greater speed from Panama City to San Francisco. Ports of call also included Acapulco, but the conflict in Mexico between Júarez and Emperor Maximilian must have necessitated some varia-

---

[57] If you want some idea of the amenities of steamboat travel at this time, turn to the chapter notes. I take my example there from Father DeSmet's account of a cruise in the following year, 1866, which was an especially busy year for river traffic.

tion in schedule. The isthmus had to be crossed on a railway so the passengers could transship on the far side the next day. George and Julia left us no diary, but luckily, Father DeSmet wrote a good account of the trip, which he made twice: in 1858 with General Harney east to west, and in 1864 west to east. From this we can assume that the young Roberts, on their first day out, "saluted" (in DeSmet's term) Monterey, San Luis Obispo and Santa Barbara. They may have called at Santa Barbara, a favorite residence of old Basque and Yankee sea captains, and then given the nod to Ventura as they threaded their way past the Channel Islands of Santa Barbara. There, if the Roberts were as fortunate as Father DeSmet, they must have sighted plenty of whales and porpoises. Riotous sea otters were also common along the California coast. A few days later they would pass the dramatic Cabo de San Lucas, the tip of Baja. DeSmet claims that he sighted Popocatépetl from the sea, but I do not see how that was possible (though I do recall sighting the Volcán de Colima in action). He says that the stop at Acapulco was necessary to take on coal and other supplies and recorded that the young men dove for coins in this day, much as they do now and must have done in Julia's time. Beyond Acapulco they coasted Guatemala, Nicaragua and Costa Rica and landed at the ancient capital of Panama City, in Nueva Granada or Colombia. It took a day to cross the isthums by train, though DeSmet notes that the isthmus is only 36 miles wide and the railroad 47 miles long, requiring less than three hours for the trip through the jungles from coast to coast. At Aspinwall the passengers transshipped and cruised north in sight of Jamaica, eastern Cuba and the Bahamas to New York. At least, such was DeSmet's cruise (and mine),though the Roberts might have called at Havana. From New York, Julia and George moved westward again to Nebraska City, Nebraska, where they settled in 1867 and George opened a law office.

It was, of course, the period of the Leonids again. And they did appear, not just once, but in all three years, 1866, 1867, and 1868, but never with the splendor of 1833. Perhaps less splendor, less alarm.

It was a tough time, however, for Maximilians, of both Mexico and Wied. In 1867 one was shot and the other just wore out. The last years of Prince Maximillian of Wied must have had its lights and its darks. Fresh luster was bestowed on the old dynasty by Uncle Max's grand nephew, Wilhelm the heir, who would help preserve Maximilian's own contributions to science, and his brilliant sister Carmen Sylva, who married Carol of Hohenzollern-Murat and became Queen of Rumania. Old Maximilian himself still seems to haunt the history of the land he explored and recorded as it has never been recorded since. A letter he wrote to Philadelphia recalling his friendship with Alexander Culbertson, came into the hands of Kessler of Helena. Then it disappeared, perhaps lost somewhere in the files of the Historical Society. Maximilian also disappeared from history. In 1866 Bismarck stirred up the Seven Weeks War, crushed Austria and caught the small principalities from Hanover to Württemberg into the iron claw of German unity and nationalism. The Duke of Nassau, who had favored Austria, lost his dukedom. Maximilian of Wied, who had so long favored Prussia in the hope that Prussia might fructify the generous German culture of the brothers Humboldt and of Weimar, witnessed instead the utter ruin of such hopes. In this twilight zone of history he lingered another year and then passed away (1867).

With typical naivete, the Bismarcks of Washington, always a numerous breed, decided this was the propitious moment to strike another blow for Manifest Destiny by promoting a new round of treaties with the Indians. Once again they appealed to Alexander Culbertson and Father DeSmet. In 1867 (?) Alec was sent up the Missouri to the River Crows at Fort Hawley, a post recently established by Louis Rivet near the Mouth of the Musselshell. (Rivet, who belonged to the Robidoux family, eventually married into the Blackfeet tribe.) We are told that Alec came up the river on the *Red Cloud* with F.X. Beidler. The trouble with this story is that among the 39 cruises to Fort Benton listed in 1867, a very busy year, I do not find any mention of the *Red Cloud*. Did it miss the list simply by not reaching Benton? At any rate, whenever and however Alec came up the river, he committed one grand indiscretion: he brought along his son Joe, cute little Joe! While the notables were assembled in august session with his dad, little Joe sat outside the council chamber with a couple of tribal elders and got the bright idea of holding a counter-council of his own. So off he trotted to his room, brought out his father's meerschaum (the gift of Prince Max?) and from the post store collected some tobacco and gun powder. Slyly, the little rascal stuffed the powder into the not-so-sacred pipe; sprinkled tobacco on top of it. Then little Mr. Business shook hands with the venerable elders, offered them the holy calumet and in his charming little way even helped them to light up. Bingo! One poor old fellow scorched his eyebrows and got the stem in his throat. Joe sprinted to his room with his new ally on his tail, and the real council almost broke up in a row. Alec saved the day by sending Joe up to Benton on a boat, but others forgave the little fellow with the excuse: "Aw, he's just a shave-tail kid!" (At least that is the story Joe told in his memoirs.)

Father DeSmet's assignment was more difficult: He must go once more to the "hostile Sioux." But his time he came by rail to Omaha and Sioux City, then by wagon, skiff and steamer beyond that. His mule team and saddle horse came up on another vessel, and how delighted he was to see them roll and frolic when they were put ashore! From Pierre to Fort Buford he made the rounds for God and country, counciling and counseling and joining eventually with Generals Sully and Eli Parker. But it was a hard trip for the elderly Jesuit, who was no longer a well man. On his return home, his diagnosis was Bright's disease.

CHAPTER XXIV

The Spoilers Come

The year 1868 should have been recorded as the Year of Lost Opportunity. On the high Missouri it dawned with an aura of bright promise. The war was over and the conflicts of the Reconstruction were far away and many people were turning westward. The Indians were not fooled by the shining aurora. On the Blackfeet winter count, the year is recalled for a drunken shoot-up, while the Sioux recorded it as the Year of the Blue Tipis because instead of canvas, the government issued blue denim.

The family Culbertson were among the thousands turning west, and so too was Father DeSmet. For DeSmet it would be the last and the most dramatic of his many adventures, the greatest of all his services for the U.S. government and yet probably the most futile. A similar pattern of hope and frustration dogged the Culbertsons.

DeSmet, serving without pay of course, was called upon to join a gaggle of generals on a train trip into Wyoming. That certainly was a new approach to the perennial question of "the hostile Sioux." The generals were Harney, Sanborn, Terry, Sheridan and Sherman, who boarded the Union Pacific (not yet transcontinental) along with the ailing and elderly Jesuit. It was a strange coalition, to say the least. In Wyoming they did confer with the Brulés of Spotted Tail but not with the main body of "the hostile Sioux?" No. Hundreds, probably thousands of the Sioux people were secluded somewhere in Montana. Sherman declared that someone must go to find them, someone must go to dialogue with them. And who did the brave generals appoint for the task? DeSmet, of course.

It was no doubt a great "honor" conferred upon DeSmet by the U.S. government, and the Belgian government was not behind hand. King Leopold named DeSmet *Chevalier de l'Ordre de Léopold I* (knight of the Order of Leopold the First). Within the Society of Jesus, DeSmet was becoming the butt of slurs and jealous innuendoes. Nevertheless, when he set forth on this, the greatest peace mission to the western Indians and the most precarious, six lamps were kept burning for him before the high altar in St. Louis. Back he went to Omaha, still not well, to catch the steamer *Columbia* up the eternal river. At every landing, it seemed, Indians swarmed to the shore to see the legendary Black Robe. From Fort Rice he set out overland with the trader C.E. Galpin, the trader's Sioux wife[58] and a body-guard of Sioux chiefs. How charmed was DeSmet with the prairies of the springtime! Wherever he walked there was beauty. And "the hostile Sioux" were themselves a people of beauty, children of God as Thaddeus had seen them many years ago. At Beaver Creek his party halted, and eighteen warriors appeared out of nowhere. They stipulaled that no white man,

[58] This remarkable person was Eagle Woman, widow of Honoré Picotte, famous in Sioux history.

Sitting Bull. Smithsonian Institution Photo No. 3193-A.

no soldier should enter their secret haven nor ever learn its location. We know simply that it was somewhere on Powder River. Desmet agreed to these terms and on June 17th was escorted into the forbidden territory. "What a lovely landscape!" he exclaimed, and very much as Garcés used to do in the southwest, he unfurled a banner with Mary pictured on one side, and the word JESUS emblazoned on the other. Under this peace symbol, with ebbing strength, he reached the camp of 5,000 warriors. He received a little refreshment and fell asleep.

When he awoke he found himself in the presence of Sitting Bull. Evidently, it was Sitting Bull who was running this whole show, and DeSmet appropriately called him the "generalissimo." In a special tipi with a body-guard of twenty warriors, DeSmet was lodged. With the help of the Galpins (i.e. Charles and Eagle Woman), he received the message: Sitting Bull could not and would not sell any of his land. He forbade the cutting of trees and especially of his favorite trees, the oaks. But he joined DeSmet in prayer to the Great Spirit and would permit his officers to go to Fort Rice for a treaty. He himself would not go. So DeSmet left his pious banner and a huge crucifix for Sitting Bull and returned to Fort Rice with Gall and many braves.

The greatest council ever held on the Plains was probably the council at Fort Rice. Some 5,000 Indians assembled there. And yet in a way it was an anti-climax to the council between DeSmet and Sitting Bull on Powder River. The treaty was signed July 2, 1868, acknowledging the Sioux title to the vast lands of Dakota west of the Missouri, east of the tops of the Big Horns and north of the Platte. No white men could settle there nor pass through the country without permission from the Indians. It was (in Stanley Vestal's terms) "a complete victory" for the Sioux, and it was officially proclaimed the following February. The Black Hills, the sacred Black Hills, were Sioux forever.

Hardly was the treaty official when the War Department violated its terms. And Father DeSmet returned to St. Louis half-dead.

The Culbertson family, meanwhile, might have settled happily for blue tipis on the high Missouri, for their dream haven of Locust Grove had ceased to be a paradise. As the money decreased, the gossip increased, and the "Indian princess"became an object of ridicule. Alec must have chosen that part of the country in the first place because of the presence of his relatives, and yet in later years, when the researcher Kessler contacted eastern descendents of the Culbertson family, he elicited but little enthusiasm and less information. There is evidence, however, that Alec's contacts with his brothers Cyrus and James at least, and with his niece Anna, were continually cordial.

Fannie, in later years, recalled hearing gossips on the streets of St. Louis whispering as she passed by at her father's arm: "Who is that old codger with the beautiful girl?" "Why, don't you know? That's Major Culbertson, who could write his check for $100,000!"

Some gossips were more generous, calling Alec "Colonel Culbertson" or asserting that Fannie was "the beauty of the family." But some, I'm sure, were much less kind.

At any rate, the creditors began to pop up out of every corner, filing one attachment suit after another against the Culbertson property. There were thirty-three of them, persons, firms or corporations. Among them one August Weber and another, represented by the Rev. Wolle, principal, the Moravian Seminary for Young Ladies of Bethleham, Pennsylvania. This item is especially curious because it evidently refers to Fannie's term there in 1865. The amount due came to $514.59, which covered books, shoes and corsets, sleighride(s) and horseback ride(s), lessons on piano and guitar, lessons in voice and French. The litigation went before the circuit court, Alec's 320 acres went to Valentine Ulrich, and Alec went to bankruptcy.

So Alec and Natawista decided to move back to Fort Benton. It was a practical solution, obviously, because the one thing Alec knew how to do was to be a trader to the Indians and also because Natty could be close to her own people again and not have to camp out on her front lawn as a sight for curiosity seekers. Besides, Julia was now well taken care of by the General, and Fannie may still have been at school (with no tuition paid?). Jack, now a young man of about twenty-five, would go to California. So in June, 1868, the Culbertsons packed up and left for St. Louis, where Jack parted for California and Alec, Natty and little Joe took off for Montana. There is no record of this, their last family trip up the treacherous old river, except that Joe says they took the *Spread Eagle*[59] to Fort Benton. He also recalled playing the violin for passengers. He must have been nine years old. Perhaps the Culbertsons came up the river with the Conrads of Virginia.

But Fort Benton, alas, was now "the Chicago of the Plains." a long, wild cry from the frontier post Alec himself had founded two score years ago. Now it was the capital of the infamous whiskey empire that reached well north into British America and well west into the gold fields. It was the outfitting center for prospectors, muleteers, stockmen, wolfers, whiskey-runners, bar-hounds and outlaws. The sort of town where buddies got tipsy together and then marched out into the street to shoot off the tip of each other's moustache at twenty-five paces. A friendly town.

Not for Indians, of course. Indians were roundly hated in Benton, though persons of mixed ancestry were more readily tolerated. If we can use the census of 1870 to form a notion of the population of Fort Benton and its environs at this era, we find it included quite a diversity: French Canadian frontiersmen in their *capotes* and red floppy caps, men like the Cadottes, families of mixed origin like Natawista's cousins the Chouquettes, those of Wren, Juneau, Gobert, Pablo, Racine, Joe Kipp, Jerry Potts, Benjamin de Roche, newcomers from the mines or the stock-drives like José of Baja and José Carrasco of Alta California and their comrades from New Mexico or Texas, perhaps Felipe Lucero and Andrew García. All of these men took wives from among "the daughters of the country." It was enough like the old fur-trading days to make returnees feel at home once more. And was it not Alexander Culbertson's town anyhow? Well, yes, but no longer his fiefdom.

Benton, since the last three years, was now a sprawl of log cabins, adobes and what-not, southward along Front Street from the old fort Alec had built. It was the baliwick of merchant princes, the brothers Baker and Powers, hard-fisted rivals. I.G. Baker, once a clerk for AFC, was now an independent king-pin and more than anyone, was Alec's successor to the reign of the high Missouri. But T.C. Power had just arrived a year ago as his chief challenger, and this very year came the brothers Conrad, Charles and William, who tossed their lot in with I.G. Baker. In the opinion of the disgruntled Indian agent, Benton was a town dominated by "merchants, thieves and black guards.'' And all that without mention of the vigilantes, the Irish Fenians or civic leaders like Johnny Healy who might play bootlegger in one act and constable in the next—in the on-going Montana tradition.

But we must admit that there is a lot of confusion in the records of this period, even in the records of the Culbertson family. Alec's own reminiscences do not go much beyond his return to Fort Benton, and Lt. Bradley's version of these reminiscences are left unfinished. Luckily, however, Joe Culbertson's memoirs begin with the family's return, picking up where his father and Bradley leave

[59] I find no record of the *Spread Eagle* on the river in 1868. Joe has things mixed up somewhere.

off. So, quite naturally, Joe himself now often becomes the central figure in the story. But his memory for dates and sequence is woefully amiss. After all, he was only a lad when these things happened. Moreover, the printed and edited versions of Joe's recollections are often at odds with his unpublished notes.

Of the episodes in Joe's account that are hard to date in sequence, one occurred on a trip he took with his parents from Benton to Union in a mackinaw. Below Milk River they were stopped by the Sioux, Medicine Bear, who had just been wounded in a fight with the Crows. So he prevailed on Alec to ferry his entire camp of two hundred tipis from the south shore to the north and to greater security from the Crow warriors. In compensation, the Sioux gave Alec more robes than he could haul.

One of the first things that happened to Alec on his return to Fort Benton was the treaty council of 1868. Not another treaty? Oh, yes! This one seems not to have been so much a fiasco as the one in 1865 (at least if we accept the account of William T. Hamilton), and Thomas Meagher was no longer on hand—he had been drowned mysteriously at Fort Benton. But this one too was made with both the Blackfeet and Gros Ventres, including even the Bloods and North Blackfeet. Just why a treaty should be made with Indians from Canada remains a puzzle. The North Blackfeet sent only one chief but the other two branches had various delegates. The new treaty had much the same terms as the unratified treaty of three years ago, although the Gros Ventres were dealt with apart from the Blackfeet since now the two former allies were allies no longer. The treaty was signed by Calf Shirt for the Bloods and by Mountain Chief for the Piegans and was witnessed by Alexander Culbertson. Even so, the treaty of 1868 was never ratified.

And like the treaty of '65, it had its ugly aftermath. During the negotiations, Mountain Chief had requested that the commissioner, William Cullen, eject some white people from the reservation because they were making a nuisance of themselves. This angered Bentonites, who began to harrass the old chief. So began a new cycle of violence, with the incidents crowding one upon the other.

The Culbertsons were probably keeping a low profile, running a store or trading post and joined by Fannie and Alec's nephew Robert Simpson Culbertson, the son of James Finley Culbertson and a veteran of the Civil War. Robert kept the store, and Fannie taught school to Sioux and Blackfeet children and roomed with the agent's family. Joe claims that the town marshall bought a rope, dug the grave and was then hanged by the vigilantes of F.X. Beidler. When a couple of night herders were slain by Crows, probably a passing war-party, vigilantes or Bentonites turned upon all the Indians they could lay hands on. When three Blackfeet appeared in town, they were lynched. These may be the three that young Joe discovered when he and a friend were taking a morning ride on the edge of town. The three corpses were hanging from a pole scaffolding with a note pinned onto the shirt of one: "These are three good Indians." A few days later, according to Joe's personal notes, a Blood Indian came down from the Whoop-up country and "stopped at our house." A man named George stormed into the house, seized the Blood, dragged him outside and shot him. In his published account, the mention of the Culbertson home is left out, perhaps because Kessler advised Joe to keep his family mostly out of his memoirs. But this version does add that the body of this lone Indian was thrown into a well and pulled out four or five days later when the owners of the well (the Culbertsons?) detected something wrong with the taste of the water. Joe comments: "Benton was not a very healthy place for any Indian to visit after the killing of these two herders," adding that some witnesses of these events became leading citizens of the state. The effect such a scene would have on Natawista can be imagined, especially if the Blood was one of her own relatives.

An incident not mentioned by Joe but taken as crucial in most accounts of the times: Alec sent a message to Mountain Chief (some sort of warning?) by means of the chief's brother, and a boy of fourteen. Both messengers were shot down in the streets of Fort Benton. This is supposed to have alienated Mountain Chief, whose daughter (or other relative), named Kakokima, was one of the two wives of Malcolm Clarke.

Malcolm had left the hide and fur trade about the time of its demise in the upper Missouri, and taken up his abode at a ranch near Wolf Creek, a stage-stop on the road to Helena. He was now one of Montana's Establishment, linked with Granville Stuart, Wilbur Sanders, John Owens. By his first wife, Kakokima, Malcolm had children Helen, Isabel, Horace and probably Nathan. His second wife, to whom he had been married canonically by Father DeSmet, was the daughter of old Isidoro Sandoval and Catch For Nothing, who gave him daughter Judith. Living with them was an old lady named Black Bear, who could remember Lewis and Clark, and a young boy Isidore. Though Mountain Chief was regarded as personally friendly to Malcolm, one of Mountain Chief's sons, Owl Child, was not. The story of his grudges seems impossible to disentangle. In the old days a family grudge was not considered a public affair, but in 1869 it was a question for the Army to deal with. So when Owl Child and his companions murdered Malcolm at his ranch, the Army was ready for action. Vigilante chiefs Beidler and Langford came over with a wagon to haul the family refugees to Helena. Rightly or wrongly, the opprobrium fell on Mountain Chief, though the Army drew up a long black list of "hostiles" and also a list of "friendlies." One of the "friendlies" was Chief Heavy Runner. There were other raids or murders, and Mountain Chief barred all whites from his camp, even whiskey traders. He did, however, allow the whites a day of grace to clear the area.

Amid all the escalating violence, Alec went about his usual way as trader and visitor among the Indians. He made one or two trips up the Whoop-up Trail to the Belly River country across the Canadian line, perhaps taking Natawista and Joe with him. It is difficult to date these trips as Joe's chronology seems somewhat awry. The trail to the Bloods of Belly River, Natawista's people, led from Fort Benton to the Marias, probably by way of John Replinger's trading post on that river near Willow Rounds, and now controlled by T.C. Powers. Replinger was a Prussian of about thirty, maybe a little less, and his post may have been one of the whiskey posts that flourished along the Whoop-Up Trail. Joe says of Fort Whoop-Up (near today's Lethbridge): "They should have named it Hell on Earth as it was certainly hell. . . (The traders from Benton) would have exterminated the BlackFeet and Blood Indians by trading whiskey to them." It was common to see an entire camp drunk night and day with five or six killings every other night. The whiskey trade was a slightly disguised form of genocide, with the rot-gut heavily laced with water, red ink, red peppers, tobacco, perhaps laudanum and even wolfer's strychnine. The best people, of course, engaged in this form of international drug-pushing. They included sheriffs, legislators, and vigilantes. Benton and its merchant princes were dependent on its free enterprise. For the Irish Fenians, whiskey smuggling killed two birds with one bottle: the Indians and the British. But for Natty, these visits to her people may have been the Great Return.

Even if Joe thought Whoop-Up was Hell, he marveled at the trip up the whiskey trail because "the country was black with buffalo" and gray wolves were still abundant. Yet trappers had poisoned buffalo, and hundreds of wolves lay dead from the poison around the carcasses. It was once again a spiral of violence.

To make matters worse, in 1869 came another epidemic of smallpox, no doubt creating new tensions among the Indians and making them desperate to drown their miseries in whiskey. The smallpox this time is said to have killed over 1,400 probably among just the Blackfeet tribes. One of the victims was Seen-From-Afar, the beloved brother, succeeded now by nephew Red Crow as chief of the Kaina. Joe indicates that his father spent the winters about 1869 and 1871 trading with the Kaina in Canada, but it is not simple to sort out all the details. General Sheridan spoke of Alec as an "Indian agent" about this time, but if the term is accurate, it must refer to some special assignment.

On his return from one of these trips, September 2nd, 1869, Alec addressed a letter to General Sully:[60] "I have recently arrived from the interior, where I have been since last winter with Bloods and Blackfeet Indians. These people are perfectly friendly with the whites." He goes on to tell of their surprise to learn of the raids. He appeals to his own "great many years" of experience among them to support his assertion that there is no general hostility, and he urges that those responsible for the troubles were just a "portion of the younger rabble, over whom the chiefs have no control, and nothing but the strong arm of the government can control."

On New Year's Day, 1870, General Sully held a council with several chiefs at the new agency near modern Choteau, where the agency had relocated from Fort Benton in 1869. Heavy Runner, two other Piegan chiefs and one Blood or Kaina chief attended. All others were reported too drunk to come. Sully warned them he must have the surrender of Owl Child and the return of stolen horses. The commandant of Fort Shaw, a native of France of the old nobility and a veteran of the Civil War, was General Philippe Régis de Trobriand, who had been patient and not very responsive to civilian demands against the Indians, but he finally called for cavalry reinforcements from Fort Ellis. Sheridan, from Chicago, ordered that the band of Mountain Chief be struck hard.

The troops were joined by several civilians as teamsters, scouts and so on, among them Joe Kipp, Joe Cobell, and both Horace and Nathan Clark, boys of 15 and 14. (One would think that in professional soldiering, personal motives of revenge should have no part. But this campaign was something less than professional.) The command of over five companies had been given specific orders: Do not strike the camp of Heavy Runner.

Marching out of Fort Shaw under the command of Major Eugene Baker, the troops gradually and cautiously approached the Marias River near the site of modern Conrad. When they discovered a tiny camp, they surrounded it, but found it to be the village of Gray Wolf. A detachment was sent up to Willow Rounds to protect the post of John Replinger. Then hurrying on through the dawn of the 23rd of January, 1870, about eight o'clock in the morning they came upon the camp of Heavy Runner. Joe Kipp called to Baker that this was the camp of the peace chief, not the blackballed one, but Baker had Kipp silenced at gun point. Heavy Runner himself came running out of his tipi toward the soldiers waving a paper. He was shot down. Soldiers began firing at will, as Indians scattered for shelter. Many were sick of smallpox and were caught in their beds. One soldier was killed. The estimate of Indians killed is 173. 140 women and children and 300 horses were taken captive. Black Eagle, one of the blackballed chiefs, escaped on horseback. Of the number killed, 53 were women and children. (This probably means children under twelve, because boys

[60] Quoted from Ege. pp. 72-73. The whole letter is informative, but I omit most of it since it is already in print and easily available. The style suggests that someone edited the letter.

Fort Benton, 1866. Photo courtesy of Montana Historical Society, Helena.

over that age were counted as potential warriors. The death toll may also include one Mexican.) A somewhat different estimate was sent in by the Indian agent, Lt. W.A. Pease: fifteen men dead (ages 12 to 37), 90 dead women and 50 dead children. The harrowing accounts of the dead and wounded were told and retold among the Piegans for years to follow. Most people now call this a massacre, but Army historians seem to prefer some other term.

After the fight, soldiers roped tipi poles and pulled them down on top of the tipi fires with the result that a number of people may have smothered from smoke inhalation. All property was set afire, and the flames no doubt provided a little warmth, at least in the temperatures of 20 or 30 degrees below zero. There probably was also a high wind chill factor. The military body-count determined that two of the black-listed chiefs, Big Horn and Red Horn, were among the dead, while one of the "friendly chiefs," Wolf Tail, was among the captives. But when Wolf Tail tried to escape, he too was killed. So much for the advantages of being "friendly" to the U.S. government.

When the soldiers discovered smallpox among the captives, they recoiled in alarm and turned their prisoners loose on the bleak and frozen prairie with hardtack and bacon, but no horses. It is hard to realize how anyone could have wandered for miles across the wind lashed winter barrens, perhaps all the way to Fort Benton, and still come out alive, but some did survive. Only God knows how. A daughter of Heavy Runner was one who lived, and later became the wife of Joe Kipp.

Rumors swept across Montana, stirring a diversity of doubts and questions, grief, remorse and exultation. Many white settlers rejoiced that the "red fiends," the Piegans, had been crushed mercilessly. The military commandants were less complacent. Of the fifteen Indians they especially wanted dead, they could be sure of only one (Red Horn), less sure about Bear Chief, hopeful that Eagle Ribs (probably Natawista's kinsman) had been wounded. But General de Trobriand reported that the Bloods were now at least "terrified" and the Piegans "completely cowed." A number of the Blackfeet with Mountain Chief and White Calf met Father Imoda from St. Peter Mission in a council on Belly River. They declared in favor of peace, and Imoda so informed General Sully in March. It was the end of Blackfeet resistance. The "Piegan War" was over before it ever really began.

The U.S. Census for 1870 lists the Culbertsons as if they were still the first family of Fort Benton and Chouteau County, as if indeed, they formed an island of domestic tranquility in this ocean of discord and bloodletting: Alex (sic) Culbertson, trader, age 61; Natawista, "keeps house", age 45; Fannie, at home, age 20; Joseph, at home, age 12; Robert, clerk in the store, age 27.

But the harmonious stability suggested by this report is quite misleading. So was the bit of the census report that I cited earlier, for neither record gives us any idea of the many people who had fled across the Canadian border.

One day, probably not long after this count was taken, Natawista was gone. At long last, the Kaina princess who had sampled every phase of the white American way of life, had lived through the Civil War, had risen to the glamor of social success and endured racism and the collapse of a fortune—at last she had enough. Her reasons? We can only guess: The January carnage on the Marias, the corpse in the well, news of the death of her brother Seen-From-Afar. . . Perhaps this was the last straw.

Joe learned that his mother had disappeared, probably in the caravan of trader John Replinger headed up the Marias. For Joe, it was a trauma he never quite recovered from. For Natawista it was the return to her people in their season of grief and ultimate defeat.

CHAPTER XXV

Vision Quest

The flight of Natawista is a watershed in the saga of the Culbertsons. Joe was a boy of eleven or twelve, and it was no doubt a serious trauma for him. Years later when he wrote of the event to researcher Kessler, he declared that he had never confided in anyone about it and even then (1919) "the tears drop out of my eyes as I write this story to you. That was the downfall of my dear old father." What he meant by Alec's "downfall" is never clarified so we can only conjecture, and ever afterward, Joe was reticent about his mother. Rarely does he mention her in his autobiography or in his letters that have come to my attention. And yet when he did come upon mention of her by someone else, the tears again flowed from his eyes, even long years later. He made up for the loss, it seems, by a great love and admiration for his father, which in turn may well have been the pillar of strength that gave Alec his resilience.

From the other children we learn little or nothing of this problem. They were, of course, all quite a bit older and independent by this period. Some time after the census of 1870 and perhaps after the departure of her mother, Fannie went back east again. Julia's husband became Nebraska's Attorney General, and he was evidently a person for whom Alec felt a special liking (in spite of the fact that Roberts became a Mason, an Episcopalian and a Republican). Janie was now dead, and Maria was probably still living on a farm in Missouri. Since neither of these were daughters of Natawista, they probably had no special concern with the matter. Of Jack, we hear nothing at this time. We do know that he returned to Montana, presumably from California where Joe says he went about 1868.

There is not much likelihood, I think, that Natawista had any special relationship with T.C. Power's agent Replinger. The Culbertsons might well have preferred the I.G. Baker firm with the Conrad brothers to the firm of T.C. Power. Probably Replinger was simply Natawista's means of transportation back to her Kaina relatives in Canada, or at least as far as the upper Marias or even the Belly River, somewhere along the "whiskey trail." Julia's family later recalled that Natawista customarily took off on her own and spent more and more time among her people, so her trip at this point may not have been as startling then as it seems to us now.

In the summer of 1870 Alec set out, perhaps with the object of looking for Natawista, though I can hardly presume he would have been so naive as to dream of coaxing her back. His own journal of this adventure is dated "Marias River, July 10th 1870." This date marks the start of the trip, since the descriptions of the parched countryside suggest a late season, and the title adds that the journey extended from July until August.

Alec's party included two teamsters, one of whom was "an Indian boy" and

"Blackfeet Indians—Three Buttes," a color lithograph by John Mix Stanley, depicts a buffalo hunt in the Sweet Grass Hills. Courtesy Amon Carter Museum, Fort Worth, Texas.

the other an Irishman named Pat, and also the "Revd Father John LaHurie." This John McHurie was probably no "Revd Father" at all, but the bogus priest Jean L'Heureux. Alec says in his journal that he was "a Catholic Missionary" who had been living among the Blackfeet Indians for the last ten years, and Joe tells Kessler, "I no pat and the priest as well as I knowd my father."(sic) Jean L'Heureux was an ex-seminarian from Quebec, expelled from a seminary in New York for reasons unspecified. He did pass many years among the Blackfeet, who called him Three Persons because he liked to tell them about the Trinity, but who seem to have regarded him with some ambivalence. He was accused of homosexual and criminal offense(s), but on what grounds is not at all clear. He was probably the "La Rue" who lured prospectors into a wild goose chase, perhaps the man who named St. Mary Lakes and River, and the one whom Granville Stuart threatened to lynch for poaching a steer. With all this colorful background, he seems nevertheless to have received some confidence from both missionaries and Mounties, as author of a Blackfeet dictionary and as an interpreter for Father LaCombe, Crowfoot, Red Crow and perhaps for the Royal Mounted Police. So it is not altogether strange that Alec should have been convinced of his sincerity.

One other question. Who was the Indian boy Alec mentions? Joe told Kessler that he himself went along on this trip so perhaps Joe was the Indian boy, but if so, why does Alec not say so? Throughout his journal, however, Alec is careful to say little or nothing that is personal or has reference to his family.

At any rate, the little expedition started out "on a fine day." made about twenty miles and camped by a cold spring near the Three Buttes in the Sweet Grass Hills. Alec points out they carried no trade alcohol, just a little serviceberry wine for their own use. Joe indicates they traveled up the Marias to approximately the scene of the Baker massacre and then cut up to the Sweet Grass

Hills. The Three Buttes had a "sugar loaf formation," says Alec, with the intervening valleys a favorite campground and hunting site of the Indians, full of buffalo, antelope, and bighorn sheep. Passing between the Three Buttes, they crossed the border of Canada and into the "rugged broken country" of Milk River. There they encountered a vast herd of buffalo. This was the rutting season, and the bellowing bulls could be heard for miles as they pawed up the earth into dust clouds and made themselves "ferocious." The river was mostly dry, and what water there was had become so filthy from the buffalo that the travelers had to dig for water for themselves and the mules.

From here on, except for their two small kegs, there was no more water, not even for the mules, until towards evening when they reached a lake that was nearly dry, probably the original *Pakohki* (Bad Water). They were now west of the Cypress Hills and had to make a dry camp. But next day they found a fresh spring and took a long time-out. There were signs ahead of an Indian camp, and "our Indian Boy more anxious than the rest" went a little way and sighted the smoke of the tipis.

We must remember that this was not long after the appalling massacre on the Marias River and that practically all the Piegans had fled across the border. Relations between Indians and whites were at a new low. And yet our travelers were "elated with the idea of meeting the camp early in the day." So they hurried on to the Buffalo Head, which had been on their horizon for the last fifty miles. They had broken the wagon hounds on boulders at the dry lake and had improvised repairs, but these gave new trouble now. So Alec himself took the boy's place at the reins, sending the boy off scouting. Back he rushed almost out of breath: "I saw three riders!" And soon they met them: a Piegan man, his wife and boy. There was much handshaking and good cheer and a smoke from Alec's meerschaum, and as they approached the camp, people began to flock about the wagons. The chief welcomed them with kindness and a "sumptuous repast," settled them in his own lodge and assigned young men to take care of the mules.

The camp was pitched in a circle about three hundred yards across to keep the horses enclosed at night against raids from Gros Ventres. As Alexander the demographer noted, this continued hostility affected the custom of plural wives and kept the population reduced so that there were not nearly enough men to take care of the women. Even with polygamy there were still lots of women no one seemed to want. The smallpox of last winter had "reduced the number of the rising generation nearly one third" so that the Piegans, by Alec's estimate, were now about 2,000 in number. And with the recent attack by the U.S. troops (evidently Baker's), Alec now expected their inevitable "extinction from the face of the earth." Yet they were happy-go-lucky, not realizing the fate that awaited them, and "strange as it may appear and greatly to their credit, (they) evince no hostile nor unfriendly feeling toward the whites, whom they know are the whole cause of their misfortune." And there follows in Alexander's text a plea that the government will now assemble these people, "humble and peaceable as they are now" and dispel their fears and make a durable peace. This is one of various indications that Alexander wrote his journal for eyes other than his own.

After three days during which their friends had "heaped upon them so much kindness," they set out with a guide for the Saskatchewan straight northward. After they reached the stream called Seven Persons or *Kit a sas ta pe* (I would spell it *ihkizíkitapi*), their guide fell behind and said he was sick. So Alec dismissed him. Again they made a dry camp with no water for the mules. But next day a herd of antelope revealed the nearness of water, which Alec sent "the boy" to find. He did, but it was alkaline and made them sick. After this, more water, also alkaline. But in the distance they espied some hills, probably the Chin, settled for a dry camp nearby and next morning reached Belly River for a good drink and a good bath. (This may be Old Man River.) Here they tried to catch a beautiful wild horse but of course could not. On the third day they reached the mouth of the *Nam-ich-ty*[61] (No River; it was nearly dry). But with good pasture and a lost horse found by "the Father" and plenty of ripe chokecherries, they lingered here. A thunderstorm and cloudburst hit them in the night.

The sequence of events becomes confusing at this point, if not earlier. Joe's brief narrative seems to indicate that near the confluence of the Belly and St. Mary Rivers, they found a Blood camp, where Natawista's brother (Joe says "my uncle") Two Shields[62] joined them as a guide. Crossing the Belly, they followed the *Nam-ich-ty* for a few days. Alec's account indicates that he himself knew this part of the country well, and they found a familiar, favorite spring. After a very hot day, the 10th of August, they were struck by a fierce storm and huddled in or under the wagon. Here Alec enumerates the persons in their group: Alexander and "the Father" and "his orphan Indian" all crammed together in discomfort and "Pat and boy" doing the best they could for themselves. So we now have five people, but no mention of the uncle. In the morning they found three inches of snow and ice. With the cold and wind, they stayed on here that day, but early next morning they hurried on to the Bow River at the place called *Son yo pan-ith coo yat* or Hill Under the Water. (This must be Blackfoot Crossing, but the spelling does little to enchance Alec's reputation as a linguist.) Alec anticipated finding the Blood camp near here because this was their customary crossing on their annual trip to The Pines (Spitzee?) for new lodge poles. And sure enough, when he sent "the boy" ahead scouting, he came back with the good news that the camp was there across the Bow.

Here again discrepancies between Alec's and Joe's accounts. According to Joe, there was no way to get their rigs across the Bow, so he and his uncle swam their horses over to the camp. Joe seems to imply that both Bloods and Blackfeet were camped there, and he refers to the chief as Crowfoot. Alec does not mention the chief's name. But the celebrated Crowfoot had not yet acquired his fame at the time Alexander wrote, whereas he had by the time Joe wrote, a half-century later. This may explain that difference in the accounts. Crowfoot told Two Shields and Joe that he wished Alexander could cross over. But in Alec's story, the Indians came swarming across the river on horseback to him and his party, evidently "glad to have met us, as they had not seen us for near six months."[63] They told Alec not to cross; they could cross to him. And they sent young men over with buffalo meat, while Alec sent them back with tobacco. Next day the tipis were transferred to Alec's side of the river, and the chief welcomed the travelers to his lodge. Traditional accounts tell us that Alexander met Calf Shirt (his famous brother-in-law) on the Bow River in 1870. Neither he nor Joe mention this, unless perhaps Two Shields is mistaken for Calf Shirt or identical with him. Alec never mentions any personal relationship in his account, and here he only stresses the politeness of their reception and adds they were happy to have reached their journey's end after nearly forty days.

[61] Maybe this should be "Just a Stream" *Namih tai.*
[62] I cannot identify Two Shields. Since Indians often had more names than one, he may be someone we know by another name.
[63] This sentence suggest the Blood camp, whereas the sentence just before it refers to the camp of Crowfoot's northern Blackfoot people.

Did they or did they not find Natawista? From neither account do we ever learn. Joe leaves us in the air, but Alec says, "Our journey. . . has been successfully compleated."

Both Alexander and Joe speak of the return trip very briefly. Joe seems to confuse the Piegan camp near the Buffalo Head with a Blood camp near the Belly. Alec has not yet mentioned a Blood camp on the Belly and Joe none near Buffalo Head. But on the way home they traveled with the Indian camp that came across the Bow to them (the Bloods?) down the Bow for three days. There they found a few buffalo but not enough, so they crossed over to Belly River three camps farther and there found plenty of buffalo and "feasted sumptuously on roast ribs and boiled humps." This is the only time Alec speaks of the Bloods' camping on the Belly. From here his little expedition seems to have followed its "outward trail" home.

Alexander concludes with a few remarks on Blackfeet customs, their preparation of bullberries, serviceberries and chokecherries with wild turnips and a few roots, their long life expectancy once they have passed childhood, and their burial customs—all very sketchily. Then he passes on to tell about the alleged priest in pious language we should rather expect from his brother Michael. The "priest" had shared all the privations of the trip courageously, had administered to the needy and instructed the nescient. In the evenings he gathered the children around his tipi to teach them the Lord's Prayer and to sing hymns that he had himself prepared for them in their own language.

This line of thought leads Alec into praise for missionaries and their efforts "to save the remnant of this tribe from ultimate extinction," a specter that seems constantly before his eyes in these times. As a model he holds up the "mountain Indians" probably meaning the Salish and Kootenais, who under Catholic missionaries had come to use the plough instead of guns. I see no evidence that at this point Alec had ever visited the missions of St. Ignatius, St. Mary, Coeur d'Alene and so on, though he may have done so a couple of years later on his return from his long train trip. For the Blackfeet tribes in particular he offers a parting plea:

". . . and strange to say, they are but little known by the people of the United States—only as bloodthirsty, savage people. This is, however, a vague idea, formed upon an ignorance of the actual character of these Indians. Those who are acquainted with them and received their hospitality and kindness will give them a more enviable reputation, and I hope (this) will be realized by the people and reciprocated by the settlers of Montana for all time to come."[64]

As Alec must have known better than anyone else, he was, in this last statement, hoping for very big things. There is considerable evidence that a large part of the "settlers of Montana" approved of actions like the Baker massacre, and within a few more years a wave of panic and hate toward Indians would engulf the state. But it is typical of Alec to hope.

He ends his story of the trips with the words: "Home again." What home, I wonder?

Ironically, off to the east of their homeward trail and just north of the Cypress Hills lay the Great Sand Hills, the *Omahk-Spdziko*, land of the ghosts. It was there, in the Blackfeet story, that the bereaved husband went to seek his departed wife. And it was there he was told he could not bring her back again but must return himself to the land of the living. (In one version he does bring her back only to lose her again.) Was Alec unconciously acting out the old Algonquian (and world-wide) myth?

[64] I have inserted punctuation and spelled out "received."

Joe gives two more descriptions of trips to the Blood country, one or both of which could have occurred earlier than 1870, say, in 1869, or also later in 1870 or in 1871. Both trips involved hostilities with other tribes. One of them coincided with a visit to the Bloods by Jerry Potts, the well known frontiersman, half Blackfeet, half Scot, who, as a little orphan boy, was for a while adopted by Harvey. Joe was staying in the camp with an uncle, and it must have been an eye-opener for the poor boy. It was a large camp spread out along Belly River with plenty of whiskey going the rounds. About three in the morning Joe heard firing at the lower end of the camp with children crying and half-drunk warriors jumping onto horses and tearing off. It was an attack by Crees, driven back by the Bloods, who captured at least two scalps and two women. Joe's uncle got one of the women, a pretty one at that, and a wife of his uncle wanted to run a knife into her. But his uncle intervened. In the story of Jerry Potts, such an attack is described and dated 24 October 1870 at twilight. The attackers were a numerous throng of Crees and Assiniboines, so the Bloods went for help. To the rescue came Jerry Potts and his old friend Star with a swarm of Blackfeet reinforcements. There is a possibility that these two descriptions refer to the same incident. Otherwise I would date Joe's adventure about a year earlier.

The other trip that Joe mentions is equally hard to date. It was a trading trip with a return in May in a party of four: Alec, Joe, a man called Kisenar and "his squaw." The name Kisenar reminds us of the boy Kisenaw at Locust Grove, but this man seems to be a white man. In the published version of Joe's memoirs, his mother is mentioned as being with the party at least at the start, but in the unpublished notes the word "father" appears instead of "mother." If "mother" is correct, then the trip would have probably occurred in 1869; if "father" is correct, then later (1871?), and the editor made the mistake. At any rate, the party had come about fifty miles with their winter's returns of hides and furs. Alec sent Joe ahead with Kisenar to scout for a campsite. Joe was riding bareback on his pinto with just a rope for a bridle, when he and Kisenar sighted six or seven Crees in the distance. Kisenar insisted on riding towards them, but smart little Joe hung back three or four hundred yards. When the Crees got to about fifty yards of Kisenar, they dropped their blankets and fired. Kisenar went down, and Joe high-tailed it back, under fire at first, about two miles to his father's wagon. They camped and waited, but Kisenar never returned. So they had to get back to Benton without a guide.

In the autumn of 1871, says Joe, he and Alec went up to the Whoop-Up country, stayed for the winter and returned in the spring.

Then Joe tells us a little more about Fort Benton as he knew it. It was rather common to have a killing or two every night. Front Street was all saloons except three stores. T.C. Powers and Brother was located on Hold Up Avenue and so were the company of Carroll and Steele and the vigilante headquarters. I.G. Baker's store was on Squaw Avenue. Joe does not mention the Conrad brothers, nor does he tell us what he thought of any of these merchant princes of the rot-gut days in Fort Benton. Maybe it's just as well for, as Joe notes, some of the top figures of Montana's commercial and political establishment had their beginnings right here. But he did think that Fort Benton was about the toughest place around, except for Fort Whoop-Up.

About 1871 or so, Alec received an offer from Jack Simmons, the agent of the Fort Peck Reservation, to go over there as trader and interpreter. So off went Alec and Joe to old Fort Browning, where Granville Stuart's brother James was store-keeper until Alec took over the job. In the spring of 1873 they moved over to Fort Peck itself, which became the main agency. So began many years in this country for both Alec and Joe.[65]

It was at this point in the story that Lt. Bradley finally caught up with Alexander Culbertson and began to write his biography.[66] James Bradley had come out of the Civil War as a sergeant, discharged in July 1865. But he found a home in the Army and was back again the following February, commissioned as a second lieutenant in the 18th Infantry. In July he became a first lieutenant. This time around he did most of his hitch in the west, in fights with Indians at Crazy Woman's Fork, Wyoming, and evidently at several other battlegrounds. One of the scouts he dealt with at this period was Jim Bridger.

But then his regiment was transferred to Atlanta, and there Lt. Bradley was back on his old turf, and now he either met for the first time or renewed an acquaintance with a Southern belle. She was Dr. Beech's daughter Mary. Dr. Beech was a surgeon at McPherson Barracks who thought his daughter was too young for a dashing, athletic Northern lieutenant. But the Lieutenant was vigorous, taut and irresistable. And when Dr. Beech said no, James and Mary eloped and got married anyhow. To avoid in-law problems, James put in for a transfer. But before his transfer came through, he was sent with his regiment to protect the good people in South Carolina from the ravishes of the Ku Klux Klan. In two or three months he got his transfer, back to the west. He and Mary set out from Atlanta by train near the end of December 1871, taking the Union Pacific into Wyoming.

That was running directly into the maw of the monster, for this was the season of the notorious blizzards that disrupted all traffic around Cheyenne. Scores of trains were blocked for nearly two months.[67] Somehow or other the Bradleys got out of the mess by taking a trip by stage (?) through the snow, snow, and more snow to Helena. James was sick. The doctors declared it was smallpox and transferred him from the St. Louis Hotel to a miner's shack (a "pest house") on the outskirts, with two medics for two months. When James was sufficiently recovered, he and Mary moved on to Fort Shaw and then to Fort Benton.

From about 1869 to 1874 Alec's old adobe fort was occupied by the Army, and it was probably here that James began his pioneering work on Montana history and on Alec in particular. From Bentonities, Jesuits, and maybe a few Indians, he acquired the information that went into his work. Since Alec is supposed to have moved to the Fort Peck Reservation, it is hard to say where or when he and James Bradley could have conferred, but one gets the impression that they must have had many confidential interviews. It is not clear that Bradley intended to write a separate biography of Alec. More probably, he intended to incorporate Alec's story into a more general history of north central Montana, to be titled "The Land of the Blackfeet." The various and extensive fragments that have been preserved were probably all to be used as parts of this work and were accomplished with the cooperation of the president of the

[65] Dates and places get jumbled at this point. In his notes, Joe suggests this trip to Whoop-Up was earlier. Other sources say that Fort Browning was abandoned about 1871, James Stuart was appointed "physician" at Fort Peck in 1870 and died in September 1873. Horace Brewster, a young bullwacker reports meeting the interpreter at Thomas O'Hanlon's post near Chinook in late fall, 1873, "an old man by the name of Culbertson." Horace warned Culbertson of a Sioux warparty in the vicinity, and Alec passed the warning to the Assiniboines (Great Falls *Tribune*, 12 March 1933, p. 6). Another story claims Alec was drinking heavily about this time. People wondered where he got the drink on the reservation till they discovered the agent had pickled a two-headed buffalo calf in a barrel of alcohol (Al. J. Noyes: *In the Land of Chinook*, p. 91).

[66] Lt. Bradley's pen name was "Cavalier."

[67] A Mexican Franciscan, Fray José Romo, en route from Egypt & Paris to Santa Barbara, one of the passengers caught in the chaos about the same time as the Bradleys, left a sketchy diary about snow, snow, snow.

James H. Bradley. Courtesy of Montana Historical Society, Helena.

Montana Historical Society[68] as it then existed, Wilbur F. Sanders. Bradley's "Blackfoot Vocabulary" reveals some linguistic competence.

And so it was that Lt. Bradley created the story of Alexander Culbertson as king of the upper Missouri fur trade. It was only the skeleton of the story, never to be fleshed out, but it was the foundation. You may prefer to say that Lt. Bradley created the Myth, and in a sense that is true. But the lieutenant's story ends early and says nothing about the sad-happy times of Natawista's flight and Alec's resilience.

---

[68] Founded in 1865.

CHAPTER XXVI

The Centennial

From now on, the life of both Joe and his father would involve the Sioux and Assiniboines more than the Blackfeet, and it was among the Sioux that history would be made in the 1870's.

In 1872 Joe had an adventure with his father that must have scared him down to the toes of his moccasins. They had come near the Bear Paw Mountains to Snake Creek and the Assiniboine camp of Chief Red Stone. When a warparty of 150 Sioux came from the Missouri looking for Gros Ventres around Beaver Creek, the young warriors of the Assiniboines joined the Sioux. Perhaps they did not know that the Gros Ventres had the new-fangled Henry rifles. After feasting and plotting, the double warparty headed for the Gros Ventre camp near modern Havre, sixty miles off, with some afoot, some on horseback and women in the party too. They began by rustling Gros Ventre horses at night and then opened fire. But the Gros Ventres soon recovered their mounts, chasing the attackers across the prairies and taking plenty of trophies for a big scalp dance. After such a fiasco, the Sioux and Assiniboine home-coming was a horror to behold and was no doubt witnessed first-hand by Alec and Joe. Women cut off their hair and the tip joint of their little fingers, keening as loud as the dogs were howling. Old men sang war songs. The wounded were dragged miserably into camp. It must have reminded Alec of the day so long ago described by Prince Maximilian.

Joe had enough. "Don't you think we'd better leave for the post?"

"Not yet, my son. They won't bother us. We'll see the thing through."

Some of the people, the old ones, went to the scene of the rout to look for the remains of sons, brothers..., finding bodies without scalps and corpses quartered.

In these times, one consolation for Alec may have been the return of Jack. It is said that both Jack and Joe spent time with him at Fort Peck and Belknap. We never learn anything of Jack's experiences in California, the place to which he was bound when we last heard of him from brother Joe. It is a curious coincidence that in 1872 another Culbertson went to California: On the passenger list of the transcontinental railroad we find S.D. Culbertson of Chambersburg, Pennsylvania (Alec's uncle?), accompanied by W.H. Scott and J. Kennedy, both also from Chambersburg. They were aboard the Overland Train as it passed through Carlin, Nevada, westbound, on October 25th.

A similar adventure now awaited Joe. In 1873 he went with his father and a Sioux delegation to Washington, D.C. Agent Simmons assembled nineteen leaders of the Yanktons with William Benwire and Alec as interpreters. With young Joe, they boarded a steamer for Sioux City and from there went by train. It was nothing like travel in the old days.

In Washington they first took lodgings in the Capitol Hotel, then paraded to the office of the Commissioner of Indian Affairs and finally to President Grant. After but a few minutes in the waiting room, they were greeted by the President who made the rounds, shaking hands with everyone. The first to be welcomed was Medicine Bear. He held onto Grant's hand a long while, then turned and commented to the others: "His hand feels the same as any other man's hand." Then removing his war-bonnet, his medicine pipe and sack and his war-shirt that dripped with scalps he made a gift of all these treasures to Grant. In return, the President gave them a little speech to this effect: "Each one of you will receive a new suit, a hat and a valise. When you get home, you will each be given a horse, a saddle and a bridle." Medicine Bear got back up and shook hands again, thanking the President: "You have many white people. They are like flies. There is no point in my people trying to fight them."

Then the party returned to the Commissioner's office and arranged for the presents. Most of the leaders got swallow-tail coats, all got stove-pipe hats, some white, some black, and each one with a ribbon around the crown. So much for diplomacy. What was negotiated or accomplished does not appear in Joe's report. Perhaps he was too young to understand it. But he does add that they visited "all the main cities" and headed finally for Council Bluffs, where they caught the Union Pacific to Nebraska, Wyoming and Idaho. (For a vivid description of this train trip at this period, be sure to read Helen Hunt Jackson's *Bits of Travel at Home.*)

Joe mentions visiting Salt Lake City, noting that they left the train "somewhere close to the Nez Percé Reservation." Now, I must say this leaves us with quite a puzzle. The Nez Percé Reservation is nowhere near Salt Lake, and one cannot but wonder why they should go so far westward out of their way. A practical route would have brought them from Corinne via the old Montana Trail through Monida Pass, perhaps to Deer Lodge and the Mullan Road. And to make the problem even more complicated, Joe claims that they crossed the Bitterroot Mountains near "the natural bridge." Presumably, they were by this time moving eastward once more, en route to Helena. But where to find the natural bridge? Informants in the U.S. Forest Service tell me that there are at least two natural bridges or natural arches known to exist in the Bitterroot Mountains: one on Blodgett Creek about six miles due west of Hamilton, and the other about thirty miles southwest of Darby on Blue Joint Creek, a tributary of the west fork of the Bitterroot. The first one is the more delicate of the two and perhaps the most accessible. The second one appears to be the remains of a volcanic neck and is near the old Nez Percé Trail. Can Joe have thought the Nez Percé Trail was the Nez Percé Reservation?

Whichever way they came, they eventually must have crossed through the heart of Montana's mining country, which would be a new experience for the Culbertsons. This is the only time of record that Alec was west of the Divide, and he would have wondered at the influx of miners from all over Europe, from every state of the restored Union, from Latin America and even many from brother Michael's China. People of all kinds had recently come up from the mines of California. Parties of Hispanics appeared here and there establishing their traditional *arrastres.* A beautiful woman named Spanish Jack dominated gambling tables in the boom town of Bear Gulch. Spanish merchant Joaquín Abascal led the boom there, and his one-time partner (and later brother-in-law), William Andrews Clark, was now climbing the ladder of fabulous fortune.

For ten days the delegates stayed at the St. Louis Hotel in Helena. From there they took the stage through Prickly Pear Canyon via the old ranch of Malcolm Clark to Sun River Crossing, where Alec could once more find himself in familiar surroundings. Here Simmons bought horses and saddles for everybody plus a wagon and team to carry all their gear. And soon home to Fort Benton, Fort Balknap, Fort Peck. They were gone only about a month, so could hardly have meandered too far astray near the Nez Percé country (unless, of course, Joe miscalculated the duration of the trip). The purpose of this jaunt, in Joe's opinion, was to impress the Indians with the big cities and the big guns. It is hardly clear what useful end was attained.

This very year (1873) Joseph LaBarge sent his new steamer up the Missouri, the one he named *DeSmet.* He begged his old friend to come visit and bless it, and it included a stateroom especially designed for the old Black Robe. Father DeSmet did visit the steamer, but, alas, it had to pull away into the river without him. The great pioneer Jesuit died shortly afterwards and so ended his earthly travels. Perhaps no white man in American history, except Garcés, was ever more loved by the Indians or loved them more in return.

In 1874 Joe went east again but not so far. He went to Parkville, Missouri, to live for a while at the farm of James Kipp. The purpose of this visit was not clear. Joe must have been about fifteen years old. His half-sister Maria had married Samuel Kipp and lived at the Kipp farm in Clay County near the post office of Barry. In later years Samuel died and Maria married Joe Walker, also of Missouri. James, "the old man," is said to have made annual trips up the river, though Joe mentions only one visit about 1879 or 1880. James died in Missouri July 2, 1880.

In the spring Joe returned home by way of Sioux City, where he ran into another Joe, this one the son of I.G. Baker of Fort Benton. The two young men boarded the *Fontenelle* and rode up the river together till Joe Culbertson got off at Fort Peck to join his father a month later at Belknap.

In the summer of 1874 (maybe this date should be '75), when Alec and Joe traveled from Fort Benton to Fort Belknap, they stopped to camp near the Bear Paw Mountains on Big Sandy Creek. After supper, as they sat at the campfire, Alec was enjoying his customary after-dinner pipe and growing mellow with reminiscence: "Joe, my son, it makes me feel sad to see those mountains and travel over this country."

"Father, why should it make you feel sad?"

"Joe, long before you were born or even dreamed of, your mother and I traveled from Fort Union to Fort Benton when there was not even a sign of a trail and the country was black with buffalo. It makes me feel bad to think of the good old days and the money I made." (More likely, the money he lost.)

"Father, weren't you afraid to go 400 miles with just a small party and the country full of Indians?"

Alec laughed: "The whole Sioux tribe knew me by the name of Red Coat *(Oga-ais-cha:* Red Shirt). And all the Blackfeet called me Beaver Child *(Cris-to-kup-a-ka* or *Xís xtaki-poka:* Wood-biter's Child). And whenever I met any of them either in a buffalo hunt or on the war path, they treated me as one of their tribe."

Joe took heart now to probe his father some more about that life on the early frontier, but Alec replied: "Joe, wait until we get to Fort Belknap and I'll tell you more."[69]

At Fort Belknap (1874) Alec met an old enemy, Lunica, who had faced him in the attack on old Fort McKenzie during the visit of Prince Maximilian in 1833. Now these two old cronies enjoyed a good laugh at their reminiscences.

[69] Narratives told by Indians generally give conversation in direct quotation (a bugbear to historians), as I have done here and elsewhere, following Joe's own style and often his very words. I have used his spelling of the Indian names for Alec but added my own suggestion for transcribing Beaver Child into Blackfeet.

One day, apparently while they were at Belknap and still basking in this father-son relationship, Alec suggested: "Joe, let's get one of your best buffalo horses. We'll take the light wagon and team and lead your horse and go on a buffalo hunt." So they did, about ten miles up Clear Creek, where they spotted a herd of at least five hundred. Driving the wagon in as close as they could, they still kept pretty much out of sight. Then, getting onto his horse, Joe worked his way into the midst of the herd. But just as he was about to shoot a fat cow, his horse stepped into a badger hole and over they went, horse and hunter. Though Joe had tied his belt to the rope around his horse's neck, they somehow escaped being trampled to death. When the dust dissipated, Alec rode up: "Are you hurt?"

So they made a noon-day camp on the creek, and while Alec was making the tea, Joe tried to creep on hands and knees through the grass up to three calves. Then a buzz in the grass. A rattlesnake. Joe lept out of the way, cleared the rattler and even shot all three calves. After lunch they butchered, loaded the meat into the wagon, and on the way home flushed out a doe elk, which Joe added to his collection. They got home before sunset, with Joe sporting his laurels.

In the spring of 1875 (by Joe's count), he and his father returned to Fort Peck. From this point on, Joe gives us more and more of his own experiences and less and less of his father's. Since this story belongs more to Alec than to Joe, I shall make no attempt to repeat all the various escapades of young Joe. However, I shall not neglect the little news about his mother that comes from an unexpected source.

The year 1874 is called in the winter count of Manistokos "When the Police Came to Many Houses": *Inákix izitotohpi Akapioyis*.[70] A massacre of Assiniboines near Solomon's Post in the Cypress Hills by a gang of Bentonite whiskey-runners had at last alerted the Canadian government to the need for law and order on the western prairies. The murder of Calf Shirt (1873) by whiskey traders at Joe Kipp's post added a note of emergency and another name to the Winter Count: "When Calf Shirt Was Killed". So westward marched the North-West Mounties. They built Fort Macleod, naming it for their commanding officer, and very soon checkmated the whiskey traders of Fort Benton. It is at Fort Macleod in its first winter of 1874-1875 that we find Natawista once more. A record of life there during this winter was written by the surgeon for the Mounties, Dr. Richard N. Nevitt.

This was a busy winter. Colonel James Macleod himself had to cover the trail between Fort Macleod and Fort Benton to change it from the old whiskey trail to a new supply route for the Mounties. Notables of western Canada hovered about the new establishment: Sir Cecil Denny, Chief Crowfoot, Father Scollen, Jerry Potts, and with a band of *métis*, even Hugh Monroe who now became interpreter for the Mounties. Dutch Fred Wachter, a whiskey trader killed Castillian Joe Arenas, and Dr. Nevitt did the post-mortem. The surgeon was an artist too and painted a portrait of Manistokos and a picture of the Horned Snake Tipi (which I suspect had some connection with the name of Natawista). He also did a portrait of Natawista but in words and under the name of "Madame Kanouse". The 29th of March, 1875, was set aside for celebration with a Catholic Mass and an "English Church Service", followed by a terrible storm. But the games attracted a huge crowd that included "the elite of the land". Ladies came on horseback, but only one on a saddle: Madame Kanouse (rhymes with "house"), whom Nevitt portrays this way.

[70] Literally "the seizers when they came to Many Houses".

You should have seen her dress. It was the Dolly Varden style, a large figured chintz just short enough to display the gorgeous stripes of a balmoral petticoat which in its turn was also just short enough to show two very small feet clad in moccasins and the end of a pair of leggings beautifully worked in beads. She also had a heavy black velvet loose-fitting overcoat and over this a most brilliant striped shawl, the stripes being about three inches broad and alternately red, blue, green and red, with a narrow line of yellow between each color. Her head gear consisted of a small plaid shawl. The other titled aristocrats were dressed also in gorgeous array, but perforce they yielded the palm to Madame.

So it would appear that for the time being at least Natawista was well provided for. But why was she called "Madame Kanouse"? Fred or H.R. Kanouse was a trader from Fort Benton and presumably a person familiar to the Culbertsons. Nevitt makes several allusions to him without suggesting any connection to Natawista. The family Kanouse probably outshone the Culbertsons in prominence at Fort Benton, since Fred's father, J.A., became a lawyer, and Fred himself a sort of self-educated lawyer and doctor to boot, as well as an Indian trader, Indian fighter, sheriff, interpreter, and perhpas a whiskey trader on the Whoop-Up Trail about 1872. But he got into a scrape with Jim "The Bluffer" Nabors and shot him. Fred was shot too but eventually escaped across the border and took up trading as a partner of Kootenay Brown at Waterton Lakes. Later he moved on to British Columbia. There does not seem to be much place in his story for Natawista, so if she had any sort of liaison with him, it must have been brief.

And neither was there any longer a place for whiskey traders in the Saskatchewan River country. The year 1875 was put down by Manistokos on his winter count as the year *Itsixawaohpi nápióhki:* When the Whiskey Was Stopped.

Because of poor transportation across Canada at this period, the North-West Mounties had to use the Missouri River as their supply line from the eastern provinces, and quite naturally Fort Benton became their depot and debarkation point. Their presence no doubt had something to do with the improved orderliness of the wicked old town. It must have been something of a relief to Alec on his occasional visits to Benton.

The times were coming fast when Alec would have to do without Joe, and Joe would be on his own. Alec foresaw this himself and realized that in his old age he would have to turn to one of his daughters, perhaps to Julia the eldest. George Roberts was by now a prominent lawyer in Nebraska. He served as Attorney General of that state for two periods: 1871 to '73 and 1875 to '79 (but not the first state attorney general as it is sometimes stated). He and Julia were living in Lincoln, but their daughter Margaret had been born in Illinois, at Lewiston, March 21, 1872. By this time they may have moved to their home at Orleans, far down on the Republican River. At any rate, on the 4th of September 1875, Alec wrote to George Roberts from Fort Belknap. He calls George "My Dear Son" and signs himself "Your Affectionate Father". He is "overjoyed" to hear from George and wishes more than ever to be with the Roberts family. For even though he does not yet feel much of "the infirmities of old age", he is "still aware of being on the down hill of life". He is happy to hear of their fine country estate and would enjoy helping Julia with the garden—whereas here "we plant plenty but the grasshoppers reap." And he turns again to thoughts of the Indians that seem to often on his mind of late:

I suppose you hear a great deal about Indians and their depredations but most of (the) rumors of that is, as a general (rule), falsehoods upon the Indians. They are perfectly peaceable and quiet. They have greater reason of complaint that we have.

He is still at Belknap(?) with the two boys, who are doing as well as can be expected, "but not very anxious I should leave them". These "boys" must be Jack (probably about thirty-two now) and Joe (about half that). Alec has learned, evidently from George's recent letter, that Fannie has gone east "somewhere". He has been urging her to visit the Roberts but as yet has no reply. He hopes "little Magge" (no doubt Margaret) will write to him, and he hopes Julia will too, and often. Then with an affectionate remembrance and God's blessing, he closes. It seems to be a letter longing for love or companionship. It was written during the calm before the storm, the eve of the Indian wars of 1876 and 1877.

So Fannie is "somewhere" in the east? Either by this time or soon afterwards Fannie came upon her relatives from China. Just how that happened we do not know but we may presume it was not by chance.

As far as we can tell, after Michael's death, two of his daughters, Helen and Alice, remained in China, the land of their birth, married eventually to ministers of religion. But Mary Dunlap Culbertson came back to the United States with her daughter Josephine, who became an artist in Brooklyn. Her other daugher Cornelia also came to the States, but whether at the same time is not clear. She was in this country in 1876, perhaps earlier, because she wanted to see the Centennial. According to a WPA story about Fannie, Cornelia and Fannie spent a year together in New York. At this time, it is added, Fannie had various suitors, including S.S. McCormick of Chicago, but Fannie proved hard to get. (Though S.S. McCormick is not identified further, I would suppose he was part of the family that developed the reaper, International Harvester and the Presbyterian Theological Seminary of Chicago.)

Though no details are given us about Cornelia's visit to the Centennial in Philadelphia, we are led to suppose that she and Fannie (who appears to be the source of the story) attended the grand fair together. The highlights of the Centennial included the special orchestra of Jacques Offenbach, Alexander Graham Bell and his telephone, and Dom Pedro II, the Emperor of Brazil, who greatly admired Bell and his invention. Offenbach's orchestra could hardly have escaped the attention of the music-loving Culbertsons, especially since Fannie was a music major, and the violinist may well have caught their eye: a handsome young Latin type named John Philip Sousa. They were something of a Centennial sensation themselves—those two lovely Culbertson cousins, one from China, the other from the Blackfeet Reservation of Montana. And if people at the Centennial had not yet heard of Montana, they learned of it from William Andrews Clark, who was sent there by Governor Potts as the territorial orator. Clark could tell the world how to make a fortune in Montana, where he was destined to become a copper king of the high Missouri, one of "the hundred men who owned America," and one of the hundred most controversial.

Alec's successors, of course, were the copper kings, the merchant princes and cattle barons, like the brothers Baker, Power and Conrad. At Fort Benton a little Civil War was still going on between Republican Powers and Democrats Bakers and Conrads. All of these merchant princes were probably involved in selling "bug juice" to the Indians along the Whoop-Up Trail and also in supplying the Indians with weapons. Conrads from the Shenandoah bought out the Bakers at Benton about 1874, and Charles Conrad began a career that paralleled that of Alec a generation earlier. Since his trade extended well into Canada, Charles took a wife among the Bloods (1876), and if it is true, as we are informed in the Conrad accounts, that she was the daughter of a chief, she may well have been a relative to Natawista. Though her father's name is not of record, hers is given as Dried Meat (Kaiyis) and Sings in the Middle. A son Joe, baptized in 1882, was then about six years old, and another son (or perhaps the same one under his father's name) was sent to Montreal for education. Kaiyis, like Natawista, returned to her people in their days of trial. Charles married again in 1881, to the sister of one of his associates in both the cattle business and the North-West Mounted Police. Except for this second marrage, his story seems a replay of Alec's. The Conrad brothers became the largest business around, with mercantiles, banks, ranches and even Missouri River steamboats, and though Charles, unlike Alec, did not dissipate his fortune, his wealth brought woes. And like Alec, in later years, he became a sort of elder statesman to the Indians. Other entrepreneurs from Virginia were the brothers Stuart: Granville, James and Robert, all of whom also took Indian wives. Granville ("Mr. Montana") had eleven children by his Shoshoni wife and on her death married a white woman. None of these tycoons, however, outrivaled William Andrews Clark. Such were Alec's successors to the title King of the High Missouri.

In the spring of 1876, when the Indian agency was moved to the present Fort Peck Agency, Joe Culbertson and his friend James Boyd moved with it. From this point onward Joe tells us but little more of his father. His own life became complicated by the tensing hostility between Indians and whites all along the frontier. When Joe ran into Charley Reynolds and Frank Girard, as they headed off to scout for Custer, he gave Frank a horse. The poor animal would die on a fatal day soon at hand.

Lt. James Bradley was transferred from Benton to Fort Shaw, west of the Great Falls. He had continued his writing and his correspondence with Wilbur Sanders but now had to abandon literary pursuits for military obligations. Off he rode in the "Montana Column" under General Gibbons, who also had to give up his literary and oratorical hobbies. For the Sioux Indians were now spinning on a collision course with the military brass. Lt. Bradley pioneered in the use of Indian scouts. With the consent of their chief, he got about 30 young Crows to act as scouts against the Sioux. One of them was the famous Curley. The Army had orders to drive Sitting Bull and Crazy Horse onto their reservations, so Gibbons marched out of Fort Shaw on St. Patrick's Day in a temperature of twenty below. Crossing half the territory of Montana, the troopers finally approahced the camp of Sitting Bull and came precariously close to attacking it even before the arrival of Custer. This, at least, was what General C.A. Woodruff reported.

The Sioux and Cheyennes were in large camps, and among them was a remarkably pretty girl named Spotted Hoop, who belonged to the tribe of Sitting Bull and on the present day was in the camp of Rain-in-the-Face. She was thinking (in Joe's story) that she had never seen such a tremendous camp. Spotted Hoop was the kind of girl men fight over, and when her husband killed another man because of her, she ran away from him. Very likely she was now looking for somebody new. But right at the moment she suddenly found herself in the midst of a different sort of maelstrom.

About noon on this day, the 25th of June, 1876, or maybe a little after noon, Spotted Hoop noticed women and children scurrying toward the camp while men began dashing about for their horses. Then shots—many shots. Sitting Bull himself, stripped for battle, whipped about the camp driving toward the center of the maelstrom. People were shouting, "Soldiers are upon us!"

Before long the attacking soldiers were driven across the river. (In later days, when Joe heard this story from Spotted Hoop, he decided that these troopers were Reno's command.) But this did not mean the battle was over. The Indians were now prepared for more action, mounted and firing and chasing the soldiers "like buffalo" (Joe's simile or maybe Spotted Hoop's). The women followed toward the battlefield higher on the ridge, and the first dead man they came upon was Tit, a black trooper whom they knew well around Standing Rock. Now the poor fellow, no "natural enemy of the Sioux, had been caught with the men of Custer. There is nothing like a "just war" for pitting good people against one another. By the time Spotted Hoop and the other women reached the scene of battle, the fighting was over.

But some of the fallen soldiers were still half alive. Their bodies were stripped, and their money, watches and chains were already looted. So the women went about cutting off fingers to get their rings. They found a great many dead Indians too, whose bodies were now removed to the camp, while surviving warriors dressed up in the soldiers' uniforms and strutted about grotesquely. "It was the finest sight I ever saw in my life,"declared Spotted Hoop. But the next morning, the vast camp split in all directions.

On the morning of the 27th, the Seventh Infantry and light artillery under General Gibbon and General Terry relieved the besieged forces of Reno. Their delight, however, was soon laced with foreboding as Reno's men reported seeing guidons of the Seventh Cavalry in the hand of the Indians. According to General Woodruff, it was Lt. James Bradley who discovered the scene of the Custer massacre. Woodruff later recalled how Lt. Bradley rode up to Gibbon and saluted: "General, I have the honor to report that I have counted 194 dead bodies; I presume they are soldiers, but they have been stripped and some are badly mutilated." If that story is authentic, then Lt. Bradley must have changed his mind upon further examination, because as Terry's scout, he made an official report to the effect that except for the customary taking of scalps, there was not much mutilation of the dead, that apparent mutilations were for the most part not caused deliberately and that the body of Custer himself had been respected. So Gibbon's Seventh Infantry buried the remains of the Seventh Cavalry. Sergeant Ferdinand Culbertson of Company A of the Seventh Cavalry recovered one of the fallen guidons from under a soldier's corpse.

It was rumored about among the Indians that the man who killed Custer was Santee, living in Manitoba, by the name of White Track or Jesse Walkpa. Joe's friend Muskrat knew him well. It is curious to reflect that the death of Custer may have been precisely the retaliation foreseen by DeSmet for the hanging of the 39 Sioux. But most of the Indians did not like to talk about what happened that day in June, 1876, the Moon of the New Life.

One morning, not long after the affair on the Little Big Horn, Joe Culbertson noticed two Indians across the Missouri River, and climbing into a skiff, he crossed over to them. They turned out to be Iron Bear and Thundering Bear, pleased to see Joe and jauntily armed with U.S. Cavalry carbines and happily mounted on horses that bore the U.S. Cavalry brand and saddles. Now, Joe was not dumb but he asked anyhow, "Where did you get all these things?" His friends willingly explained as they loaded their gear into his skiff and, leading their prize steeds, crossed the wide Missouri.

A few days later Joe took a dispatch about 125 miles down to Fort Buford, where he caught the *Deer Lodge* back up to Fort Peck. This errand may have been the start of his service with the Army as a scout.

It must have been a grand Fourth of July, that Centennial Year. In Philadelphia at the Fair it was the peak of euphoria, the celebration of these national gods, Progress and Manifest Destiny.

In Fort Benton, Montana Territory, the celebration would be a little more

Joe Culbertson, U.S. Army Scout.
Photo courtesy of Mollie F. Culbertson Sedgwick.

muted. The Culbertson Hotel under the management of Robert, changed its name to suit the occasion and became the Hotel Centennial. The Union was saved, the slaves "freed", the Indians corraled, the land exploited and fortunes amassed . . .

News of the incident on the Little Big Horn must have reached the ears of many a celebrant both east and west on the Fourth of July.

CHAPTER XXVII

The Stag at Eve

"We must act with vindictive earnestness against the Sioux," declared Sherman to Grant, "even to their extermination, men, women and children. Nothing less will reach the root of the case." One dare not suppose that either of them learned this sentiment at West Point, but in the Northwest the urge toward revenge and genocide was prevalent. There is the story of one old pioneer who, when asked on his death-bed if he had any regrets, simply replied: "Just one. I ain't never killed me an Indian." To die without fulfilling his quota!

It was in this atmosphere that both Joe and his father passed the crucial times of '76 and '77, caught between poles of conflict, trapped too, perhaps, in their own habitual ambivalence. Alec leaned toward the role of the elder peacemaker, while Joe, young, reckless and looking for action, was both a scout for the U.S. Army and a personal friend of some of the Army's bitterest adversaries.

Joe was also quite a ladies' man, and that trait gave a new dimension to his career when he set eyes on Spotted Hoop, the follower of Sitting Bull. Or was it the other way around? The story as Joe tells it has Spotted Hoop setting eyes on him. She had been captured by Bear Coat (General Nelson Miles), just where or when is not altogether clear. Many of the Sioux took refuge in Canada after the Custer debacle, but they would often drift back across the border. Some of Spotted Hoop's people surrendered to Miles at Fort Keogh (Miles City), where Joe was stationed about 1876-77. But Spotted Hoop must not have been retained long in close confinement because we find her attending an Indian dance at the mouth of the Redwater. Also attending was General Miles' scout Joe Culbertson, riding a bay.

"Who's that man?" Spotted Hoop asked the women around her.

"That's Joe Boy—the scout for Bear Coat."

So Spotted Hoop began to follow Joe around. Or at least that's the way Joe liked to see the affair.

In June of 1877, Joe set out for the friendly camp of the Yanktons at Wood Mountain across the line in Canada. He may have been acting as a sort of spy for the Army, though he was accompanied by friends who hardly fit that category: Dave Burshia, Nick Álvarez and Joe's "wife". Perhaps this "wife" was Spotted Hoop. The Burshia and Álvarez families were neighbors of the Culbertsons on the Fort Peck Reservation, where the population was officially divided into Yankton (or Yanktonai) and Assiniboines, both Sioux in origin but mutually hostile.[71] Burshia was classified as Yankton, Nick and his family as Assiniboines. (Nick's father Philip had married an Assiniboine as his first wife, but as his second wife a Yankton niece of Sitting Bull.)

[71] It was a common practice of the government to enclose traditional hostiles on the same reservation. Divide and rule?

When they reached the Yankton camp about three o'clock on the third day out, Joe was promptly taken into custody by three Royal Northwest Mounted Police. Both Nick and Dave Burshia managed a quick retreat back across the border. Next day Joe was conducted to a post about thirty miles away and brought before Major Walsh, Captain Allen, Sitting Bull himself, and about twenty of Sitting Bull's warriors. The Sioux leader claimed that Joe was a spy.

But Major Walsh warned that not a hair of Joe's head should be harmed (thus precluding a scalping party). Sitting Bull changed his attitude, though perhaps not his suspicions, shook Joe's hand and asked:

"What are you doing in this country?"

"I'm on a visit to my father-in-law, Black Horn."

"That's good," said Sitting Bull and left the scene. He had too much sense, as a guest in Canadian territory, to press the issue.

In a few days, Captain Allen with a sergeant and perhaps an interpreter set out to accompany Joe back to Wolf Point on the Fort Peck Reservation. Nothing is said about whether Joe's wife was still with him. But Allen asked Joe if he would like to go back to Wood Mountain and interpret for the Mounties. Joe agreed to that. Though he was already a scout (for General Baldwin, USA?), Joe probably did not mind being a sort of double agent. It is not obvious how he got clearance from the U.S. Army for all this running back and forth, unless of course the U.S. officials wanted him to do just that very thing. Anyway, he did return north with Allen, apparently performed whatever duties he was supposed to do for the Mounties and then returned in February to Poplar with one of the Mounties and also with Black Horn. There may be some connection between Joe's adventure and the Treaty of 1877, which the Canadian government made with the Indians at Banff. One of the interpreters there was Isidore Sandoval II, and Bad Head (Joe's grandfather?) appeared as very old but still "influential."

Just when Joe married—or began his liaison—with Spotted Hoop is not evident. He gives the date as 1880. His dates are quite unreliable, however. His first known son, Joseph William Culbertson, is reported to have been born at Poplar on March 31st of either 1878 or 1879. Spotted Hoop was probably Joe's contact with Sitting Bull.

Joe admired Sitting Bull. He describes the famous medicine man as kindly, dignified, a good talker "like a brigadier general of the U.S. Army," always well dressed and careful to keep a neat tipi and good horses. "In my twenty years experience as an Indian scout," Joe adds, "I will always say that I think that Sitting Bull was the greatest Indian among his people. . ." It is typical of Joe's ambivalent nature that he was also friendly with the man who assassinated Sitting Bull, even though he deplored the deed.

The same sort of ambivalence shows up in his account of Spotted Hoop: "very pretty and a very good woman." She liked to go with Joe on his hunting trips. "Little did you think," Joe once reminded her, "when you were cutting the fingers (of Miles' and Custer's fallen troopers), that you would have one of General Miles' scouts as your husband. I suppose if I had been killed in that battle. . ., you would have cut my fingers off to get my ring."

Spotted Hoop's head fell and she said nothing except, "That was in the past."

But she had a jealous eye and a quick draw, and Joe was an avid enthusiast for dancing. One night, when she caught Joe dancing with someone else, she took a shot at him. She missed. Not long afterwards, Joe let her go to visit her people at Standing Rock. She did not return. Joe commented, "I felt a little sorry. . ., but I never insisted very much on her returning home, as I thought she might take another shot at me and make it count."

Of course, Joe could not be expected to give up dancing. Like his father, he played the fiddle and performed at most of the dances in his part of the prairie, sometimes traveling miles during the wintertime. His companion was a black musician named Dick Wilson, and their favorite march was the *Arkansas Traveler*, with the gentlemen promenading their Sioux consorts arm in arm. Such affairs were known to get pretty hectic before the exit, grand or otherwise.

In Montana, racism reached a new peak after the Custer affair and the exodus of the Nez Percés. As Looking Glass, White Bird and Joseph led their "non-treaty" followers streaming over Lolo Pass, many Montanans went into a state of panic. With General Howard in hot pursuit, the Nez Percés were detained near Missoula while Delaware Jim once more interpreted as go-between. But the Nez Percés slipped by Fort Fizzle into the Bitterroot, southward. Gibbon set out from Fort Shaw across Cadotte Pass to intercept them with three companies that included Lt. James Bradley, who had to lay down the pen again and take up the sword. On August 9th, 1877, Gibbons struck the Nez Percé camp at the Big Hole. Lt. Bradley was assigned to lead a charge of regulars and volunteers into the willow breaks around the lower camp. "Don't go in there!" someone called. "It's certain death." But Lt. Bradley spurted ahead and was immediately shot dead. Though the ensuing battle was called "magnificent" by General Woodruff, it has acquired a much less flattering reputation from historians. Driven across Yellowstone Park, the Nez Percés were trapped at last near the Bear Paws. White Bird and his followers escaped into Canada.

With Lt. Bradley gone, his biography of Alec Culbertson was never finished. Mary Bradley returned to Georgia with her two little daughters.

In violation of the terms of surrender, the Nez Percés were shunted about first to malaria-ridden Leavenworth, then to Indian Territory. It is an ironic footnote that among the followers of Chief Joseph was *Tzi-kai-tza*, seventy-odd years old and believed to be the son of General William Clark. With many of Joseph's people, he was driven into exile to perish in ignominy.

These rambunctious times of 1876-77 coincided with the last days of Alec's career as a trader. With the buffalo vanishing from hunting lands, with the Sioux of Sitting Bull and the Nez Percés of White Bird still refugees in Canada or drifting back and forth across the border on the warpath, with various bands of *métis*, Salish and Blackfeet and other traditional enemies wandering displaced and disoriented over the land, this was not an easy period for free traders. Yet that is evidently just what Alec and a number of other hardy souls were about. Since Joe Culbertson tells us almost nothing his father's last years and activities or even whereabouts, we have to probe whatever slim evidence we can scrape together elsewhere. One tenuous account[72] dates Alec's employment at Fort Belknap as trader, hunter and interpreter as running only from 1873 to 1875. Another account, written by Charles Aubrey, Alec's cousin by marriage, gives us this statement:

> In the year 1877 I was located at Marias River and engaged in the Indian trade. A few miles above me, at Willow Rounds, Col. Culbertson, of the American Fur Company, had a winter trading post; below me a wandering trader was located.

Charles Aubrey got his memories mixed up. For of course, Alec was no longer representing AFC in 1877, but Aubrey again refers to the three traders with himself as the man in the middle. He also enumerates the various tribes whose members came to trade on the Marias that winter: Salish, Nez Percés, even

---

[72] Julia Schultz's oral interview.

Klamaths—not to mention the Blackfeet. It would have been very dangerous for any Nez Percé to appear freely in Montana at that time, according to Andrew García's autobiographical account. Charles' wife Louise and her sister Melinda (Chouquette) were supposed to be cousins of Red Crow of the Bloods and nieces of Natawista, and as you'll recall, protegées of the Culbertsons of long ago. One cannot but wonder if Alec still kept up some contact with Natawista or her family.

Details that may substantiate Aubrey's date of 1877 (or the winter of 1877-78 by implication) are his stories of the wandering Nez Percés and of Walking Coyote. This was the young Salish who rounded up a few buffalo at Charles' instigation— at least in Charles' account—and drove them over the Divide to St. Ignatius Mission, where they eventually became the foundation of the famous herd of Pablo and Allard.

Many another besides Alec and Aubrey plied their trade across this region during these tumultuous times, either at small outposts or roaming about with covered wagons and Red River carts. There was the veteran Joe Kipp, for instance, with his occasional partner the greenhorn James Willard Schultz. There was the mule-skinner Andrew García, who has left us an even more realistic picture of the free trader's life than has Schultz himself. Many Indians from Canada, Dakota, Montana and Idaho began to converge on the Judith Basin and central Montana for the final hunts of the buffalo. The late seventies was a time of desperation for Indians threatened with starvation as the buffalo disappeared, and as the Crees, *métis* and the refugee Sioux and Nez Perces worked their way back and forth across the Medicine Line. The white population reacted with anger and even panic. It was at this time that Angus MacDonald's half Nez Percé son Duncan made trading and diplomatic trips to the Nez Percés through what is now Glacier National Park and recorded his adventures for the Deer Lodge press.

Joe Culbertson remarks of the last hunting days with his usual ambivalence:

> I think (the Indians) were the happiest people on earth in those days. I am an Indian myself and half civilized. It even makes me feel bad to look back at the good old days that have passed when the buffalo was plentiful.

So were the times good or bad? Joe wavers. But how ephemeral was the happiness to be! The year 1876 had been "The Year of the Good Winter." The good signs proved tragically deceptive, and, alas, 1879 was marked down on the winter count as "The Year When First There Were No More Buffalo." The Indians could not believe the end was coming (very much like the rest of us in similar circumstances), seeing only the abundance at hand. But suddenly the end came. And the process was irreversible. The "Good Winter" of '78 left a dry prairie that burst into flame driving the herds from west of the Cypress Hills down into Montana, to return north never more. The Indian camps clustered about the Great Sand Hills as if waiting there for the famine to send their people to the ghosts for good: Crowfoot's people and Red Crow's on the west (with Natawista perhaps among them), Crees and Assiniboines toward the south, Sitting Bull and his refugees on the southeast—all waiting, but for what? Crowfoot was one who saw the end at hand. "There will not be enough to eat for so many tribes," he warned Sitting Bull, and with his own bands, the Bloods, Crees and *métis* followed the herds into Montana. Precarious as it was for the Sioux to cross the Medicine Line, many did cross in quick sallies or secluded camps. As it was Crowfoot's foresight that realized the awful truth, so it was his personal courage that kept the peace between Blackfeet and Crees. But even Crowfoot could not put down the whiskey traders. Up they popped, far from the reach now of Royal Mounties. Evenutally, U.S. troopers appeared in the Judith country to herd the Piegans

Fort Benton and the Missouri River, 1878 (?). Photo courtesy Montana Historical Society, Helena.

back to their desolate agency and the starvation that awaited them there, while Crowfoot and Red Crow had to lead their painful trek back across the Medicine Line to another country where there was nothing left to eat.

In the time of these sorrowful events came Alexander Culbertson's last tours. There is some evidence (hardly compelling) that he made his final boat trip up the fickle river about 1879. Often in these last days he rode alone across the prairie lands that no one knew better than he, carrying his blankets and his provisions on his horse, and no doubt with the necessities at hand for a smoke of his pipe and a sip of his favorite tea. He found weapons to be quite a nuisance in these times when everyone else regarded them as life insurance. He dared to go unarmed even into the camp of Sitting Bull, somewhat like his old friend DeSmet. Since Natawista may have been in the buffalo camps, we cannot but wonder if he saw her again. According to a family report, she was spending the summer of 1879 on a visit (!) to her people.

Yes, it had been a long, long trail a-winding from the days of the barefoot lad with the big Culbertson feet tracking over the Blue Ridge or the Alleghenies, from the days of the young engagé who stood firm on his bond, no more, no less, from the wild young rascal who dashed off with the warriors on horseback over the Croquant du Nez—only to come home unhorsed. A long way too from the plush old captalist who could write his check for $100,000 . . . Now here he stood alone on a prairie empty of buffalo. And day or night, welcomed into the outlawed Indian camps.

Such is the picture, at least, that we get from Alec's obituary. But the documentary evidence about his last few years is fragile at best. The letter he wrote to George Roberts in '75 sounded as if he might have been ready to move to Nebraska even then. Yet the reference I have just cited suggests that he lingered in Montana almost till the last. There is also the obvious fact that he had to spend enough time in Montana, and perhaps even Fort Benton, to tell his story to Lt. Bradley.

Alec's reputation stood Joe Boy in good stead and probably saved his scalp even if it did not provide him with the same immunity from Indian hostility.

On a run between Belknap and Fort Peck, for example, Joe and a snow-blind comrade were waylaid by a Santee Sioux. But the "hostile" turned out to be Struck the Ree, an old friend of Alec. So instead of bushwacking them, he took Joe and his companion into camp for the night, then sent a guide with them for three day's travel to conduct them safely to Fort Peck.

Joe may not have seen much of his father during the summer of 1879. About the first of June Joe had gone up to Fort Benton with T.C. Powers, and thereafter he had to run errands back and forth between Benton and Fort Assiniboine, which was just then under construction near present day Havre. The Army was supposed to check the influx of Crees, *métis* and other Indians from Canada via the Milk River valley, a traditional Cree hunting ground. Joe is quoted as saying that he parted from his father in the summer of 1879 and that Alec "was leaving Montana forever."[73]

So we can assume that this was the season, when Alec at last found his way down to Orleans, Nebraska, the home of Julia. It was a rational move. He had two daughters in Nebraska at this period, and daughters must be more consoling than sons to a man of Alec's age. Fannie was married in February, 1879, at Kearny, Nebraska, to a young lawyer and Republican politician of that community named Louis S. Irvin. Old Fort Kearny was part of Alec's one-time stamping grounds. So it is possible that he was able to visit both his daughters this year. Perhaps he even went down there for the wedding and then stayed on at Julia's. He must have brought with him his little family archive, the volumes of Audubon's work that the artist had given him personally, the manuscript of Denig on the "Tribes of the Upper Missouri", perhaps some odds and ends of his own composition, some pictures, Indian craftwork and other such memorabilia. This would explain how Julia acquired some of these items and also her mother's old jewelry. For it was to Julia, whom he had so long ago left lone and forlorn at the Bethlehem boarding school, Julia the daughter left out of the trusteeship—it was to Julia that Alec turned in his final hours.

One day when Joe was at Fort Assiniboine, his relative "Colonel" R.L. McCulloh, the one who had so much enjoyed the long-ago summer at Locust Grove, called him aside for some frank talk.[74]

"Joe, did you hear the news?. . . I'm sorry to tell you. Your father is dead."

Alec died at Julia's home on the 27th of August, 1879. He was buried at Orleans. George and Julia moved to Idaho several years later, but George had Alec's remains reinterred about 1904, also at Orleans.

The country where Joe was running errands to and from that sad summer of '79 was just the country where he and his father had ridden together and camped and reminisced together at that mellow campfire as only father and son can do.

---

[73] The file on Julia Schultz in the Montana Historical Society.

[74] McCulloh had been moved from Chambersburg to St. Louis as a boy, but it is not clear whether he knew Joe. Neither is it clear why Joe called him "Colonel", though Robert was in the Army during the Civil War for nine months. He is said to have arrived at Fort Assiniboine in September, 1879, with his sometime partner Charles Broadwater.

Epilogue

Before you close the covers of this book, you will want to know something about what happened to the rest of the people whose trails you have been following across its pages. Joe Culbertson is the only one of his family who has left us any extensive record of himself. His story would make another book. Some of his adventures were quite hair-raising—literally. But the hair was never Joe's. He liked best to be remembered as "General Miles' old scout", though he scouted also for Generals Baldwin and Wheaton and in company with other scouts more famous than himself: Yellowstone Kelly, Johnny Bruyère, Charlie Reynolds, Vic Smith.

Sometimes Joe visited his brother Jack. The two halves of Jack never did seem to fit together, and he has remained a mystery throughout this saga. He did have a family of his own and at least one wife. The Dawson County census of 1880 lists John Culbertson, ranch man, born in Dakota; his wife Mary, Indian, 24 years old, born in Dakota; a son John, three years old, born in Montana. For a while Jack conducted a trading post for Leighton and Jordan at the Big Bend of the Milk River. Once, when Joe was running a dispatch from Fort Peck to the Big Bend, he realized he was being tracked by a couple of warriors. He made a quick slip into some badlands and then to Jack's place by morning. His comment reveals an attitude typical not only of himself but probably of his father too: "I never believed much in fighting when there was a good chance of get away." Whether Jack fitted that same mold we cannot tell.

Evenutally, Jack moved to a ranch near the present town of Culbertson, named probably after him. Here he ran a store or post that stood half-way between Fort Buford and Fort Poplar and catered to the soldiers passing between the posts. Family tradition claims that his mother came to visit him from time to time. It seems natural that Jack would be the one Natawista would come back to, for he, after all, was her first-born, the fruit of those carefree happier days—if ever there were. The girls were both taken from her at an early age, and Joe was more his father's son than his mother's. But Natawista could not afford to remain on the U.S. side of the border indefinitely since now she was enrolled in Canada among the people of Red Crow, her nephew, and there the erstwhile Queen of the High Missouri subsisted on the simple rations of poverty. Gone were the days of the fabulous gowns, the rings and the rubies. Bad Head (her father?) was reported in 1880 as very old, blind, with one old wife and the blue jacket of a minor chief. He died in the fall of 1884. So probably Natawista divided her time between Jack in Montana and Red Crow in Canada, and perhaps as long as Jack lived.[75]

[75] I am including this information on Jack and Natawista with the generous permission of O'Neil Jones, who gleaned these details from persistent interviews with members of Jack's family.

That was not long. One day in the fall of 1888 Jack was over the state line in Williston, North Dakota, near the Missouri River above Tobacco Gardens. He went into the bar of Newton and Gibson. For reasons not on record he got into a fight and was killed. A minimal effort was made to treat the case legally, and a post mortem revealed four wounds on his head, "none of which could have caused death" but any one of which might have caused loss of consciousness. It was thought by the examiners that after Gibson knocked him down, Jack tried to get up but fell back and smothered in the dirt on the bar room floor. Believe that if you can. Not everyone swallowed the story then, as is evident from comments in the newspaper. Do you suppose Natawista was visiting Jack at the time he was killed? The date was October 13th—Indian summer and a likely season for a last visit before the winter closed in.[76]

Back in Canada, Natawista lived with her nephew Old Moon near Stand Off, Alberta. These were years of poverty and hunger. In the spring of 1893 the agent addressed a report to the Indian Commissioner on the 6th of April telling of the sickness that then prevailed among the older Bloods and citing the example of "Mrs. Culbertson, the sister of Red Crow". Not long after that Natawista died. The Register for the Oblate Fathers of the Blood Reserve records her funeral on 14 June, 1893, naming her Nellie Culbertson, sister of Chief Red Crow. ("Aunt" would be more accurate.) Her grand-nephew was in attendance. She was buried at the Catholic Mission in Stand Off.[77] With Jack now gone, there is no sign that Joe or the girls even knew about it.

This was the year when Joe seems to have married again, this time to Isabel LaRocque. She was from Qu'Apelle, Saskatchewan, the daughter of Jean Baptiste LaRocque and Julia LaMare, a family of French and Chippewa origin. When Isabel was about six, her family moved down into Montana with their eight children, like so many other *métis* families in their two-wheeled Red River carts. The LaRocques were evidently staying near the Bear Paw Mountains at the time Chief Joseph and his Nez Percés swept through Montana. Isabel married a white man, Abbott in the employ of Joe Kipp as a trader at old Fort Browning. They had two sons. After Abbott died, Isabel married Joe, and apparently they were both congenial about accepting each other's offspring.

Many other *métis* fled from Canada because of Riel's rebellions. The last of these conflicts occurred in 1885, but tensions between *métis* and Montana whites flared long after the execution of Riel himself, in fact on into the next century with the harrassment of the "landless Indians." Since both Jack and Joe were married to, or on good terms with refugees, one wonders if this racial hostility had something to do with the killing of Jack and with the attack on Joe that occurred at Tobacco Gardens. Joe was serving the Army at Fort Buford about 1893 or '94 and was out walking with Isabel one summer evening. As they crossed the Garden Coulee, someone shot Joe in the hip and groin. Joe was a rugged rascal and recovered well. He recalled his mother's story: Beware of Tobacco Gardens.

With the demise of AFC, the new corporate interests that took over Montana were the railroads and the mining companies. Marcus Daly's Amalgamated and James J. Hill's Manitoba Railway were powerful allies. Hill cared nothing for man or mountain that stood in his way and proposed packing the Blackfeet off to the hositile Dakotas (while an Army boss wanted them shipped to the Flatheads). Hill antagonized the stockmen by luring nesters onto the range. Stockmen in turn were often hostile to settlers, Indians and *métis*. So it would

---

[76] Cleve Culbertson was brutally lynched for murder in Williston in 1913. His father was J.W. Culbertson of Wyoming but whether any relation to Joe or Jack I cannot tell. (Williston *Herald* 18 Dec. 1913.)
[77] Information provided by Hugh A. Dempsey.

seem that the Culbertsons, or what was left of them, who were a little bit of everything, got caught in the middle once again. But Jim Hill's son Louis tried a conciliatory approach, fascinated as he was by both the scenery and the natives. Among the friends he cultivated along his father's railroad, now the GN, were ranger Dan Doody of Nyack, prima donna Mary Garden, Albert, Crown Prince of the Belgians and Joe Culbertson of Poplar. Louis and Joe, in times to come, would visit the annual Indian fair, go off on hunting trips together and even plan a movie about Custer.[78]

Joe made friends among his old enemies the Sioux and even accompanied the Sioux chiefs to Washington to intercede for the band of Sitting Bull. He toured with General Hugh Scott and made contact with his mother's relatives, the Aubreys and the Wades-in-the Waters. One way or another he kept track of Julia and Fannie. He enjoyed rubbing elbows with the notables of Montana at Helena or at the fashionable Alhambra Hot Springs. For years he kept fond hopes of publishing his memoirs. He handed out documents, photos, relics, even his own manuscripts to people he took to be his friends. Probably through Robert McCulloh, he was presented to Charles Kessler of Helena, who wanted to write a biography of Alexander. Joe and Julia loaded Kessler with memorabilia. When he proved tardy about returning such treasures or getting Joe's autobiography into print, poor Joe would live in agony from one mail to the next. Eventually, Kessler grew discouraged by the indifference of some of the Culbertson relatives in the east, abandoned his project, moved to California and left his collection to the archives established in Los Angeles by copper king William Andrews Clark. So once again the Culbertson story was shelved in vaults of oblivion, while Joe's part of it appeared publicly only in a distorted form.

Typical of Joe's bid in the game for fame was his little misadventure on one of his returns from Helena and Kessler aboard Hill's railroad. Imagine his chagrin on being tossed into jail in Great Falls! "Just four little beers!" he cried, protesting that he must have been under surveillance on the train, followed, drugged and rolled . . . Well, perhaps, but Agent Mossman of Fort Peck Reservation had to come and get him loose. Righteously, Joe swore he'd go to "the springs to be boiled out" and then convert to a new man. Alas, the new man's prospects of fame never rose from the ashes.

Various census reports (federal, state, Indian Bureau), compiled during the last decade of the 19th century, describe the Culbertsons of Montana something like this: Joseph, Sr., age 42 in 1900, judge of the Indian court and a member of the Blackfeet tribe; his wife, Isabel, born 1869 in Canada of the Chippewa tribe, speaks English but cannot read it; Joseph William, son of Joseph, Sr., by a Sioux woman, born in March 1878, attended the Industrial Boarding School on the Standing Rock Reservation and then Carlisle Academy (near the Culbertson ancestral home); Maggie, daughter of Joseph, Sr., by a Sioux mother, born in May, 1892; Lizzie, daughter of Joe and Isabel, born February, 1894; Samuel, son of Joe and Isabel, born in July, 1898 (though mistaken as a daughter by the census-taker). Isabel's two sons by Abbott were George, age 15 in 1900, and Frank two years younger.

The family of Jack Culbertson is harder to keep track of after his death, but he had at least two children, John and Mary. A young John Culbertson is listed as a boarder (cow hand?) on the ranch of Howard Eaton[79] near Medora in the

---

[78] See *After the Buffalo Were Gone,* Northwest Area Foundation, St. Paul, 1985.
[79] Eaton was the friend of Theodore Roosevelt and the Marquis de Morès, a tourist guide in Glacier National Park and the Southwest.

Bad Lands of the Little Missouri. In 1899 we find a Jack Culbertson included in the family of a Yankton named Iron Leggins; two years later he is 20 years old and married to Rosie; two or three years more and he is single.

Scattered over Montana and the west there were other Culbertsons, now almost too numerous to interrelate. Alec's nephew Robert was raising a family of his own at Fort Benton, the last of the line on Alec's old home turf. It may be more than coincidental that Alec's daughters resided in Nebraska where both their husbands were lawyers and leaders of the Republican Party. But the family of Julia and George moved to Idaho, where George practiced as attorney for the Union Pacific and became the first Attorney General of that state. He would represent Idaho at the Roosevelt inaugural and again at the fiftieth anniversary of the battle of Gettysburg, when he once again climbed over the old stone wall into the apple orchard to greet the two "Dutch" sisters who had given him asylum with his boot full of blood. His daughter and Julia's, Margaret, became director of the State Historical Museum and Library in Boise and gave considerable help to Kessler. Caroline, their other daughter, preserved something of the Indian side of the family story and so too did son Alexander C. Roberts of Spokane.

Louis and Fannie Irvin also left Nebraska. In 1889 Louis was appointed by President Harrison as a special agent for the Treasury Department and was sent to San Francisco, a city with which his family would be associated for quite some time to come. The Irvins had to shift about the country, however, to El Paso, St. Louis, District of Columbia, Los Angeles, Long Beach, but San Francisco appears to have been the city they came back to. Son Pierre reached even more distant ports of call in the Navy. Fannie was the only one of the Culbertson children who came back to live among the Blackfeet, for when Louis was lawyer for the Blackfeet tribe, they made their home at Midvale (East Glacier) among the offspring of Alec's old cronies and Natawista's cousins: the Dawsons, Clarkes, Sandovals, Monroes, and Spotted Eagles. . . Joe too would come there among the old-timers like himself, probably at least for a chat about the long ago. Fannie outlived all the rest of Alec's children, drawing her life into a magic circle to die in Great Falls, just a little way up the Golden River from her reputed birthplace, Fort Benton. Fannie was the proud beauty of the family. Though, to judge from portraits, I cannot imagine that Julia was far behind.

Of all the old generation of fur trading days, it was Captain Joseph LaBarge who survived the longest, until 1899 in fact. With him faded the last remmant of the old days. But he left a large family to cope with the new. The corporate giant he had so often served and so often defied, was there no more. In its place were other corporate tyrants, merchant princes, copper kings and the moguls of the railroads that had now suppanted the steamboats.

It is on the reservations that the historical snoop finds names that evoke memories of the past: Mitchell among the Yanktons and Assiniboines, Bruyère and Lavatta with the Yanktons, Dan Martín(ez) among the Assiniboines, Boyd, Burshia, LaRocque and so on. . . And of course, Philip Álvarez. Philip was still very much alive at Poplar. His son Nick (Omasute and Shoots Them) had accompanied the Army expedition to capture Gall in 1881, became an Army interpreter and a blacksmith at Wolf Point. Philip's oldest daughter Belle, grandniece of Sitting Bull, was probably in school at Fort Shaw, leaving Eliza, Louise and Joseph at home with her father. Eventually, she married the well-known humorist and columnist John Tatsey, who was a grand-nephew of Natawista. Joseph Álvarez, probably a son or grandson of Philip, became a trumpeter with Sousa's band and seems to have been in France during World War I with Joe Culbertson's son Sam. When Sam came home, he swept Agent Mossman's daughter off her feet and into wedlock—much to Mossman's chagrin and Joe's ticklish delight. Joseph Álvarez came home and married Joe's daughter Lizzie. So here again we find the closing of a magic circle.

At the turn of the century, amid the racial tensions and the smallpox that again swept Montana's high-line, there was still another circle to close—not a magic one to be sure, but the period of thirty-three plus years. The Leonids began their vast ballet in 1898 with a repeat performance each year till 1901. There were a couple of tyrants in the solar system, named for the gods Jupiter and Saturn, who pulled the dancers out of their routine. But even with such a prolonged display, it was nothing like the old days when Prince Maximilian marked it in the Winter of the Falling Stars. Even so, things worked out in their spirals, as the Sioux proverb tells us: Your deeds are your children. They will return.

KYÉNE

Genealogy Charts

Culbertson

4 brothers (Robert, Joseph, Alexander & Samuel) Culbertson
came from N. Ireland & settled in Penn. by 1743

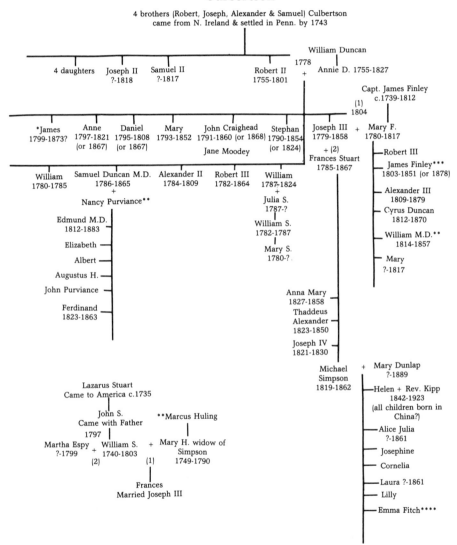

All twelve were born on Culberston Row, PA.
** Huling & Purviance are French (Huguenot) names. William the M.D. married Nancy C. McCulloh,
daughter of Thomas G. McCulloh and Margaret Purviance.
*** James Finley married Elizabeth B. Wallace. Their son Cyrus J. died in California 1851, may
be the one who hunted buffalo with Alec. Another son was Robert Simpson of Fort Benton.
**** The date on Michael Simpson's daughters is problematic

Princes

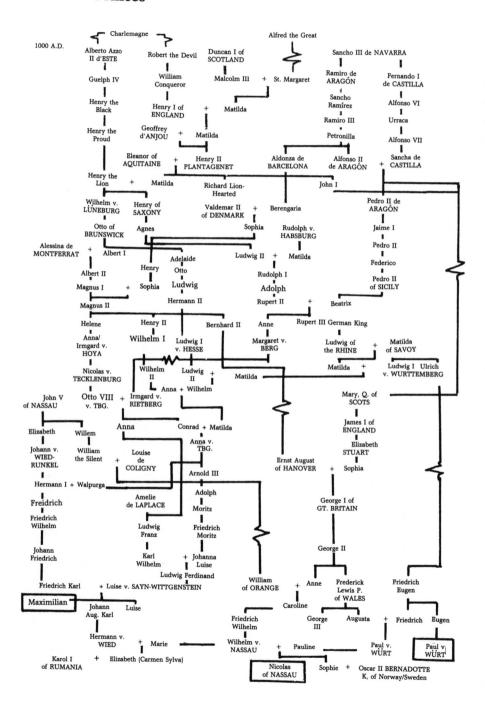

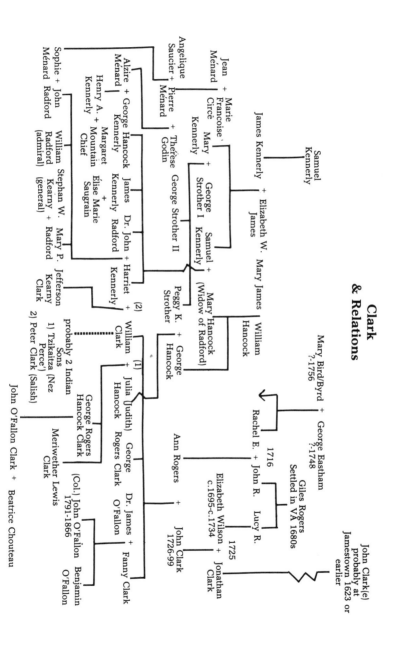

Clark
& Relations

Chouteau
Laclède

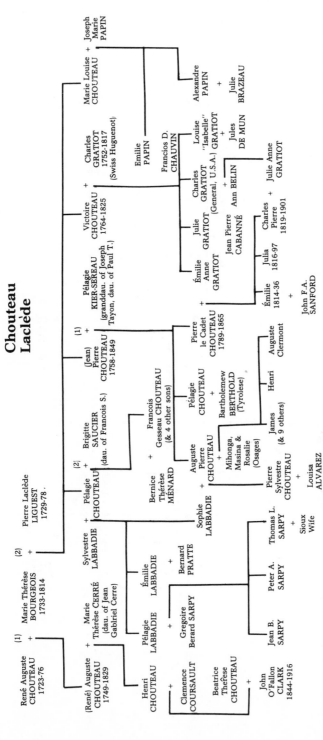

MARIE THÉRÈSE BOURGEOIS: Madame Chouteau, the matriarch of the family and its real founder. She could defy church and state and get by with it. All her offspring by Laclède-Liguest are, of course illegitimate but were obliged by law to retain the name "Chouteau" (that of her legal husband) rather than that of their real father.

CHARLES GRATIOT I: His French Huguenot family fled to Switzerland from persecution and there he was born. He was a co-worker with George Rogers Clark during the Revolution, along with Jean Gabriel Cerré, father of Marie Thérèse Cerré on ths chart, and the famous Father Gibault. His son Charles II, the General, was chief engineer of the Army, serving at West Point and many other places.

CHARLES PIERRE CHOUTEAU (son of Pierre le Cadet, the real head of American Fur Co. for years and the builder of the great Chouteau fortune) was a Missouri River steamer captain. He was both the nephew and the son-in-law of General Gratiot, also a friend of Alexander Culbertson, Fr. DeSmet and numerous others.

For JOHN O'FALLON CLARK see my chart on Clark. Ditto for MÉNARD.
JULIE BRAZEAU probably is of the family which gave its name to the mountain peak in Jasper National Park.
JOHN F. A. SANFORD: a Virginian. He "owned" the famous slave Dred Scott in the suit Scott vs. Sanford.

Notes

PROLOGUE: The principal source is Alexander von Humboldt & Aimé Bonpland: *Personal Narrative of Travels to the Equinoctial Regions of America During the Years 1799-1804,* translated from the French in 3 volumes; Chapter X. There are various editions.

The Quotations, page 2: The Sioux proverbs derives from the "Phillips County Interviews" on tape in the Library of the Montana Historical Society, Helena. The brief citation from the legend of Shining Shirt is my own paraphrase. Sources for this legend include Ella E. Clark: *Indian Legends from the Northern Rockies,* pp. 92-95, 125-128; Harry Holbert Turney-High: *The Flathead Indians of Montana,* pp. 41-43; Lucylle Hartz Evans: *St. Mary's in the Rocky Mountains,* p. 7; J. Neilson Barry: "Spaniards in Early Oregon", Washington Historical Society Quarterly, January, 1932; Jack Holterman: *Place Names of Glacier/Waterton National Parks,* pp. 51-52.

CHAPTER I: Sources on the origins of the Culbertson family: *Biographical Annals of Franklin County,* pp. 434-441 (Culbertson material probably the work of James Gray Rose, Who may be borrowing from William Alexander Parsons Martin); Jeannette Erickson: personal correspondence, 30 July, 1982; Ida Eliot Snively: manuscripts at the Pennsylvania Historical Society "Genealogy of the Culbertson Family," "Genealogy of the Stuart Family," "The Culbertsons of Culbertsons' Row"; Lewis R. Culbertson: *Genealogy of the Culbertson Families;* Montana Historical Society: *Contributions.* Sometimes overlooked is the Huguenot element in the family revealed by the surnames Huling and Purviance. And what of Culbertson itself—'son of Colbert'? *The Alleged Royal Descent of the Culbertsons:* I must confess that I do not believe that the Culbertsons, not even those from the line of Frances Stuart Culbertson, are descended from Mary, Queen of Scots. It is, possible that they descend from some earlier generation of the Stuarts and even from Duncan I, supposedly slain by Macbeth in 1040. Such, at least, was the tradition, though conservative historians claim that the founder of the family was one of the Celtic Bretons of northwestern France, Alan Fitz-flaad, who arrived in England around 1100. Alan's son was selected Steward of Scotland by David I, and the title STEWARD became hereditary for a custodian or seneschal of the royal authority in Scotland. From this title derives the surname STUART and its variants. Persons interested in this question should consult the works of Arnold McNaughton, M.D.A.R. von Redlick, Gerald Paget and A.C. Addington metioned in the bibliography.

But if proof of blood relationship remains elusive, the evidence for poliltical affiliation is clear. The brothers Culbertson migrated to the colonies in 1743, while Lazarus and son came in 1735. This was the period of the collapse of the Stuart cause. The supporters of the Stuarts called Jacobites were an incongruous mix of Scots, Irish, French and Tory English. Their name derives from *Jacobus,* Latin for "James", and it was James I, the son of Mary, who gave his name to Jamestown, Virginia, the James River and the version of the Bible. But James II was replaced by the House of Orange, while "James III" (the Old Pretender) failed to attain the throne, which was offered instead to the House of Hanover. Ironically, both the Houses of Hanover and Orange, owed their claims and ancestry to the House of Stuart. This summary may clarify the attitudes of families in this book, their choices in politics, their allegiance to the Olyphants, Lowries and Mackeys.

CHAPTER II: Sources on early families of St. Louis include Foley and Rice: *The First Chouteaus;* William Clark Kennerly: *Persimmon Hill;* James Kennerly: *Diary, 1823-1826;* Stella M. Drumm: "The Kennerlys of Virginia"; J. Thomas Scharf: *History of St. Louis;* "Catholic Marriages, St. Louis, Missouri, 1774-1840" and "Catholic Baptisms, St. Louis, Missouri, 1765-1840" both published by the St. Louis Genealogical Society; R.C. Ballard Thurston: "Some Recent Finds Regarding the Ancestry of General George Rogers Clark"; Frederic L. Billon: *Annals of St. Louis;* the *Dictionary of American Biography.* Some of the research on early St. Louis families was done for me by Mrs. Coralee Paull.

Spanish Settlers in Early St. Louis: It is sometimes said that there were four—and only four— early Spanish settlers in St. Louis. Questionable as this statement is, it refers to the four Spaniards brought to San Luis or St. Louis by the first Spanish Governor Commandant of Upper Louisiana, Don Pedro

Piernas. The four were 1: Benito Vásquez (1750-1810) from Galicia in northwestern Spain, who married Julie Papin from Canada; 2) Martín Milony Duralde, evidently a Spanish Basque, the son of Pedro Duralde and María de Elizaga, born in Viscaya, Spain, perhaps in the town of Cumbre, which was under the ecclesiastical jurisdiction of the French Diocese of Bayonne; 3) Eugenio Álvarez (c. 1736-1816) from Madrid or Toledo and the son of Augusto (?) Álvarez and María Bravo; he married Josephe Crépeau from Vincennes; and 4) Josef Álvarez Hortiz (Ortiz) (1753-1808), son of Francisco Álvarez and Bernarda Hortiz; he was born in Lienira, Estremadura, and married Marguerite Marianne Becquet from New Chartres, Illinois. The Reconstructed Census of 1776 of St. Louis lists another man, Francisco Álvarez, a soldier from Spain. It is the surname Álvarez that concerns us especially, but it is sometimes difficult to sort out the various persons who bore this name. There were evidently two or three with the baptismal name Manuel. Still another *may* have been the grandfather by a former marriage of the Philip (Felipe) Álvarez of the narrative to follow. While both names Álvarez and Vásquez are encountered frequently in annals of the fur trade, Martín Duralde is of interest for political reasons. He married Marie Joseph Perrault of Quebec and moved to New Orleans, where he became a member of the U.S. territorial legislature. His daughter Clarisse married the first U.S. governor of Louisiana, William Charles Cole Claiborne, gave him a son of the same name and quietly succumbed to the yellow fever that then was so prevalent in New Orleans. Martín and Marie Joseph Duralde also had a son Martín Duralde II, who married Henry Clay's daughter Susan.

CHAPTER III: For years it seemed that practically the only source available in English regarding Prince Maximilian was the edition of his own *Travels in the Interior of North America* in the four volumes of Reuben Gold Thwaites. It included the art work of Charles Bodmer. History books repeated each other from this single source as if their authors neither cared nor dared to venture farther afield. Then the Prince's *Travels in Brazil* (or part of it) came into rare use, and the *People of the First Man* more recently supplemented these earlier works with some of the Prince's field notes. In 1983, the 150th anniversary of Maximilian's trip to North America, public interest was at last aroused, in part by the Joslyn Museum and the Smithsonian, and a fresh assessment was in order. A big step forward is the publication of a new and more complete edition and translation of Maximilian's diaries by William J. Orr and Joseph C. Porter, along with additional biographical data. Some observations about the House of Wied-Neuwied occur in the memoirs of Queen Marie of Rumania, the granddaughter of Victoria, and still more in the memoirs of Carmen Sylva (Queen Elizabeth of Rumania), the grandniece of Maximilian. Sources of the genealogy of the House of Wied and the related houses of Nassau and Württemberg derive from Prince Isenberg and Baron Freytag: *Europäische Stammtafeln* in five volumes, the *Genealogisches Handbuch des Adels*, 1951, 1959 (especially for the maternal lines), and Charles Recker's article "The Counts of Tecklenburg and of Ravensberg" in *The Augustan*, XXI: 1, the Augustan Society, Torrance, CA. (The Tecklenburg research was accomplished in my effort to trace the Tecklenburg descent, of my grandmother.) A helpful source for both Maximilian and Bodmer includes the brochures of the Joslyn and Smithsonian on their exhibits.

Paul of Württemberg: Any talk of Maximilian inevitably invites comparison with Prince (Duke) Paul of Württemberg. Both men were naturalists, both were inspired by Alexander von Humboldt, both were especially concerned with the American Indian, both brought an Indian protege to reside in courtly Europe, both traveled in the U.S. and Latin America and attempted to travel under assumed names, more or less incognito, Maximilian as the Baron von Braunsberg and Paul as the Baron von Hohenberg. Remarkably too, they both made similar criticisms of Americans and seem to have held similar liberal attitudes. Paul must be carefully distinguished from his cousin of the same name and title. For his far wanderings and romanticism Paul has also been dubbed "the Gypsy Prince." Sources on his adventures include Louis C. Butscher's articles "Prince Paul Wilhelm" as given in my bibliography; the Prince's own *Travels in North America, 1822-1824*, in the English edition by Nitske and Lottinvile; Larry S. Thompson's *Montana Explorers*, Volume I. This last work gives a brief outline of Paul's second trip to America, 1829-1831, citing as evidence of his visit to Montana and the headwaters of the Missouri, the big bill that Paul ran up at Fort Union from May to August, 1830. Larry Thompson traces Paul up the Missouri and down the Yellowstone and suggests that Sacajawea's son may have "joined him on some of his later expeditions." The records of this second trip have, however, been lost, though we know that in 1831 Paul passed the winter on a trip to Mexico City, Vera Cruz, then back to New Orleans (his favorite resort) and through the northeastern U.S. In 1839-1840 he went up the Nile and in 1849-1856 came again to the U.S., Mexico, California and also to South America, and sailed around the world in 1857-1859. Marshall Sprague's *Gallery of Dudes* has an excellent account of Maximilian but only a couple of mentions of Prince Paul, though he does add that Maximilian got information from Paul in preparation for his visit to the U.S. A packet of special source materials on Prince Paul was graciously sent to me by Dr. Robert Schweitzer from the Württembergische Landesbibliothek, Stuttgart.

The Moravian Seminary: Since this institution was destined to figure decisively in the saga of the Culbertsons, we can afford to take a careful look at it through the Prince's eye. It may well have been Prince Max, in the days to come, who passed on these impressions to Alec and suggested that he educate his daughters here. By tradition, the Moravian Brethren were missioners among the Delawares and Iroquois. The Moravian College, as it is called today, is still a thriving institution and one of the oldest educational establishments in the U.S., older in fact than the U.S. itself. It was the first boarding school for girls in the Thirteen Colonies, founded by the Countess Benigna von Zinzendorf. Her father, Count Nikolaus Ludwig von Zinzendorf, was a follower of John Hus of Bohemia and so became an exile in America, where began to preach to the Indians in the 1730's. At Christmas, 1740, he visited and named the village of Bethlehem.

Paul of Württemberg, who did *not* think highly of the communes of Wurttembergers under Rapp, speaks well of the Moravians (p. 450, Bek edition). Their schools, he says, "are used by many Americans of high station for the education of their daughers." And he adds that "little Bethlehem" outdid New York and Philadelphia by a performance of Haydn's oratorio "Creation".

CHAPTER IV: The standard sources of the Missouri fur trade are largely secondary: John E. Sunder: *The Fur Trade of the Upper Missouri, 1840-1865;* Hiram Martin Chittenden's two works, *The American Fur Trade of the Far West* in 2 volumes, and the *History of Early Steamboat Navigation on the Missouri River* (published as two volumes in one and including the biography of Captain Joseph La Barge); George Catlin: *Letters and Notes on the American Indians,* 2 volumes, various editions; LeRoy R. Hafen (editor): *Mountain Men and the Fur Trade of the Far West,* 10 volumes (more adequate for the central Rockies than for the northern areas). The Historical Society of Montana's *Contributions,* in 10 volumes, offer much information (and some misinformation), including a biographical sketch of Alexander Culbertson in Volume X and Lt. Bradley's Papers scattered through Volumes II, III, VIII, and IX. (Not all Bradley's Papers have been published to date. He did a "Blackfoot Vocabulary" still in manuscript but rather good for his times and circumstances.) In this chapter, of course, we still depend on Maximilian's account and especially in the new Orr-Porter edition.

Some persons mentioned in this chapter need to be identified: *Manuel Lisa:* One of the founders of the Missouri fur trade, of Hispanic origin and an entrepreneur of amazing ability. He established the first post in Montana, Fort Ramón near the Big Horn, in 1807. His "country wife" Mitain was an Omaha whose heart-wrenching story appears in various accounts of the early fur trade. By her Lisa had a daughter Rosalie and a son Ramón (Raymond, Christopher). Lisa took the daughter to St. Louis and she is supposed to have married a white man. But when Lisa tried to take the son away from Mitain, the Indian Agent Benjamin O'Fallon intervened. The story must have been known to Alexander Culbertson and should have taught him a lesson but evidently did not. It is almost a pre-run of his story. *François Roi* (Roy, Le Roi) was from Rheims. Prince Max, punning on his name, called the new planatation the *Royaume.*

William May was an ubiquitous trapper and the grandson of John Sevier, governor of Tennessee. *Sevier* is a Huguenot name derived from the Spanish Basque family Xavier. This was the family of St. Franicis Xavier.

Joseph La Barge (1815-1899): The son of a *québequois* whose ancestors hailed from the south of France, and the grandson of Spanish soldier Álvarez Ortiz, Joseph blended the disparate elements common to the Creole heritage. Like his father, who had come all the way from Quebec to St. Louis in a birchbark canoe (via Ottawa River to Lake Michigan to Green Bay to Wisconsin River to the Mississippi with 8 miles of portage), he was a man inured to the frigid north. Like his mother with her Spanish piety, he was at home in the warm, casual south. His family members were long-time friends of Daniel Boone. When the Marquis de Lafayette was a guest of the Chouteaus, Joseph, an eager lad, jumped onto the rear axle of the Marquis' carriage so that he could greet the hero in his native tongue. But then he was an agile athlete from early youth and gained the reputation of out-jumping, out-running and out-swimming all the boys of his neighborhood. As he grew older as a swimmer, he could over-take a yawl, a deer or an elk. A British traveler named James Stuart wanted to adopt him and take him abroad, but (quite understandably) his parents said No. Instead, they sent him off to begin studies for the priesthood. But handsome young Joseph preferred dalliance with young ladies and occasional mischief in the company of his friend Édouard Liguest Chouteau. Prestigious as their families might be, both boys were expelled and had to find their own way home on a Mississippi River boat. So Joseph learned about steamers.

At first he turned to the Indian trade and took a hitch with AFC. He lived with the Loup Pawnees and learned their language. He witnessed the steamboat attack on the women of Black Hawk's followers as they were struggling to swim the Mississippi. In spite of his personal or family friendship with the Chouteaus, he soon learned to be wary of the Chouteau Company, American Fur, and of its methods and monopolistic designs. When Joseph dared to go into opposition to AFC, he came close to extinction. Justly or not, he suspected the Company's agents were trying to lure him into a trap and murder him. So after a job with Robidoux, he returned to his boyhood fantasy, the river boats, first as a clerk, eventually as a pilot and captain. He was probably the most famous of the Missouri River captains. Another captain was his brother Jean (John), who, however, died fairly young.

CHAPTER V: The main source for the epidemic of 1833 is S.F. Cook as listed in the bibliography. Similarly, for the Prophet Dance and the native revivalism, see Leslie Spier. Most of the narrative of this chapter comes from Lt. Bradley's Papers and Maximilian's journals. *Seen From Afar:* This chief of the Kaina, so important to the success of Alexander Culbertson, deserves special attention. Oral tradition suggests that in a sense he and Alexander made each other. Stories about Seen From Afar or Far Off In Sight are told by Adolf Hungry Wolf in his book *The Blood People* , pp. 156-7, 272. J.W. Schultz gives less reliable accounts, naming him Far Off In Sight, but since one of Schultz' stories is dated 1880, the accuracy of the narrative and even the identity of the chief must be called into question. There may be a confusion of father and son. In some accounts, the Blackfeet name is spelled Peenaquim or Pinukwiim, the spelling used by Schultz. The difference in transliteration between these forms and mine is not as great as it seems, since there is evidence that W and Y are interchangeable. (The same difference may be noted in Alexander's spelling of the name *Natawista* and my spelling as given on page 57. The true Seen From Afar, *Pinukwiim* or (as I prefer it) *Piinakoyim*, had an alternate name, *Ap-unistai-nakoyim*, White Calf Vanished or White Calf Out of Sight. Perhaps the play on words is intentional. Instead of *Pi-* (far off), *-sai-* has been inserted, changing the meaning from "Seen Afar" to "Seen No More"; *-nukwiim* or *-nakoyim* remains in both names and mean "seen, is seen". The *-sai-*, however, raises a problem because it also means "out" as well as "not", and one translation of the name suggests that it refers to a white calf bobbing in and out of sight along the top of a ridge. The root *unista-* raises another question because it means "calf", to be sure" but has a homonym meaning "spirit", related perhaps in both meaning and etymology to "manito." White Calf was also the name of the last of the Piegan chiefs, who did have some Kaina connection.

CHAPTER VI: Maximilian and Lt. Bradley are still our mainstays for this chapter, both of whom contribute to the story of Loreto. Other sources on Loreto are these: Chittenden: *The American Fur Trade*. . . , pp. 671-672, 674; Washington Irving: *The Adventures of Captain Bonneville*, pp. 129, 134-136; Larpenteur: *Journal*, Volume I, pp. 168-170; Frances Fuller Victor: *The River of the West*, pp. 133-135; James Carnegie, Earl of Southesk: *Saskatchewan and the Rocky Mountains*, pp. 160-162; Claude E. Schaeffer: "Echoes of the Past on the Blackfeet Reservation: Loreto, the Young Mexican Trapper" in *The Montana Magazine of History*, Volume II, No. 2, April 1952, pp. 11-26; Mrs. M.E. Passmann: an article preserved in the Library of the Montana Historical Society, Helena.

The story of Loreto gives us a glimpse into a phase of the fur trade Alexander Culbertson tells us nothing about, and an important phase at that: the annual trappers' rendezvous. Loreto attended both the rendezvous of 1832 at Pierre's Hole, Idaho, just west of the Grand Tetons, and that of 1833 at Green River. At these wild frolics, trappers assembled to represent all the companies, and Indians came by the hundreds from various tribes. Rivalry gave way to revelry in a mix of drinking, gambling, dancing, wrestling, shooting, racing horses and playing practical jokes. (Example of a practical joke: baptize your buddy with alcohol then strike a match.)

At the rendezvous of Pierre's Hole, Loreto belonged to the Rocky Mountain Fur Company and brought along his wife and tiny son. Her name was *Sinopáki* (Fox Woman) with the war alias of Kills on Both Sides, and she was a Piegan whom Loreto had ransomed from the Crows. When the rendezvous was over, Loreto moved his little family out with his Company's brigade under Jim Bridger, north into the country of the Blackfeet, where you traveled in brigades if you valued your scalp. And whom should they meet in this country? The Blackfeet, of course, headed by Eagle Ribs. Among Eagle Ribs' warriors *Sinopáki* recognized her own brother. Running her horse over to meet him, she carried along her baby strapped onto her saddle in his cradle board. But Jim Bridger, faking a peace offer, pulled a gun and fired on Eagle Ribs. In the ensuing brouhaha, the horse fled back across the lines to Loreto. Realizing that his little son could not survive without his mother, Loreto seized the baby and dashed across the no man's-land to restore him to *Sinopáki*. This act of valor became legendary along the frontier and was recorded by Washington Irving. Details vary somewhat in the different accounts.

But this misadventure cost poor Loreto wife and child. After a year of wandering, perhaps among the Nez Percés, from whom he may have acquired the Indian name of Spotted Eagle, he was back for the rendezvous of 1833. Came now revelers old and new: Fontenelle and Drips representing AFC, Captain Bonneville and Sir William Drummond Stewart, Charles Larpenteur and Baptiste (Pampi) Charbonneau, Wyeth and Cerré, Robert Campbell and even William Henry Harrison's son Ben, sent out west by his father to cure himself of alcoholism—at a trappers' rendezvous! Don Manuel Álvarez of the Santa Fe Trail was there too with a marvelous story of his visit to the geysers of the upper Yellowstone. The joys of the season, however, were marred by tragic attacks from animals with rabies. This summer Loreto, perhaps still seeking his little family, severed his ties with Rocky Mountain Fur outfit and joined up with American Fur instead. When the rendezvous ended on the 24th of July, he may have gone down the Yellowstone with Don Manuel, who quit the fur trade this year, and/or with Wyeth and Cerré. Anyhow, he was assigned to the Piegan post, where he joined Sandoval and perhaps another *paisano* named Pablo. If Washington Irving's rumor was true, he also found his wife and child.

For those interested in the botanist Nathaniel Wyeth, there is a colorful account in Larry S. Thompson's book, *Montana Explorers: The Pioneer Naturalists*, Volume I, 1985.

CHAPTER VII: This chapter owes most to Maximilian. For details on the meteor showers, any handbook of astronomy will do, Robert H. Baker's, for example. But for some details, local sources are needed, e.g. David Lavender's *Bent's Fort*, p.150. My disparaging remarks on the fur trade, which disturb some people (happily, since there is no point in writing anything that disturbs no one), owe some material to Calvin Martin: *Keepers of the Game*.

CHAPTER VIII: For this chapter we rely on standard sources for the fur trade, Sunder, Bradley, Hafen's *Mountain Men . . .* (see Volume IX). There is still something here from Maximilian and/or his English editor. Joel Overholser of Fort Benton and Hugh A. Dempsey have supplied me with details by correspondence and conversation. The correction on the eclipse of the sun was sent to me by Owen Gingerich of the Harvard and Smithsonian observatories. This chapter also includes a reference about Catlin from Catlin. Denig's *Five Indian Tribes of the Upper Missouri* here joins my list of standard sources. This work was apparently attributed in part at least to Alexander Culbertson, and he may have contributed to it, but John Ewers, the editor, has now established it to be the work of Denig. Volume X of *Contributions* includes a sketch of Alexander's life from which I occasionally borrow. See also Larpenteur's *Forty Years . . .*

CHAPTER IX: Sources on Michael Culbertson are listed in Chapter I: Notes. The basic material on West Point derives from Sidney Forman: *West Point*, but some very pertinent matter was supplied to me by private correspondence from archivist Kenneth Rapp of West Point, and this includes information about the academy itself and General Gratiot in particular: *Dictionary of American Biography*, Volume VII, pp. 503-504; St. Louis *Republican*, 19 May 1855 (an obituary); George McCullum, *Detroit News*, 3 January 1943.

CHAPTER X: Sources on Natawista include Mildred Walker Schemm: "The Major's Lady" in the *Montana Magazine of History*, January 1952; Dabney Taylor (a descendent through Julia): "The Major's Blackfoot Bride" in *Frontier Times*, 1969. Hugh Dempsey has provided me with genealogical data on Natawista and her relatives. (It must be remembered that some uncertainty remains in such material.) The sketch of Marcelino Baca derives from Hafen's *Mountain Men*. Sources on Audubon include his own *Journals*, Edward Harris: *Up the Missouri with Audubon*, Larry Thompson: *Montana Explorers*, Volume I. A letter from Father A. Duhaime, OMI, of Cardston, Alberta, 8 May 1979, and another from Hugh Dempsey 27 April of the same year were helpful for this chapter.

CHAPTER XI: While we continue to depend on Lt. Bradley and *Contributions*, we have to keep in mind that Bradley probably propagates the opinions and mistakes of Alexander Culbertson. Another source for this chapter is Larpenteur's *Forty Years a Fur Trader*.

Marcelino Baca: His story is told by Janet Lecompte in Volume III of Hafen's *Mountain Men . . .* Over six feet tall and novelesquely compared to Hercules for strength and to Apollo for beauty, Marcelino was bond to become a romantic legend of the fur trade. He was in Bridger's brigade from the Yellowstone to the Sierra Nevada (with Loreto?) and ranged on his own from Powder River to the Platte. Once shot in the ankle by Blackfeet, he coiled himself into a ball and rolled down the hill to safety. On the Platte in 1838, at least so the story goes, he was captured by Pawnees, who in their tender mercy were just about to eat him alive, slice by roasted slice. But lo! Who should intercede but the chief's daughter. (That's better than Pocahontas.) She got him. He took her to wife, naming her Tomacita, and in time married her in the church at Taos.[80] *Pindray* (Peindry): Sunder, p. 74, mentions two French "counts" on the Missouri, the Comte d'Otrante (d'Otranto) and the Comte de Peindry. He cites Chittenden, pp. 155-156. Louise Berry, p. 507, also mentions "Peindry" and Otranto. I have no quarrel about Otranto, but I think they are all in error regarding "Peindry". I suggest this man was really the Marquis Charles de Pindray, whose story is told by H.H. Bancroft in the *North Mexican States and Texas*, vol. II, pp. 675-676, and by Rockwell D. Hunt and Nellie Van De Grift Sanchez in *Short History of California*, pp. 484-485. The handsome Marquis, also compared to both Herculues and Apollo, cut quite a figure in San Francisco in 1851 but, in agreement with an agency of the Mexican government, led an expedition to Guaymas to protect the mines of Sonora from Apaches. Before long, he was found shot to death.

To appreciate the quandry in which AFC found itself, we should recall that Fort Laramie (Fort John) and the ill-starred outpost at the top of the Missouri were both peculiarly strategic. Laramie was AFC's toe-hold on the Platte, which might easily slip into the control of the rival Creole trading family, the Robidoux. But the Blackfeet trade of the upper Missouri was now about to fall into the hands of the Hudson's Bay unless Alexander Culbertson could retrieve it at the last minute.

Material on the Presbyterian missionary ventures can be found at the Presbyterian Historical Society in Philadelphia: e.g. REF BX 2570 P7 MS v. 4-8, Nov. 1844, #677.

De Smet: The best source on Father De Smet is the edition of his *Life, Letters and Travels* by

---

[80] But for a different version of this story that makes Jim Bridger the hero and the Utes his captors, see Great Falls *Tribune*, 9 April 1933, p. 6. It became a part of the oral folklore of the frontier.

Chittenden and Richarson in 4 volumes originally but now issued in two. Not to be overlooked is De Smet's own *Oregon Missions* and his *Voyages aux Montagenes Roucheuses* published in Lille and Paris in 1875. Eventually, De Smet went back and forth to Europe 19 times. After his visits to the Far West in 1840 and '41, he went to Europe and brought back missionaries to America, including the famous Antonio Ravalli, traveling around the Horn via the Malvinas (Falklands), Valparaiso, Callao and up to Oregon. The next year (1845) he attempted to contact the Blackfeet by way of Lake Columbia, Vermillion River to Lake Louise (?), and down the Bow, fascinated by a tremendous aurora borealis (the dance of the manitous at the gates of the hereafter). Guided by James Bird and a Cree métis, he turned south, and when Bird deserted him, he and the Cree trudged on through the snows of autumn and "a labyrinth of narrow valleys" in quest of Hugh Monroe. They never found Monroe but only the signs on his passing near the "mountain of Quilloux" (Chief Mountain?). After wintering at Fort Edmonton, he returned west by dog-sled, traveling with Crees and Iroquois, to Columbia Icefield and Columbia River. Now in 1846 we find him trying again to reach the Blackfeet.

CHAPTER XII: Sources for this chapter include Clark Kennerly's *Persimmon Hill* and Hazard Steven's biography of his father Isaac I. Stevens. To balance the son's panegyric, there is a professional biography of Stevens by Kent D. Richards, listed in my bibliography. If you want the sources for J.W. Schultz's stories about Seen From Afar (whom he calls Pinukwiim), James Bird, Mad Wolf, Lame Bull and Morning Eagle, see his *Blackfeet and Buffalo*, pp. 41, 149-193, 347-367. the last citation tells a story reminiscent of that of Marcelino Baca. How much of all that you care to believe I leave to your discretion. Another reference to James Bird (Jr.) is the essay about him by John E. Wickman in Volume V of Hafen's *Mountain Men*. For Jean Baptiste (Pampi) Charbonneau see Ann W. Hafen's essay on him in the *Mountain Men* series, Volume I. Though the main essay on Alexander Culbertson in the *Mountain Men*, by Ray H. Mattison, appears in Volume I, casual references to Alec's role in the reorganization of the Company occur in volumes VIII, p. 154, and IX, pp. 317-318. For the additional comments on Seen From Afar, see my reference to Adolf Hungry Wolf's book in the notes to Chapter V. For John Palliser, see his book *The Solitary Hunter*.

CHAPTER XIII: This chapter depends in large measure on Thaddeus Culbertson's own account, which appeared as Bulletin 115, the Bureau of American Ethnology, 1952. The editor, John Francis McDermott, is a descendent of the family Chouteau.

CHAPTER XIV: Besides the usual support on the *Contributions* (especially Volume X) and the *Life, Letters and Travels* of De Smet, this chapter owes much to Rudolph Friedrich Kurz' *Journal*, printed as Bulletin 115, Bureau of American Ethnology, reprinted by Ye Galleon Press.

Hispanic Engagés: In an attempt to explain the introduction of adobe architecture to Fort Benton, let me enumerate the engagés of Hispanic origin. Though the original Pablo and Sandoval had both been killed by the date we are now concerned with, and Loreto was either dead or gone west in the flesh, the children of all three by their Piegan wives were still at hand. The son of Loreto may have been the young leader Spotted Eagle noted in the Fort Benton annals, later a medicine man but improbably an adobe-mixer. John "Oregon" (Aragon?) was present for a short time but drowned during a trip down the river with Harvey in the spring. Pete Martínez may have been in the area this early and perhaps also some of the men who bore the Hispanic surnames that appear on the census of 1862. Manuel Martín, the famous guide and hunter, was also an adobe-maker at Fort Owen/St. Mary, and was on the plains with Father Point in 1842, but whether he came again is not known. Joseph Ramsey (Ramírez?), the companion of Pallister, was at Fort Union, as were Philip Álvarez, Joniche Barro (Barra?), Joe Dolores. Any or all of these men could have done service at Benton too. Philip Álvarez sired progeny that would form relationships with the families of both Alexander and Natawista and also with that of Sitting Bull. He had come up the river as a steamboat cook and became a tailor and wrangler for Alec and Denig at Fort Union. Though he is said to have been related to Sandoval, he appears in the census of 1870 as born in Missouri about 1829 and in the census of 1900 as a native of Texas or Mexico, born in September 1822 of a father from Spain and an Aztec mother. The records confused his surname to Alverz, Alvary, Alves, Alvoris. Philip became interpreter at Union, Poplar and the Blackfeet Reservation for Spanish, French, Sioux, Cree and Blackfeet, though how efficiently in all of these it is hard to tell. Whether he derived from any of the families of his surname in St. Louis is also conjectural, but one of them may have had a son in Mexico of a previous marriage. Philip's son Nick thought (erroneously) that his "Spanish" father had come up the river with Lewis and Clark and (more probably) that he had first appeared on an expedition known as "Travelers Pulling a Boat". Near White Earth River, when the expedition encountered the first Assiniboines, Philip joined the Rock Band, married Nick's Assiniboine mother and let the travelers go on without him. (See James Larpenteur Long: *The Assiniboines*, pp. 162-177; the *Contributions* citing fur trade ledgers; U.S. Census reports.)

CHAPTER XV: The inside view of the House of Wied-Neuwied comes mostly from Carmen Sylva's memoirs, *From Memory's Shrine*, with the informative pages in this order: 85,209,44, 154-156, 167, 171-172. The memoirs of Queen Maria of Rumania are also helpful, especially Vol. I, pp. 240-246, 257. See also my references to Maximilian and Catlin. The letter from Prince Hermann to Adolph of Nassau is a manuscript in the private archives of the House of Luxembourg and was copied for me with the gracious permission of the Grand Duke of Luxembourg and the kind assistance of Professor Jean Schoos. Translations for this correspondence were provided to me by Professors Gertrud Lackschewitz and Anne Broeder-Cevrero, and I must add that some of the translation proved a special task in itself because of Prince Hermann's archaic script and peculiar handwriting. This letter seems to be the only surviving evidence of any details of Hermann's trip to America now available in the archives in Wiesbaden. Casual and somewhat misleading references are found in Sunder, p. 151, and Louise Barry, pp. 1182 and 1185. Sunder, however, is much more adequate regarding other phases of the Missouri cruise, especially p. 146. See Stevens' *Pacific Railroad Reports*, Vol. I.

The information about Governor Stevens comes from the biographies by his son Hazard and Kent Richards previously mentioned. An incidental note regarding Stevens in St. Paul is that he stirred the interest of a strange young man of that city in his scheme for a transcontinental railway. The young beaver's name was James J. Hill.

Newspaper items on Princes Hermann and Nicolas in America include one from the St. Joseph *Gazette*, 1 June 1853, p. 2, col. 4, and another from the New York *Tribune*, 14 November 1853, p. 6, col. 5. These articles were Louise Barry's source and were copied for me by the Kansas State Historical Society. Limited information on Prince Nicolas appears in the *Almanach de Gotha* for 1914, and more detailed data in *Nassovia* in articles written by Christian Spielman.

The *Nassovia* is available in this country at the Harvard University Library.

Carmen Sylva: In a book overweighted as this one is with muscle men trying forever to prove they are the "right stuff", a figure like Carmen Sylva will be a welcome relief to some and will appear intrusive to others. For those who prefer her and her special insights, here are some additional details: She was, of course, the daughter of Marie of Nassau whom Prince Maximilian labeled "the Will-o'-the Wisp, the "Flibbertigibbet." She grew nevertheless into the beautiful and gracious queen Elizabeth I of Rumania. Immersed from girlhood in music, poetry, weaving and painting and tutored at the piano by Clara Schumann herself (the widow of Robert Schumann), she became keenly attuned to Beethoven, Schiller and Villon and was known as the "poet queen". Charming but unpredictable, she wrote novels, memoirs, verse, romantic fantasies in both German and French. Her autocratic husband, both a Hohenzollern and a Murat, tolerated her romanticism so long as it remained on paper only. But, alas, when she contrived a real-life romance between her favorite nephew Nando and her favorite lady-in-waiting Hélène, her husband sent her into exile, first to Venice with Hélène (not too harsh an exile) but then to her mystic mother Marie in the dark and snowy woods of Wied.[81]

With her tragic sense of life, Carmen Sylva, sank for months into bed and wheel-chair, but eventually she received a healing of sorts, not from a mesmerist nor from her mother so much as from the devotion of the children of Nando. (Nando eventually married, not Hélène of course, but Marie of Rumania.) Perhaps you know the "Carmen Sylva Waltz", a typical concert piece by Rumania's waltz-king Jon Ivanovici, or perhaps you have read or heard about the book Pierre Loti wrote of her exile. I have cited her comments on several occasions, but here is another on her mother's mysticism and the method of prayerful healing as one in which the patient did not remain merely passive: "Certainly my mother often appeared to us no longer to tread the earth, she seemed to float rather than walk. . . (The cure was) the art of transforming pathological phenomena into therapeutical processes."

CHAPTER XVI: We continue to rely on the two biographies of Governor Stevens and his own *Pacific Railroad Reports*. Alexander's report on "The Blackfoot Nation" is printed in *Not in Precious Metals Alone*. See also Lt. Doty's "Visit to the Blackfoot Camp", edited by Hugh A. Dempsey. *Edwin Denig:* The anthropologist John C. Ewers regards Denig as "the real author" of much of the material attributed to Hayden and also "the most prolific and the most knowledgeable writer" on the upper Missouri tribes of his time. (Ewers, 1961, xxxvii.) He was of great help to various artists, scientists and wayfarers: Audubon, Kurz, Thaddeus Culbertson, De Smet, Hayden, Henry Schoolcraft (who was Longfellow's main source of Hiawatha). He also worked closely with Ferdinand Culbertson and now with Governor Stevens. For the story told by Kurz, see Kurz, p. 180.

Lt. Saxton and the Nez Percés: On his trip east, Saxton reached the confluence of the Snake and the Palouse and was met there by delegates of the two tribes the rivers were named for. They wanted to know why Saxton and his soldiers were crossing their country. Saxton replied he was too sleepy and tired to talk to them. So the 50 warriors waited until he deigned to reappear, supposedly fed and rested. At the smoke and "war talk", Saxton announced that "the chief of all the country between the mountains and the Pacific Ocean" (Stevens) would come to them, adding "I want you to be ready to help him." Pointedly, he gave them a demonstration of target practice. The Indians assisted him, his troops and baggage across the river and explained the cause of their worries: A "Spaniard" had warned them that soldiers were coming to take over their homes. "Show me the men who tried to excite you," cried Saxton, "and I will hang them on the next tree!" Bully bluster of this sort was then much in vogue. I am at a loss to say why the Nez Percés did not just dump Saxton into the river.

---

[81] See the story of Carmen Sylva by Pierre Loti.

Little Dog: Unfortunately, most of what we find on record about Little Dog is gleaned from non-Indian sources and particularly unreliable sources at that, e.g. William T. Hamilton. Hamilton says that Little Dog was prone to secret religious moods and undertook vision quests in the Sweet Grass Buttes. He submitted to the tortures of the Sun Dance with the traditional thongs skewered through gashes in his breast. He would erect a painted war pole and ride around camp singing war songs and urging the people to battle. About 1845 (according to Bradley) he led his warparty in an attack on a wagon train somewhere around Fort Hall and in the midst of the destruction discovered a box of "brass buttons without eyes". This he hid among rocks along the Snake River. Years later he realized that his buttons were really gold coins but refused to go back to recover them. For by this time he had turned from hawk to dove, war chief to peace chief. Once, says Hamilton, he lead a warparty against the Flatheads, only to be warned by the stars not to carry out his raid. Maybe it was more moonlight than starlight because his eye fell upon the daughter of the Flathead medicine man Bear Tracks. Little Dog kidnapped her. But when she explained that she loved a Kootenai chief, he returned her to her father's lodge. (There is talk of flowers at this point in the story, since the girl's name is supposed to be Pretty Flower.) In response to this act of reconciliation, Bear Tracks brought horses and other gifts to the Blackfeet. No matter how many yards of yarn there are in this account, there is in fact good evidence of peace between the Flatheads and the band of Little Dog. It is reasonable to suppose that Little Dog's politics were influenced by his visions, not by some predilection for white people.

CHAPTER XVII: Stevens himself is a basic source for this chapter, augmented as usual by his son's biography of him. See also "The Blackfoot Peace Council" by Albert J. Partoll, James Doty's two entries as listed in my bibliography and the "Phillips County Interviews." Robert Burns, S.J., gives excellent background on the Jesuits and the Indian wars.

Henry Kennerly's Recollections: Some details of this chapter derive from Henry Kennerly's "Recollections" in MS form and compiled many years after the events. There is difficulty reconciling some items in Henry Kennerly's account with the Fort Benton and Fort Sarpy Journals, which both appear in the *Contributions.* (Note especially *Contributions,)* Vol. X, pp. 44, 48, 273.) In regard to Kennerly's movements and companions, we learn in the Fort Benton Journal that on 12 September Michel Champagne and James Chambers (the factor of Fort Sarpy) left Benton on a skiff to meet the boat coming up the river from Fort Union. On 17 September two men were sent to the mountains for timber in company with "Mr. Vaughn Kinerly and Willsen" (Agent Vaughan or his son, Henry Kennerly and E.S. Willson of St. Paul). It was a rainy day. On 30 September, Sunday, Kennerly and Willson returned to Fort Benton from the Sweetgrass Buttes, having left "Mr. Culbertson yesterday morning who probably camped on the Marias last night with 'Lame Bull'. . .'' In the Fort Sarpy Journal (*Contributions,* Vol. X, p. 140) we discover the entry for 6 September written probably by James Chambers: "Col. Cummings Mess. Kennerly and Champagne learned that Mr. Culbertson had gone down to meet the Boats. . .'' We cannot solve the differences between the Journals and the "Recollections" simply by assuming that the Journals are more reliable. Any attempt to solve them would have to involve the question of how far Kennerly and his companion(s) could have traveled in thirteen days.

CHAPTER XVIII: The narrative of Alec's maneuvers as usual comes from Lt. Bradley's Journal. The archives of the Moravian College in Bethlehem, PA, still preserve the record of Julia and Fannie. Ship Passenger Lists, New York Harbor, #175515 gives data on the *Kathay* and its voyage (though not much). The story of the Mackeys and the Culbertsons' part in it is given briefly in Sunder, pp. 178-180, in *Contributions,* and in Ewers' *The Blackfeet,* pp. 222-223. However, much of my account comes from James Trott, who generously provided me with many details from the Presbyterian Historical Soceity, including the appraisals of Elkanah Mackey about the Culbertsons. The material is scattered through files labeled "Presbyterian Church, USA" or simply PC—USA, with difficult designations like REF BX 2570 P 7 MS v. 4, so that the researcher requires assistance on the spot. Some items have been organized into a report, used by both John Ewers and James Trott regarding the "Missionary Endeavors" of the Presbyterians among the Blackfeet and written by Guy S. Klett, 1941. James Trott has also prepared a report on the Mackeys, presently in MS, from which he kindly allowed me to quote. Michael's lecture and his book *Darkness in the Flowery Land* are listed in my bibliography. For other details, consult Sunder pp.183-86; Schultz, J.W.: *Blackfeet and Buffalo,* pp.347 ff.; John Owen's Journal and the Fort Benton Journal for the appropriate dates; Alec's letter to Julia as cited in the bibliography; see Ewers' *The Blackfeet,* pp. 222-23 for Lame Bull's strange speech. Hugh Dempsey in conversation called my attention to the special relation between Alec and Seen From Afar.

Chapter XIX: There is the usual background material from Lt. Bradley, now reinforced by Sunder, pp. 183-186, 190-192, 202 ff.; Boller pp. 22-23, 202-203; see the references used in the last chapter for the Presbyterian interests (REF BX 2570 P7 MS. v. 4; James Trott and Grey S. Klett. See also John Evers:

The Blackfeet p. 202; Hugh Dempsey: "A Blackfoot Winter County''; Robert Burns, S.J., p. 329; William

T. Hamilton: "A Trading Expedition. . ." in *Contributions*, Volume III; De Smet: *Life, Letters and Travels*, p. 1500; John Owen's *Journal;* Peoria *Daily Transcript;* Peoria *Journal* (an article by Ernest E. East, 25 July, 1936; Michael Culbertson's works in the bibliography.

The Trouble with William T. Hamilton: I have a lot of trouble with William T. Hamilton, favorite though he may be with historians. If his story of the trading expedition of 1858 is to be taken seriously, it is only fair to ask a few questions about it: What business did Col. Wright have in sending Hamilton and MacKay as spies into the northern Plains military district? If he had to know about the Blackfeet, why not consult the commandant of that district or the traders like Alec Culbertson? Why meddle in a relatively peaceful situation so far from his own turf? Why did Vaughan, nobody's fool and suspicious of intruders (e.g. Gore), apparently allow Hamilton a free hand? How did it happen that Crows and Blackfeet camped so close together and engaged in nothing more warlike than horse-racing and trading, especially since the Crows were not signatories to the Judith Treaty? Strange, isn't it, that Hamilton, guardian of the peace, exploits the horse race to start trouble. Also worth scrutinizing is Hamilton's account of how he bamboozles both the Jesuits of Cataldo Mission and the Indians under their persuasion. Are we to suppose that he also bamboozled Little Dog?

The sons of Little Dog are not easy to identify. According to the *Blackfeet Heritage*, p.152, one of them became a leader of the Indian police. The elder Little Dog, (Hamilton's "friend"?) is reported as the son of Medicine Old Man and his wife Strikes With a Gun, while the junior, the policeman, was the son of Good Strike Woman. If the policeman was 54 years old when the *Heritage* sources were compiled for the allotment system, he would have been very young in 1858, too young, I think, to take part in that wild horse race. And Little Dog, the elder, had insisted at the Judith Treaty on barring the western tribes from using the northern passes over the Divide. Yet in Hamilton's story, the Kootenais are encamped at St. Mary Lakes, which in fact was their traditional campground if they came from the area of Macleod, Alberta, but if so, why were they so hated by the Bloods and why would they flee over the Divide? And that escape over the pass with the whole camp of men, women, children, dogs and horses, all under attack—would that be physically possible on a precipitous trail, blockaded perhaps with windfalls? None of these difficulties prove that Hamilton's story is fiction, but they do raise some doubts.

Richard de Aquila Grosvenor (1937-1912), a son of the Marquess of Westminster, had just taken his M.A. at Trinity College, Cambridge, and was now finishing off his education with globe-trotting. In later years he became a liberal whip in parliament and a leading railway magnate. Prominent too in his work on behalf of his employees, he was raised to the peerage in 1886 as Baron of Stalbridge. (*Dictionary of National Biography*).

CHAPTER XX: Sources for this chapter include Mildred Schemm's article, "The Major's Lady, Natawista", Peoria *Daily Transcript* Ernest E. East's article in the Peoria *Journal*, 25 July, 1936, Robert McCulloh's recollections in Kessler's Collection; Sunder, pp. 210-212. Julia Schultz's interview, Selina Monroe's interview, and Dabney Taylor's article.

CHAPTER XXI: Much of the information on Michael Simpson Culbertson after his experience at West Point derives from the Presbyterian Historical Society in Philadelphia and from the Graduate Theological Union Library of the San Francisco Theological Seminary in San Anselmo, California. I owe a great deal to researchers in these two libraries, most especially to James H. Trott of Philadelphia (originally of Fort Benton) and Michael D. Peterson of the San Francisco Seminary Library. Among the general sources are these: *The Biblical Repertory and Princeton Review; The Centennial Memorial of the Presbytery of Carlisle;* "Foreign Missionary Papers, Calendar, China;" *The Jubilee Papers;* Joseph M. Wilson: *The Presbyterian Historical Almanac.* Michael Simpson Culbertson's essay "The Revolution in China" appears in the *Princeton Review*, April 1854, pp. 321-348. A fund of manuscripts is the "Presbyterian Church, USA, General Assembly, Minutes and Reports," from which I have drawn material on p. 72; "The Home and Foreign Record": April 1855, p. 111; Oct. 1855, p. 303; Dec. 1855. In this Chapter I cite time and again from "REF BX 2570 87 MS, volumes 4-8: #1; #157, #229,#238, #219, #198, #210, #212, #219, #245, #242, #252. (I cite them here in the order of their application to the text.) The #245 is reenforced by the *Biblical Repertory* (Index), p. 326. Michael D. Peterson discovered numerous mentions of Michael Simpson Culbertson in the *Jubilee Papers of the Central China Presbyterian Mission, 1844-1894*, Shanghai, American Presbyterian Mission Press, 1895, pp. 11, 37-38, 42-45, 59-61, Michael's own writings are listed in my bibliography. A Chinese point of view is represented by Jen Yu-Wen: *The Taiping Revolutionary Movement.* For those interested in a perspective on the Tai Ping Rebellion and the Manchu regime that differs from the one suggested in my account, I recommend the novel by Pearl Buck: *Imperial Woman.* I have also drawn on personal correspondence from Kenneth Rapp, archivist of West Point, N.Y.: 29 April and 16 May 1983.

James Trott called my attention to an item he unearthed in the archives of the Presbyterian Historical Society that may throw light on Mary Culbertson's visit to Japan: In 1841 James C. Hepburn, M.D., his wife and the Rev. Walter M. Lowrie reached Singapore. Two years later they tried to enter China. But because of ill health, the Hepburns returned to the U.S. in 1846 and in 1859 went to Japan. Perhaps Mary and Helen visited them there.

One thing that became apparent to me and also, I believe, to other researchers is that Michael Culbertson has been passed over by historians and that his true stature in the history of Chinese missions may be determined by future studies. I hope my brief introduction to him proves to be a foundation. To compare a Catholic missionary in China, see my article on *Carolis "Restless Pilgrim."*

The Term Question: However casually today's readers may regard this issue, it was of prime importance to the missionaries of the 1850's. It was one phase of the far-reaching Rites Controversy, which, in the eyes of many historians (among them Pearl Buck) caused quite a rumpus among Protestants, brought the Catholic missions in China to disaster and Christianity itself into disrepute. It helped create the vacuum the communists have filled. In any case, Western chauvinism and arrogance as well as typical bureaucratic bungling in Rome, London or New York must share the blame. Even so, there was good reason for the missionaries of every faith to insist on carefully chosen language. Notice how a loose interpretation of the Bible helped to spark the revolt of the Tai Pings. For many primal people, like the Jews of the Old Testament, the name of a thing is the thing itself and the spoken word a bond of covenant. Confucius himself cautioned his followers that the misuse of language results in the misuse of thought. The written character in Chinese often expresses much more meaning than can normally be conveyed by the spoken language. A good example is the translation of "Jesus", which turns out to be more fortuitous and less controversial than the terms for "God". The first syllable *Ye* was selected simply for its phonetic value, but the second syllable *su* was written by a character that signifies "resurrection" and also includes the radical for "fish", corresponding to the ancient Greek Christian symbol found in the catacombs. The term "God", however, presents an altogether different problem, for in Chinese the words *Tảo, Tiȃn* and *T'ảï-Ji* are used to express the Absolute, the Unconditioned, the One. Any term added or substituted *subtracts* from the meaning rather than enhancing it and so projects anthropomorphism. No name for God, of course, can ever be more than approximate.

CHAPTER XXII: Sunder provides the general background for the Missouri area during the Civil War period. The cruise of the *Spread Eagle* and other steamboat activities are covered in all the literature of the time, as in Chittenden's *History of Early Steamboat Navigation. . .* (always the basic source on La Barge), De Smet's *Life, Letters and Travels.* Lewis Henry Morgan's *Indian Journals* add special details for the trip Morgan was on. For particulars on individual Army personnel, refer to the books by Cullum and Heitman in my bibliography. See Schnick, B.S.: *The Burning of Chambersburg.* The somewhat questionable remarks about Alec in the war derive from Kessler's MS. We are still indebted, of course, to Lt. James Bradley. See De Smet, Volume II, pp. 1510-15 for his remarks on gold, and p. 807 for his trip to California etc. The *Diario* of Martínez y Saez is in the Museo de Ciencias Naturales in Madrid and was researched for me by my friend of many years, Padre Ricardo Martínez de Velasco.

The Fool Soldiers: When Santee Sioux dragged their white captives, women and children, from Shetak, Minnesota, to the wilds of Dakota, they were reported by the Galpins. Some young Teton Sioux known as the Fool Soldier Band and numbering a mere dozen, courageously negotiated the release of the white women and children and brought them into Fort Pierre. They were led by Martin Charger, who was alleged to be the Indian grandson of Meriwether Lewis. It is not recorded that the U.S. Army was overjoyed to have a handful of Sioux youths do their job for them, and no compensation was ever made to the Fool Soldiers. See Doane Robinson: *History of South Dakota,* Vol.I, pp. 210-213; 1904); Lt. Col. John Pattie "Dakota Campaign" in Vol. V, pp. 283-291 & p. 350 of the South Dakota Historical Collections; Historical Signpost series of the South Dakota State Historical Society, p. 190. Many thanks to Evelyn Sheets of Trenton, Missouri, for calling my attention to this episode. Pattie claims that about 7,000 Sioux were driven from Minnesota into Dakota. If so, this could explain some of the hostility mentioned in this chapter.

The Killing of Owen MacKenzie: This disaster comes as a surprise if we recall that there was good rapport between Owen and Malcolm Clarke: they dined together at Fort Union in October of 1855, and in December, 1857, Owen paid some money to Clarke at Fort Campbell. A newspaper item in the Forsyth *Independent* for 10 April 1939 by Mrs. M.E. Plassmann (cited from her book) gives a different version of this killing. The date is wrong but some of the other details may be correct since Mrs. Plassmann says she heard the story from an eye witness. She says the *Nellie Rogers* was an AFC vessel near the mouth of Milk River when the event took place. There was some tension between Malcolm and Owen over Harvey, who was disliked by many AFC people and of whom even "Major Culbertson" was afraid. Malcolm was not, and Alec kept the two men apart, leaving Malcolm in "the northern country". Owen, says Mrs. Plassmann was one of Harvey's men (a point one may argue about), and now when Owen in a drunken state, tried to board the steamer Malcolm ordered him back. Owen persisted and Malcolm shot him. At a meeting it was decided that Malcolm need not go on to St. Louis to give himself up for witnesses would testify in his behalf.

CHAPTER XXIII: In this chapter we encounter William T. Hamilton once more in his story "Council at Fort Benton". How much of his self-glorification one can believe is a question I leave to the reader. Some details on Little Dog are given by Lt. Bradley.

Research in the archives of the Quaker pioneers of Philadelphia has not brought to light any reliable information on George Robert's origins, but his trip up the Missouri is mentioned in C.J. Atkins: "Log of the Benton", North Dakota Historical Society Collections, Volume II, pp. 307-9 and note.

The Cruise of the "Ontario", 1866: De Smet's *Life, Letters and Travels,* I, pp. 87-8; II, pp. 846 ff.; I, pp. 732-37 provides us with details of the trip during the heyday of the river traffic. This was Father De Smet's final cruise as far as Fort Benton, and his details of it, according to historian Chittenden, are "undoubtedly the most complete that have come down to us." The *Ontario* departed from St. Louis on April 9th and reached Benton on the 7th of June. DeSmet had a passport issued to him on the date of departure by General W.T. Sherman. The *Ontario* was a sternwheeler of 450 tons, three boilers, and drew thirty inches of water when light and required up to twenty cords of wood a day. It had two 132 horsepower engines and against the current could travel at five or six miles an hour, or with the current fifteen to eighteen. The crew included captain, two pilots, two clerks, an assistant pilot, two engineers, two mates, two watchmen, a steward, three books, one barkeeper, seven cabin boys, one baggage smasher, eight white deckhands, nineteen blacks for miscellaneous functions, four firemen, one chambermaid. There were thirty staterooms, 7 feet x 6, with two berths. The first class passengers numbered fifteen men, twelve women, five children, ten Catholics, the rest Protestants, free thinkers and a few Jews. DeSmet said Mass in his stateroom often with the door open to the congregation. There were games of cards, dice, checkers and so on, and evening charades, but mostly dancing to live music and moonlight concerts on deck with refreshments.

There is much that DeSmet tells us about the river itself, its dangers, bluffs and "Bad Lands," the geology and the performances of the buffalo. DeSmet visited the Sioux at Forts Sully and Rice, deploring the mortality from hunger and disease. At Fort Union he baptized a number of children, and this must have been the occasion when, on the 25th of May, he baptized Nick Alvarez, the son of old Philip by his Assiniboine wife. (Nick was probably six at that time.) DeSmet noted signs of hostility on all sides, attributing the ultimate blame to the whites. As soon as the steamer had entered Sioux territory, the pilot-house was boarded up, cannons were mounted in the bow, sentinels posted and weapons checked. But the warparties that appeared did not offer battle. Even so, at Benton it was clear that the new outbreak of conflict had obliged the Jesuits to close down their missionary activities among the Blackfeet and flee from St. Peter Mission back across the Divide. (We recall that this was the year that Little Dog and his son were assassinated.)

The item on the letter of Prince Maximilian is derived from the Kessler Collection, MS, #265. Joe Culbertson's memoirs tell the story of his boyish mischief. See also the file on Julia Schultz and her interview.

CHAPTER XXIV: DeSmet's *Life, Letters and Travels* include the story of his last great adventure with Sitting Bull. Material on Fanny Culbertson derives in part from her interview by WPA worker(s). From here to the end of this book, we turn to the autobiography of Joe Culbertson, a chaotic work with probably the most clumsy piece of editing in the literature of the Northwest done by some representative(s) of the GN Railway. The conflicts at Fort Benton are detailed in Ege's book, *Strike Them Hard.* Accounts of the carnage by Baker's men are given in many books, by Ege, J.W. Schultz, etc. A unpublished (to date) account by Michael Olinger is more balanced than most, but the details vary considerably from one writer to the next. Ege seems to have begun by trying to justify the Army but hestitates midway. The circumstance that his book appeared about the time of the MyLai massacre may have had something to do with it. The culminating horror of the captives turned loose on the winter prairie with only a pittance of food and no transportation is treated nowhere that I know of in any detail and so left to our imagination.

Star: The man so named (*Kakatosi* in Blackfeet) is probably Frank Pablo Star or Starr, brother of Michel Pablo the well-known buffalo herder and a son of the New Mexican killed long ago at Pablo's Island. The George Starr of more recent record was a son of Frank, born about 1869, who became a guide in Glacier National Park, a tribal judge and representative in travel.

CHAPTER XXV: Alec's own "Journey to Bow River", edited by Hugh Dempsey, gives much of the background of this chapter, supplemented by comments by Joe Culbertson in his memoirs and in an exchange of letters with Charles Kessler. Some original material in manuscript form was loaned to Kessler by Joe's sister Julia. We go back to Lt. Bradley once more and include a brief bit from the *Diario* of Fray José Romo, OFM, in the Archives of Mission Santa Barbara, California.

CHAPTER XXVI: Most of the story now derives from Joe Culbertson, either in his autobiography, the published and the unpublished forms, or in his correspondence with Kessler. There is also Kessler's correspondence with other members of the family, notably Julia and Julia's daughter. Occasional items are provided by Rasmussen's *San Francisco Passenger Lists,* Volume II, pp. 171-2. Information on natural bridges or arches in the Bitterroot area was provided to me by Mr. Dick Strong of the Hamilton Ranger Station. Hugh Dempsey's "A Blackfoot Winter Count" offers data on Bad Head and his successors. The material on the winter events at Fort Macleod comes from Dr. Richard N.Nevitt's reminiscences, listed in the bibliography. The interview of Frances Culbertson, previously cited, is still useful here. Hugh Dempsey sent me the information on *Kaiyis,* the Blood wife of Charles Conrad, later supplemented by data on the Conrad genealogy.

CHAPTER XXVII: The title of the chapter derives from Sir Walter Scott's *The Lady of the Lake:* "The stag at eve had drunk his fill/where danced the moon on Monan's rill. . ." Sherman's proposal of genocide is quoted from TIME Magazine, 5 November, 1984, p. 87. Much of the rest of the chapter depends on Joe's reminiscences. The piece on Aubrey derives from his article "The Edmonton Buffalo Herd." Julia Schultz's oral interview is the source for occasional information in this, as in earlier chapters, and is on file at the Montana Historical Society in Helena. The source of the data on Alec's grave is Charles E. Hanson, Jr.: "Marking the Grave of Alexander Culbertson."

EPILOGUE: This final piece depends largely on Joe Culbertson's material, but the last portion of Natawista's story comes to me by personal correspondence from Hugh Dempsey. The U.S. Census as well as the state census schedules and those taken by the Bureau of Indian Affairs provides us with information used in this chapter.

Bibliography

The Biblical Repertory and Princeton Review; vol. XXVI for 1854; Index volume 1825-1868; Philadelphia PA.
Biographical Annals of Franklin County (PA).
Bismarck Daily Tribune; 24 Oct. 1888, Bismarck, ND.
Blackfeet Heritage, 1907-1908, Blackfeet Heritage Program, Browning, MT 1980.
Bradley Papers, Montana Historical Soceity, Helena; v. BRADLEY
Burke's Royal Families of the World, Burke's Peerage, Ltd., London, vol. I, 1977.
Catholic Marriages, St. Louis, Missouri, 1774-1840; St. Louis Genealogical Society, St. Louis, no date.
The Centennial Memorial of the Presbytery of Carlisle, vol. II, Biographical; Harrisurg, PA, 1889; v. ROSE.
Dictionary of American Biography, 21 volumes.
Dillon Examiner: 12 September, 1932, Dillon, MT.
Encyclopedia Americana, various editions.
Encyclopedia Britannica, various editions.
Foreign Missionary Papers, Calendar, China, REF Bx. 2570, MS, vol. IV; Presbyterian Historical Society, Philadelphia, PA.
Forsyth Independent Forsyth, MT., 10 April 1939.
Glasgow Courier, Glasgow, MT: 1 June, 1923
Great Falls Leader Great Falls, MT: 6 February 1939.
Great Falls Tribune, Great Falls, MT: 21 June 1938; 5 & 7 Feb. 1939; 16 July 1945; 25 Dec. 1960; 26 May 1962, 9 April 1933.
Helena Herald, Helena, MT: 24 Sept. 1879.
Helena Independent, Helena, MT, 22 July 1933.
History of Idaho, the Gem of the Mountains, vol. II, 1920.
Idaho Statesman: 8 Dec. 1963 (article by Suzanne D. Taylor).
Kessler Collection; Montana Papers, William Andrews Clark Memorial Library, University of California at Los Angeles, MSS.
Montana Historical Society: *Contributions,* especially volumes II, III, VII, X; Helena, MT.
Moravian Archives, Bethlehem, PA.
National Archives; v. also U.S. Census.
Nebraska Blue Book, 1915.
Not in Precious Metals Alone: A Manuscript History of Montana, Montana Historical Society, Helena, MT 1976.
Pennsylvania Historical Society: materials on the Culbertson genealogy, MSS; Philadelphia, PA.
Peoria Daily Transcript, Peoria, IL; 2 Feb., 1860, p. 4.
Peoria Journal, Peoria, IL: 25 July 1936.
Phillips County Interviews (tapes), Montana Historical Society, Helena.
Presbyterian Church, USA, General Assembly, Minutes and Reports, 1855, 1856, 1857; Presbyterian Historical Society, Philadelphia.
Progressive Men of Montana; no date but compiled about 1900/1902.
River Press, Fort Benton,MT: 24 January 1923.
State Historical Society of Idaho: 12th Biennial Report of the Board of Trusteees, 1929-1930, Boise, 1930.
State Historical Society of Nebraska, Lincoln.
State Historical Society of North Dakota, Bismarck.
State Historical Society of South Dakota, Pierre.

U.S. Census Reports, National Archives.
U.S. Military Academy Archives, West Point, NY.
Williston Herald, Williston, ND: 16 July 1925, 18 December 1913.

ADAMS, Alexander: *John James Audubon,* G.P. Putnam's Sons, 1966.
ADDINGTON, A.C.: *The Royal House of Stuart,* 4 volumes. ALLEN, J.J.: "From St. Louis to Fort Union in 1862".
ALLEN, J.J.: *From St. Louis to Fort Benton in 1862.*
AUBREY, Charles: "The Edmonton Buffalo Herd", MS in Montana Historical Society, recently published in *We Seized Our Rifles,* edited by Eugene Lee Silliman, Mountain Press, Missoula, MT.
AUDUBON, John James: *Journals,* various editions, e.g. Donald Culross Peattie, editor: *Audubon's America.*
BAKER, Robert H.: *Astronomy,* various editions.
BANCROFT, Hubert Howe: *California Inter Pocula, 1848-1856,* San Francisco, 1888 and reprints.
BANCROFT, Hubert Howe: *History of California,* 7 volumes, San Francisco, 1884-1890 and reprints.
BANCROFT, Hubert Howe: *History of Washington, Idaho, and Montana, San Francisco, 1890.*
BARRY, John Neilson: "Spaniards in Early Oregon", Washington Historical Quarterly, 23: 1932, 25-34.
BARRY, Louise: *The Beginning of the West, 1540-1854,* Kansas State Historical Society, Topeka, 1972.
BILLON, Frederic L.: *Annals of St. Louis,* 1886.
BOLLER, Henry A.: *Among the Indians,* edited by Milo M. Quaife, Chicago, 1959 & University of Nebraska Press, 1972.
BRADLEY, James (Lt.): See Bradley Papers and Montana Historical Society: *Contributions.*
BROWNING, Charles H.: *American of Royal Descent,* Genealogical Publishing Company., Baltimore, 1969.
BURNS, Robert Ignatius, S.J.: *The Jesuits and the Indian Wars of the Northwest,* Yale University Press, 1966.
BUTSCHER, Louis C.: "Prince Paul Wilhelm and his 'Account of Adventures in the Great American Desert' ", New Mexico Historical Review, July 1942, Albuquerque.
CARMEN SYLVA (Elizabeth of Wied, Elizabeth I of Rumania): *From Memory's Shrine,* translated by Edith H. Lippincott, 1911.
CATLIN, George: *Letters and Notes on the American Indians,* edited by Michael M. Mooney, NY 1975; other editions.
CHITTENDEN, Hiram Martin: *The American Fur Trade of the Far West,* 2 volumes, Academic Reprints, Stanford, CA, 1954.
CHITTENDEN, Hiram Martin: *History of Early Steamboat Navigation on the Missouri River,* 2 volumes in one, Ross & Haines reprint, Minneapolis, 1962.
CHITTENDEN, Hiram Martin: v. DE SMET.
CLARK, Ella E.: *Indian Legends from the Northern Rockies,* Oklahoma University Press, Norman, 1966.
COHEN, Paul A.: *China and Christianity (1860-1870),* Harvard University Press, Cambridge, MA, 1967.
COHEN, Stan & Don Miller: *Military and Trading Posts of Montana,* Missoula, 1978.
COOK, S.F.: "The Epidemic of 1830-1833 in California and Oregon", University of California, 1955.
CRAWFORD, Lewis F.: *History of North Dakota,* American Historical Society and Historical Society of North Dakota.
CULBERTSON, Alexander: "Journey to Bow River" (1870), edited by Hugh A. Dempsey, *Alberta Historical Review,* vol. 19, number 4, autumn 1971.
CULBERTSON, Alexander: Letters, 9 June 1956; 9 May 1866; 4 Sept. 1875; Montana Historical Society Archives, Small Collection 586 (which also holds a manuscript copy of the previous item by Alexander Culbertson).
CULBERTSON, Alexander: "Report on the Blackfoot Nation" in *Not in Precious Metals Alone.*
CULBERTSON, Joseph: Letters etc. See Kessler Collection.
CULBERTSON, Joseph: *Life of Joseph Culbertson,* Frank Delger, Wolf Point, MT 1958.
CULBERTSON, Joseph: Notes (including the material on which the previous item is based); see Kessler Collection.
CULBERTSON, Lewis R., M.D.: *Genealogy of the Culbertson and Culberson Families,* revised edition, Zanesville, Ohio, 1923.

CULBERTSON, Michael Simpson: *Darkness in the Flowery Land; or, Religious Notions and Popular Superstitions in North China,* Charles Scribner NY, 1857.

CULBERTSON, Michael Simpson: "The Religious Condition of the Chinese and Their Claims on the Church".

CULBERTSON, Michael Simpson: "The Revolution in China".

CULBERTSON, Thaddeus A.: *Journal of an Expedition to the Mauvaises Terres and the Upper Missouri in 1850;* edited by John Francis McDermott, based on a text previously edited for the Smithsonian Institution; Bureau of American Ethnology, Bulletin 147, 1952.

CULLUM, George W. (General): *Biographical Register of the Officers and Graduates of the U.S. Military Academy, West Point, N.Y.* vol. I.

DE SMET, Pierre-Jean, S.J.: *Life, Letters and Travels;* edited by Hiram Martin Chittenden and Alfred Talbot Richarson in 4 volumes; reprinted in 2 volumes by Kraus Reprint, NY, 1969.

DE SMET, Pierre-Jean, S.J.: *Voyages aux Montagnes Rocheuses,* Lille & Paris, 1875.

DE VOTO, Bernard: *Across The Wide Missouri;* Houghton Mifflin, 1947.

DEMPSEY, Hugh A.: "A Blackfoot Winter Count", Glenbow Occasional Paper No. 1, Glenbow Institute, Calgary, Alberta; revised and expanded in *The Blackfeet Tribal News,* Browning, MT, October 1984.

DEMPSEY, Hugh A.: "Jerry Potts, Plainsman", Glenbow Occasional Paper, No. 2, Glenbow Institute, Calgary, Alberta.

DEMPSEY, Hugh A.: "Indian Names for Alberta Communities", Glenbow Occasional Paper No. 4, Glenbow Institute, Calgary, Alberta.

DEMPSEY, Hugh A.: personal correspondence, 12 Dec., 1980, etc.

DEMPSEY, Hugh A.: editor: see CULBERTSON, Alexander; DOTY, James; NEVITT, R.B.

DENIG, Edwin Thompson: *Five Indian Tribes of the Upper Missouri: Sioux, Arikaras, Assiniboines, Crees, Crows,* edited by John C. Ewers, University of Oklahoma Press, Norman, 1961.

DONALSON, Andrew (Lt.): See STEVENS, Isaac Ingalls: *Reports...*

DOTY, James (Lt.): *Journal of Operations of Governor Isaac Ingalls Stevens of Washington Territory in 1855,* edited by Edward J. Kowrach, Ye Galleon Press, Fairfield, WA, 1978.

DOTY, James (Lt.): "A Visit to the Blackfoot Camp", edited by Hugh A. Dempsey, Alberta Historical Review, summer 1966.

DRUMM, Stella M.: "The Kennerlys of Virginia" in the Missouri Historical Society Collections, vol. 6, no. 1, Oct. 1928, St. Louis.

EAST, Ernest E.: article in the *Peoria Journal,* q.v.

EGE, Robert J.: *Strike Them Hard! Incident on the Marias, 23 January, 1870.* The Old Army Press, Bellevue, Nebraska, 1970.

EWERS, John C.: *The Blackfeet; Raiders on the Northwestern Plains,* University of Oklahoma Press, Norman, 1958.

EWERS, John C.: *Indian Life on the Upper Missouri,* University of Oklahoma Press, Norman, 1968.

EWERS, John C., editor, See DENIG.

FAHNE, A.: *Wesfalien Geschlechter.*

FARNHAM, : *The Jubilee Papers.*

FINERTY, John: *War-Path and Bivouac,* edited by Milo Milton Quaife, University of Nebraska Press, 1966.

FOLEY, Michael F.: *The United States and the Blackfeet Tribe: 1855-1950's,* Indian Claims Commission, Docket Number 279-D, MS; also printed serially in *The Glacier Reporter,* Browning, MT, 1984.

FOLEY, William E. and C. David Rice: *The First Chouteaus: River Barons of Early St. Louis,* University of Illinois Press, 1983.

FORMAN, Sidney: *West Point: A History of the United States Military Academy,* Columia University Press NY, 1950.

FRANK, Baron Freytag von: See ISENBERG.

GOWANS, Fred R.: *Rocky Mountain Rendezvous: A History of the Fur Trade Rendezvous, 1825-1840,* Brigham Young University Press, Provo, Utah, 1976.

HABERLY, Lloyd: *Pursuit of the Horizon: A Life of George Catlin,* Macmillan, NY 1948.

HAFEN, Ann W. contributor to the following item.

HAFEN, LeRoy R., editor and contributor: *Mountain Men and the Fur Trade of the Far West,* ten volumes, The Arthur H. Clark Co., Glendale CA, 1965-1972.

HAMILTON, William T.: "The Council at Fort Benton" in *We Seized Our Rifles,* edited by Eugene Lee Silliman, Mountain Press, Missoula, MT 1982.

HAMILTON, William T.: "A Trading Expedition..." in Montana Historical Society, *Contributionsm,* vol. III.

HANSON, Charles E., "Marking the Grave of Alexander Culbertson" in *Nebraska History*, Nebraska State Historical Society, Lincoln.

HARRIS, Edward: *Up the Missouri with Audubon*, edited by John Francis McDermott, University of Oklahoma Press, Norman, 1951.

HARWOOD, Michael: "Mr. Audubon's Last Hurrah" in *Audubon*, National Audubon Society, Nov. 1985, NY.

HEITMAN, Francis B.: *Historical Register and Dictionary of the United States Army; 1789-1903*, Washington, D.C, 1903.

HOLTERMAN, Jack: *Place Names of Glacier/Waterton National parks*, Falcon Press, Helena, Billings, 1985.

HOLTERMAN, Jack: "Restless Pilgrim" in Southwestern Mission Research Center: *SMRC Newsletter*, insert, edited by Bernard Fontana, Tucson, AZ., December 1984.

HUMBOLDT, Alexander von: *Ensayo politico sobre el Reino de la Nueva Espana*, edited and annotated by Juan A. Ortega y Medina, Mexico, D.F., Editorial Porrua, 1966.

HUMBOLDT, Alexander von and Aime Bompland: *Personal Narrative of Travels to the Equinoctial Regions of America During the Years 1799-1804*, translated and edited by Thomasina Ross, 3 volumes, George Bell and Sons, London, 1900.

HUNGRY WOLF, Adolf: *Charlo's People: The Flathead Tribe of Montana;* Good Medicine Books, No. 10, Invermere, British Columbia, 1974.

HUNGRY WOLF, Adolf: *The Blood People: A Division of the Blackfoot Confederacy*, Harper & Row, 1977.

ISENBERG, Prinz von & Baron Freytag von Frank: *Europaische Stammtafeln*, five volumes, various dates.

ISNERT, Cornelius M., contributor: See HAFEN, LeRoy R.

JEN, Yu-wen: *The Taiping Revolutionary Movement*, Yale University Press, 1973.

KENNEDY, Michael Stephen: See LONG, James Larpenteur.

KENNERLY, James: "Diary, 1823-1826", edited by Edgar B. Wesley.

KENNERLY, Henry A.: "Recollections. . ." MS (a copy in Glacier Natinal park Library).

KENNERLY, William Clark: *Persimmon Hill* (as told to Elizabeth Russell), University of Oklahoma Press, Norman, 1948.

KURZ, Rudolph F.: *The Journal of Rudolph Friedrich Kurz*, edited by J.N.B. Hewitt, Ye Galleon Press, Fairfield WA, no date. This is a reprint of Bulletin No. 115, Bureau of American Ethnology, Smithsonian Institution, Washington, D.C.

LARPENTEUR, Charles: *Forty Years a Fur Trader on the Upper Missouri:* The Personal Narrative of Charles Larpenteur; 1833-1872, edited by Milo Milton Quaife, Lakeside Press, Chicago, 1933.

LASS, William E.: *A History of Steamboating on the Upper Missouri River*, University of Nebraska Press, 1962.

LECOMPTE, Janet, contributor: see HAFEN, LeRoy R.

LONG, James Larpenteur: *The Assiniboines*, edited by Michael Stephen Kennedy, University of Oklahoma Press, 1967.

LONG, Philip S.: *Jerry Potts, Scout, Frontiersman and Hero*, Cypress Books, Billings, 1974, 1976.

LOUDA, Jiri & Michael Maclagan: *Heraldry of the Royal Families of Europe*, Clarkson N. Potter, NY, 1981.

MACLAGAN, Michael: See LOUDA.

MARIE, Queen of Rumania: *Ordeal: The Story of My Life*, Charles Scribner's Sons, NY, 1934, 1935, 2 volumes.

MARTIN, Calvin: *Keepers of the Game: Indian-Animal Relationships and the Fur Trade*, University of California Press, 1978.

MARTIN, William: See pp. 5, 146-8, 205.

MATTISON, Ray H., contributor: See HAFEN, LeRoy R.

MAXIMILIAN, Alexander Philipp, Prince of Wied-Neuwied: "A Journey Through the Nebraska Region in 1833 and 1834: From the Diaries of Prince Maximilian of Wied", translated and edited by William J. Orr and Joseph C. Porter in *Nebraska History*, fall, 1983, Nebraska State Historical Society.

MAXIMILIAN, Alexander Philipp, Prince of Wied-Neuwied: *People of the First Man*, edited by David Thomas and Karin Ronnefeldt, with watercolors by Karl Bodmer, E.P. Dutton, NY, 1976.

MAXIMILIAN, Alexander Philipp, Prince of Wied-Neuwied: *Travels in Brazil, in 1815, 1816, and 817*, London, 1820.

MAXIMILIAN, Alexander Philipp, Prince of Wied-Neuwied: *Travels in the Interior of North America, 1832-1834*, volumes 22, 23 and 24 of *Early Western Travels*, edited by Reuben Gold

Thwaites, with an additional volume of the sketches and paintings of Karl (Charles) Bodmer; also a reprint of the 1843 edition, AMS Press, NY, 1966.

McDERMOTT, John Francis, editor: *Travelers on the Western Frontier,* University of Illinois Press, 1970.

McDONNELL, Anne, editor and contributor: *Contributions* of the Montana Historical Society, Helena, 10 volumes.

McNAUGHTON, Arnold: *The Book of Kings,* vol. II, Times Book Co., Quadrangle, NY, 1973.

MILLER, Don: See COHEN, Stan.

MORGAN, Lewis Henry: *The Indian Journals,* edited by Leslie A. White, the University of Michigan Press, 1959.

MORLEY, James Henry: *Diary, 1862-1865,* MS, Montana Historical Society, Helena.

MURPHY, James E.: *Half Interest in a Silver Dollar: The Saga of Charles E. Conrad,* Mountain Press, Missoula, MT 1983.

NEVITT, R.B.: *A Winter at Fort Mcleod,* edited by Hugh A. Dempsey, Glenbow Alberta Institute, 1974.

OGLESBY, Richard E., contributor: See HAFEN, LeRoy R.

O'MEARA, Walter: *Daughters of the Country,* Harcourt, Brace and World, NY, 1968.

ORR, William J.: See MAXIMILIAN.

OVERHOLSER, Joel F.: "Fort Benton: World's Innermost Port" in the supplement to the *River Press,* 22 Oct. 1980.

OWEN, John: *The Journals and Letters of Major John Owen,* edited by Seymour Dunbar & Paul C. Phillips, 2 volumes, 1927.

PALLISER, John: *The Solitary Hunter,* Long, 1856.

PARTOLL, Albert J.: "The Blackfoot Indian Peace Council" in *Frontier Omnibus,* edited by John W. Hakola, 1962.

PAUL WILHELM, Prince of Wurttemberg: "Account of Adventures in the Great American Desert"; see BUTSCHER.

PAUL WILHELM, Prince of Wurttemberg: *Travels in North America, 1822-1824.* translated by W. Robert Nitske, edited by Savoie Lottinville, University of Oklahoma Press, Norman, 1973.

PENSON-WARD, Betty: Who's Who of Idaho Women of the Past.

PLASSMANN, (Mrs.) M.E.: Article in the *Forsyth Independent,* 10 April 1939.

QUAIFE, Milo Milton, editor: See BOLLER, FINERTY, LARPENTEUR.

RASMUSSEN, Louis J.: *Railway Passenger Lists of Overland Trains to San Francisco and the West,* vol. II, San Francisco Historic Records, Colma, CA, 1968.

RAYMER, Robert George: *Montana, the Land and the People,* vol. III, 1930.

REDLICH, Marcellus Donal Alexander R. von: *Pedigrees of Some of the Emperor Charlemagne's Descendents,* vol. I; Genealogical Publishing co., Baltimore, 1972.

RICE, C. David: See FOLEY, William E.

RICHARDS, Kent D.: *Isaac I. Stevens: Young Man in a Hurry,* Brigham Young University Press, Provo, Utah, 1979.

ROBINSON, Doane: History of South Dakota, vol. I, 1904.

ROSE, James Gray (probable author of the biographical material in the *Centennial Memorial of the Presbytery of Carlisle,)* q.v.

SAEZ, Francisco de Paula Martinez y (AKA Francisco Martinez): *Diario* in the Archives of the Museo de Ciencias Naturales, Madrid, Spain.

SCHARF, J. Thomas: *History of St. Louis.*

SCHEMM, Mildred Walker: "The Major's Lady: Natawista"in *Montana Magazine of History,* Helena, January 1952.

SCHNECK, Benjamin Schroeder: *The Burning of Chambersburg.*

SCHULTZ, James Willard: *Blackfeet and Buffalo,* edited by Keith C. Seele, University of Oklahoma Press,Norman, 1962.

SCHULTZ, James Willard: *Floating on the Missouri,* edited by Eugene Lee Silliman, University of Oklahoma Press, Norman, 1979.

SCHULTZ, James Willard: *Signposts of Adventure,* Houghton Mifflin, 1926.

SCHULTZ, Julia in Phillips County Interviews, q.v.

SILLIMAN, Eugene Lee, editor: *We Seized Our Rifles,* Mountain Press, Missoula, MT 1982.

SNIVELY, Ida Eliot: Compilation of papers in manuscript: "Genealogy of the Culbertson Family", "Genealogy of the Stuart Family", "The Culbertsons of 'Culbertson's Row'", in the Pennsylvania Historical Society, Philadelphia.

SPIELMANN, Christian: "Prinz Nicolas von Nassau zum 70. Geburtstage", translated for me by Hanns-Marcus Muller of Cologne.

SPIER, Leslie: *The Prophet Dance of the Northwest and Its Derivatives,* Menasha, Wisconsin, 1935.

SPRAGUE, Marshall: *A Galaxy of Dudes,* University of Nebraska Press, 1966, 1967.

STEVENS, Hazard: *The Life of Isaac Ingalls Stevens by His Son,* 2 volumes, Houghton Mifflin.

STEVENS, Isaac Ingalls, contributor: *Reports of Explorations and Surveys to Ascertain the Most Practicable and Economical Route for a Railroad from the Mississippi River to the Pacific Ocean,* Washington, D.C., 1860, 12 volumes; see especially vol. XII, Book I.

SUNDER, John E.: *The Fur Trade of the Upper Missouri, 1840-1865,* University of Oklahoma Press, Norman, 1965.

TAYLOR, Dabney: "The Major's Blackfoot Bride" in *Frontier Times,* Dec.-Jan. 1969.

THOMPSON, Larry S.: *Montana's Explorers: The Pioneer Naturalists, 1805-1864,* Montana Graphic Series #9, Montana Magazine, Inc., 1985, Helena.

THURSTON, R.C. Ballard: "Some Recent Finds Regarding the Ancestry of General George Rogers Clark", Filson Club History Quarterly, Louisville, Kentucky, January 1935, Kentucky Historical Society.

TROTT, James H.: unpublished MS on the Mackey missionary venture to Montana.

UPHAM, H.D.: "Upham Letters from the Upper Missouri, 1865", edited by Paul C. Phillips, Sources of Northwest History, No. 19, University of Montana.

VESTAL, Stanley: *Sitting Bull: Champion of the Sioux,* University of Oklahoma Press, Norman, 1957.

WEISEL, George F.: *Men and Trade on the Northwest Frontier,* Montana State University, Missoula, 1955.

WILSON, Joseph M: *The Presbyterian Historical Almanac and Annual Remembrance of the Church of 1863,* vol. V, Philadelphia, 1863.

Index